D0408885

All About All About Eve

All About "all about eve"

The Complete
Behind-the-Scenes Story
of the Bitchiest Film Ever Made

Sam Staggs

St. Martin's Press ✖ New York

A portion of this work appeared in *Vanity Fair* in somewhat different form.

Book Design by James Sinclair

Library of Congress Cataloging-in-Publication Data

Staggs, Sam.
    All about All about Eve: the complete behind-the-scenes story of the bitchiest
film ever made / Sam Staggs.
        p. cm.
    Includes bibliographical references and index.
    ISBN 0-312-25268-4
    1. All about Eve (Motion picture) I. Title.
PN1997.A323 S73 2000
791.45'72—dc21   99-056341

First Edition: March 2000

10   9   8   7   6   5   4   3   2   1

To Robert Sanchez, Glenn Russell, Evan Matthews,
Steve Lambert, Tim Boss, Cary Birdwell,
John Conway, Gary Schwartz,
and Warren Butler—who know all about movies

contents

Author's Note

ince *All About Eve* is, to me, one of the most entertaining movies ever made, I have tried to write an entertaining book about it. I like to think of my work as "fan scholarship," or even "camp scholarship," and why not? Surely a book about a particular movie should echo the "voice" of the movie itself.

To come at a Hollywood classic from every angle, as I've attempted to do, you have to immerse yourself in all aspects of the production, as the moviemakers did. It's necessary to memorize the script. To learn your way around the sets and observe carpenters, electricians, stylists, and script-girls. Study every performance. You have to become a shadow director, as well as a shadow star, someone who sees everything but who remains out of camera range.

My chief method in tracing the route of *All About Eve* has been a production history of the film. The complete story, however, began long before anyone conceived such a picture, and continues long after: through the Broadway musical *Applause* and including quotations, references, and allusions to *Eve* right up to the present day.

I wanted to write not as a detached observer but rather from the point of view of an audience member trying to figure out why I like the movie so much, and why I still find it fresh after thirty or forty viewings. My approach is emotional—that's the fan response. But without research and a rigorous quest for accuracy and balance, the entire book might amount to little more than a studio press release.

Writing about the Hollywood of fifty years ago is a slippery job at best because so many of the people—and the documents—are gone. And of course those in the motion picture industry, like the rest of us, have remembered what was favorable to themselves. Each one framed his or her narrative with an eye to flattering close-ups.

In trying to separate fact from myth, I have retained a constant skepticism. Many of the anecdotes recounted here derive, with variations, from several sources. I've also included several from a single source, and a few from sources not entirely convincing. The quotes from various persons connected with *All About Eve* sometimes sound scripted, but they're real. Attributions are given in the endnotes.

I might have caught a glimpse of the heart of the mystery from the rear, an unflattering angle which, paradoxically, has always excited me, possibly because it is in some way involved with my passion for "backstage," for observing what is magic from the unusual, privileged angle.

—Gore Vidal, *Myra Breckinridge*

Chapter 1

Fire and Music

1951

terse headline in *Variety* on September 27, 1951, told the news: MANKIEWICZ, 20TH SEVER CONTRACT. Many in the industry were surprised that Joseph L. Mankiewicz, the Hollywood director and screenwriter, was quitting 20th Century-Fox, where he had spent the better part of a decade. His separation from Fox was amicable, as such things go; his valedictory to Los Angeles less so. Mankiewicz referred to the City of Angels as "an intellectual fog belt."

Manhattan, he felt sure, would salute him. There he could breathe finer air. He expected to be smartly quoted all over town, and when he tossed out a bon mot his New York listeners wouldn't miss a beat. Nor would anyone complain "What's that supposed to mean?" as they had done since his first day in the intellectual fog belt.

Two Bekins moving vans that would transport everything the Mankiewicz family owned across the country to their new home in New York were packed. One van was filled with household goods. The other contained what was irreplaceable: the writings of Joseph L. Mankiewicz, his papers, his many awards and citations.

Mankiewicz told a reporter he was off to Broadway to "make my pitch for the theatre." Although he spent the rest of his life in New York, he never completed a play, and he never directed one.

1995

Celeste Holm, in her apartment on Central Park West, answered the phone herself. After hearing a description of the book in progress, titled *All About All About Eve*, she asked, "Why the hell do you want to write that book?"

"Why? Because millions of people love the movie. And also because no one has told the story of how it came about and why *All About Eve* is considered both a Hollywood classic and a cult film."

"I don't get it," she snapped. "A work of art speaks for itself! I think a book like that is a waste of time. If people are interested, let them see the movie."

"I've seen it thirty times."

"Then see it thirty more!"

"Look, Miss Holm, it's not backstairs gossip I'm after. But since Mankiewicz lost all his papers in the fire—"

"I guess you want to talk to me about Bette Davis?" Celeste Holm demanded, and without waiting for an answer she continued. "I've talked to everybody in the world about that movie!"

"Bette Davis? No. I'd rather hear about you."

"All this crap about books—I don't get it."

"Suppose I send you a detailed letter about the book. Your memories of shooting *All About Eve* are important."

"Well . . . maybe. I don't know. Good-bye."

She never answered the letter.

1996

Told about the unproductive phone conversation with Celeste Holm, Kenneth Geist, Joseph L. Mankiewicz's biographer, remarked, "When you're the last Mankiewicz survivor in New York, you've probably had enough."

All About All About Eve

Also by Sam Staggs

MMII: The Return of Marilyn Monroe

1976

"I'm not a dinosaur, you know," harrumphed Celeste Holm when a reporter in Los Angeles asked her if *All About Eve* is the movie people best remember her for.

"Didn't you see *Tom Sawyer* last year?" she scolded. "I played Aunt Polly. That was a hit too. . . . Actually, I can tell a lot about somebody just from the movie of mine he mentions first. If you like *All About Eve* so much it probably means you're a Bette Davis nut, a late-show freak. The Broadway musical fans want to know about my playing Ado Annie in the original production of *Oklahoma*. And the socially conscious crowd, the urban liberals, talk about *Gentleman's Agreement*."

1951

Volumes of plays—Ibsen, Oscar Wilde, Kauffman and Hart, Rostand, Molière, Beaumont and Fletcher, even Clyde Fitch and old melodramas—all of these crackled in the fire as if this were Berlin in 1933. Theatre histories, the works of Sigmund Freud, scripts and diaries, biographies of Minnie Fiske and Sarah Siddons and the Barrymores blazed up for a few minutes and then were gone. Mementos saved from movie sets melted like candle wax.

The fire grew and fattened, consuming every molecule of oxygen. It lapped up half a lifetime of memories. The highway itself seemed on fire, while inside the overturned Bekins van ugly smoke gnawed away at wooden crates, cardboard boxes, and metal file cabinets, which, despite their greater strength, would not survive.

A distant siren started up as photographs of Bette Davis charred in the flames like bacon strips. Nearby, a carton flared and that was the end of letters covering several decades: to and from Joe Mankiewicz and his brother, Herman, their sister, their parents, wives, nieces and nephews, and telegrams to them from half of Hollywood. Packed on the bottom of this box was a book of addresses: Celeste Holm in Manhattan, Thelma Ritter in Queens, Mr. and Mrs. Gary Merrill in Maine, Darryl Zanuck's private phone number in his spacious suite of offices at 20th Century-Fox. When the call came, Joe Mankiewicz must have felt that the grandest era of his life had perished. The loss was devastating. Destroyed were hundreds of files dating back to 1929, the year he arrived in Hollywood as a twenty-year-old whose first assignment at Paramount was writing titles for silent movies. Had they survived, those files—along with manuscripts, correspondence, countless personal and professional items detailing two decades of Hollywood history—would now belong to an important university, or perhaps to the Academy of Motion Picture Arts and Sciences in Beverly Hills.

Years later, an interviewer asked Mankiewicz to enumerate all the awards for his most famous picture, *All About Eve*. He shook his head and said nothing, remembering the enormity of the fire. But losing track of the many awards for that film was the smallest part of his misfortune. "Forgive me," he said at last, "but I can't attach much importance to the fact that somewhere in those melted filing cabinets was the dust of a few more back-patting certificates or statuettes. I don't mean to sound ungrateful. It's just that I miss so terribly all of my project notebooks, my manuscripts, my letters and diaries—the private documentation of my twenty-year stretch out there."

Joe Mankiewicz liked fire imagery; he often used it in his work. Three examples from *All About Eve* come to mind. Bette Davis on Miss Caswell, played by Marilyn Monroe: "She looks like she might burn down a plantation." Addison DeWitt describes Eve's first onstage reading of Lloyd's play as "something made of music and fire." And when Bette says "Remind me to tell you about the time I looked into the heart of an artichoke" and Eve replies "I'd like to hear it," Bette's sardonic punch line is "Some snowy night in front of the fire."

In his two or three best works, Mankiewicz was a comic, cynical Prometheus who snatched fire from Hollywood and sent it out across the world to millions of delighted moviegoers. The Mankiewicz flame from his best work as a writer/director—*The Ghost and Mrs. Muir* (1947), which he didn't write, and *A Letter to Three Wives* (1949) and *All About*

Eve (1950), both of which he wrote and directed—burns as bright today as it did a half-century ago.

Joe Mankiewicz owed his start in Hollywood to his older brother, Herman J. Mankiewicz, the witty, hell-raising screenwriter best remembered as co-author of *Citizen Kane*. It was Herman who brought Joe out to California in 1929 and introduced him to the right people. In later years Joe repaid the favor many times.

The other author of *Citizen Kane* was Orson Welles. It's not clear whether Herman Mankiewicz or Welles wrote the scorching end of that movie, but if it was Mankiewicz, the thundering irony is almost too painfully clear. That final operatic holocaust of Charles Foster Kane's effects recurred somewhere on a stretch of highway that day in 1951 when Herman's kid brother, Joe, lost the papers and mementos that meant more to him than anything else he had acquired in Hollywood.

Did Joe Mankiewicz, too, have some secret, half-forgotten "Rosebud" that vanished in the moving-van fire? And if so, did his, like Kane's, represent an unhealed wound? Or—more likely—was the Joe Mankiewicz "Rosebud" a comic one, etched in irony and drenched with a certain kind of wit that later would assume the flashy name of "camp"?

That final fire at Xanadu, and the later one that consumed the Mankiewicz moving van, rhyme like a combustible couplet. It's right out of a movie, you think. And then you say: Why not? In Hollywood, where life and art always overlap, who can tell the difference?

"I am too beautiful to be a *hausfrau!*" shrilled the young woman, slinging the script across the sofa into a mound of cushions. "I vant to be an actress again!"

"But you're a splendid housekeeper, my dear, you said so yourself. You said, 'Every time I get a divorce, I keep the house.' "

Her husband's cool rejoinder was too much. She burst into tears and slammed out of the room, followed by Josephine, her devoted boxer bitch, whose sharply barked laments on the stairs echoed those of her mistress.

A few miles west of Hollywood, in the mountain vastness of Bel Air, there lived a happy couple. He was Russian but, owing to his Oxbridge accent, his suave brittleness, and his waxy polish, he passed for an Englishman. The lady was a Magyar from Budapest who had once passed for an actress, though her stage debut was far away and long ago. As a thespian, this young woman was forgotten by the world, since her acting résumé contained but a single line.

Few in Hollywood had heard of an operetta called *Der Singende Traum* ("The Singing Dream"), much less of the soubrette with the given name of Sari who frolicked across the stage in Vienna a few years before World War II. But Sari Gabor Belge Hilton Sanders remembered the applause. She recalled gypsy violins at romantic suppers with gentlemen after performances, and ranks of roses in her dressing room. She craved new glories in America.

Sari Gabor, nicknamed Zsa Zsa, was desperate. Everyone she knew was famous: her sister Eva, starring on Broadway in *The Happy Time*; two of her ex-husbands, Turkish government press director Burhan Belge, and Conrad Hilton, the multi-millionaire hotelier; and Zsa Zsa's third husband, George Sanders, had just landed the role of Addison DeWitt in Joseph Mankiewicz's next movie, *All About Eve*.

At the age of thirty, give or take a little, Zsa Zsa had prospered, certainly; she wasn't the former Mrs. Hilton for nothing. But to be an actress, to make films like her sister Eva and so many other girls she knew—now there was something worth making sacrifices for.

George and Zsa Zsa had been married not quite a year. Their nuptials (a word often used by Louella Parsons and Hedda Hopper to announce a new Filmland alliance) had taken place on April 1, 1949, in Las Vegas. And George had been making movies ever since. He and Zsa Zsa had recently returned from Spain, where he filmed *Captain Blackjack*.

Later that afternoon, tears dried and makeup freshened, Mrs. George Sanders reemerged.

"Vy not, Georgie?" she said, smoothing the lapel of his smoking jacket. "Phoebe, ze high school girl—it's a small role vich comes only at ze end of ze picture."

"My dear, I believe you might be a trifle mature for the part. Let's see, Phoebe must be seventeen or so, and you were born in—"

"Look at ze script, George," Zsa Zsa implored. "Zis girl stands in front of three long mirrors. Sink how lovely—three Zsa Zsas."

A waft of his wife's perfume brushed his nostril, and George wavered. "Look here, I suppose . . ."

"Three Zsa Zsas at ze end of the picture," she gurgled, tilting her exotic Hungarian head.

George disliked it when she gurgled. He reconsidered the threefold prospect of his wife.

She sucked in her breath and chattered on: "It's only a walk-on at ze end, you know."

George Sanders frowned. "It's more than a walk-on," he informed her with a certain superiority. "Besides, it's unlikely that Darryl would give the role to an untried actress. And I'm not the least convinced that you know how to behave on a set."

"Tell Darryl Zanuck that if I'm no good, ze studio can cut me off." She made a sweeping gesture with her arms.

George Sanders didn't say the first thing that came to mind. Instead he paused for a long moment, looked down at his drink, then slowly replied, "Don't be silly. Acting isn't for you."

A half-century later, one might say that he was absolutely right. And wrong!

For Zsa Zsa soon made her debut in *Lovely to Look At* (1952), quickly reached her A-list zenith in John Huston's *Moulin Rouge* the same year, and has been the Potboiler Princess ever since, most famously in *Queen of Outer Space*.

It was 1950, and Hollywood seemed fascinated with itself.

At Paramount, Billy Wilder was putting the finishing touches on *Sunset Boulevard*, with Gloria Swanson as silent screen star Norma Desmond, a glamorous old vamp, and William Holden as a down-at-the-heels screenwriter. Nicholas Ray was directing *In a Lonely Place* at Columbia, with Bogart also playing a screenwriter—this one suspected of a film-noir murder. Over at MGM they were contemplating *Singin' in the Rain*, the gloriously energetic, tuneful, tap-dancing story of Lina Lamont (Jean

Hagen), another silent star—this one with a screechy voice that dooms her when talkies arrive. Even Marlene Dietrich was about to play a sultry actress resembling herself in the early airplane film *No Highway in the Sky*, speaking throaty lines such as "My films are a few cans of celluloid on the junk heap someday." And at 20th Century-Fox, Joseph L. Mankiewicz had just started *All About Eve*, a film that, while technically about Hollywood rather than Broadway, in fact amounted to exploratory surgery on the dysphoric underbelly of show business.

It was something of a miracle that his movie got made at all, at least the way it did, for Bette Davis hadn't spoken to Darryl Zanuck, the producer, in nine years. And besides, Claudette Colbert had already signed to play the role of Margo Channing. *Variety* and *The Hollywood Reporter* had announced the Colbert coup late in 1949.

Zanuck, moreover, had John Garfield in mind for Bill Sampson, Margo's lover. He also thought José Ferrer would make a fine Addison DeWitt, and he wanted Jeanne Crain for the role of Eve Harrington. All these possibilities, and others, Zanuck jotted in pencil on the inside back cover of Mankiewicz's original treatment of *Eve*. Zanuck's early casting notes reveal Barbara Stanwyck, in addition to Claudette Colbert, as a possibility for Margo Channing. From the start, however, he favored Celeste Holm for Karen, Hugh Marlowe for Lloyd Richards, and Thelma Ritter for Birdie.

In early April 1950 Bette Davis was finishing *The Story of a Divorce* at RKO. This film, later retitled *Payment on Demand*, was her first after leaving Warner Bros., where she had been under contract for eighteen difficult years.

One day, during a lull in shooting while Curtis Bernhardt, the director, conferred with his cameraman, Bette got word that she was wanted on the telephone. Since filming had stopped for a time, she was able to leave the set and take the call in her dressing room. She had on one of the rather matronly dresses designed for her to wear in the picture.

"Hello, Bette, this is Darryl Zanuck," said the production chief of 20th Century-Fox. His high-pitched Nebraska accent, full of sharp *r*'s and words bitten off at the end, was in marked contrast with Bette's *r*-less New England speech, naturally full of broad *a*'s that had broadened even further as she acquired the florid stage diction of the time.

Bette knew Zanuck's voice—and she didn't believe this was Zanuck. Always suspicious, on screen and off, she assumed it was a friend playing a joke. After all, the last thing Zanuck had said to her, during their falling-out in 1941, was "You'll never work in Hollywood again!"

"Hello, Darryl dear," Bette crooned, sounding more Broadway-British than ever. "Lovely to heah from you."

"Bette, I've got a script I want you to take a look at," Zanuck said. "I think you'll like it. And I hope you'll want to do it."

"Anything you say, my deah." She sounded even saucier on the phone than she did on-screen. "If I like it, I *will* do it," she said with a trace of malice and a soupçon of insolence. Bette couldn't figure out which one of her friends was pretending to be Darryl F. Zanuck, so she decided to have a little fun herself, string him along, do an imitation of Bette Davis. Why not? Everyone else did.

By the end of the conversation, she expected this young man—who on earth could it be?—to end his charade with a guffaw. All the while, of course, Bette was puffing her cigarette like . . . well, just like Bette Davis.

"The only thing is, Bette, if you like it you've got to be ready to start shooting in ten days, wardrobe finished and all."

"Right away, Darryl deah." Bette said it as though she were Judith Traherne, the Long Island playgirl and horsewoman she played in *Dark Victory*.

"So you're interested in the script?" Zanuck continued, making allowances for star extravagance.

"Anything you say, Darryl dahling."

"Wouldn't you like to know the name of the picture?"

"Oh, why not surprise me?" Bette said airily. She flung her cigarette hand over her shoulder like a boa.

"Bette, this script is by Joe Mankiewicz. It's the picture Claudette Colbert was going to do before she broke her back."

"Broke her back?" Bette yelped.

And then it dawned!

"Darryl! Is that really you?"

They talked for four or five minutes, during which Zanuck made her one of the best offers any film actress ever received. Bette jumped at the chance to read the script of *All About Eve*, which ultimately, as the critic Ethan Mordden has said, "might be the film that ruined Davis or the film that made her immortal." Perhaps it did both.

Betty Lynn, playing the daughter in *Payment on Demand*, recalled later that Bette's eyes were blazing when she returned to the set. Speaking at breakneck speed, Davis told her younger co-star that the phone call was from Zanuck and that he was sending over a script that had Hollywood in a buzz.

Bette's Quarrel with Darryl Zanuck

In January 1941 Bette Davis was elected the first woman president of the Academy of Motion Picture Arts and Sciences. It was a high honor, and Bette set out to serve with distinction. She soon locked horns, however, with some of her older colleagues. The first disagreement came when Bette suggested that holding the usual Academy Awards banquet in the Biltmore Hotel "might seem frivolous in light of the terrible struggle that our British and European friends are engaged in against the Nazis. Some have suggested we cancel it. I think a better solution would be to hold the ceremony in a theatre, charge a minimum of twenty-five dollars a seat, and donate the proceeds to British War Relief."

Surprisingly, this plan was opposed as "undignified" by some members.

Next, Bette raised the issue of extras. Pointing out that many of them did not speak English and that few were capable of judging technical excellence in films, she suggested that they no longer be permitted to cast votes in the Oscar competition. This suggestion also met with disapproval from many members.

Her other recommendations also caused shock and consternation, so that Bette soon felt she had been chosen only as a glam-

orous figurehead whom no one cared to take seriously. A few days after the first meeting over which she presided, Bette resigned despite a warning from Darryl Zanuck, who had sponsored her for the presidency. How dire his prophecy, and how blind: "You'll never work in Hollywood again."

Jean Hersholt, who was elected to replace Bette, was a diplomat and a skilled politician. He soon maneuvered to deny extras the right to vote, and he paved the way to moving the awards ceremony from banquet hall to theatre. His success in the wake of Bette's failure no doubt implies sexism on the part of the male-dominated Academy. But Bette's bluntness and impatience, her refusal to compromise, surely helped alienate many whom she might later have persuaded.

An even smaller part than that of Phoebe, the young schemer who ends *All About Eve*, was the role of Miss Caswell. If Zsa Zsa Gabor had read the script carefully, she might have tried to grab that little bonbon of a role: Miss Caswell, given name Claudia, whom George Sanders describes as "a graduate of the Copacabana School of Dramatic Art." In the script, Mankiewicz describes her merely as "a blonde young lady."

Ironically, though Zsa Zsa coveted the part of Phoebe, she was fleetingly considered for "the blonde young lady." On the 20th Century-Fox casting director's list, under the heading "Miss Caswell," are the following names, most of them forgotten but two or three are unforgettable: Virginia Toland, Barbara Britton, Karin Booth, Marie McDonald, Mary Meade, Joi Lansing, Adele Jergens, Marilyn Maxwell, Gale Robbins, Joyce Reynolds, Leslie Brooks, ZaZa [sic] Gabor, Lois Andrews, Myrna Dell, Angela Lansbury, Pat Knight, Cleo Moore, Ellie Marshall, Marilyn Monroe, Dolores Moran, Marian Marshall, Randy Stuart, Marjorie Reynolds, Arleen Whelan, Angela Greene, and Rowena Rollins.

At every studio, such lists amounted to little. They were devised when the casting director and his associates, thinking out loud, jotted a quick roster of possibilities. In this instance, at Fox, the casting office soon received a skeleton list from Zanuck and Mankiewicz. Later the casting director winnowed these starlet names. It's impossible to determine how Zsa Zsa made it that far, though it's likely that George Sanders mentioned her to Mankiewicz. Life at home no doubt became sweeter with the announcement, "I've submitted your name." But Zsa Zsa wasn't yet blonde, nor had she launched her Hollywood career. Soon she and all the others were out of the running.

Instead, Marilyn Monroe played Miss Caswell, and of the actors who appeared in *All About Eve* she is the only one whose career was to ascend. For others in the cast—Bette Davis, Anne Baxter, Gary Merrill, Celeste Holm, Hugh Marlowe, George Sanders, Thelma Ritter, and for Mankiewicz himself—*All About Eve* was the climax. Never did a single one of them surpass, or even equal, what he or she did so brilliantly, with such verve and wit, in this film. For all of them the picture was a watershed that separates what they hoped to accomplish in the movies from the actual roles that life, or Hollywood, dealt from its unmarked deck.

Marilyn Monroe went up, and up, and up, but for the others a long descent began the day *All About Eve* was in the can. If not for this movie, half the cast would be forgotten.

The Casting Couch

Nancy Davis Reagan didn't know in 1950 that she was under consideration for the role for Karen Richards. When I queried her in 1998, she said she had never heard that her name was on the casting director's list. Nor was she aware that the man she would marry two years later, in 1952, was also in the running for a part in *All About Eve*. And yet there is the name Ronald Reagan, along with twenty-four other contenders, jotted down for the character of Bill Sampson. If Reagan, not Gary Merrill, had gotten the part, it would have been his second movie with Bette Davis. It might also have changed the course of history.

Consider how Hollywood history might have been different if the casting director had prevailed in his various recommendations. The following lists are not complete; rather, they are selections of the most intriguing possibilities.

KAREN RICHARDS

Nancy Davis
Alexis Smith
Ann Sothern
Shirley Booth
Patricia Neal
Margaret Sullavan
Ruth Warrick
Jessica Tandy
Barbara Bel Geddes
Arlene Dahl
Joan Fontaine

BILL SAMPSON

Robert Cummings
William Holden
Edmond O'Brien
Zachary Scott
Glenn Ford
Ronald Reagan
Montgomery Clift
Robert Young

ADDISON DEWITT

José Ferrer
Clifton Webb
Claude Rains
Basil Rathbone

Charles Laughton
Vincent Price
Adolphe Menjou

EVE HARRINGTON
Jeanne Crain
Ann Blyth
Elizabeth Taylor
June Allyson
Olivia de Havilland
Donna Reed
Mona Freeman

MARGO CHANNING
Katharine Hepburn
Ginger Rogers
Greer Garson
Joan Fontaine
Joan Crawford
Paulette Goddard
Rosalind Russell
Hedy Lamarr
Gloria Swanson
Norma Shearer

MAX FABIAN
Everett Sloane
Walter Slezak
Fred Clark
George Jessel
Zero Mostel

Chapter 2

When Was It? How Long?

Our story actually begins several years before Joe Mankiewicz began filming *All About Eve*. During the 1943–44 Broadway season, at the Booth Theatre on Forty-fifth Street in New York, the Austrian actress Elisabeth Bergner (1897–1986) was appearing in a stage thriller called *The Two Mrs. Carrolls*. In the play, Bergner had the role of a devoted and unsuspecting wife who is slowly being poisoned by her husband.

The play is creaky by today's standards. It was creaky in the forties, but without the competition of television drama, such plays often did very well, and *The Two Mrs. Carrolls* turned into a fashionable hit. (One reviewer called the play "the largest bundle of nineteenth-century heroics the twentieth has ever offered with a straight face.")

In Europe Elisabeth Bergner had been called "the Garbo of the stage." Bergner herself once summed up her career with this line: "Schiller, Goethe, Shakespeare, Ibsen, Strindberg, Hauptmann, Chekhov, Shaw, Barrie, and Shakespeare again and again and again."

She made movies in Germany (*Fräulein Else*, 1929; *Der Träumende Mund* ["Dreaming Lips"], 1932), and also in England, where she had emigrated. When the British film *Catherine the Great* was banned shortly after opening in Berlin in 1934, Hitler's chief propagandist, Dr. Alfred Rosenberg, wrote in the Nazi Party newspaper *Völkischer Beobachter*: "The attempt to present in Berlin émigré Jews, especially the warped Elisabeth Bergner, and to make money from them in Germany, represents an inartistic effort that must be resisted."

Since the German-speaking countries were dangerously inhospitable, Bergner and her Hungarian husband/manager, Paul Czinner, remained in England. There she filmed *As You Like It* (directed by Czinner) in 1937 with the promising young actor Laurence Olivier. In this film, perhaps her best known, Bergner is a riveting presence. She has the wide, pleading eyes of a northern Renaissance Magdalene and, around her mouth, traces of a smirk. Her exuberant, full-bodied voice resembles an unlikely admixture of Eva LeGallienne and Mae West.

Two years after *As You Like It*, Bergner starred in *Stolen Life* with Michael Redgrave, which Warner Bros. remade in 1946 starring Bette Davis and Glenn Ford. Hollywood released this later version—the story of twin girls, one good, one bad, and both of course played with gusto by Bette—as *A Stolen Life*.

Having come to the United States when a German invasion of Great Britain seemed likely, Elisabeth Bergner was content to appear in plays by authors other than the great European dramatists. After all, the competition was formidable—Helen Hayes, Katherine Cornell, Lynn Fontanne—and many actors whose first language wasn't English ended up playing stock parts: peasants, spies, fortune-tellers, and Nazi brutes.

We don't know Bergner's thoughts on Martin Vale (nom de plume of Marguerite Vale Veiller), the author of *The Two Mrs. Carrolls*, but from all accounts the actress threw herself into the play and gave it her best. In fact, she seems to have poured into this melodrama not only more than it deserved but more, almost, than it could take. Bergner wasn't merely histrionic; she was over the top.

One reviewer, commenting on "the way she laid down a rose, the way she staggered up and down the stairs," concluded that "Miss Bergner is a prize package of theatrical trickery who overdid the cuteness and melting connubiality." In other words, she chewed the scenery.

George Bernard Shaw put it this way after seeing her in his *Saint*

Joan: "Miss Bergner played Joan as if she were being burned at the stake when the curtain went up, instead of when it went down."

Elisabeth Bergner gave almost 400 performances of *The Two Mrs. Carrolls*. It was during the run of this hit that she inadvertently played out, offstage, the events that would later come to be associated with Margo Channing. What happened to Margo in the film had already happened in real life to Elisabeth Bergner: There really was an Eve.

At this point in the narrative I introduce Mary Orr, who lives on West Fifty-seventh Street in New York. She is a playwright, an actress, and the author of novels and short stories. I recently spent an afternoon with her, and this is what she told me.

"My husband, Reginald Denham [1894–1983], directed *The Two Mrs. Carrolls* on Broadway with Elisabeth Bergner. After Elisabeth left the play in New York—which must have been in the summer of 1944—for a brief vacation before starting the national tour, her husband, Paul Czinner, called my husband on the phone. Actually, Reggie and I weren't married at that time, but we both knew that he would be my husband before long.

"Incidentally, you know, don't you, that Paul Czinner [1890–1972] managed every detail of Elisabeth's career, and had done so throughout their marriage? He was one of the producers of *The Two Mrs. Carrolls*. Well, one day Paul called up and said, 'Reggie, could you come to New Hampshire and spend a weekend with us? I think we should discuss who is going to play opposite Elisabeth on the road, because Victor Jory won't go.'

"I think Victor had had enough of Elisabeth, to tell you the truth. But anyway, he had refused the tour and they had to find a new leading man. So my husband said to Paul Czinner, 'I have to drive Mary up to Maine next weekend. She's acting in summer stock in Skowhegan.'

"I was a young actress in my twenties then, considerably younger than Reggie, and I had to take whatever acting jobs came along, even if it meant that Reggie and I would spend most of the summer apart. That wasn't easy, you know, because we were very much in love.

"Anyway, Reggie said to Paul, 'We could make a detour on our way to

Maine, spend a long weekend with you and Elisabeth, and then I can drive Mary to Skowhegan on Tuesday.'

"And that was what we did. We drove to New Hampshire, and it took a long time in those days because there were no interstates. Reggie and I stopped at Woodstock, Vermont, which was the nearest town to where this farm was that Elisabeth and Paul had taken for the summer.

"Now, Elisabeth was a very interesting character. I want you to realize that. Why? Well, for one thing, off the stage she was a little German *hausfrau*, and then on the stage she was another person. Absolutely.

"Elisabeth and Paul invited us to dinner. Paul Czinner had recommended the little Woodstock Inn in Woodstock, Vermont. At that time it was a plain and simple country inn; now it's a Rockefeller-type resort. Well, Reggie and I checked into this inn and Reggie called Paul and said, 'We're here.' Paul said, 'As soon as you've had a shower and changed, come on over,' and he gave Reggie directions through the New Hampshire countryside to the farm where he and Elisabeth were spending the summer. It must have been about twelve miles east of Woodstock.

"We found it. My husband was a good driver. I never drove. Never had the eyesight to pass the test, but anyway we had a pleasant visit with them. Elisabeth was as nice to me as if I had been her equal in the theatre. She made no distinction.

"While having drinks, we brought Paul and Elisabeth up to date with the latest theatre gossip from New York. Finally Paul looked at Elisabeth and said in his Hungarian accent, 'I sink you should get busy vith the dinner, Reggie and Mary must be hungry.'

"Elisabeth, whose accent was almost more British than German, stood up and said, 'Come on in the kitchen with me, Mary, and I'll teach you how to cook Wienerschnitzel.'

"While the men were still talking about Victor Jory's replacement, I went into the kitchen with Elisabeth. I watched one of the world's great actresses bread veal and peel potatoes. Now, at that time she was already in her late forties but she looked young. She was always young-looking because she was small and moved around like a girl.

"She did this and that in the kitchen, whatever you do when you make Wienerschnitzel, but she talked up a storm all the while. Before long, coming to a pause in her dinner preparations and also in her running monologue, she looked at me and said, 'You're a young actress. Let me tell you about the one—'

"Now I must tell you that Elisabeth always called her 'that terrible girl,' 'that awful creature,' or 'that little bitch.' She never called the girl by name, although later I learned that the girl's name is————" And here Mary Orr said, "But be careful, please, what you say about her, because she's unpredictable. In a minute, you'll understand what I mean. What's that? Oh yes, she's still alive. She's no longer a girl, of course, after all these years. But I can assure you she's still very much alive. I've met her!"

(And so for reasons of punctilio I'll use the name "Miss X"—at least for now.)

"Anyway, the girl used to stand in the alley beside the Booth Theatre night after night, wearing a little red coat. I suppose she somehow saw every performance of *The Two Mrs. Carrolls*. Or maybe she only claimed she did.

"Elisabeth told me all this right there in the kitchen. 'So, Mary,' she said, 'wouldn't you be curious? I was too, and so one night I invited her into my dressing room.'

"It seems that from that very night the 'terrible girl' took over Elisabeth's life. The girl lied to her, deceived her, did things behind her back—even went after her husband, Paul Czinner! And why not? He was in a position to do things for her. He was a well-known film director, and his shrewd management had been indispensable to Elisabeth's career.

"Years later someone hinted at a lesbian relationship between Elisabeth and the girl. At that time I certainly never thought of such a thing. You didn't think about such things, back then.

"This is such a story! Are you sure you want to hear all of it?" Mary Orr asked.

I assured her I was fascinated, and so she continued, "Well, one night Elisabeth invited the girl to come to her dressing room for a visit. She was touched that a young fan would feel such devotion toward her. And the girl had a faint accent. She was English, she told Elisabeth and Paul, and, like them, she had fled to America for fear the Germans might invade Great Britain. Elisabeth said the girl's eyes filled with tears. I wouldn't be surprised if Elisabeth's did, too. After all, she possessed all the emotions of the theatre.

"So there they were at the Booth Theatre, on Forty-fifth Street, in Elisabeth's dressing room one night after the performance. If they had turned on the radio they might have heard, 'This is Edward R. Murrow, in London. Today more bombs fell on this city. . . .' But they didn't. Instead they all became friends.

"A few days later Elisabeth arranged for the girl to become a secretary of sorts to Paul. And of course the girl performed to perfection. What did girls do in those days? Back then I'm sure she made coffee for the boss, and for the boss's wife, or maybe it was tea, since they all had English connections—although some of them, as you'll see presently, were more English than others.

"What else did she do? She handled correspondence, ran errands, maybe typed, and I wouldn't be surprised if she massaged Elisabeth's ego—maybe even her legs and feet as well, after a long day of acting. Whether she did the same for Elisabeth's husband is anybody's guess."

Here Mary Orr takes a break to rest her voice. Her deft characterizations, full of detail, seem to have brought back colleagues long dead. As her narrative unfolds they make their silent entrances and exits once more there in her apartment, among her own relics of a life in the theatre.

Irene Worth is another actress connected to our story. Born in Omaha, Nebraska, in 1916, she made her Broadway debut in 1943 in *The Two Mrs. Carrolls*. It is not important to know what role she played, for it was flimsy compared to her later career. After her unremarkable beginning, Irene Worth went on to create the role of Celia Copplestone in T. S. Eliot's *The Cocktail Party* at the 1949 Edinburgh Festival, and her classical roles range from the Greeks to Shakespeare, right up to the best female parts in Ibsen, Shaw, Chekhov, and Beckett.

Seldom memorable in her sporadic film roles, Irene Worth acted with Bette Davis and Alec Guinness in *The Scapegoat* in 1959. Bette played a crumbling bedridden countess; Miss Worth had a less vivid part.

But all of this was years in the future for the ingenue who landed a part in *The Two Mrs. Carrolls.* In 1943 Irene Worth got the role, did her job, and some time later went to England, where she made her career. None of this would concern us here except for a rumor that has buzzed around for years. That rumor casts Irene Worth as "the terrible girl" who inspired Hollywood's Eve Harrington. "She clawed her way to the top," declare the rumormongers. The savory little story is just what's needed to confirm every tale of theatre skullduggery.

But it isn't true.

Roy Moseley, in his 1990 book, *Bette Davis: An Intimate Memoir* (along with earlier writers who had broached the subject), unwittingly fueled the rumor with this anecdote:

> *All About Eve* was based on Elisabeth Bergner, who was appearing on Broadway when a young actress playing a small part came to her to say she would be quitting. Miss Bergner asked "Why?" and the young actress said, "Because I'm not good enough, not good enough to be with you. You're so magnificent!" Miss Bergner persuaded the young actress to stay on. Her name was Irene Worth and she grew into a star herself. The difference was that Bergner and Worth remained friends. This was the basis for the story of *All About Eve* but, of course, without the sense of evil which pervades the film.

Moseley was in a perfect position to verify his facts, since he writes elsewhere in the book that, as a theatrical agent in London, he represented Elisabeth Bergner during the 1960s. Oddly, however, he jumbled the story. But no matter how we view that scene of unworthy Miss Worth proclaiming, "I'm not good enough, not good enough"—as though she were one of the hundred neediest cases—still, it's important to know that she didn't carve her career from the flesh of another grande dame.

But her link to our saga is crucial, because shortly after Elisabeth Bergner and Paul Czinner took Miss X under their wing, Irene Worth announced that she was leaving.

In the meantime, according to Mary Orr, Miss X hadn't been content merely to stand at the stage door, a loyal fan in a red coat. Nor was she satisfied with her subsequent status as secretary to Paul Czinner and factotum to her idol, Miss Bergner. With Irene Worth on the way out, a replacement must be found. Miss X volunteered to read Miss Bergner's role at the auditions so that Miss Bergner would not have to be bothered. Later that day, Miss Bergner was surprised to learn that Miss X had read. It was . . . terribly kind. And Elisabeth Bergner was generous. She, along with her husband and his co-producer, Robert Reud, decided to do something for Miss X.

The three of them went to Actors' Equity to seek permission for the young Englishwoman to make her Broadway debut. Actors' Equity investigated. A few days later Paul Czinner got a phone call. "No trouble at all," he was told by the Equity rep. "The girl's not English, she's American. I guess you couldn't tell the difference between an English accent and one of ours, could you?"

Czinner and Bergner accepted the young lady's explanation. She told them she had to find out—in the company of experts—whether her British accent was as persuasive as she hoped.

Irene Worth, at her last performance, received several bouquets from producers and co-stars, and then—

But now Mary Orr is back, voice rested, and once more she takes up the narrative.

"Irene Worth had good connections in England, some big shot, I can't remember who it was. He helped her get started in London, I think.

"As for 'the terrible girl,' Elisabeth thought her talented. I can't remember, really, whether she became Elisabeth's understudy, but it stands to reason that she would, even though she was much too young for the part. And the girl went on to win some kind of award.

"It was a thing called the John Golden Award. It was supposed to help young actresses. Help them do what? I'm not sure. But Golden did give the award, and 'the terrible girl' won it that year." (Actor-director John Golden [1874–1955] also had two theatres named for him. The first, on West Fifty-seventh Street, later became a cinema. The second John Golden Theatre on West Forty-fifth Street, was so named by Golden himself when he took it over in 1937. And the front of the latter theatre is the one you see—exteriors only—in *All About Eve*.)

"How far did she go in undermining Elisabeth's career, you ask? Not far at all. Maybe she coveted Elisabeth's starring role in *The Two Mrs. Carrolls*, but she never got it. Apparently she just gave Elisabeth a few unhappy nights. I don't think it went much further than that.

"And yet, to return to that evening when Elisabeth Bergner told me the story in that farmhouse kitchen while she was furiously making Wienerschnitzel, you know, she just went on babbling about 'that terrible girl' who seemed to have provoked a crisis in her life. At the time, I assumed it had upset her because she had been so kind and then she felt she had been stabbed in the back. It certainly became an obsession with Elisabeth about that girl. Much later, I began to wonder if there had been a closer relationship than what Elisabeth told me. Maybe she had been terribly hurt. Broken-hearted. I don't know; that's just a guess.

"After dinner that night, as Reggie and I drove back in the moonlight to the Woodstock Inn, I asked him a question. 'Did you ever see a girl in a red coat who hung out at the stage door every night?'

"He said, 'Oh yes, I suppose I do remember her. Why?'

"I told him the story just as Elisabeth had told it to me. He was amazed, but after hearing it he recalled the girl who seemed to attend every night's performance.

"As the director of *The Two Mrs. Carrolls*, he had a lot on his mind. All during the run he'd see the show once or twice a week, then he'd tell Elisabeth, 'You're overacting; don't do that,' or whatever.

"I remember the first night of previews, when the villain suddenly appeared through the window, it produced several loud screams from the audience and when Reggie went backstage after the show Elisabeth dressed him down. She said, 'How could you do that—they screamed at me! I won't stand for it!' Of course, that's exactly what Reggie had aimed for. He was so put-out he grabbed her by the shoulders and said, 'You silly bitch, that's what we want them to do, scream their heads off!'

"Paul Czinner was in the dressing room, and the moment Reggie finished scolding Elisabeth he turned to Paul and said, 'I'm frightfully sorry!' As an Englishman, he was embarrassed to have lost his temper.

"Czinner replied very calmly, 'A little discipline for her is good. You should see vot Max Reinhardt vould do for her in Berlin!'

"The play ran forever, and then they took it on the road. One night when it was in Chicago, Elisabeth called up after a performance and said in mock horror, 'Reggie, you must come here immediately! We have lost the scream!'

"You'll have to forgive me, I'm telling you all these old tales, which can't interest you very much. After all, you're working on *All About Eve*. Are you sure you want me to go on? Well, it's all fascinating to me, naturally, but that's because I lived through it.

"My goodness, how did I get so far off the main path? To go back to my story, the next morning in Vermont I noticed Reggie getting up at some ungodly hour, about six o'clock. We hadn't known each other too long then, you see. We weren't accustomed to sharing a bedroom.

"I was bewildered. I said, 'Why are you getting dressed at this hour?' and he said, 'I'm going bird-watching.' He had never mentioned so much as a pigeon to me before that.

" 'Look out the window and see the robins,' I grumbled, burying my face in the pillow.

"To which he replied, 'Now look here, I'm an Englishman and all the birds up here are life species.' Do you know what that means to a birder? It means they're seeing a bird of a special species for the first time. That's what every ornithologist lives for. It's like hitting the jackpot.

"I groaned and turned over again. I looked at him and said, 'What am I going to do in this stupid little inn all day long?'

"And you know what he answered? He said, 'Sit down and write that story you told me last night. That's a hell of a story, and if you don't write it, who will?'

"What did I know about writing short stories? I had written a piece for the *Pictorial Review* about a young actress struggling to get on Broadway—it was about myself, really—and then Reggie and I wrote *Wallflower*, a play that opened on Broadway at the Cort Theatre in January of 1944, about six months before the trip to Vermont that I've just told you about. I hadn't written a lot, but then I was only twenty-six.

"Well, after Reggie went out to his birds, I had my breakfast downstairs—no room service in that little inn—and I thought a long time. Finally I went to the office and asked, 'Is it possible to borrow a typewriter?' They said, 'We put an old one down in the cellar just last week when our new one came. Can you use the old one?' I said, 'I can't type anyway, so it won't matter whether I have the old one or the new.'

"They brought the typewriter up to our room. They supplied me with plenty of Woodstock Inn stationery, and I stuck the first sheet into the machine. Did you ever read Moss Hart's *Act One*? There's a line in it where he says, 'The worst moment in a writer's life is when he stares at the paper in the typewriter and the paper is white.'

"I stared at that piece of stationery, thinking, How do I tell this story? Should I have Elisabeth talking, or do I tell it through the eyes of the girl? Finally I decided to tell it through my own eyes.

"Reggie returned at five o'clock. We were going back to Elisabeth and Paul's for dinner. He said, 'Well, Mary, what have you done all day?' and I screamed, 'Get away! Don't bother me!'

"He disappeared for another hour or so, and when I finally stopped he asked, 'What's this all about?'

"I said, 'I've been writing that story.'

"He said, 'Smashing! Read it to me,' and I said, 'No, I won't read it to you. It's not finished.'

"So for three more days, while we spent a long weekend at the Woodstock Inn and Reggie went bird-watching every day, I worked on that story, which, as you know, is 'The Wisdom of Eve,' the basis for Joseph Mankiewicz's movie, *All About Eve*.

"Eventually, the night before we were to leave for Skowhegan, I said, 'I finished the story today.'

"Reggie said, 'Give it to me and let me read it.'

"I said, 'No, Reggie, I'll read it to you, because you know I can't spell, and my terrible punctuation would put you off.'

"He never said a word while I read him the story, from the first line: 'A young girl is on her way to Hollywood with a contract for one thousand dollars a week from a major film company in her pocketbook,' to the last: 'She's going to marry my husband, Lloyd Richards.'

"When I finished he just stared at me. I said, 'Well, what do you think?' and he said, 'Who the hell taught you to write?' I said, 'God, I guess,' and Reggie said, 'That's a great story, Mary. We must do something about it.'

"My agent turned it down cold. She said, 'You can't write stories—

you should stick to plays, like *Wallflower*. You'll never get this published in any magazine!' I understand she was terribly upset a few years later when *All About Eve* won six Oscars.

"In the end, it was Reggie who sold the story.

"A man named Dale Eunson, from Montana, wrote a play called *Guest in the House*, which Reggie directed on Broadway. Dale had also been a screenwriter in Hollywood, and he had written several novels set in his home state. Somehow he became editor of *Cosmopolitan*.

"One night Dale and his wife gave a party at their house on East Sixtieth Street, and Reggie and I attended.

"The first thing you're asked at a theatrical party is, 'Do you have a job? What are you doing?' When Dale asked Reggie that, Reggie said, 'I haven't a job at the moment, but Mary's written an extraordinary story and since you're the editor of *Cosmopolitan*, you ought to read it. You'll like it. It's about the theatre.' Reggie didn't mention that every other magazine in town had turned it down.

"Dale said, 'Send it to me,' and I did, and he bought it the next day, for eight hundred dollars. The story was published in the May nineteen, forty-six issue."

All About the Many Versions of "Eve"

The following chronology of "The Wisdom of Eve," *All About Eve*, and *Applause* was compiled in 1970 by Roderick L. Bladel, of New York, and is used here with his permission. I have updated it somewhat.

1. Mary Orr's short story, "The Wisdom of Eve," *Cosmopolitan*, May 1946, p. 72. Leading characters' names: Margola Cranston and Eve Harrington.
2. Mary Orr's radio play, *The Wisdom of Eve*, performed on *Radio Guild Playhouse* on NBC, January 21, 1949.

Important plot change: Margola, now called "Margo," misses a performance, which she had not done in the short story. This radio production may have been directed by Harry W. Junkin; the supervisor of the *Radio Guild Playhouse* series was Richard McDonagh. Claudia Morgan played Margo Cranston, and Marilyn Erskine was cast as Eve Harrington.

3. The film *All About Eve*, written and directed by Joseph L. Mankiewicz for 20th Century-Fox. Released October 1950. The screenplay was published by Random House in 1951, and again in 1972 in Gary Carey's book for Random House, *More About All About Eve*.

4. *All About Eve*, radio version performed on *Screen Guild Theatre*, March 8, 1951, with Bette Davis, Anne Baxter, and George Sanders reprising their roles from the film.

5. One-hour radio version of the Mankiewicz *All About Eve* on *The Theatre Guild on the Air* series, NBC, November 16, 1952, starring Tallulah Bankhead as Margo Channing and Mary Orr as Karen Richards.

6. The stage version of *The Wisdom of Eve* by Mary Orr and her husband, Reginald Denham, using the characters and situations of the first radio version, carefully avoiding any Mankiewicz dialogue and plot changes. Published in 1964; available for amateur production through Dramatists Play Service, 440 Park Avenue South, New York, NY 10016.

7. *Applause*, stage musical with libretto by Betty Comden and Adolph Green, music by Charles Strouse and lyrics by Lee Adams. Work on the libretto was begun by Sidney Michaels, who was replaced by Comden and Green. Mankiewicz's name does not appear on the program of

Applause, which gives this line of credit: "Based on the film *All About Eve* and the original story by Mary Orr." *Applause* opened March 30, 1970, at the Palace Theatre in New York and ran for 896 performances.

Chapter 3

Minor Awards Are for Such as the Writer

cattered through various books are abbreviated accounts of how Mary Orr's story "The Wisdom of Eve" found its way to Joseph L. Mankiewicz: A story editor at 20th Century-Fox read it in *Cosmopolitan*, thought of Mankiewicz, acquired the story, and soon the director set to work. In reality, however, the route was long and marked by surprise.

Mankiewicz himself said that after winning two Academy Awards (Best Director and Best Screenplay) for his 1949 film *A Letter to Three Wives*, he began thinking of the Oscar—and all such awards—as a symbol or a totem. Keenly aware of the conniving and skullduggery that often net such laurels, he realized that the subject "would make an excellent frame for a film about the theatre." Mankiewicz found his "McGuffin"—the device to get the story going—in the Orr short story.

After this story appeared in the May 1946 issue of *Cosmopolitan*, it seems to have been offered to all the major film companies, including 20th Century-Fox, but no one wanted it then. At the time, much of the fiction that appeared in national magazines was routinely sent, either by agents or by authors themselves, to Hollywood. Story departments at the studios also vetted the magazines for potential material. It was eventually through this latter channel that Mary Orr's story reached Mankiewicz. Curiously, however, it was not until 1949—three years after publication—that the story came to the attention of James Fisher, then head of Fox's story department. Fisher, following standard procedure, sent copies of the story to the studio's contractual producers, writers, and directors. Among the recipients was Joe Mankiewicz.

Half a century later, Mary Orr is still perplexed that it took her story three years to arouse interest. In retrospect, it seems made for the movies.

One reason there were no immediate takers in Hollywood is that Eve Harrington, in the story, suffers no retribution for her lies and deceit. From that first line, quoted earlier, where she's on her triumphant way to Hollywood, to the final one where she has stolen Lloyd Richards from Karen, his wife, Eve is shining proof that immorality pays off—at least in show business. Eve, in the story, is a woman who "has it all" decades before the phrase became a shibboleth for ambitious American career women. She has celebrity, money, and a very useful fiancé.

By the 1940s, however, Hollywood movies had become suffocatingly moralistic. Transgressors—especially women—had to be punished. It was a gentleman's agreement.

Even Joe Mankiewicz, who sneered at Hollywood hypocrisy, made sure, by picture's end, that Eve is headed for a lifetime of empty tomorrows for her sins against Karen Richards and Margo Channing—both "good" women. Yes, Margo is "good" even though she sleeps with her boyfriend out of wedlock, hits the bottle when she's down, and brawls when she's mad.

Mary Orr's Eve keeps her ill-gotten gains, but in the Mankiewicz script it's Margo Channing who wins big. For Margo holds on to her career, marries the man she loves, and even gets the last word, to Eve: "You can always put that award where your heart ought to be." This is Mankiewicz morality, a bit more realistic than Hollywood's facile loftiness of the time, yet conventional enough to placate film-industry censors who insisted on penalties for the wicked, viz Eve.

Is It Over—Or Is It Just Beginning?

"Margo Channing's career is over at forty."

—Molly Haskell, *From Reverence to Rape* (1974)

"Bette Davis's Margo Channing in *All About Eve* knows . . . that though her audience approval may be like waves of love coming up each night, it won't keep her warm when the wrinkles set. She ultimately opts for retirement and the role of wife to her younger director-boyfriend."

—Marjorie Rosen, *Popcorn Venus* (1974)

"In the classic Hollywood film about the theatre, *All About Eve*, Margo Channing, the great star played by Bette Davis has, finally, to say that what she really, *truly*, wants is to be a 'real' woman; that is, a 'married lady' busy 'doing things around the house,' instead of starring in a major new play."

—Harriett Hawkins, *Classics and Trash* (1990)

"At one fell swoop, in admitting that, yes, a woman must choose between happiness and a career, Margo seemed to undo all that Bette's gutsier characters had proved about a woman's capacity to function bravely and effectively on her own. Successful in the world as she may have been until now, Margo finally—wisely, the film insists—accepts that the time has come for this power-ful, independent woman to stop fighting, step back, and let her husband take care of her."

—Barbara Leaming, *Bette Davis: A Biography* (1992)

Fueled by feminist critics, the rumor has spread that Margo Channing gives up her Broadway career because she's getting married at last. Thus, *All About Eve* seems to fit neatly into prevalent theories about Hollywood's attitude toward women, about gender in fifties films, and so on. In this case, however, the neat fit comes from hearing only part of what Margo says.

She, Bill, Karen, and Lloyd are seated at a table in the Cub Room of the Stork Club. Margo and Bill have announced their forthcoming marriage, and Margo says, "Lloyd, will you promise not to be angry with me?" The reason she anticipates his anger comes a few lines later: "I don't want to play Cora." (Cora is the star role in Lloyd's new play, *Footsteps on the Ceiling*.)

Karen is more shocked than Lloyd, and so Margo responds to her: "Now wait a minute, you're always so touchy about his plays, it isn't the part—it's a great part. And a fine play. But not for me anymore—not for a foursquare, upright, downright, forthright married lady."

Lloyd's next line is politically correct: "What's your being married got to do with it?"

Margo: "It means I've finally got a life to live! I don't have to play parts I'm too old for—just because I've got nothing to do with my nights! Oh, Lloyd, I know you've made plans. I'll make it up to you, believe me. I'll tour a year with this one, anything, only—only you do understand, don't you?"

The most important point is that Margo says nothing about giving up her career. Any actor who offers to "tour a year" with a play is not on the verge of retirement. She has toured before; Eve says she first saw Margo when she was onstage in San Francisco. Obviously, Margo plans to marry and to go right on acting.

What some critics haven't heard, apparently, is Margo declining only the role of Cora, one of those "parts I'm too old for." Margo is finally willing to admit how inappropriate the role is for her. Earlier in the film she had referred to Cora as "still a girl of twenty." And Margo is twice twenty. How could anyone *not* admire her good sense? Some women of forty could play "a girl of twenty," but Margo Channing is not one of them.

There is no hint from Bill that he wants Margo to retire, or even to curtail her career. On the contrary, he compliments her several times on her talent and also on specific performances. Even if he wanted her to give up the theatre, he probably wouldn't say so. It's Bill who is named Sampson, but the strong-man of this story is really Margo.

Another reason, perhaps, why "The Wisdom of Eve" wasn't quickly snapped up by a studio is its backstage setting. Films—honest films—about Hollywood and its denizens were dangerous. To studio moguls they represented a kind of nest-fouling. Besides, skeletons belonged in the closet, not on public display, and the studios spent thousands each year in hush money to keep closet doors shut. Furthermore, though Mary Orr's story is ostensibly about the theatre, it's easy to substitute "Holly-wood" for "Broadway."

On the West Coast, that swap made movie people squirm. At the time, show-biz self-contemplation was expected to take the form of harmless entertainments like *Stage Door*, teary fables (*A Star Is Born*), or frothy, lavish musicals such as *The Barkleys of Broadway* and *Summer Stock*. As Ethan Mordden has written about this backstage subgenre in his book *Movie Star*, "Films about Hollywood must either explore the cor-ruption and silliness or must lie at length, for there is little that is truly exhilarating or noble or even nice about the place."

For whatever reasons—and perhaps the only reason was oversight—Hollywood ignored "The Wisdom of Eve" for almost three years. Mary Orr, of course, didn't sit around waiting for a call. With her husband she collaborated on *Dark Hammock* and *Round Trip*, plays that opened on Broadway and in which she also appeared. Orr continued writing short stories, and she acted in scores of radio plays.

But actors, then as now, went through lean times, and in January 1949 Mary Orr's career was at its leanest. One day she went to NBC looking for work, and someone sent her to see Harry Junkin, the director of a dramatic series called _Radio Guild Playhouse._

"I can't give you a job, Mary," Junkin told her in a voice not far from hysteria. "I haven't even got a script for next Friday! You think you're desperate? What about me?"

Ever resourceful, Mary Orr looked at him and said, "Harry, if I go home and write you a script over the weekend, will you give me a part—provided there's a part in it that suits me?"

In a sense, she was right back at the Woodstock Inn, staring at a blank page. For although she had collaborated on Broadway plays, she had never tried her hand at radio drama. Mary Orr began to wonder if she would have to master a new genre every year. What next—a masque?

So far, 1949 was not going the way Orr wanted it to. She was out of work, her husband was out of work—and not only that, he was in Polyclinic Hospital with both legs smashed. Early one morning, out bird-watching, Reginald Denham was taking binoculars out of a suitcase in the trunk of his car when another vehicle ran off the road, plowed into him, and crushed his legs between the bumpers. At first the doctors thought they might have to amputate. Nine months later, he left the hospital.

"I had to pay all those bills," Orr recalls. "What was I to do? After I left NBC I went to visit Reggie and I told him that if I could think up a radio play Harry Junkin would not only buy it from me, he'd let me act in it, too."

Denham said, "Go home and dramatize 'The Wisdom of Eve.' "

Mary Orr said, "But this is radio! I don't know how to—"

"You act on radio all the time," said her husband with a groan as he tried to shift his bandaged legs. "You know about voice-overs and the techniques they use on the air."

And so the play, like the story, was written over a weekend.

"I'm a very fast writer," Mary Orr says. "Once I get started I don't look up. And I never go back and make changes."

On Monday morning she delivered the play to Harry Junkin, who paid her $250 for it. Four days later, on Friday, January 21, 1949, _The Wisdom of Eve_ was broadcast, with Claudia Morgan as Margo. (In the short story, the character was called "Margola," with accent on the first syllable; this radio play is where she became "Margo.") Marilyn Erskine played the part of Eve, and Mary Orr was Karen Richards.

Radio Guild Playhouse was one of NBC's sustaining programs, meaning that it was a prestigious offering and therefore not interrupted with jingles for shampoo or toothpaste. The show originated live from New York at 8:00 P.M., but this early-evening broadcast went only as far as Chicago. Because of the time difference between the East and West Coasts, a *second* live broadcast was done at 11:00 P.M. Eastern Time, to accommodate listeners in the Pacific Time Zone who wanted to hear a play at the normal hour, eight o'clock. Actors who worked in such dual-broadcast programs often had time to return home or go out to dinner between the first and second shows. Or get drunk. According to Tom Hatten, a radio enthusiast and a CBS show-business correspondent in Los Angeles, "The big problem was keeping the actors sober for the second show."

It was lucky for Mary Orr that a second, prime-time broadcast was beamed all the way to California, for someone in Hollywood had the radio on that January night. And they liked what they heard.

Three days later, on Monday, NBC called Mary Orr at her apartment to give her the news. 20th Century-Fox had telephoned with a movie offer. What did she think of $5,000 for all rights to her original story and to this new play based on it?

In 1949, $5,000 was almost enough to live on for a year, even in New York. Even with hospital bills. And even after NBC deducted its percentage, which came to $750.

Mary Orr, like many people in the arts, didn't know how to strike the best deals for herself. Having left the agent who said, "You'll never get this published in any magazine," Orr had handled her own literary affairs for a time before meeting Marcella Powers, a young agent at Music Corporation of America (now ICM). Understandably, Orr does not recall every detail of the negotiations, but she believes that it was Miss Powers who advised her on the thornier points of the contract that 20th Century-Fox drew up.

Technically, what Fox offered Mary Orr was an option. In the studio era (as now), only the author of a blockbuster best-seller might expect an outright offer to purchase film rights for a work. Far more likely, the work in question was optioned for a period of time—six months, a year, eighteen months—during which the studio sought to line up a good screenwriter, interest stars or their agents in the property, charm exhibitors with its commercial appeal, and so on.

Fox's acquisition of the option on "The Wisdom of Eve" gave the studio exclusive control of the story in exchange for the $5,000 paid to Mary Orr. Considering that she was not a famous author, and that she was selling a short story rather than a novel, the option fee seems generous. (By comparison, in 1950 Alfred Hitchcock acquired rights to Patricia Highsmith's first novel, *Strangers on a Train*, for only $7,500.) Mary Orr's deal in 1949—roughly the equivalent of a modest year's salary—was far more lucrative than the $2,000, $5,000, and $10,000 option fees that producers routinely offer today for first novels and other lesser works.

Between them, Miss Orr and Miss Powers cannily refused to relinquish all rights to the material. Instead, Mary Orr retained stage rights, so that today if the dramatic version of "The Wisdom of Eve" is performed anywhere, she gets a royalty. On the other hand, Fox refused to let her have mechanical rights, meaning that she gets nothing from television broadcasts and video rentals of *All About Eve*. But that was standard practice; even Joe Mankiewicz retained no mechanical rights to the film. He was paid for writing and directing, and got nothing else.

A more troubling aspect to Mary Orr, some fifty years later, is the matter of credit. She says, "A movie company takes advantage of anyone, if they can. You expect that. At the time, I was interested in the five thousand dollars they were paying for that little thing I had written in four days. I got the money and that's that. But apparently Mankiewicz never wanted my name mentioned at all in connection with the work."

Mary Orr's name does not appear in the screen credits of *All About Eve*, although in the screenplay published by Random House in 1951, and reprinted in 1972, the title page reads: "All About Eve / A Screenplay by / Joseph L. Mankiewicz / based upon a short story by / Mary Orr." In 1951, the preposition is "upon." By 1972 it has been shortened to "on." Because she retained stage rights, however, by the time the musical *Applause* opened on Broadway in 1970, Mary Orr received credit and Mankiewicz did not.

Darryl Zanuck seems to have found it anomalous that Mary Orr's name was missing from the official screen credits of *All About Eve*. In a memo written in early November 1950, shortly after the film's premiere, and sent to Fox story editor Julian Johnson, Zanuck inquired about the omission of Orr's name. On November 10 Johnson replied that "no credits are put in a contract which are not required. No author credit was demanded and none was put in the contract." Presumably, Mary Orr's agent could have gotten screen credit for her client if she had thought to ask for it.

But to quote Max Fabian in the film, "This is for lawyers to talk about." The legalities outlined here—who gets how much money and for what, whose name goes above the title, below it, and whose name gets left out—are standard points in every Hollywood contract, and have been for the better part of a century. Since they are haggled over so fiercely and often generate displeasure that lasts for years, they are matters of some interest in tracing the genesis of any film. Seen in the wider context of filmmaking, however, the deal that Mary Orr struck with 20th Century-Fox was sweeter than it might have been.

Is Mary Orr justified in claiming that Mankiewicz somehow sought to suppress her name in connection with *All About Eve*? It seems unlikely that he did. Even if he had tried, he could not have buried the fact that his screenplay was based on her story. Not surprisingly, Orr is restrained in her admiration for the film. Few writers like the changes another writer makes in adapting their work.

Mankiewicz and Orr, who never met, didn't like each other. More accurately, neither one liked the *idea* of the other. Her comments to me implied a certain disgruntlement that *All About Eve* is so much more famous than "The Wisdom of Eve."

In 1989, at the age of eighty, Mankiewicz discussed his career with Peter Stone, himself a screenwriter. Their conversation appeared in the August 1989 issue of *Interview*, under the title "All About Joe." That piece, which reads like a catalogue of slights to Mankiewicz during his sixty-year career, prompted the interviewer to remark, near the end of their talk, "Joe, throughout our entire conversation, I hear one thing over and over: anger." Mankiewicz replied, "I am angry—very angry," and explained that "I've never been recognized by my own country for my body of work. All over the world, but not in my own country."

Surely his grievance was misplaced, for Mankiewicz has often been ranked as one of this country's most important filmmakers, along with Billy Wilder, Alfred Hitchcock, George Stevens, Frank Capra, John Ford, William Wyler—in short, he belongs to the Hollywood pantheon. What's more surprising, however, is what Mankiewicz had to say in that interview about the real Eve, Elisabeth Bergner's "terrible girl," and what he implied about Orr, creator of the fictional Eve:

"About three years ago they presented me with the Lion d'Or at the Venice Film Festival. And I got this telephone call from an absolutely desperate-sounding woman. She said, 'Mr. Mankiewicz, this is Eve.' I said, 'Eve?' She said, 'Yes, the Eve you wrote the movie about. I was the girl who stood outside the theatre.' I said, 'Oh, I didn't know that.' "

"You didn't believe her at this point?" asked Stone.

"Not a word. So she says, 'I know you don't believe me, so I'm going to send you something.' Sure enough, she sent me a copy of this autobiography by Elisabeth Bergner, the great German actress. She wrote about a play she had done in New York, *The Two Mrs. Carrolls*. This girl, wearing red stockings [*sic*], was there outside the theatre every single night of the run. Bergner tells this story to a group of people, one of whom was a shy, quiet woman who never opened her mouth. A couple of months later, Bergner picked up a magazine, and to her absolute amazement, she read the whole story. And the author of this magazine story was that woman who seemed so shy: Mary Orr."

"The woman who never opened her mouth, just listened," said Stone.

"As Bergner told the story, which was filled with many of the incidents that were also in the picture."

"So the girl on the phone really *was* Eve."

"Exactly. Hollywood bought the story, it became *All About Eve*, and Mary Orr made her fortune out of this. The only people who did not make anything were Eve and Elisabeth Bergner. And me . . . except for my salary."

"And two Academy Awards," Stone pointed out.

"I earned them."

At the time of this interview Mankiewicz was old and bitter. But age, and feeling undervalued, don't really explain his claim that Mary Orr "made a fortune" from 20th Century-Fox. Even if he didn't know the exact amount she was paid for the rights to her story—and it's likely he didn't—he surely knew that magazine stories sold to Hollywood have rarely made a fortune for their writers.

In the interview, Mankiewicz seems to feel slighted that he, along with Eve's prototype, and Elisabeth Bergner as well, didn't get a cut of Mary Orr's "fortune": *The only people who did not make anything were Eve and Elisabeth Bergner. And me . . . except for my salary.*

Though Mankiewicz perhaps didn't realize it, he was quoting Elisabeth Bergner almost verbatim in the italicized lines above. Her book, wittily titled *Bewundert Viel und Viel Gescholten*—"Greatly Admired and Greatly Scolded"—devotes five pages to "the terrible girl," although Bergner never employs that epithet in print. Bergner, in her eighties when the book was published, remembered certain details differently from Mary Orr. Bergner got the story title wrong, the amount of time necessary for publication, and at some point the girl had stopped wearing a red coat and put on red stockings instead. In general, however, Bergner's version follows the one that Orr told me.

Here's how Bergner concludes her five-page anecdote about the would-be usurper:

"But I'm telling this story now only because Reggie Denham asked about The Girl With Red Stockings. He didn't know the outcome of the story which I've just told the reader. . . . Mary Orr was there and heard the story for the first time.

"A few weeks later in New York, I was at the hairdresser's when I picked up a magazine. There was this whole story printed under the title 'Girl With Red Stockings.' Without the names, of course. It was about the great actress and the girl who always stood outside the stage door and who told big lies in order to break into the theatre.

"And the author of this magazine story was Mary Orr, the shy, quiet girl who had listened to my story that night. . . . Hollywood bought the story for Bette Davis, added some love intrigue, and it became the film

All About Eve. This film became an international success and eventually a Broadway musical as well. *And Mary Orr and all the parties concerned grew very rich from it. The only ones who didn't earn anything from it were the real participants: the girl, my husband, and I.*" (Emphasis added.)

The peculiar, rankling relationship of Mankiewicz and Mary Orr resembles the struggle of an estranged couple for custody of an only child. That child is none other than Eve Harrington.

A few years after her phone call to Joe Mankiewicz, "Eve" made a call to a New York journalist named Harry Haun and poured out her story to him.

Haun sounded both amused and perplexed as he told me about "Eve" one bright, sunny morning in his apartment on Riverside Drive in New York. He is a burly native Texan who for many years has been a journalist specializing in celebrity profiles. Among those he has interviewed are Celeste Holm and Joseph L. Mankiewicz.

One day in the early 1990s, four decades after *All About Eve* was made, Haun answered his phone at the *New York Daily News* and heard an energetic voice telling him that she was the real Eve. Someone had sent her a copy of Haun's article on the movie in *Films in Review* for March/April 1991.

The caller was Miss X, who told Haun her real name: Martina Lawrence. But Haun already knew a Martina Lawrence: that's the name of one of the twin sisters Elisabeth Bergner played in the 1939 British film *Stolen Life.* (The other twin was called Sylvina Lawrence. By the time Bette Davis starred in the Hollywood remake in 1946, the twins had become Kate and Patricia Bosworth.)

Haun, considering the possibilities, set up a tea party so that Miss Lawrence could at last tell her version of the story. He also invited Mary Orr. If Joseph Mankiewicz hadn't been infirm, Haun might have persuaded him to complete the family circle: Eve's "parents" and their unholy offspring.

Harry Haun's original plan was a luncheon, but Mary Orr demurred. She told him, "I don't want to suffer through lunch. I'll come if you make it tea." He chose the upstairs at Sardi's because it's uncrowded in the afternoon.

Haun recalls that "the girls eyed each other curiously, suspiciously." Mary Orr remembers that "Martina and Harry did all the talking. I sat and listened."

What did they discuss?

"At first, she wanted Harry to help her write her side of the story. Then she wanted *me* to rewrite the story from her point of view. I said, 'I have no interest in doing that.' I got the feeling she was desperate to find someone to help her. At the end of tea I excused myself. You see, I had nothing to say to her. I had satisfied my curiosity to see her after all those years."

For indeed, Mary Orr and Martina Lawrence had met before. It was after "The Wisdom of Eve" appeared in *Cosmopolitan* in 1946, but before *All About Eve* was filmed.

"She came to my home one day, very angry," Mary Orr recalls. "We lived on Central Park South then, in an apartment on the second floor. Somehow this girl got past the doorman and made her way upstairs. I suppose she had found my name in the phone book. She had discovered that issue of *Cosmopolitan* in a stack of old magazines at a dentist's office.

"Now, this was a couple of years after it was published. She rang my bell and when I answered she pushed in past me. She was livid. I had no idea why she had come, but she threatened to sue me. She had recognized herself in the story but, the statute of limitations having expired, she never found a lawyer who would take the case.

"She lives in Venice, I believe. One of the things she said the day she broke into my apartment was, 'You owe me a fare to Italy.' And now, nearly a half-century later, she was in New York on a visit, trying to find somebody to write her story. That story—oh my, she thinks it's her claim to fame, even though it was detrimental to her."

In his article for *Films in Review*, Harry Haun added a postscript about Martina Lawrence: "A former librarian who lives in Venice and works in a bookstore there . . . she insists she was never the premeditated plotter Mankiewicz made her out to be—that her skullduggery only existed in the mind of Elisabeth Bergner."

Mary Orr's characterization of Martina Lawrence, and Harry Haun's, left me unsettled. I felt as though I had been reading Henry James at his most ambiguous. Indeed, the *donnée* of this story was right out of James: a forlorn little American selling books in Venice for fifty years, trying in vain to make someone believe her. Martina Lawrence might have materialized from *The Wings of the Dove* or *The Aspern Papers*.

Did she, I wondered, represent innocence betrayed, or evil understated?

What if she was really just an ingenue who wanted a part in a play? Suppose Elisabeth Bergner projected wickedness onto a young girl's innocent admiration? Bergner was a star. She could boost reputations, or destroy them. What if the unreciprocated advances of an aging actress had ruined the future of a naive girl in a little red coat (or was it red stockings?) who stood near the stage door night after night just to catch sight of her idol? And suppose this girl was not terrible at all. Suppose she was merely a fan—like the rest of us.

Or just the opposite. Suppose the girl was a Machiavellianess who would stop at nothing. In that case, "The Wisdom of Eve" merely suggests all she's capable of.

That version would play like this: After a baroque flirtation with the vulnerable, middle-aged, émigrée actress, the caressing little serpent coiled around her victim, injecting malice with each caress. She would do anything at all for a part in a play. She would even, like a female Iago, turn her mentor's "virtue into pitch."

Eventually I met Martina Lawrence face to face, but only at the eleventh hour. And rather than solve the mystery, she deepened it. But that conundrum comes later. For now, the one sure thing is this: If she hadn't existed, neither Mary Orr nor Joe Mankiewicz could have imagined her quite so well.

Chapter 4

Zanuck, Zanuck, Zanuck

*I*n the spring of 1950 Joe Mankiewicz received his first two Oscars—Best Director and Best Screenplay—for *A Letter to Three Wives*. By that time 20th Century-Fox, where Mankiewicz was under contract as a writer-director, had optioned Mary Orr's story. A year earlier this story had been given to Mankiewicz, who read it and apparently knew from the start that here, in a few pages, was the embryo of the picture he wanted to make about the theatre.

On April 29, 1949, Mankiewicz had written a memo to Darryl F. Zanuck, production chief of the studio. The memo recommended that Fox exercise its option on "The Wisdom of Eve." Mankiewicz also noted in his memo to Zanuck that the story "fits in with an original idea [of mine] and can be combined. Superb starring role for [Fox star] Susan Hayward."

The deal with Mary Orr and her agent was soon made, but Mankiewicz had little time to think about how he would treat the material, for he had just finished directing *House of Strangers* with Edward G. Robinson and Susan Hayward. With an opening date of July 1, Mankiewicz still had to supervise post-production work on the film.

Much more demanding was his next assignment, *No Way Out*, a tense racial drama starring Richard Widmark, Linda Darnell, and Sidney Poitier. During the early summer he and Lesser Samuels collaborated on the screenplay for this movie, which was shot from October 28 through December 20. (The picture was not released, however, until August 1950.)

Between completing the screenplay of *No Way Out* and the start of production, Mankiewicz in the summer and early fall of 1949 also wrote the treatment of the movie that would become *All About Eve*. To do so, he left home and sought the relative isolation of the San Ysidro Guest Ranch near Santa Barbara. There he followed his habit of writing at night: "I was alone and I would write from about eight P.M. until two or three in the morning, while listening to the radio. Next day I would play tennis and go for long walks, then start back to work after dark."

Like many writers of the time, especially male writers, Mankiewicz never learned to type. As the *Hollywood Reporter* once phrased it, he "penned his scripts in longhand." From these manuscripts his secretary, Adelaide Wallace, would make typescripts with impeccable margins and faultless spelling.

Mankiewicz said later that he worked on the treatment for three months, and the rough draft of the screenplay for six weeks. The treatment—which is a synopsis or detailed plot outline—was called *Best Performance*, Mankiewicz's original title for *All About Eve*. It ran to eighty-two pages, double-spaced.

It is impossible to reconstruct a complete and precise chronology of *Eve*'s evolution from story, to treatment, to script, and finally to completed film. But the copy of Mankiewicz's treatment that Zanuck used to write his suggested revisions is dated September 26, 1949. This indicates that Mankiewicz worked on his treatment during the summer and early fall of 1949, spending, as he recalled later, three months on it.

He would not, of course, have worked on treatment and script simultaneously. It seems likely, therefore, that with so many projects underway, Mankiewicz waited until he had finished shooting *No Way Out* in late December of 1949 before he began transforming his *Best Performance* treatment into the actual script that would later be renamed *All About Eve*. Zanuck was eager to see it.

Darryl Zanuck's biographer, Mel Gussow, describes the producer's collaboration with Mankiewicz as one of "mutual trust with a healthy degree of mutual suspicion . . . they worked superbly together. Each honestly admired the other. Zanuck knew that there was no one better with dialogue on the lot and Mankiewicz knew that his outspoken comedies could not be made except in such an atmosphere of freedom as provided by Zanuck."

Zanuck produced three of the films Mankiewicz directed at Fox: *No Way Out*, *All About Eve*, and *People Will Talk*. Their actual collaboration, however, was more intricate than the above statistic indicates, for Zanuck, as studio production chief, was to some extent de facto producer of every film done on the lot. He and Mankiewicz retained their wary cordiality until 1963, when Zanuck fired Mankiewicz as director of *Cleopatra* and recut that ill-fated epic. ("He *rechopped* the picture," said Mankiewicz.)

Zanuck ran the show at Fox. He was responsible for all A product (as opposed to cut-rate B pictures), in addition to which he personally produced one or two films a year. Naturally, he reported to the president of the company and the board of directors, most of whom were in New York, but generally they left the day-by-day business of *making* the movies up to him.

Reading Mankiewicz's treatment of *Best Performance*, Zanuck followed his custom of making notes in pencil throughout the text and inside the back cover. At one point he underlined a phrase in Addison DeWitt's voice-over narration: "Eve . . . but more of Eve, later. All about Eve, in fact." The phrase Zanuck underlined was "all about Eve," which may have been the first dawning of the new title. At any rate, sometime during January 1950 the project acquired its new name.

Elsewhere in the pages of Mankiewicz's initial treatment, Zanuck expressed his concern about premature revelation of Eve's villainy to the audience. "Beware of Birdie's jealousy as it will tip off that Eve is a heel," he wrote. Where Eve makes a sexual overture to Bill Sampson in her dressing room and kisses him, Zanuck's reaction was: "This is all wrong. She is too clever to jump in so quickly." The kiss was eliminated, but the overture stayed. Several long speeches were reduced to a few lines, with Zanuck's marginal note, "This should cover it all." There were professorial admonitions to "Make clear. This can be confusing." Perhaps anticipating audience incredulity and wondering if viewers would suspend disbelief, Zanuck reacted to Karen's draining the gas tank of the Richards' car to make Margo miss her performance with: "This is difficult to swallow." It stayed in, and it's still a bit difficult to swallow.

A major concern to the producer was a series of scenes, in the treatment, that depicted Eve's calculated designs on Lloyd Richards. Zanuck wanted to cut the entire four pages that showed Eve and Lloyd spending time together in little cafés on side streets, in Lloyd's apartment with Karen present and later without Karen, in Eve's furnished room, and Lloyd going to see Eve late at night after a phone call from a friend of Eve's. Zanuck noted: "Dull, obvious, dirty. . . . This is wrong. . . . All relationships with Eve and Lloyd [should be] played offstage by suggestion. . . . We get it by one brief scene at rehearsal." Most of the superfluous material was deleted.

Like most treatments, Mankiewicz's is a typical writer's "workshop" where he lays out all his materials, from which he will soon extract and polish the actual script. What sets this treatment apart, however, is the degree to which Mankiewicz has already nailed down the structure of his screenplay. Even at this stage, the material is unmistakably Mankiewicz's own; it bears his fluency, his wit, and also his excesses. It's an excellent example of how to transform a well-tailored treatment into an even better script.

Perhaps most surprising is the discovery that many of the film's best lines—"Fasten your seat belts, it's going to be a bumpy night," and "You can always put that award where your heart ought to be," to cite two of the most famous—were already there at this early stage of *All About Eve*.

Instructive, too, are the changes and omissions made either by Mankiewicz or Zanuck. For example, in the treatment Karen and Lloyd "wish Bill all sorts of bad luck" as he leaves to go to Hollywood. In the film Karen says, "Good luck, genius," and Lloyd merely shakes Bill's hand. Someone realized that most moviegoers would be confused by the theatre shibboleth "break a leg."

There's even a whiff of deference to McCarthyism. In the treatment,

Mankiewicz has Eve tell Margo, in a cab from LaGuardia after they've put Bill on the plane, that she—Margo—needs galoshes. Eve knows this because she has watched Margo's comings and goings so closely. Referring to Eve's surveillance, Margo quips, "You're not on one of those congressional committees, are you?" This sly political reference must have given Zanuck the willies, for he slashed through it with a heavy pencil—markedly heavier than elsewhere—as though the House Committee on Un-American Activities were reading over his shoulder.

At the end of the treatment, the young girl, Phoebe, doesn't slip into Eve Harrington's apartment as she was to do later, in both script and film. Rather, she calls out from the shadows near the entrance to Eve's Park Avenue building. Eve invites her in for a drink. And the girl is not a highschool student but a young working woman who "worships Eve from afar." Nor does Phoebe hold Eve's award to her breast while bowing into an infinity of mirrors; that cinematic finale came later. The treatment ends as Addison DeWitt's taxi "drives off and is lost in the lights of the city."

After incorporating various changes suggested by his producer, Mankiewicz delivered his first draft of the screenplay—dubbed the "temporary script"—to Darryl Zanuck on March 1, 1950. According to 20th Century-Fox's records, Mankiewicz's services as writer (for accounting purposes) terminated on March 24, 1950. Adhering to studio bookkeeping policy, Fox subsequently started Mankiewicz's "assignment as director" at the beginning of April.

Mankiewicz was luckier than most screenwriters: His scripts were lightly edited, if at all. (Unlike the writer who once told a companion at the premiere of a film he had written, "Shh! I thought I just heard one of my lines.") In the case of *All About Eve*, the trajectory from treatment, through various drafts of the shooting script, to the actual film was uncluttered by compromise. In this sense, *Eve* "belongs" to Mankiewicz as a novel belongs to its author. He owns it as few studio directors ever owned their films.

Zanuck, of course, served as "editor" to the Mankiewicz screenplay, as he had done on the treatment. After reading Mankiewicz's lengthy first-draft "temporary script" in March 1950, he praised it highly but suggested some changes and cuts. Zanuck wrote in a memo, "I have tried to sincerely point out the spots that appeared dull or overdrawn. I have not let the length of the script influence me. I have tried to cut it as I am sure I would cut it if I were in the projection room."

The "temporary script" of March 1 ran to 223 pages. After Zanuck's cuts and Mankiewicz's own, the next—and final—version had slimmed to 180 pages. Most of the changes involve shortening or condensing.

Overall, the "temporary script" is not radically different from the final version. But there are some intriguing changes. For example, the "temporary" has a five-page scene in Max Fabian's limousine after Margo's cocktail party. Karen and Lloyd ride with Max and they all talk about Margo's outrageous behavior at the party. They also discuss Eve as a possible understudy for Margo. Karen and Lloyd urge Max to give Eve the job. Max demurs. It's a long, chatty scene that stops the story dead.

Deleted, also, was a four-page scene in the Richards' country house. Dialogue from this scene was saved, however, and added to the lines spoken in the car by Margo, Karen, and Lloyd.

Elsewhere in the "temporary script" are such unpolished, rather pedestrian speeches as this, spoken by Addison to Eve: "What do you take me for? A talented newsboy like Bill Sampson? Or Margo—a gifted neurosis? Or Lloyd Richards—a poetic bank clerk? A refined Girl Scout—like Karen? Look closely, Eve, it's time you did. I am Addison DeWitt. I am nobody's fool. Least of all yours."

In the revision, Mankiewicz turned it into this trenchant exchange:

ADDISON

What do you take me for?

EVE

I don't know that I take you for anything. . . .

ADDISON

Is it possible—even conceivable—that you've confused me with that gang of backward children you play tricks on? That you have the same contempt for me as you have for them?

EVE

I'm sure you mean something by that, Addison—but I don't know what.

ADDISON

Look closely, Eve, it's time you did. I am Addison DeWitt. I'm nobody's fool. Least of all yours.

Anyone comparing these two versions of the *All About Eve* screenplay would likely agree that the deleted passages were love handles on an otherwise shapely script. Since Mankiewicz, as screenwriter, was inclined to overindulge, we can assume that it was Zanuck who reduced *Eve* from 223 pages to a svelte 180 by toning the muscle and losing the flab.

Zanuck, unlike the semi-literate moguls of Hollywood legend, was considered an astute judge of scripts, and his editorial suggestions were usually followed—even by Mankiewicz, who had enough power and prestige to buck the front office when necessary. While many of Zanuck's suggestions at the time of the first draft of *Eve* were reflected in the revised shooting script, Mankiewicz disregarded one change that Zanuck recommended. "On page 32," Zanuck wrote, "I think the use of my name in a picture I am associated with will be considered self-aggrandizement. I believe you can cut it with no loss." The producer's name occurs four times just after Bill Sampson, making his first appearance, flings open the door of Margo's dressing room.

BILL

The airlines have clocks, even if you haven't! I start shooting a week from Monday—Zanuck is impatient, he wants me, he needs me!

MARGO

Zanuck, Zanuck, Zanuck! What are you two—lovers?

The in-joke stayed in the script. Gary Merrill and Bette Davis read their lines as written, their exchange was filmed, and the scene remained in the picture. To this day it gets a laugh, one reason being that it's an early tip-off—although a red herring—to the movie's gay subtext.

Across town at Paramount, Billy Wilder, Charles Brackett, and D. M. Marshman, Jr., were also dropping names in their *Sunset Boulevard* screenplay. "Seems like Zanuck's got himself a baseball picture," sneers producer Fred Clark when he rejects one of William Holden's Casey-at-the-bat story ideas. "I think Zanuck's all wet," says Holden, the failed screenwriter.

By early April, Mankiewicz had finished revising the draft of his screenplay. The version that now emerged was the shooting script, identified on the title page as "Revised Final—April 5, 1950." (This designation appears on Bette Davis's copy of the script, which I consulted at Boston University, where her papers are deposited. Other members of the cast and crew would have used copies of the same version.)

Adam's Rib

From the Book of Genesis: "And the Lord God caused a deep sleep to fall upon Adam, and he slept; and he took one of his ribs, and closed up the flesh instead thereof.

And the rib, which the Lord God had taken from man, made he a woman."

The Book of Mankiewicz gives a similar account of Eve's creation, only in this case it's Eve Harrington. For Joe Mankiewicz, at a young age, also lost a rib. Many years later he told an interviewer, "I remember that in 1918 I was sick for a year during the famous influenza epidemic. I caught double pneumonia, followed by pleurisy, and they removed one of my ribs."

Mankiewicz's sister, Erna, told Joe's biographer, Kenneth Geist, that during surgery on her little brother the doctors inserted a silver rib to replace the one they had removed. Mankiewicz himself denied this, however, saying that if he had indeed received such a valuable substitute, "I'd have had a mortgage on it long ago."

The story is worthy of a zealous press agent. But Erna Mankiewicz was no fabulist. She was a schoolteacher who surely would have bridled at any attempt to fictionalize her brother's life.

Much had happened to the material between Mary Orr's "The Wisdom of Eve" and this completed version of the screenplay. Most obviously, it had grown from a prose work of fewer than a dozen pages into 180 pages of narrative and dialogue. Included in this metamorphosis was Mankiewicz's recharacterization and expansion of Mary Orr's characters—Margola Cranston, now rechristened Margo Channing; Karen Richards, Lloyd Richards, Eve Harrington, Miss Caswell—and his invention of half a dozen new ones: Addison DeWitt, Bill Sampson, the Old Actor at the Sarah Siddons Awards, Birdie Coonan, Max Fabian, and Phoebe. (Mankiewicz had also dropped a character from the story: producer-director Clement Howell, Margola's English husband.)

In Mary Orr's story Karen Richards is the narrator. There she, too, is an actress, but Mankiewicz, in his script, has made her just a "happy little housewife." Margola's maid, who bears no resemblance to Birdie, is named Alice; she neither speaks nor is she described. Margola lives in Great Neck, Long Island, in a forty-room house called Capulet's Cottage. In the story, Margola is not forty but somewhat older. Karen Richards says, "If she ever sees forty-five again, I'll have my eyes lifted."

Mankiewicz kept not a line of dialogue from Mary Orr's story, but he did retain what served him far better: the breezy, brittle tone. The story's high-gloss opening sentences match Addison DeWitt's lacquered narration at the start of the movie. We don't know to what extent Mankiewicz consciously mimicked Mary Orr's tone, but he must have recognized the story's hard-edged irony as the right key in which to play his own composition.

Mankiewicz and Zanuck, while in basic agreement on the *All About Eve* screenplay, were not the final arbiters on all points, however. The imprimatur of Joseph Ignatius Breen, chief administrator of the Production Code, was necessary for this picture as for virtually every other one. Breen was, in effect, the head censor of Hollywood at the time, an ardent Catholic who had been director of Code Administration since 1933, first under Will Hays and, since 1945, under Eric Johnston.

References to "the Hays office" and later to "the Johnston office" actually meant the Motion Picture Producers and Distributors of America (MPPDA), which was created by the film industry in 1922 and whose grip tightened in 1934 after Catholic bishops formed the Legion of Decency and threatened to bar American Catholics from seeing all movies. (Some attributed this more rigid enforcement of the Code to Mae West's racy on-screen dialogue and suggestive wiggles. Pauline Kael, for example, says that if West's on-screen bosom-heaving and dirty songs "led to the industry's self-policing Production Code, they were worth it. We enjoyed the crime so much that we could endure even the punishment of family entertainment.")

Breen and his minions were empowered to review scripts as well as films, suggesting changes at all stages and granting a seal of approval to films that met the standards of the Code. Only rarely would a producer buck the power of the Production Code by releasing a film without the requisite seal. Two famous instances of Code nonapproval are Howard Hughes's *The Outlaw* in 1943 and Otto Preminger's *The Moon Is Blue* ten years later.

Familiar Code regulations included these: "Scenes of passion should not be introduced when not essential to the plot"; "Sex perversion or any reference to it is forbidden"; "The sanctity of the institution of marriage and the home shall be upheld"; and "Pointed profanity . . . or other profane or vulgar expressions . . . is forbidden."

Although the Code was not only fussy but also obsessive, its guardians often missed subtle suggestiveness, both verbal and visual. Screenwriters and directors knew this, and so a script usually included bargaining material—that is, scenes or bits of business and lines of dialogue that the moviemakers didn't expect to get Production Code approval for, but that they included for trading purposes.

Today *All About Eve* strikes viewers as "adult" in the sense that it is sophisticated, but in 1950 much of its dialogue stopped just short of raciness and some of its situations didn't conform to Code standards of "good taste" (e.g., Bill, explaining to Margo why he didn't immediately come up to her room: "I ran into Eve on my way upstairs and she told me you were dressing." Margo: "That's *never* stopped you before.").

Like the other studios, 20th Century-Fox employed experts to forewarn of anticipated problems when the script was submitted for Production Code approval. Colonel Jason S. Joy, Fox's director of public relations, acted as ex officio liaison to Joseph Breen and the formidable script-vetters of the Johnston office.

Colonel Joy was ideal for the job, since he himself had formerly worked in the Hays office. A native of Montana, he came to Hollywood in 1926 from the American Red Cross. He left the Hays office in 1932 to join the Fox Film Corporation—three years before it merged with 20th Century to become 20th Century-Fox.

By the time of *All About Eve*, Colonel Joy was a gray-haired man in his sixties. With his conservative eyeglasses and loose-fitting business suits, he might have belonged to that multitude of character actors who played uncles and businessmen and politicians in movies and television shows. Even his voice, which was pleasantly staid, added to the typecasting.

During Colonel Joy's time at the Hays office, the Production Code lacked real teeth. Tolerant and enlightened, Joy did not have a large appetite for censorship, and his admonitions were frequently ignored. According to film historian Kenneth Macgowan, "Some producers played ball, some did not. Others sent in only parts of their scripts, and paid little or no attention to Joy's criticism."

But the Code, and its enforcers, grew increasingly rigid under Breen, who blamed the Jews in Hollywood for just about everything. Writing to Father Wilfrid Parsons, editor of the Catholic publication *America*, in 1932, he characterized the Jews as "a rotten bunch of vile people with no respect for anything beyond the making of money. Here [in Hollywood] we have Paganism rampant and in its most virulent form. Drunkenness and debauchery are commonplace. Sexual perversion is rampant . . . any number of our directors and stars are perverts. Ninety-five percent of these folks are Jews of an Eastern European lineage. They are, probably, the scum of the earth."

Despite Breen's anti-Semitism, he seems not to have singled out Jewish writers, directors, and producers for increased scrutiny. To Breen, perhaps, after years of stanching the corrupt ooze of Hollywood, there was neither Jew nor gentile but only a vast freemasonry of debauched pagans. Mankiewicz was Jewish; Zanuck was not. Breen's fiery righteousness engulfed them both.

Beginning in March 1950, a routine but surreal correspondence started up, first among those at 20th Century-Fox who were concerned with making *All About Eve*, and later between them and the resident censors at the Johnston office. Surviving letters and memoranda from these exchanges convey some of the difficulties that moviemakers faced. No one escaped the pinch of the Code straitjacket.

On March 15, 1950, Colonel Joy delivered the Mankiewicz script to Joseph Breen. Two weeks later, in a letter dated March 30, Breen wrote: "We have read the final script for your proposed production titled *All About Eve*, and wish to report that this basic story seems acceptable under the provisions of the Production Code.

"However, we direct your attention to the following details: At the outset, we direct your particular attention to the need for the greatest possible care in the selection and photographing of the dresses and costumes of your women. The Production Code makes it mandatory that the intimate parts of the body—specifically the breasts of women—be fully covered at all times. Any compromise with this regulation will compel us to withhold approval of your picture."

This curious opening of Breen's letter wouldn't surprise us if it were addressed to Howard Hughes. After all, *The Outlaw* had made Jane Russell's breasts notorious and wags were still joking that the title should have been "The Sale of Two Titties." But Joseph Mankiewicz? Nowhere in the script was there a hint that décolletage might upstage drama. Nor was any female star in the cast known for cheesecake. It's possible, of course, that Marilyn's starlet reputation had preceded her. More likely, however, this mammary caveat was—to mix an anatomical metaphor—a knee-jerk reaction from Breen. It seems no one read the paragraph carefully, for in the party scene Marilyn ended up just about as strapless as possible.

Next, Breen asked that on page 15 "the use of the word 'sex' be changed to something less blunt in the circumstances." The offending line, spoken by Margo in the dressing room when she quotes the lady reporter from the South, was: "Ah don' understand about all these plays about sex-stahved Suth'n women—sex is one thing we were nevah stahved for in the South!"

Colonel Joy asked Mankiewicz for the change, and got it. "Sex" turned into "love."

On the next page of the script Margo said, "Honey chile had a point. You know, I can remember plays about women—even from the South— where it never even occurred to them whether they wanted to marry their fathers more than their brothers." Breen found this dialogue unacceptable. Later, when Colonel Joy suggested that the line be changed to the more Freudian "whether they had a fixation for their fathers or their brothers," Mankiewicz snapped in a memo to Zanuck, with a copy to Colonel Joy: "I do not like Jason's substitution of 'fixation' for 'marry' in Margo's teasing line about Lloyd's plays. I cannot imagine even censors objecting to the line as it is now written—delivered in a light, ribbing tone. The proper word, in any case, would be 'screw.' "

Mankiewicz sounds disingenous. The censors *did* object, and eventually a compromise was made. Jack Vizzard, one of Breen's underlings, noted in a "memo for the files" on May 4 that "a protection shot will be developed at this point, since it *sounds* as though the dialogue is talking about incest." Mankiewicz kept the line in his script, but the protection shot was eventually used in the film.

In the script, Mankiewicz describes Margo's dressing room and then adds, "A door leads to an old-fashioned bathroom." Birdie, of course, makes several trips into and out of this bathroom. But it made Breen nervous. His letter states, "We presume that there will be no notice of a toilet in the bathroom in these scenes."

When Colonel Joy, in a subsequent memo, conveyed Breen's apprehension to Mankiewicz, the retort was: "By my Oscars, I promise to show no indication of a toilet. Has it ever occurred to Joe Breen that the rest of the world must be convinced that Americans never relieve themselves?"

Next was a line that, if retained, would have made Thelma Ritter as notorious as Jane Russell, though for a different reason. Mankiewicz has Birdie say, in the dressing-room scene, "I'll never forget that blizzard the night we played Cheyenne. A cold night. First time I ever saw a brassiere break like a piece of matzo." Breen, not tickled, noted dryly that "the reference to the brassiere should be changed or eliminated."

And so it was, as Mankiewicz surely expected. It's likely he conceded that Borscht Circuit line as a gambit for retaining Birdie's crack. "Everything but the bloodhounds snappin' at her rear end." Breen also found this one "vulgar" and recommended that it be changed or eliminated, presumably because verbal references to the posterior were off limits although visual ones were not.

Colonel Joy, as go-between, reported Breen's request to Mankiewicz, adding helpfully, "Insomuch as Bridie's line is at the end of the shot, perhaps you can let it go the way it is and clip off 'rear end' if we have to, although I don't think we will." Mankiewicz replied impatiently, "The word *should* be 'arse.' What do you suggest we substitute for 'rear end'? 'Backside'? 'Butt'? What would you think of 'snappin' at her transmission'?"

In the pantry scene where Margo supplies Max Fabian with bicarbonate of soda for heartburn, the script reads simply, "Max burps." This troubled Breen, who wrote worriedly, "We presume there will be nothing coarse about the burp." But the Production Code, to his chagrin, lacked a subsection on prohibited human rumbles, and so Gregory Ratoff, as Max Fabian, produced one of the great screen belches, perhaps surpassed only by Elizabeth Taylor's in *Secret Ceremony*—although hers seems unscripted, a comic fringe benefit of the fried chicken she devours in a scene with Mia Farrow.

Curiously, Breen had missed an earlier Max Fabian burp. On page four of the script, at the Sarah Siddons Awards, Mankiewicz had indicated that Max "drops the powder into some water, stirs it, drinks, burps delicately, and closes his eyes." Perhaps it was the word "delicately" that made this foreshadowing burp acceptable.

On page 119, the word "tart" was unacceptable to Breen and so it disappeared.

A few pages on, Breen and his fellow readers discerned a nuance that any literary critic might envy. Karen and Lloyd are arguing over Eve. Lloyd says, "That bitter cynicism of yours is something you've acquired since you left Radcliffe," and Karen snaps back, "That cynicism you refer to, I acquired the day I discovered I was different from little boys!" Her line always gets a laugh, one reason being that its meaning sounds submerged and elliptical. It could mean all sorts of things, or merely the obvious.

But Breen had little doubt. When told of it, Mankiewicz snorted. Zanuck swore. Colonel Joy pointed out diplomatically to Mr. Breen that perhaps someone had misconstrued the comic intent of that exchange between husband and wife. Breen wrote back: "The dialogue is still considered highly questionable. The lines seem open to an interpretation that the reference is to menstruation."

Joseph Breen yielded on the line, but the matter of bathrooms would not go away. We can imagine the grimace on Breen's face as he finished dictating a long memo: "We suggest that you soften the reference to the 'Ladies' Room' by possibly referring to it as the 'Lounge Room' or the 'Powder Room' or something similar. The line, 'I understand she is now the understudy in there' seems somewhat vulgar, and we ask that it be changed."

Now it was Mankiewicz's turn to grimace. Of all the idiotic, half-baked— He sighed and puffed harder on his pipe. "Changing 'Ladies' Room' to 'Powder Room,' " he wrote in an exasperated memo, "is not only childish but will most certainly hurt Bill's comment" (referring to Eve Harrington, Bill says, "I understand she's now the understudy in there."). Exhausted by such extreme literal-mindedness, Mankiewicz concluded rather pedantically, " 'Understudy' refers to *ladies* and not to *powder*."

On this point Mankiewicz prevailed, and on Breen's final point he also refused to budge. Referring to the hotel-room scene where Addison slaps Eve, Joseph Breen wrote demurely: "We ask that the slap across the face be eliminated."

It wasn't, and when Breen saw this slap on screen in its context of implied sado-masochism, he may well have bemoaned his leniency in letting the pagans retain such perversion.

Chapter 5

Miss Channing Is Ageless

or Claudette Colbert April really was the cruelest month—at least in 1950, for that's when she lost the part of Margo Channing. Colbert was forty-seven at the time, late autumn for a movie actress in those days. The first long shadow had crept across her career six years earlier when she played—reluctantly—the role of mother to adult Jennifer Jones and adolescent Shirley Temple in *Since You Went Away* (1944). Anyone in Hollywood could have told you that her best films were behind her: *Cleopatra, Imitation of Life, It Happened One Night*, all released in 1934; *Drums Along the Mohawk* (1939); *Palm Beach Story* (1942); and many others. She no longer got the star treatment—or the star roles—of earlier years, when she was, in the words of her *Midnight* co-star Don Ameche, "completely spoiled."

As long as Oscar nominations, and one Oscar, were appearing on schedule, and a Colbert movie was practically guaranteed at the box office, she demanded that cinematographers shoot her from certain angles; above all, they must photograph only her left profile, for she considered her right one unflattering. (Colleagues called the right side of her face "the dark side of the moon" because no one ever saw it.)

Claudette also insisted that the studio have a driver on call for her around the clock, whether she went anywhere or not.

The words used to describe Colbert were "high-spirited," "silken," "charming," "sophisticated," "strong-minded." She was a lady, even when her left nipple bobbed above the white surf as she bathed in asses' milk in *The Sign of the Cross* (1932). Accordingly, one definition of a Hollywood lady might be that, in such circumstances, her left profile will always upstage her left nipple. Claudette Colbert was untouched by scandal and aloof to feuds, although she did quarrel with Noël Coward once, provoking him to say of the petite actress, "If she had a neck I would wring it."

Darryl Zanuck had loftier ambitions for Colbert when he thought of her as Margo Channing in *All About Eve*. For one thing, she had class, and Fox put a premium on class. Then, too, Colbert's forte was comedy, and she knew how to wear elegant clothes. She also had a sly wit, which seemed right for Margo, and Colbert's on-screen persona was a woman who always did the right thing. Margo Channing didn't always do the right thing but her character was sympathetic, and who wouldn't pull for Claudette Colbert against the nasty usurper, Eve? In Fox films, Zanuck liked good characters good and bad ones sexy.

And Claudette was certainly good. She once said she got tired of playing noble roles and would have liked to play more feline characters. That's why Margo Channing thrilled her. Mankiewicz seemed happy that she would be his star. Perhaps he responded to what a critic later called "the hard-softness of Colbert's sophistication."

Colbert could hardly wait to finish *Three Came Home*. The director, Jean Negulesco, wanted realism in this World War II drama in which British and American families on Borneo are sent to prison camps by the Japanese invaders. Colbert knew all along that she was giving an outstanding performance, so when Negulesco directed her to play a jungle rape scene in the most harrowing way possible, she complied. The scene called for her to fight off a prison guard, the would-be rapist. As the cameras whirred, Colbert thrashed about, she fought and kicked and bit as though her life depended on it, as indeed the character's did.

When Claudette screamed, then fell writhing to the ground, it looked like the climax of the scene. An instant later, however, the cast and crew realized it was something more. Negulesco rushed to her, along with his assistant and several other actors in the film. Someone called an ambulance and a couple of hours later word reached the set that the star would remain hospitalized indefinitely with a ruptured disk.

Colbert knew then that she would never make *All About Eve.* "I cried for days," she said many years later. "Days! I cried for years."

But studios will always be kind, especially when they stand to lose money on an injured star. "Fox couldn't have been nicer," Colbert went on. "They waited for me as long as they could. They waited two months, and Joe Mankiewicz was adorable. He used to send me flowers tied to a pogo stick."

In her later comments Colbert throws light on how Mankiewicz conceived *her* Margo Channing: "Joe's idea originally was that Anne Baxter as a young girl looked very much like me. And that was the point of it— that this young girl had a fixation about the older actress. She looked like her, and she thought she could be better. When Bette did the role, it became a whole different thing."

Suddenly, hearing that, you can almost imagine Colbert in the role. For the first time, the original casting makes sense. Otherwise, it's rather a stretch to imagine her as Margo because Colbert has the "unyielding good taste" not of Margo Channing but of Karen Richards. Colbert—flamboyantly bitchy? Colbert delivering such lines as, "Remind me to tell you about the time I looked into the heart of an artichoke"? Colbert gulping a martini and then swooping down the stairs like a maddened bat?

No. Colbert's Margo would have been far more secure than Bette's. Davis was brass; Colbert platinum. *Her* Margo, threatened by Eve and attacked by Addison, would have been moderately surprised but lightly self-mocking. ("Colbert would have been a piss-elegant drunk," Mankiewicz said later.) With Claudette Colbert as Margo, the problem of Eve Harrington might have resembled a drawing-room comedy where an upstart must be dealt with in Act II and put in her place by the end of the third act.

Years later Mankiewicz admitted that he still thought about Colbert in the role: "The question of aging would have been emphasized if Claudette had played Margo. Margo can't play her usual roles because she's too old. But, in the eyes of the public, Bette Davis was never really young. And so that dimension of the aging actress is somewhat eclipsed with Bette playing Margo Channing."

When Colbert talked about the movie in later years she said, "Bette did a great job! I know how much it meant to her at the time, because she had her share of personal and professional woes." Asked if she felt any bitterness over the loss, Claudette replied, "It wasn't my conception of the role, but I resent those false reports that portray me as ungracious to a fellow artist who gave as much to the role as Bette did."

Bette and Claudette crossed paths occasionally over the years, and neither hissed. Sometime in the 1960s, after both women had long since grown used to playing someone's mother, Claudette told Bette, "I envy you your career. Do you know why? It's because you played older women before you had to. Now you'll never have to cross the age bridge."

In her autobiography, *The Lonely Life*, Bette wrote: "I say thank you to Claudette Colbert for hurting her back. Claudette's loss was my gain. No broken back—no Gary Merrill. I must confess, in the years that followed I felt less and less thankful to Claudette's broken back."

With Colbert's back in a steel brace and the rest of her in traction, a replacement had to be found. No doubt Mankiewicz was fearful that Zanuck might use Colbert's indisposition as an excuse for offering Margo to the actress he had favored from the start: Marlene Dietrich.

Zanuck and Mankiewicz had tussled over this one before. Mankiewicz objected strenuously to Dietrich. Later he explained why: "I was, and am, a great admirer of Marlene. But from what I knew of her work and equipment as an actress, I simply could not visualize—or hear—her as a possible Margo." Anyone who questions Mankiewicz's judgment in this instance should imitate Dietrich's voice and accent while repeating the line "Fasten your seat belts, it's going to be a bumpy night." It takes forever.

Dietrich, an on-screen paean to artificiality, might have stolen *All About Eve*, but it would have been petty theft. The script was already a tribute to artifice. The right actress to play Margo was therefore one with dirt on her shoes—an American Anna Magnani—and one earthy enough to make you believe it when she calls herself "a junkyard" and orders new girdles a size larger. But Dietrich, even in 1950, was far beyond girdles. As an actress, she was approaching those unworldly contours befitting the inflatable dress she wore in her nightclub act during the long twilight of her career.

Mankiewicz wanted Colbert's replacement locked in as fast as possible. Otherwise, Zanuck might revert to Susan Hayward, whom Mankiewicz had originally mentioned as a possible Margo Channing and who was right there on the Fox lot, under contract and available. Now, however, she seemed wrong to Mankiewicz, one reason being her age: Hayward was only thirty-two; Margo was forty.

Mankiewicz had a viable second choice, an actress who had long ago learned every theatrical trick and who was famous for her stage work in London and New York. Gertrude Lawrence was fifty-one, but with her swooping archness, her great-lady-of-the-stage mannerisms, and a zany sophistication that had served her well in Noël Coward comedies, she deserved the compliment that Lloyd Richards, in the *Eve* script, paid his leading lady: "Margo, you haven't got any age."

Gertrude Lawrence was an extravagant performer, extravagant in the Josephine Baker mode except that Lawrence didn't use tail feathers and peek-a-boo outfits. The obverse of Baker, actually, Lawrence achieved extravagance by suppressing it, so that her preposterousness remained mostly subliminal. Beautifully dressed and coiffed, with a hint of madness under the makeup, Lawrence suggested camp By Appointment to His Majesty the King. Though not well remembered today, Lawrence was a celebrity when Mankiewicz considered her for *Eve*. (Julie Andrews, who played her in the 1968 movie musical *Star!*, captured none of the above.)

In certain photos Gertrude Lawrence resembles Dietrich: hands in slacks pockets, eyelids down. In other pictures she has the searching eyes, the absurdly thin and arched eyebrows of Elisabeth Bergner. Elsewhere—in family snapshots of Gertrude digging in the garden, without makeup and with a head scarf knotted in front—she could pass for Minnie Pearl.

Her Margo Channing would have lifted the picture into the clouds of cracked-soprano loopiness, evoking weird echoes of the British jazz age:

long cigarette holders, smoking jackets, and fox-trots. There's a certain wan sweetness about Gertrude Lawrence and her era, which by 1950 had already vanished. But to have made it Gertrude Lawrence's movie in the way that it became Bette Davis's, Mankiewicz would have had to rework *All About Eve*. With Bette the movie flames, because she plays Margo as a walking bonfire. Gertrude's Margo Channing would have sparkled, occasionally going off like a Roman candle.

Mankiewicz claimed he sent Gertrude Lawrence his treatment and she liked it enormously. But getting the actual script into her hands was another matter. More than twenty years after *All About Eve*, Mankiewicz said, "To this day, I don't know whether Gertie ever did read it; I'm quite sure that if she had, she would have crawled to California to play it."

Here is the Mankiewicz version of his dealings with Gertrude Lawrence:

"All scripts were first submitted to, and approved by, her lawyer, Fanny Holtzmann. Miss Holtzmann read the screenplay and called me at home to say she found it very good. There were only two changes she would insist upon:

"One: The drunk scenes would have to be eliminated. It would be preferable, in fact, if Miss Lawrence neither drank nor smoked at all on the screen.

"Two: During the party sequence, the pianist was not to play 'Liebestraum.' Instead, he would accompany Miss Lawrence as she sang a torch song about Bill."

Mankiewicz makes lawyer Holtzmann sound creepily protective. But unless he omitted some key part of the story, Holtzmann's alleged first stipulation makes no sense. Gertrude Lawrence was often photographed with a cigarette in her hand, and she was no teetotaler onstage or off.

Holtzmann's second condition does ring true. What better place to showcase Gertrude Lawrence than at a piano in the middle of a cocktail party? And the suggested song—"Bill," with music by Jerome Kern and lyrics by P. G. Wodehouse and Oscar Hammerstein II—might have worked well as Margo's anxious but witty homage to Bill Sampson just when she's terrified of losing him to the younger, fresh-faced Eve Harrington.

Lawrence made only a handful of movies. Her last was *The Glass Menagerie*, filmed in Hollywood in 1949. Though it wasn't released until the fall of 1950, glowing reports of her performance in it were current in Hollywood as soon as the movie was completed. That's another reason Mankiewicz wanted her.

Lawrence's husband, Richard Aldrich, wrote that, while Gertrude was vacationing in Florida, Mankiewicz "approached her agent to secure her for the lead in his forthcoming picture *All About Eve*. On her return to New York she discussed the proposal with Fanny Holtzmann. The script, which I read at Gertrude's earnest request, gave promise of becoming one of the best pictures of the year. Not least of the inducements of *All About Eve* was the salary which the studio was prepared to pay to get Gertrude.

" 'I'm turning it down,' she informed me.

" 'Are you sure that's wise?'

" 'I'm sure it's very foolish—financially speaking. And it won't help my career. But I told you—I want to be Mrs. A. *Now* will you believe me?' "

The war, and their careers, had kept Richard Aldrich and Gertrude Lawrence apart for much of their marriage. Her desire to play "Mrs. A"—Mrs. Aldrich—led her to take a year off. That was 1950, the year of *All About Eve*.

Lawrence also had something else in mind. She had seen Rex Harrison and Irene Dunne in *Anna and the King of Siam* and loved the movie. According to her husband, "When she refused the offer to star in *All About Eve*, she asked Fanny to look into the possibility of securing for her the right to have a musical made" from the Harrison-Dunne film. Having acquired these rights, Gertrude went to Rodgers and Hammerstein, "who contracted to write, compose, and produce the musical which became *The King and I*."

Gertrude Lawrence played Anna Leonowens in this smash musical until she was hospitalized with hepatitis in the late summer of 1952 and, instead of convalescing as she had planned, she slipped into a coma and died.

And that, in a very long nutshell, is how Claudette, Susan, Marlene, and Gertrude did not play Margo Channing.

Chapter 6

The End of an Old Road, the Beginning of a New One

We left Bette Davis in a blaze of nerves on the set of *Payment on Demand* after her phone call from Darryl Zanuck. Following that conversation she went through a pack of cigarettes in two hours. It was all she could do to finish the day's shooting, especially because her scenes called for restraint.

A messenger arrived at RKO in the late afternoon carrying a large envelope with Bette's name on it. Excited as she was, she didn't know quite what to expect. How long had it been since she had read a good script? This one, despite the ballyhoo, might be no more than a cut above the others.

"Good night, good night," she said briskly to director and colleagues. She started reading the script as her chauffeur drove off the lot, and her enthusiasm grew with each page she turned. Over an hour later, when the driver reached her Tudor-style house perched on a rocky cliff at 1991 Ocean Way in Laguna Beach, Bette knew this was the best script she had read in years. Possibly the best one ever.

Bette jumped out of the car and raced inside, not pausing at any window to regard the vast Pacific that seemed part of her own real estate. She was bustin' to finish the script.

She stopped just long enough to pour herself a glass of scotch, then marched into her bedroom and, provisioned with plenty of cigarettes, didn't come out again until she had not only finished reading *All About Eve* but had started to learn her lines.

Next morning she phoned Darryl Zanuck. Their conversation was full of goodwill. The most important line in it, of course, was Bette's: "Darryl, I'd love to play Margo Channing."

As soon as she hung up she called Mankiewicz. He invited her to dinner to discuss Margo Channing and the shooting schedule. No one remembered later where they ate, or what, but when decades had passed Bette still recalled what Mankiewicz told her about Margo: "He said she was the kind of dame who would treat her mink coat like a poncho!" And in the movie she does just that. Margo, leaving for the airport with Bill, stretches across the dressing-room chaise longue to scoop her fur coat off the floor.

Bette had five days left on *Payment on Demand* at RKO. She had looked forward to a vacation; now that was out. On the contrary, she must double up. Edith Head, at Bette's insistence, was to design the Margo Channing outfits (but no one else's) for *All About Eve*. Bette immediately started going to Edith for dress fittings at night after a long day's work at RKO to finish up *Payment on Demand*.

The reason for this breakneck schedule was that the Curran Theatre in San Francisco had been rented for two weeks of location shooting to begin April 11. With a play closing and another to open soon, the Curran was available for only two weeks in April.

Since a number of scenes in *All About Eve* take place in a cavernous Broadway playhouse, it made artistic sense to shoot them in a real theatre. Apparently it made financial sense as well, for 20th Century-Fox, in budgeting the film, had decided that location filming in an actual old New York–style theatre was preferable to building a theatre set.

Lyle Wheeler, the art director, had scouted Los Angeles theatres but found nothing appropriate. The Ethel Barrymore in New York was briefly considered, but scheduling proved difficult, and the cost of flying cast and crew that far was prohibitive. Eventually Wheeler hit upon the solution of using the ornate old Curran, built in 1922 and only four hundred miles away. But this decision meant there was no flexibility in the starting date. Since Margo Channing was needed in virtually every scene to be shot at the Curran, Bette Davis didn't get a single day off between pictures.

On April 5, 1950, Bette celebrated her forty-second birthday on the set of *Payment on Demand*. After cake and champagne, the cast and crew surprised her with a huge ostrich egg. For a moment Bette looked blank, then she read the inscription and laughed: *Thanks for being a Good Egg*.

Two days later, on April 7, Bette signed her contract for *All About Eve*, and four days after that, on the eleventh, production began in San Francisco.

"Darryl Zanuck had a hair fetish. He didn't like too much of it. I had a hairy chest and a messy head of hair." This is Gary Merrill on how Mankiewicz overruled Zanuck in casting him, rather than John Garfield, as Bill Sampson. Since the time of *All About Eve* is one Broadway season, October to chilly late spring, Bill needn't bare his chest. And in the movie his head of hair is more kempt than Margo's.

"I never tried to get the part in *All About Eve*, never called an agent," Merrill said some years later. "I thought about who might be chosen to play the part, but did nothing about it. I was lying on the beach at Malibu when the phone rang, and I almost missed hearing it. The call was from Joe Mankiewicz, asking if I would test with Anne Baxter for *Eve*."

Along with Zanuck's aversion to hirsute actors, he wasn't easily convinced that Gary Merrill could play the Broadway director who loves Margo Channing but who also stands up to her. Zanuck grumbled that Gary Merrill "had only played around airplanes," and he was right, for Merrill's Hollywood career hadn't led him beyond portrayals of lieutenants, commanders, and the like in such military aviation films as *Winged Victory* (1944), *Slattery's Hurricane* (1949), and *Twelve O'Clock High* (1949).

"On Sundays," Merrill wrote in his memoirs, "a large film studio is nearly deserted. The empty sets for westerns, New York streets, or Arabic marketplaces are rather eerie. One Sunday in 1950 I had been called to the studio for a makeup test with Miss Bette Davis."

Bette Davis: "This was the first time I met Gary. They did photographic tests of us together. I was to look older than he as Margo. I did."

Gary Merrill: "On that Sunday I went to the test stage, and there, being turned this way and that, as though she had just been picked up from a counter at a jewelry store, was the Queen, Bette Davis."

Bette Davis: "I had seen the film *Twelve O'Clock High* and an actor in it named Gary Merrill. I had never seen him before and I was greatly impressed by his performance and looks."

Gary Merrill: "The makeup people should have been pampering her but instead they were twirling her around, examining facial lines. They were trying to see if our age difference would be too noticeable. The professional attitude Bette adopted throughout the ordeal was impressive."

Bette Davis: "Hollywood always wanted me to be pretty, but I fought for realism."

Gary Merrill: "Bette had a few character lines around those incredible eyes, but here was a magnetic woman with a compelling aura of femininity who might also be willing to confront dragons. I was irresistibly drawn to her."

Bette Davis: "People get the idea that actresses my age are dying to play younger women. The fact is, we die every time we play one."

Gary to Bette: "Certainly wonderful of you to come to the studio on a Sunday."

Bette to Gary: "For this part, I would come to the studio seven days and nights a week."

Gary Merrill: "Never in the history of motion pictures has an actress been so perfectly cast."

And so, sizing each other up, they both liked what they saw. But before the romance of Bette and Gary could take wing, each one had to shed a marital encumbrance.

Bette's third marriage—to William Grant Sherry, variously characterized as "a muscle-bound sailor" who was "an artist of sorts" with a "bohemian attitude and blunt manner"—had been rather ludicrous from the start. According to one of Bette's biographers, she "decided to marry him only a month after she picked him up at a party" in 1945. Already this sounds like the scenario of a boisterous Bette Davis picture, but it gets better—meaning much worse—during the next five years.

It's easy to see why Bette fell for Sherry the Hunk. Hedda Hopper's mouthwatering description would almost qualify for the pages of *Honcho*: "In a suit you couldn't possibly guess what a handsome Greek God he was. Now he'd run up fresh from the sea with the water still glistening on his mahogany tanned skin. He was in navy trunks, and with a physique that would do for Atlas, stood before me, muscles rippling evenly under a firm skin, young, strong, and handsomely male. He has an even, confident, ingratiating smile, kindly but masculine as a left hook."

Bette was starving, and here was her banquet.

But someone might just as well have sprinkled gunpowder on the bridal veil, for during the honeymoon trip to Mexico City Bette nagged and taunted, the bridegroom exploded, and somewhere in the middle of a cactus desert he shoved her from the car. A quickie Mexican divorce was the obvious solution, but the unhappy couple seemed determined to live miserably ever after.

The air was sulphurous. Other disputes ensued, one of which climaxed with the new husband hurling a steamer trunk at his cowering helpmate. But love caressed the turbid waters; the tempest subsided. And on May 1, 1947, Bette Davis gave birth to Barbara Davis Sherry—B.D.—who in years to come would be both the apple of her mother's eye and the dagger in her heart.

In October 1949 Bette filed for divorce. The next day Sheilah Graham headlined: BETTE DAVIS ACTS TO RUB OUT 3RD MARRIAGE. Graham, better remembered today for her liaison with F. Scott Fitzgerald than for her prose, continued: "Screen tragedienne Bette Davis chalked up another real-life setback late today when she filed suit for divorce from her artist-husband William Grant Sherry, accusing the muscular one-time masseur of rubbing her the wrong way." The flippant tone of the column infuriated Bette, and she later retaliated by having Sheilah Graham barred from the set of her next picture.

Tempers cooled, and a few weeks later Bette and Sherry announced a reconciliation. Their riotous marriage lurched forward.

On December 31, 1949, to celebrate New Year's Eve, they went to the movies. They saw *Twelve O'Clock High*, starring Gregory Peck, Hugh Marlowe, and Gary Merrill.

In the spring of 1950 Bette started filming *The Story of a Divorce*, a more fitting title, under the circumstances, than *Payment on Demand*, which the picture was eventually called.

One night during that crowded month of April 1950, Bette didn't make it home to dinner. The cast and crew of *Payment on Demand* surprised her with a forty-second birthday party two days before the actual date, April 5. Waiting at home for his wife, Sherry, by turns worried and annoyed, decided to pay a surprise visit to RKO. The studio gateman who let him in informed Sherry about the surprise party for Bette in the commissary. This was news to her husband. He hadn't been invited.

By now the party was over, so Sherry made his way to Bette's dressing room. There he found her and co-star Barry Sullivan in a very jovial mood, relaxing with post-party drinks and cigarettes and bursts of laughter. A terrible row took place. Sherry, perceiving Sullivan as "the other man," slugged him, and the next day Bette filed for divorce again. It was while Bette was in the midst of this marital commotion that Darryl Zanuck phoned to offer her *All About Eve*.

Gary was married at the time to Barbara Leeds, a blue-eyed actress who wore her blonde hair in bangs and had a wide-open smile on a friendly face. Leeds was a Doris Day look-alike. Gary was thirty-six; his wife was thirty-three. They had married in 1941.

After his first encounter with "the Star" that Sunday for the makeup tests, he returned to his beach house in Malibu and entertained his wife and their Sunday-afternoon guests with stories of meeting Bette Davis. "I was appalled," he said, describing the callous treatment she got from the makeup artists. He had developed a big, protective feeling toward her, as though she were a lamb loose in the Hollywood jungle.

He was right to call her "the Star." Certainly Bette deserved the uppercase that he, a character actor, couldn't help vocalizing, and perhaps the quotation marks in his voice as well. But Bette Davis, in April 1950, was a fading star. *Winter Meeting* (1948) had been the first of her pictures to lose money. Her behavior had become less professional and more unbearable on the set of each new and lackluster movie.

After *Beyond the Forest*, in 1949, it seemed impossible for her career to get any worse. And since "camp" as an aesthetic concept hadn't yet been invented, no one realized that this movie would fester into immortality once Edward Albee featured a Davis line from it—"What a dump!"—thirteen years later in his play *Who's Afraid of Virginia Woolf?*

On a hot day in August 1949 Bette left the Warner Bros. lot for the last time as a contract player at the studio that had hired her in 1932. Over the years at Warner she had quarreled and shouted. There had been lawsuits and threats. In Gary Merrill's words, she had been "willing to confront dragons." But so, it was said, had Jack Warner—a most unlikely incarnation of St. George. How could Miss Davis and Mr. Warner, as they politely referred to each other in correspondence and statements to the press, survive apart? Their fights were so invigorating.

As an actress, Bette Davis had also matured and perfected her craft at Warner Bros. Sometimes, especially when the joke was on someone else, she had even laughed. When she tried really hard, Bette could recall days of fulfillment when the Academy nominated her, nights of vindication when she won. There, at the studio, despite every conceivable setback, she had waxed from bette davis to Bette Davis, and then all the way, at last, to BETTE DAVIS. But she, like everyone else in town, being weighed in the scales of box-office gross, was found to have the precise value of her latest picture. And so she searched in vain for friends, colleagues, any longtime familiar face as she pulled up to the studio gate that final time. It was nearly the end of Hollywood's first half-century, and on that piercingly clear summer afternoon everybody she knew was busy on a new picture. As the former Queen of Warner Bros. drove away, no one waved good-bye.

Zanuck wanted Jeanne Crain to play Eve Harrington. Though the years have reduced her star to the size of an asterisk, in 1950 she was famous. Under contract to Fox, Crain had become a favorite with fans and theatre exhibitors of the period.

On-screen she seemed passive and one-dimensional, especially in such treacly fare as *Home in Indiana* (1944) and *State Fair* (1945). She was not without acting ability, however, and in 1949 she was nominated for an Oscar for her performance in *Pinky* as a black girl passing for white. That was also the year Mankiewicz used her in *A Letter to Three Wives*.

Despite her good performance as one of the ensemble in that picture, Mankiewicz was unenthusiastic when Zanuck urged him to cast her as Eve. When he told Zanuck that Jeanne Crain could never summon the "bitch virtuosity" needed to play Eve Harrington, Zanuck yielded. Mankiewicz then named the actress he considered right for the part.

"Anne Baxter as Eve?" Zanuck mused. "Joe, why the hell do you think she's better than Jeanne?"

Mankiewicz sold Zanuck on Baxter, and since she was also under contract to Fox at the time, Zanuck okayed her for the part.

Anne Baxter's version of how she came to play Eve Harrington differs from Mankiewicz's. She claimed that the role was offered to her because Jeanne Crain got pregnant. And since Crain eventually bore seven children, the odds seem to favor Baxter's account.

Chapter 7

San Francisco, An Oasis of Civilization in the California Desert

ette Davis was so rude, so constantly rude. I think it had to do with sex." That's how Celeste Holm remembered her co-star thirty-eight years after *All About Eve*. It's a tantalizing thing to say, but Holm didn't elaborate. One wonders whether she meant that Bette's alleged rudeness had to do with rivalry between stars of the same sex, or whether Bette, like a lioness in rut, snarled when the number-two cat on the set—in this case, Celeste Holm— rubbed too close to her new mate—in this case, Gary Merrill.

The two women did not like each other. They met for the first time at a party shortly before the entire cast and crew left for San Francisco. When Mankiewicz introduced them, Celeste said, "I am so looking forward to working with you."

Bette said, "So am I."

It seemed they were off to a good start, even though Bette, during her reign as Queen of Warner Bros. if not of the jungle, was known as a cut-throat.

Compared to Bette, Celeste was something of a newcomer to pictures. Although she had won an Oscar for *Gentleman's Agreement*, it was only for a supporting role. Would Bette Davis hold that against her? You hear all kinds of things in Hollywood, Celeste reflected, and if half the things you hear about Bette are true . . .

It's possible that Bette viewed Celeste as something of a goody-goody with a sharp eye for the publicity value of righteousness. It was only a year before, after all, that Celeste starred as a tennis-playing nun in the Loretta Young vehicle, *Come to the Stable.* And a few days before she and Bette started work on *All About Eve*, Celeste read a lofty poem called "The Shadow of the Voice" during the Easter sunrise service at the Hollywood Bowl. The next day she was prominently pictured in the *Los Angeles Times.*

Then, too, Bette was forty and then some. Celeste hoped it wouldn't bother her that she, Celeste, playing Margo Channing's best friend, was so much younger. And looked so much younger. Celeste Holm was thirty.

A couple of weeks after Celeste and Bette's first encounter, this strange group of stars began to descend on San Francisco. Celeste Holm, Gary Merrill, and Hugh Marlowe flew from Los Angeles on Darryl Zanuck's seaplane. But flying, in those days, was not considered the safest way to travel. Bette Davis got the real star treatment. She went by train.

On Monday, April 10, the Zanuck seaplane took off. "Noisy! Oh, my God," moaned Celeste.

Gary was crowded beside Celeste, with Hugh scrunched up behind them in the plane's rear seat. The roar of the engine grew even louder as the plane reached its cruising altitude. Small talk was out. Gary and Hugh studied their scripts, while Celeste filed her nails.

But Celeste liked to talk. She wouldn't be drowned out by the motor. "Well," she said, turning to Gary, "I wonder what—" but her words mixed with the rumble of the engine.

"I can't hear you!" he yelled.

"*I said, I wonder what it's going to be like working with the Queen Bee!*"

Gary chuckled. He leaned close to her ear and called out, "I know one thing—it'll all be over in eight weeks."

Celeste laughed, and Gary laughed, and Hugh Marlowe wondered whether these shouted remarks wouldn't strain their voices on the day before shooting was to start.

When the plane landed and the three of them were en route to their hotel, Celeste eyed Gary again. She seemed to be studying his face. Gary didn't know it then, but Celeste's mother was a professional portrait painter and Celeste, too, had a lively interest in art. (As Karen Richards in *Eve,* she's a Sunday painter.)

"Are you Lithuanian or something?" she suddenly asked.

Gary was nonplussed. What a strange question, he thought.

"Pure early American," he snapped. And he got one of those looks on his face, the kind he uses on Anne Baxter in the film when she tries unsuccessfully to seduce him in her dressing room.

"He was so defensive," Celeste said later. "I love roots. I'm Norwegian on my father's side, and on my mother's side I'm everything. But I must have stepped on some kind of toes there. Gary does look Lithuanian, or something interesting. I guess everybody was nervous when we got to San Francisco."

Perhaps Gary's nerves made him peevish. After all, this was the biggest step of his career. And a few days earlier he had indeed met the Queen Bee, as Celeste blithely called her. He had been having drone fantasies ever since.

Then, too, Gary was a Merrill from Connecticut, so being labeled Lithuanian disturbed him on several levels. Next to a tenor, a deep-rooted New England actor is the touchiest thing in show business, or so an onlooker might have thought on that chilly day in San Francisco when Gary's grumpy retort wounded Celeste's feelings. Perhaps he felt some manly twinge when asked whether he was Lithuanian. For during the recent war, a third of the population of Lithuania had been cut down by invading armies. The question, if not impertinent, seemed to suggest all sorts of bad luck.

When Bette's train pulled into the station in San Francisco, a battalion of reporters and photographers swarmed around it. The train stopped, passengers disembarked, and finally, amid a flurry of porters, railroad personnel, and studio emissaries, Bette descended onto the platform. Reporters called out questions while others scribbled answers and flashbulbs popped.

Bette's entourage included her three-year-old daughter B.D. and the child's nanny, a young woman named Marion Richards; Bette's secretary; and a bodyguard to protect them against William Sherry, Bette's estranged husband, who had made threats.

As they made their way into the station, Marion Richards was aghast to realize the photographers were taking pictures of her. "I was wearing sunglasses and my hair was the same color as Miss Davis's," she said later. "When we left the train they rushed up and began to photograph me. I said, 'No, please, you're making a mistake. That's Miss Davis back there, in the fur coat, carrying the little girl.' "

The nanny, who had lived for some time in the house with Bette and William Sherry, knew Bette's moods. She didn't want to provoke one, however inadvertently. Bette shot her hapless employee a couple of looks indicating that she wasn't happy at being upstaged, even accidentally. Having reclaimed the limelight, however, Bette let the incident pass without comment as she handed over her little daughter.

Half of Hollywood, or so it seemed, had arrived in San Francisco. For weeks now, Fitz Fitzgerald of the Fox Location Department had been arranging hotel reservations for all fifty-five members of the cast and crew. Most of them stayed at the Fairmont. He had also drawn up schedules of departure and arrival times for everyone, whether they were flying in, coming by train, or driving up from Los Angeles. In addition, Fitzgerald obtained the necessary permits for shooting. While he was doing all this, the head of the studio's Transportation Department had put a fleet of trucks on the road to haul necessary shooting equipment.

Bette having made her star's entrance, other trains and other planes filled San Francisco with celebrities. Thelma Ritter flew in from her home in Queens, New York; Anne Baxter arrived late that night because she hated to leave her husband, John Hodiak. George Sanders and his wife, Zsa Zsa Gabor, arrived on the same flight as Marilyn Monroe.

Long after George and Marilyn were dead, Zsa Zsa wrote about the trip: "I had met Marilyn in the commissary and noted that she was extremely adept at wiggling her ass and batting her eyelashes. On the plane to San Francisco, I had the window seat, Marilyn the aisle—with George, appropriately, sandwiched in the middle. Marilyn spent most of the trip batting her eyelashes at George, who turned to me when we were alone and said, with a mixture of sympathy and pride, 'Poor girl, she has it bad.' 'George,' I said in fury, 'don't flatter yourself, she's having sex with everybody.' "

Marilyn later said this about her first encounter with Zsa Zsa: "I saw she was one of those blondes who put on ten years if you take a close look at them."

Marilyn's memory of Zsa Zsa as a blonde is inaccurate, however. It probably dates from a year or so later, because in 1950 Zsa Zsa still had the dark auburn hair she was born with. But Marilyn was right: Her adversary did look mature. Not only was her hair undistinguished, but her teeth hadn't been capped and her nose was considerably less svelte than it later became. Zsa Zsa's eternal youth lay ahead.

If every copy of the *All About Eve* script had been lost, Mankiewicz could have fashioned a similar vivisection from what his cast said to, and about, one another. But he was too busy to take notes. He had been in San Francisco for several days planning, with cinematographer Milton Krasner, how to use the Curran Theatre to maximum effect during the scant two weeks it belonged to them.

Monday, April 10, had been a long day for everyone. Now, at last, with flowers in every suite and champagne cooling in buckets, those who had come to make this movie were ready to get started.

These actors had, in a sense, spent years and years preparing just for the next day, just for April 11, 1950, the first day's work on *All About Eve*. What did it all mean? So far they knew only that they had witty lines to speak, a terrific story, and that Joe Mankiewicz outranked the directors they usually worked with.

But so much could go wrong. It had happened in the past, to them, to others. They felt anxiety; they felt a tingling anticipation. And something else, just beyond the borders of consciousness, some vague pattern that the mind glimpses but cannot grasp. Bette summed it up later: "There was just a smell about it—you just *knew* it had to be great and that it would be great for all of us."

The phone rang in Bette's suite. Marion Richards answered in the sitting room. "Miss Davis," she said when she knocked on Bette's bedroom door, "it's Mr. Merrill. He's calling up everyone to go down to the bar for drinks."

Gary got no refusals. There wasn't a teetotaler in the bunch.

Celeste said, "That first night we all went for drinks at the Fairmont, where they had a bar that went around and around. Everybody was showing off. Bette had taken one look at Gary and Gary had taken one look at Bette, and something had happened."

When the long evening finally wound down they all went back to their rooms. But Zsa Zsa wouldn't stop talking. "Later that evening," she said, "I was able to prove my point. Our hotel suite was right next door to Marilyn's and I took George aside and said, 'Why don't we keep our door ajar tonight and watch how many men go into Marilyn's room?' Ever the voyeur, George agreed and watched with me as four different men from the movie's crew each, in turn, visited Marilyn's room and made love to her.' "

Marilyn's rejoinder: "People had a habit of looking at me as if I were some kind of a mirror instead of a person. They didn't see me, they saw their own lewd thoughts."

The first day of filming, Bette Davis awoke without a voice. She tried to speak but no words came.

The trouble had started a few nights earlier in Los Angeles when William Sherry dropped by her house at Laguna Beach. He had come to try to talk her out of a divorce.

Bette peered out. Sherry called to his wife. His voice sounded round and firm and manly, like his biceps. But for Bette the charm had worn off. She wanted more than muscles.

Sherry's timing wasn't good. It was late and Bette needed sleep. The arrival of her third husband annoyed her. Whatever he had to say he could say to her lawyer. She greeted him curtly: "You can't come in." Instead, Bette pranced out on the front lawn in her nightgown. Moonlight frosted ocean waves as the tide heaved against the rocks. Under different circumstances she might have dissolved into his arms with one of those romantic lines such as "Don't let's ask for the moon—when we have the stars."

Instead she looked at him and said, "I thought I told you not to come here, Sherry."

He said he'd like to come in, try to work things out, get back together. That did it. Playing Bette Davis roles all these years had left its mark. "Haven't you heard?" she taunted. "I'm making a new picture. You know who with? Joe Mankiewicz. He's a *real* man. He's a genius. He makes a living *all his own!*"

Bette's taunts hit Sherry like a kick in the groin. "Shut up!" he yelled as he made a lunge.

Bette ran inside her house and locked the door. She'd show him. There followed a lava-spill of abuse half remembered, perhaps, from Mildred, Bette's character in *Of Human Bondage*. She wanted Sherry to hear every word, even with the heavy Tudor wooden door slammed in his face. Before the scene played out, she had vented so long and loud that her husband, as though emasculated, had slunk away into the shadows. He quietly got in his car and drove away.

Bette, though very weary, didn't sleep at all that night. Her throat ached and toward morning she spat blood into a handkerchief.

And now, to wake up in San Francisco ready to begin the first mile of that long comeback road, and discover that her voice had failed . . .

"Call a doctor!" she rasped into the phone.

The specialist told her to rest her voice for a day or two. He assured her the problem was neither serious nor permanent.

But Joe Mankiewicz turned pale when Bette arrived at the Curran Theatre and pulled him close to whisper something desolate. "Oh, what am I going to do about it?" she moaned.

Joe didn't panic. He patted her shoulder, smiled, and said, "Honey, we're going to keep it." Actually, Joe liked this new sound, her injured voice. "It's the whiskey-throated voice that Margo should have," he said. "A bourbon contralto."

"Now I sound like Tallulah Bankhead," Bette muttered.

"Don't admit it," cautioned the sly director.

Bette loved this sort of secret.

"And one more thing," Mankewicz added. "Even when your throat improves, I want Margo to sound like this. Can you keep it up for a month?"

He called rehearsal. Although Bette had to guard her voice, she could compare her interpretation of Margo Channing with the director's.

She could even mouth her lines as long as she "saved" most of her voice; opera singers do it at rehearsals all the time. Later Mankiewicz said, "Bette was letter-perfect. She was syllable-perfect. The director's dream: the prepared actress."

On the first day of shooting, very little film was actually shot. Mankiewicz and his cast and crew were getting used to one another and to the Curran Theatre, which echoed their noisy preparations. Electricians were everywhere, rigging lamps and laying cables, while set dressers rearranged furniture, hung drapes, and tested props. Carpenters already had erected scaffoldings, and now they checked them one last time to make certain every plank was in place. Early on, these same carpenters had built a long, sturdy platform that extended out from the stage and over a section of the theatre's orchestra seats to provide unhampered working space for Krasner's camera and the Junior Crane on which it was mounted.

Now an apprentice carpenter fixed a balky door; another tried to remove a squeak from a loose floorboard. Camera assistants and soundmen laid tracks, adjusted booms, and tested acoustics. Mankiewicz seemed to be everywhere at once, conferring with the crew, talking with the cast. By late afternoon he and Milton Krasner, his director of photography, were ready for their final survey. At last the set was ready; it looked perfect.

Mankiewicz had guessed it earlier, but at day's end he felt confident he'd be able to make the picture he wanted. In retrospect, he summed it up like this: "Bette's professional attributes were not unique within the *Eve* company. Without exception, the entire cast was no less conscientious."

We get an idea of Mankiewicz's rehearsals from Bette's recollections: "The rehearsal period was very important. A great director will let his cast run through the script three or four times. The actors would do it how they felt it, how they saw it. He would then start correcting this or that. All this was prior to the director's trying *anything* with the camera. You see, the camera should *follow* the actor."

In some cases, of course, the camera follows a stand-in. On March 15 Mankiewicz, along with Milton Krasner, a couple of Krasner's assistants, and Gaston Glass, the picture's first assistant director, had flown to New York. There, using doubles for Bette Davis and Celeste Holm, they shot background plates of the John Golden Theatre which would tie in with the scenes to be filmed inside the Curran. (Background plates are scenes filmed at locations remote from the studio, then projected on a background screen in the studio with the players performing in front of them. The camera is synchronized with the background projector so that the shutters of both machines open and close simultaneously.) In the film, we never see the outside of the Curran Theatre—only the John Golden.

Shooting after midnight in front of the Golden, Krasner and his assistants got unexpected help from a member of the NYPD. The policeman, an amateur photographer, told Krasner: "You've not got very much depth in the background over there. How'd you like some of those neon signs in the distance to be lighted up?" Krasner liked the suggestion. The officer sent a rookie to speak to several shop owners and café managers a block away, who agreed to light up their signs.

While in New York Krasner also made background plates of the exteriors of the 21 Club and Eve's Park Avenue apartment building. These were used as establishing shots for interior scenes to be filmed later at the studio. As there was no snow in Westchester for the country road sequence (which eventually had to be photographed at the Canadian border), they moved on to New Haven for additional footage.

There, exteriors of the Shubert Theatre and the Taft Hotel were photographed, with doubles used for Anne Baxter and George Sanders. Eventually, back at Fox, these New Haven background plates were projected on a screen behind a treadmill as the two actors strolled down this "virtual" street, with Addison telling Eve: "And tomorrow morning, you will have won your beachhead on the shores of Immortality."

Chapter 8

How Could I Miss Her? Every Night, Every Matinee

 clever graffito sums up Hollywood's most famous costume designer: "Edith Head gives good wardrobe." Bette Davis explained why: "While other designers were busy starring their clothes in a film, Edith was making clothes to suit a character." And that's why Bette chose Edith to design Margo Channing's outfits.

At the time, Edith was chief designer at Paramount, where she had just dressed Gloria Swanson for *Sunset Boulevard*. Then Bette got the part in *All About Eve* and the race was on to complete Margo's wardrobe in time for filming.

Charles LeMaire, executive director of wardrobe at Fox, happened to be Edith's friend. He had already dressed Anne Baxter, Celeste Holm, Thelma Ritter, Barbara Bates, and an unknown blonde named Marilyn Monroe for the film. (After Claudette Colbert's injury forced her to drop out, the outfits LeMaire had designed for her were recycled for other Fox stars in later films.)

Reading the script, LeMaire realized that *All About Eve* could end up a very good picture indeed, the kind of film where the costumes themselves help characterize the women who wear them.

The theatrical setting added to LeMaire's enthusiasm, for he himself had started out as a costumer on Broadway. Born in Chicago in 1897, LeMaire performed in vaudeville in his teens and early twenties. In 1921 he moved backstage to wardrobe. Soon he had a reputation, thanks to his showgirl costumes for such Jazz Age extravaganzas as the *Ziegfeld Follies, George White's Scandals,* and the *Earl Carroll Vanities.*

Later he helped create circus spectacles for Ringling Bros. and Barnum & Bailey. In the forties, LeMaire was on radio with *Fashion Show of the Air.* Before going to Hollywood, he operated a dressmaking establishment in New York.

"Sure I would have liked to dress Bette Davis," LeMaire recalled, "but I was already on another film. I had confidence that Edith could do it, so I asked for her on loan." While LeMaire was arranging to borrow Edith Head from Paramount, Mankiewicz phoned her and said, "I love your work. Just do what you think is right."

Edith said, "Bette and I had done a few films already and we had a good working relationship. She trusted me." During her final week on *Payment on Demand* at RKO, Bette left the studio every day in the late afternoon and rushed to Paramount for conferences and fittings with Edith. The two women had most recently worked together on *June Bride* (1948), a comedy in which Bette played a magazine writer. For that role, Edith designed a coat dress with both open and concealed pockets (the latter for pencils, memo pads, and the like). Bette liked the coat dress so much that she had six of them made for herself in various colors.

"She was wearing one the day we started working on *All About Eve*," said Edith. "She strode about, hands deep in her pockets, studying the fabrics, the sketches. For each costume, I'd place my favorite sketch on top, then alternates. In nothing flat, she'd whipped around the room, selected each of the top drawings, and was saying, 'When do we fit?' "

"Edith always took time to read the script and understand the character," Bette said. "She managed to make you look as good (or as bad!) as the script allowed."

If Mankiewicz thought he alone knew the secret of Bette's Tallulah-esque way of speaking, he was wrong. Edith Head, immediately spotting Bankhead as Margo Channing's prototype, had her researchers bring in every still of Tallulah they could find. "I steeped myself in Tallulah," said the crafty Edith, "and everything looked as if it was made for her, yet the clothes complimented Bette. She is such a good actress that she makes clothes belong to her."

Edith suggested that Bette wear mostly full skirts in the picture, but a suit with a tight skirt in the theatre scene where, after berating Bill, Lloyd, Eve, and Max, Margo ends up alone onstage in the empty theatre. Since this suit was needed early on for sequences to be filmed at the Curran, Edith set to work on it right away.

Toward the end of this scene, the script indicates that "Bill grabs her, pulls her down on the bed." The night Bette came for the fitting, she tried on the gray suit. "I hope you've made it very strong, Edith," she said.

While Edith circled Bette, stopping to eye her from various angles, a seamstress made minor adjustments with pins. Suddenly Bette wheeled across the office—"she has a walk like a whiplash," Edith said—seized two big ottomans, and shoved them against the couch. Then she zipped back over to Edith and the seamstress, who knelt down to stick a pin in the hem.

A moment later Bette screamed, swept across the room, and dived onto the improvised bed. "We thought we had gouged her with a pin," Edith said. "Or that she was having a fit. But as Bette got up, laughing, she said, 'That's exactly what I want—strong clothes to help me move. Guess it'll work.' "

That dive-bomber business wasn't in the script, of course, but Bette had already decided how she would play the scene. And Edith had decided on accessories for the suit. She planned for Bette to wear a white handkerchief in the suit's left-hand pocket, a tailored blouse with a black bow tie, and strapped black patent leather pumps.

Mankiewicz always required costume tests to make sure his stars looked exactly right, and in spite of his tight schedule with *Eve*, he demanded the same tests now. Principal actors were photographed wearing each costume. Then Mankiewicz himself, or the costume designer, wrote suggestions right across the photos. Bette, he thought, looked too tightly tailored in Edith's costume, so he ordered some modifications. The result was that, in the film, Bette's blouse had frills and a white tie at the neck. She also wore a small diamond pin in place of a handkerchief, and black kid pumps without straps. The suit remained untouched.

April 12, Wednesday morning, day two of *All About Eve*. By seven o'clock hairdressers and makeup artists were at work on Anne Baxter and Celeste Holm, for this morning they were to film the first meeting of Eve Harrington and Karen Richards. This was an important scene because it gained sympathy for the stagestruck young Eve, whose idolatry of Margo Channing seemed so innocent. Indeed, it set the tempo and timbre of Anne Baxter's entire performance. While Anne was made to look dowdy in a trenchcoat, Celeste was glamorized in mink. As makeup was carefully applied, and hair combed and sprayed, both actresses brushed up their lines with the script clerk.

Mankiewicz, too, had been on the set long before shooting was scheduled to begin. If any problem arose, it was his duty to solve it. Besides, he was a perfectionist. Part of his job, too, was to determine the camera setups. From there the cinematographer assumed responsibility for lighting the set.

Milton Krasner and his assistants, along with electricians and grips, had also been at work since the crack of dawn to prepare the lighting for the first scene, which was a night shot in the alley beside the Curran Theatre. To film this night scene in daytime, Krasner had the whole area covered with tarpaulins to obscure the sun and its reflections. Then appropriate lighting was set up to create the low-key illumination that would mimic night. Sound men tested their channels, prop men checked props, and the assistant director took a last-minute look at everything. At 9:00 A.M. the cameras rolled.

What we see at the beginning of the scene is Karen Richards getting out of a taxi. She takes a step, hesitates, looks curiously about, then makes her way into the alley, heading for the stage door. As she passes a recess in the theatre's exterior wall, Eve steps out of the shadows and calls out softly, "Mrs. Richards." The scene takes up three pages in the script.

To film it took half a day. From nine o'clock until long past lunchtime, they did it over and over again. At first the lighting wasn't exactly right, Mankiewicz thought, and so they did another take. This time Krasner wasn't satisfied; they repeated it. A streetcar grinding up a nearby street spoiled the third take, then Anne Baxter flubbed a line. Before Mankiewicz got what he wanted they had repeated the scene more than a dozen times. Only after the fourteenth take did the director finally say "Print it." At last, well on toward two o'clock in the afternoon, hungry actors and crew members escaped the alley and hurried next door to Clift's Redwood Room for lunch.

"Miss Holm seemed anything but exhausted by her ordeal of fourteen takes," wrote John Hobart of the *San Francisco Chronicle*, who had waited more than an hour to interview Celeste that day. "The blonde actress looked bright-eyed enough to cope with fourteen more."

Fresh from her Easter Sunday performance at the Hollywood Bowl a few days earlier, Celeste sounded very New Age. According to the reporter, "Miss Holm has developed a personal philosophy that seems to have worked out well. She believes it is 'important in life to know one's self and to know what general direction one wishes to take, that with this self-knowledge decisions become relatively unimportant, for the right things will happen to you.' "

When lunch was over, Celeste, Anne, Joe, Milton, and the others reassembled to shoot the continuation of the sequence. This takes place backstage as Karen leads Eve to Margo's dressing room. The short scene having gone well, by six o'clock the day's shooting was over. Exposed film was packed up and airmailed to Fox's lab in Los Angeles. The next day—Thursday, April 13—was Bette's first appearance before the cameras. Thanks to the throat specialist, her voice had improved. Her pain had diminished, and so had her panic.

Now Mankiewicz had a new fear. What if Bette's voice stayed husky for a week or so, then healed? That would be a calamity. Besides, hearing Bette in this lower register convinced him that it was exactly the way Margo Channing must talk.

By now everyone on the picture knew why Bette's voice had dropped. Reporters who visited the set, however, were told that she had strained it on her previous film. This version appeared in all the papers, no doubt to the amusement of the San Francisco doctor who treated her, and who knew the real story.

Mankiewicz ribbed his star that day on the set. "I'm glad you're feeling better," he said. "But I warn you—if your voice improves too much we're going to start off each morning with a screaming scene."

Chapter 9

To Margo. To My Bride-to-Be

uring the first week of filming, Bette Davis and Gary Merrill fell in love. Celeste Holm: "And from then on she didn't care whether the rest of us lived or died. Why, I walked onto the set the first or second day and said, 'Good morning,' and do you know her reply? She said—"

Bette Davis: "Oh shit, good manners."

Celeste Holm: "I never spoke to her again—ever."

Gary Merrill: "There is truth in the idea that an actor's personality is created in the parts he or she plays. My role was that of Bill Sampson, who was in love with Margo Channing, and as the film progressed I became infatuated with Bette."

Bette Davis: "On my first day of shooting, as Gary and I rehearsed our first scene together, I took a cigarette out of a cigarette case and waited for Bill Sampson to light it. He went on with his lines. I kept waiting for a light. When I realized he was ignoring the gesture, I asked if he were going to light my cigarette? He looked me squarely in the eye and said . . ."

Gary Merrill: "I don't think Bill Sampson would light Margo's cigarettes."

Joe Mankiewicz: "He's right, Bette. Bill would never light this dame's cigarette."

Bette Davis: "I looked at Gary for a minute. *Of course Bill Sampson wouldn't.* I wondered if that was Gary Merrill speaking to Bette Davis, to establish who was boss, or was it his opinion of what the character would do? I'm not quite sure to this day."

Joe Mankiewicz: "Margo Channing waits for no man! Margo wouldn't stand for Bill's 'babying' her, not for a minute."

Bette Davis: (pause) "You're quite right, Mr. Merrill. Of course Bill wouldn't light her cigarette."

Gary Merrill: "At first, since I love kids, I played games with Bette's three-year-old daughter, B.D., who was on location. As B.D. (her name is Barbara Davis, but Bette always called her B.D.) became more comfortable with me, so did her mother. And as I earned more of their trust, Bette opened up and began confiding in me about her problems."

Bette Davis: "The unholy mess of my own life—another divorce, my permanent need for love, my aloneness. Margo Channing was a woman I understood thoroughly. I had hard work to remember I was playing a part."

Gary Merrill: "Before long we were walking about holding hands, going to the movies. . . . From simple compassion, my feelings shifted to uncontrollable lust."

Bette Davis: "The last place I expected to find love was on a movie set."

Celeste Holm: "It was not a very pretty relationship; they laughed at other people. Bette and Gary formed a kind of cabal, like two kids who had learned to spell a dirty word."

Bette Davis: "There was one bitch in the cast—Celeste Holm."

Gary Merrill: "Would Miss Davis like coffee? A cigarette? A sandwich? Someone murdered?"

Bette Davis: "I sensed in Gary my last chance at love and marriage. I wanted these as desperately as ever. I had been an actress first and a woman second."

Gary Merrill: "I walked around with an erection for three days."

Bette Davis: "I started falling in love with him when I observed how he could relax in bed all day long for two solid weeks."

Zsa Zsa Gabor: "There was one bed on the set and every time we came back after lunch, it was obvious that Gary and Bette had been using it during the break."

Bette Davis: "*That bed* was for a scene in *All About Eve* but it was so comfortable that, between shots, the whole cast stretched out on it. Most of us would lie there for a few moments then pop up for cigarettes or something. Not Gary. He just lay there, completely at ease, until his scenes were called."

Gary Merrill: "We only played two love scenes before I said, 'Will you marry me?' "

Bette Davis: "I had fused the two men completely—Bill Sampson and Gary Merrill. Margo Channing and Bill Sampson were perfectly matched. I was breaking every one of my rules. I always swore I'd never marry an actor."

Chapter 10

A Graduate of the Copacabana
School of Dramatic Art

s early as *All About Eve*, the root system of the Monroe legend had begun to spread, though no one guessed then at its vitality. Marilyn's brief scenes in the picture, along with her earlier appearance in John Huston's *The Asphalt Jungle*, are mere buds. But the twig surged, redoubled, and took over the forest.

After interviewing about a dozen young actresses, including Sheree North, for the role of Miss Caswell, Mankiewicz proposed the name of Marilyn Monroe. Zanuck hit the ceiling. He had dropped her from the Fox roster a couple of years earlier because, Marilyn herself later claimed, he considered her unphotogenic. She had played bit parts in several Fox pictures, and Zanuck had excised her from all but one or two. On the day of her dismissal a studio official explained: "Mr. Zanuck feels that you may turn into an actress sometime, but that your type of looks is definitely against you."

The screenwriter Ben Hecht once defined a starlet as any woman under thirty who is not actively employed in a brothel. According to Mankiewicz, Marilyn's two or three years as a member of the 20th Century-Fox "stock company" left little time for acting. "For the most part she auditioned a great deal, late afternoons, in executive offices."

Why did Mankiewicz want her to play Miss Caswell? "There was a breathlessness and sort of glued-on innocence about her that I found appealing." But Zanuck might have foisted another girl as the "graduate of the Copacabana School of Dramatic Art" if Marilyn's protector, Johnny Hyde, hadn't intervened.

Hyde, fifty-four years old at the time, was a short, wizened man with severe heart trouble. He was also a top agent at William Morris. Though married, Hyde was in love with Marilyn and by all accounts he treated her well. Unlike most other men she knew at the time, he also respected her and seems to have recognized the talent that her insecurities concealed. Without Hyde's interest, Marilyn might have remained unknown.

Johnny Hyde brought her to see Joe Mankiewicz. Hyde wanted his girlfriend/client to work often, and in important films. "He haunted my office," Mankiewicz said. Even after choosing Marilyn for the part, Mankiewicz had no intention of defending her against Zanuck's caprice. "I wasn't about to tear up my contract and stomp out if she didn't get the part," he said.

Once Hyde had convinced the director that Marilyn was the one, he set to work on Zanuck. Hyde, because of his status as a top movie agent, was in a position to overcome Zanuck's resistance, if not his reluctance. "On March 27, 1950, Marilyn Monroe was signed for five hundred dollars a week—on a one-week guarantee," Mankiewicz later recalled. With this initial agreement came a long-term contract with Fox, which remained in effect, with modifications, through June 1962, when the studio fired her for the second time. Two months later Marilyn Monroe died.

Today Marilyn, in her fleeting scenes in *All About Eve*, is intoxicating. At the time, however, she commanded scant attention. Reviewers overlooked her when the picture came out. Until *Niagara*, three years later, it was cheesecake more than film roles that kept her going. In the years following *All About Eve*, Marilyn's co-stars seemed dazed that their own careers faltered while hers mushroomed. After her death, when the myth obscured the facts, various members of the cast ransacked their memories for details of the fledgling goddess during that long-ago April.

"And that poor Monroe child—Marilyn—Marilyn was terrified of Bette Davis!" This is George Sanders speaking in 1970, two years before his suicide. "During one scene in a theatre involving Marilyn, Bette Davis, and me, Bette whispered after a shot, within poor Marilyn's hearing: 'That little blonde slut can't act her way out of a paper bag! She thinks if she wiggles her ass and coos, she can carry her scene. Well, she can't.' "

Reporting Bette's unkindness to Marilyn, George Sanders overlooked his own. Ten years earlier, in his *Memoirs of a Professional Cad*, Sanders himself had written condescendingly: "Even then, on the set of *All About Eve*, Marilyn struck me as a character in search of an author and I am delighted she found Mr. Miller eventually."

The Love Songs of Addison DeWitt

If George Sanders had been more ambitious, he might have left acting for a career in opera. During an appearance on Tallulah Bankhead's radio show in the early 1950s, he sang the aria "In lacerato spirito" from Verdi's *Simon Boccanegra*. His well-trained voice was so pleasant that many in the studio audience did not believe it belonged to George Sanders. They left convinced that he had mouthed a recording of someone else's singing.

Sanders' vocal coach in Hollywood was Maestro Cepparo. One day, without George's knowledge, the maestro planted the manager of the San Francisco Opera Company near the open door while George sang several arias. According to George's friend Brian Aherne, who was present, the gentleman immediately offered George the role of Scarpia in *Tosca* for the upcoming opera season. To the astonishment of all present, Sanders said he did not want to become an opera singer. He politely but firmly declined the offer.

He did, however, record an album called *The George Sanders*

Touch in 1958. On it he sang not arias but standards, including "September Song," "As Time Goes By," and "More Than You Know." Included on the album was a song of his own composition, "Such Is My Love." Sanders's biographer, Richard VanDer-Beets, describes the actor's singing voice as "a rich baritone."

In 1955 Marilyn herself told Joan Collins (who at that time was filming *The Virgin Queen* with Bette), "That woman hates every female who can walk. She made me feel *so* nervous. She didn't talk to me at all, just sort of swept around the set, nose and cigarette in the air. She's a mean old broad."

Celeste Holm's opinion of Marilyn has wavered. In 1978 she declared, "I saw nothing special about her Betty Boop quality. I thought she was quite sweet and terribly dumb, and my natural reaction was, 'Whose girl is that?' " Ten years later Holm's appraisal had become less brittle, more patronizing: "I always felt sorry for her. She had a pretty little figure and little button nose. She was a very strange girl, full of the unexpected. She wanted so much to amount to something. Poor little thing." In recent television interviews Holm has implied that she instantly spotted a future star in the uncertain young actress. Time has been good to Marilyn, at least in the eyes of this colleague.

Barbara McLean, who edited *All About Eve*, was perhaps a more reliable talent scout than Monroe's co-stars. In 1951, when director Henry King was casting *Wait 'Til the Sun Shines, Nellie*, Marilyn tested for a part. McLean, watching the test results with King, predicted: "That girl's going to be a big star." King answered, "Well, I haven't got time to wait." McLean's rejoinder: "I'd sure take her if I was directing the picture."

Anne Baxter wrote in her memoir, *Intermission*:

About a year earlier, I'd made a movie called *A Ticket to Tomahawk*. Marilyn Monroe played one of a trio of the required dance-hall girls. The whole nutsy shebang was a spoof on Westerns, a form of high camp far ahead of its time. We shot on location 9,000 feet up in the Rockies. We were thereabouts for eight long weeks.

All of us lived in Durango at the Royal Motel, a euphemism, and ate at the local greasy spoon called the Chief Diner. Marilyn Monroe came in with a different crew member every night, wearing the same sweater. She was eminently braless and I particularly remember the pink V-necked angora sweater. It was said she slept in it. We never saw hide nor hair of her, or of her two roommates [i.e., the other dancehall girls] outside of dinnertime or during their occasional days of shooting. They slept whenever possible and all day Sunday. Or were closeted in the only phone booth, calling Hollywood.

As it turned out, *A Ticket to Tomahawk* premiered in San Francisco during the filming of *All About Eve*. A few days before the world premiere at the Fox Theatre, at Market and Ninth, on April 20, 1950, local papers carried ads showing an Indian seated cross-legged holding up a sign: HEAP BIG FUNNY PICTURE! Few others agreed. Next day the papers ran a smattering of modest reviews.

Gregory Ratoff, playing producer Max Fabian in *All About Eve*, was enthralled by Marilyn's Miss Caswell. Off-screen, he prophesied in his ebullient Russian accent: "Thees girl ees going to be a beeg star!"

Gary Merrill told an anecdote about a cast party that Bette hosted in a San Francisco restaurant: "Marilyn Monroe was seated next to Hugh Marlowe. The party went on quite late but Marilyn excused herself early because she had to work the next morning. We all knew that the scene was really Bette's scene, and that Marilyn had only a few lines. After she left, we all wondered what was going to happen to the dumb blonde. The next day Bette and Marilyn played their scene. I recall that Marilyn had four or five lines. Bette had more, but she was an experienced actress and accomplished the scene with little bother. It had to be done in ten takes, however—Marilyn kept forgetting her lines. Obviously, this problem did not injure her career."

Bette herself never had much to say about Marilyn, the only member of the cast whose fame was to equal Bette's own. In her first autobiography, *The Lonely Life*, published in 1962, Bette doesn't mention her at all. In *This 'N That* (1987), Bette's rather sketchy second volume of memoirs, she is noncommittal: "Trivia fans remember *All About Eve* because in it Marilyn Monroe gave her first important performance on the screen."

Zanuck and Marilyn retained a mutual disrelish. As the years went by, each commented on the other. When Zanuck, a consummate businessman, saw Marilyn's star on the rise in 1951, he issued a press release naming her "the most exciting new personality in Hollywood in a long time." A couple of years later, watching the rushes from *Gentlemen Prefer Blondes*, he didn't believe Marilyn was doing her own singing. When Marilyn got wind of his disbelief, she marched into the boss's office and sang "Diamonds Are a Girl's Best Friend" just for him—no doubt with an angry edge that we don't hear when she's performing with Jane Russell.

Zanuck's office was sixty feet long and had a grand piano in it. Picture him in a dash to the keyboard, where he starts to accompany Marilyn just as she reaches the second verse. But something is wrong with this picture: This is Fox, where they *didn't* make MGM musicals.

Even in the mid-fifties, when Marilyn was an enormous star, Zanuck refused to renegotiate her contract. He also cast her in roles she didn't like, which is one reason she rebelled. In 1954, at the time of one such rebellion, Zanuck issued a peevish statement to the press that said in part: "There has been so much talk about Marilyn Monroe that there is now a danger women moviegoers will say, 'So, she makes men excited—enough of her.' In the future she will make only two films a year and there will not be so many photographs of her sent around."

Legal battles followed. Marilyn left Hollywood and spent more than a year in New York, returning to the studio in triumph early in 1956. Coincidentally, a month later Zanuck resigned and didn't return to Fox until six years later. In 1960 Marilyn told an interviewer, "Mr. Zanuck has never seen me as an actress with star quality. He thought I was some kind of freak."

At the time of Marilyn's death in August 1962, Zanuck was in France, where he had spent most of his time since leaving Fox in 1956. (He had nothing to do with the studio's firing her earlier in 1962, during the chaotic filming of *Something's Got to Give*.) Learning that Marilyn was dead, Zanuck issued a statement. His sounds less self-serving than many others: "I disagreed and fought with her on many occasions, but in spite of the fact that I have not seen her for six years, we were always personal friends. Like everyone who knew Marilyn Monroe or worked with her, I am shocked. Marilyn was a star in every sense of the word. I do not claim to have discovered Marilyn Monroe. Nobody discovered her. She discovered herself. I was merely an instrument that provided her with the vehicles in which she was able to reach the theatre-going public of the world."

Ten years after Marilyn's death, Mankiewicz said: "I thought of her as the loneliest person I had ever known. Throughout our location period in San Francisco, Marilyn would be spotted at one restaurant or another dining alone. Or drinking alone. We'd always ask her to join us, and she would, and seemed pleased, but somehow she never understood or accepted our unspoken assumption that she was one of us. She remained alone. She was not a loner. She was just plain *alone*."

Marilyn's life is like a Hollywood remake of *Rashomon*; every version of it contradicts the others. For instance, it's odd that Mankiewicz doesn't mention Marilyn's scene with Bette Davis, which, according to Gary Merrill, required ten takes. It's the kind of amusingly ridiculous incident an efficient director like Mankiewicz would be eager to talk about. Or perhaps he considered it routine. After all, Celeste Holm and Anne Baxter, two seasoned players, required fourteen takes in their first scene together.

Another instance of Whose Version Do You Believe? involves a story about Marilyn's reading matter on the set of *All About Eve*. Mankiewicz saw her one day with a book in her hand. Surprised, he called her over, asked what she was reading, and she didn't answer; she just handed it to him. The book was Rainer Maria Rilke's *Letters to a Young Poet*. Mankiewicz asked if she knew who Rilke was and she said no, so he told her a little bit about the German poet. Perplexed and intrigued, Mankiewicz asked if someone had recommended the book to her. Marilyn shook her head and answered, "No. Nobody. You see, in my whole life I haven't read hardly anything at all. I don't know how to catch up. So what I do is, every now and then I go into the Pickwick Bookshop and just look around. I leaf through some books, and when I read something that interests me I buy the book. So last night I bought this one. Is that wrong?"

Mankiewicz told her it was the best possible way for anyone to choose what to read. "She was not accustomed to being told that she was doing anything right," he said. "She smiled proudly and moved on. The next day Marilyn sent me a copy of *Letters to a Young Poet*. I have yet to read it."

In view of all that's been written about Marilyn Monroe's desire for culture and her efforts at self-improvement, the story rings poignantly true. But Marilyn herself told a story that was different in every particular. In her autobiography *My Story*—a posthumously published book that some Monroe biographers consider spurious but that nevertheless sounds convincing—Marilyn described Mankiewicz as "a different sort of director than Mr. Huston. He wasn't as exciting, and he was more talkative. But he was intelligent and sensitive." And, she continued, "I felt happy on the set."

Marilyn, who according to one source dictated this memoir to a journalist in the mid-fifties, recalled that during the filming of *All About Eve* she was reading *The Autobiography of Lincoln Steffens*. (A turn-of-the-century muckraker, Steffens [1866–1936] reported on municipal corruption, labor problems, and social ills. He published *The Shame of the Cities* in 1904; his *Autobiography* came out in 1931.) According to Marilyn, "It was the first book I'd read that seemed to tell the truth about people and life. It was bitter but strong. Lincoln Steffens knew all about poor people and about injustice. He knew about the lies people used to get ahead, and how smug rich people sometimes were. It was almost as if he'd lived the way I'd lived."

Here is Marilyn's version of the Mankiewicz book discussion, taken from *My Story*:

> The Lincoln Steffens trouble began when Mr. Mankiewicz asked me one day what was the book I was reading on the set. I told him it was the Steffens autobiography and I started raving about it. Mr. Mankiewicz took me aside and gave me a quiet lecture.
>
> "I wouldn't go around raving about Lincoln Steffens," he said. "It's certain to get you into trouble. People will begin to talk of you as a radical."
>
> "A radical what?" I asked.

"A political radical," Mr. Mankiewicz said. "Don't tell me you haven't heard of Communists."

"Not much," I said.

"Don't you read the papers?"

"I skip the parts I don't like," I said.

"Well, lay off boosting Mr. Steffens, or you'll get into bad trouble," said Mr. Mankiewicz.

I thought this was a very personal attitude on Mr. Mankiewicz's part and that, genius though he was, of a sort, he was badly frightened by the front office or something. I couldn't imagine anybody picking on me because I admired Lincoln Steffens. The only other political figure I'd ever admired was Abraham Lincoln. I used to read everything I could find about him. He was the only famous American who seemed most like me, at least in his childhood.

A few days later the publicity department asked me to write out a list of the ten greatest men in the world. I wrote the name Lincoln Steffens down first and the publicity man shook his head.

"We'll have to omit that one," he said. "We don't want anybody investigating our Marilyn."

I saw then that it wasn't just a personal thing with Mr. Mankiewicz but that maybe everybody in Hollywood was just as scared of being associated with Lincoln Steffens. So I didn't say anything more about him, to anybody, not even to Johnny Hyde. I didn't want to get *him* in trouble. But I continued to read the second volume secretly and kept both volumes hidden under my bed.

Whether Marilyn literally hid those books under her bed or not, it's the right metaphor for America's red scare in 1950. And nowhere was the scare more hysterical than in Hollywood. Perhaps Mankiewicz, a political liberal, was frightened, even though he had never belonged to a left-wing organization. Certainly he was aware that innocuous pursuits, such as reading books critical of America, could sometimes make one the object of unpleasant scrutiny. In fact, the red baiters gave Mankiewicz himself quite a scare over a loyalty oath, although his brush with the Hollywood Inquisition came later in 1950, several months after his admonition to Marilyn. (Kenneth Geist, in his biography *Pictures Will Talk: The Life and Films of Joseph L. Mankiewicz*, gives a full account of Mankiewicz versus the McCarthyites.)

Whether Marilyn read Rilke or Lincoln Steffens on the set of *All About Eve* is not of surpassing significance, except that Mankiewicz seems unfair in characterizing her as vacuous and cognitively haphazard. Those who knew her well have said she read a lot. At various times she read Shakespeare, Proust, Emerson, Joyce, Freud, the Bible. It's just possible that she had a genuine interest in Rilke. The German actress Hildegard Knef, who was acquainted with Monroe at the time, said that Marilyn asked her a number of questions about German literature. And the day they met, Marilyn was carrying a copy of Rilke's poetry under one arm.

Chapter 11

Killer to Killer

t the end of the first week of filming, everyone joined Mankiewicz to view the rushes. These various rudimentary scenes had been developed at the studio in Los Angeles, spliced into coherence by film editor Barbara McLean, and flown back to San Francisco.

Months of anxious preparation had led up to these images on a small portable screen. Here at last was the evidence to exhilarate or depress. Were they making an outstanding film, or just another picture? How well they all remembered big productions that began in giddy optimism and then petered out. In such cases, only frustration came from watching rushes—scenes that misfired, sequences that fell drably short of expectations.

On that Saturday night, after watching the results of their best professional efforts, they were all excited. Even this crude preview of *Eve* bolstered their faith. They were good; they were great. Monday morning, on the set, they were even better than before.

"Every day was like a glorious relay race," Anne Baxter recalled of the time spent filming *All About Eve*. She added, "None of us, Marilyn Monroe included, *none* of us could wait to get to work." In spite of the discontents common to every movie set—rivalry, suspicion, gossip, hang-overs, upstaging, missed cues, catty remarks, delays, overtime, rumors, deadline pressure, sexual jealousy—even with a full measure of these, the making of *All About Eve* came to be a happy memory for Anne Baxter. *Excellence* was the word she chose to sum it up. "I was good, I was respected, I had a great part, the script was superb, the actors were per-fect and perfectly cast." Although Baxter played a treacherous bitch, she made friends with her on-screen adversary, Bette Davis. (Their friendship lasted, and one May morning in 1983, while visiting Anne Baxter in Connecticut, Bette stepped out of the shower and toweling her-self dry, discovered a lump in her breast. Anne comforted her seventy-five-year-old houseguest as best she could, never dreaming that Bette would outlive her by four painful years.)

Rapprochement with fellow actresses was rare for Bette Davis. A friend said, "Bette was really fond of only four female co-stars: Olivia de Havilland, Mary Astor, Anne Baxter, and Gena Rowlands, whom she favored above the others." From colleagues, Bette demanded as much as she put forth. If they couldn't, or wouldn't, reciprocate, look out. Having worked with Errol Flynn in *The Private Lives of Elizabeth and Essex* in 1939 and finding him insufficiently intense, Bette bad-mouthed him for the next fifty years. And then there was Susan Hayward, who played Bette's daughter in *Where Love Has Gone* (1964). "She wouldn't give me anything in our scenes," Bette growled. "It was like playing to a blank wall." On the last day of filming Bette took off her wig, flung it in Susan's face, and barked a valedictory "Fuck you!"

But Bette considered Anne Baxter superb in *All About Eve*. "Margo and Eve's relationship worked on two or three levels," Bette explained. "Anne was really playing a double role: one thing on the surface, another underneath. I called it the 'sweet bitch.' Her part was more dif-ficult than mine."

Anne Baxter, who made her Broadway debut at age thirteen, later revealed that she had patterned Eve Harrington on her own first under-study. That girl, she said, "was nice to everybody but me and would always be in the wings watching me like a hawk. In the movie I tried to follow Bette around with my eyes to get that feeling across."

The Fate of Understudies

- Backstage at *Phantom of the Opera* (1943), the star soprano of the Paris Opéra, Madame Biancarolli, is drugged (by Claude Rains, the Phantom) so that his protégée (Christine DuBois, the star's understudy) can go on. Later Madame Biancarolli is murdered by the Phantom.
- In *The Actor's Nightmare*, a play by Christopher Durang, a man finds himself more or less forced to go onstage as an understudy having absolutely no idea of his lines or business. He flounders in Noël Coward, Shakespeare, Beckett, and finally in Robert Bolt's *A Man for All Seasons*, at which point he is executed—apparently for real.
- In 1934 Max Reinhardt came to Los Angeles to direct a stage production of *A Midsummer Night's Dream* at the Hollywood Bowl. The production became famous for several reasons, one of them being that it presented an unknown young actress named Olivia de Havilland. She had appeared in a local production of the play the previous year while a freshman in college and was briefly an understudy in the Hollywood Bowl production. Reinhardt chose her as a last-minute replacement for the star, Gloria Stuart, who was unable to go on. The following year Reinhardt used de Havilland in his film version of the play, and she has been a star ever since.

Anne Baxter called her director "Joe the Mank." And since he had just won two Academy Awards for *A Letter to Three Wives* on March 29, a couple of weeks before they all arrived in San Francisco, Anne and others in the cast glued two large plastic Kewpie dolls—representing his two new Oscars—to the lectern where Joe kept his annotated copy of the script.

She had a secret crush on him. "John Hodiak and I were happily married then, but Joe's wit, his modest perspicacity, and my latent father complex drew me to him like a magnet," Anne Baxter confessed long afterward. "In fact, all the ladies on the set melted and gravitated to him as I did." Bette, in fact, suspected more than a crush. While making the picture, and long after, she reportedly believed that Anne and Mankiewicz had had a backstage affair. For twenty years Bette retained a nagging suspicion that Mankiewicz had somehow favored Anne Baxter, and that the favoritism involved sexual politics. According to Bette's longtime secretary, Vik Greenfield, Bette at last came out with it. "We went to see Anne Baxter in _Applause_," Greenfield said, "and when we were backstage, Bette asked Anne if she had an affair with Joe during the making of _All About Eve_. 'No,' said Baxter. 'I always thought you did,' said Bette."

True or false? Why, one wonders, would Bette wait so long to ask the burning question? Surely the delay wasn't caused by natural timidity. And since their paths often crossed, Bette could have interrogated Anne years before.

Anne Baxter corrected another misapprehension. Gossip to the contrary, she always denied there was any kind of feud between her and Bette on the set. "The studio tried to play that up all during the filming," she said. "But I liked Bette very much. She'd come on the set and go 'S-s-s-s' at me, but it was just a joke between us." Interviewed in the early eighties for the BBC documentary, _Bette Davis: A Basically Benevolent Volcano_, Baxter said, "She never threw fits without a damn good reason." She was referring to Bette's entire career, not to the placid set of _Eve_.

An interviewer asked Celeste Holm about working with Anne Baxter. "Oh, she was fine. But of course you know she was what's-his-name's granddaughter."

"Frank Lloyd Wright," supplied the interviewer.

"Frank Lloyd Wright," repeated Holm. "And so she was very sophisticated and very, 'Have you read the latest Christopher Fry?'"

Perhaps this breezy, left-handed compliment owes something to an anecdote that Anne Baxter had told earlier about Celeste. When cast and crew left San Francisco to complete filming at the studio in Los Angeles, they were scheduled to shoot on Stage 9, one of the smaller soundstages on the Fox lot. As Anne recalled, "Our assistant, Stan

Hough, didn't want to crowd the sets, and after pushing and fitting five portable dressing rooms here, there, and everywhere, he left Celeste Holm's outside. Out in the cold was more to the point. Celeste took one look and tearfully flounced back to her permanent dressing room.

"Joe was horrified and furious. He all but foamed at the mouth. He knew how vital it was that we work easily together.

"Everything stopped for two solid hours while Joe, all three assistants, Celeste's agent, and several emissaries from the front office made elaborate apologies. She came back on the set chin high, wet eyes shining resolutely—we couldn't help wondering if she'd toured in Saint Joan."

Celeste counters that this slight occurred because, sometime earlier, she had quit the studio and Zanuck now wanted to punish her. "Mr. Mankiewicz insisted that I play the part of Karen and Mr. Zanuck didn't want any part of that. So when I arrived, my dressing room was out in the alley and everybody else's was inside. Mankiewicz said, 'What are you trying to do? Kill an actress?' "

In San Francisco Bette Davis was forced to use a small, dingy dressing room. She claimed she didn't mind at all. She was even quoted as saying that Hollywood spoils actors by treating them too royally. "This cubbyhole," she said nobly, "is all an actress needs. A place to hide while she changes clothes. I think those ankle-deep carpets, mirrored walls, and elegantly furnished suites Hollywood gives newcomers tend to magnify their opinion of themselves." (P.S.: When Bette arrived back in Los Angeles, 20th Century-Fox saw to it that she got the plushest dressing suite in town.)

George Sanders, commenting on his two top female co-stars in *All About Eve*, sounded like one of those studio publicists hatching up a feud: "Bette upstaged Anne Baxter at every turn, and drove Anne to distraction. Playing a woman of forty who was jealous of a much younger woman, Bette played it as if it were happening to her personally. Anne caught the underlying tensions and viciousness. It is to her credit that it spurred her to act even better than she would have with a gracious co-star."

Bette returned his fire. She had heard about Sanders' bisexuality from Henry Fonda, an actor who disdained all deviation from what he considered the norm. This led Bette to characterize Sanders as a "bitch." Bette said he was more of a bitch to work with than Miriam Hopkins had been (which, coming from Bette, was saying a lot) and that he upstaged her at every opportunity. "He won that goddamned award [meaning his Oscar for Best Supporting Actor of 1950] at my expense!" she snarled.

Was Bette justified in her disdain for Sanders? Curiously, he is perhaps the only person ever to admire the character of Eve, whom he called "the nearest thing to a heroine in our story." Most of us see Margo as that heroine. After all, the beleaguered Margo survives not only her double-crossing friend, Karen, her unsupportive boyfriend, Bill Sampson, and the disloyal playwright, Lloyd Richards, but also "that venomous fishwife" Addison DeWitt and Eve, his unholy ally.

Sanders found nothing heroic in Margo Channing. He characterized her as "a vain, aging, flamboyant, temperamental woman . . . How many members of the audience could, or would have cared to, identify themselves with her?" The answer, of course, is that she's the only one in the picture anyone *can* identify with—at least for very long. (Thelma Ritter's friend-indeed role is too brief and too one-dimensional to arouse more than passing empathy.)

"Her lack of fundamental graciousness toward her co-players disgusted me," Sanders sneered. He was referring, now, to Bette Davis, not Margo Channing. But just how gracious was he?

"George Sanders never spoke to anyone," Celeste Holm said. "He was a brilliant actor, but he wasn't much fun."

George Sanders: A Psychological Self-Portrait

"The kind of actor I have become has been determined to a large extent by the weakness of my character. On the screen I am usually suave and cynical, cruel to women and immune to their slights and caprices. This is my mask, and it has served me faithfully for twenty-five years. But in reality I am a senti-

mentalist, especially about myself—readily moved to tears by
cheap emotions and invariably the victim of woman's inhuman-
ity to man."

—Sanders, *Memoirs of a Professional Cad*

"George slept soundly in his portable dressing room between shots,"
Anne Baxter said. "It bothered me only once. Eve's climactic scene,
when Addison DeWitt confronts her with her real self and lays down
their private ground rules, was a formidable challenge. It required a
gamut of emotions, building to and culminating in hysteria and ending
in acrid defeat."

Baxter explained that she was a "starting-gate actress," meaning she
was ready to act long before she walked onto the set. In fact, even as she
climbed into the makeup chair, she was already in character. For her,
rehearsals differed very little from takes. But George Sanders "yawned
his way through rehearsals."

So when Baxter and Sanders did the first take of that climactic scene
between Eve and Addison, it was like "opening night" for her, but for
George it was more like closing.

"Take it easy, Annie," Mankiewicz cautioned in a whisper.

"Godalmighty, Joe, I don't know *how*. Can't we stick a pin in George?"

"He'll warm up," Joe whispered. "Just be damned sure you don't
exhaust yourself. *Save* yourself the first few takes."

She tried to save herself, to hold back, but "by take five I was a rag."

Mankiewicz called a short break and took George aside. He and
Sanders talked quietly. Baxter remembered that Mankiewicz laid a hand
on "George's elegantly tailored shoulder" while they spoke.

She walked around, taking deep breaths and trying to relax without
losing her emotional climax.

"Take six. Take seven—and George went off like a rocket."

This sequence, where Sanders slaps Baxter and she flings herself
across the hotel bed, is a little S&M masterpiece. Eve taunts Addison as

if to provoke his wrath. She succeeds; he strips her emotionally and dominates her. Both grow more aroused as Addison's vehemence reaches an erotic crescendo. The scene ends when Addison, having conquered her, makes Eve recite a brief masochist's catechism:

ADDISON

Are you listening to me?

EVE

(She lies listlessly now, her tear-stained cheek against the coverlet. She nods.)

ADDISON

Then say so.

EVE

Yes, Addison.

ADDISON

And you realize—and you agree how completely you belong to me?

EVE

Yes, Addison.

The subtext of sexual frenzy, so camouflaged that Sanders and Baxter may well have been unaware of its implications despite their brilliance in the scene, suggests a lot about both characters. Just prior to the lines quoted above, Addison sneers at Eve: "That I should want you at all suddenly strikes me as the height of improbability." The most obvious interpretation of this line is, "That I should want such a weak, pathetic character as you." Another possible meaning is, "That I should want you at all *now that I've got you.*" Or still another: "That I should want you *or any woman.*"

Shortly before this scene, Addison appears as an unmistakable voyeur. Standing outside Eve's dressing room when she tries (with no luck) to seduce Bill Sampson, Addison is obviously aroused. His expression implies a vicarious thrill, perhaps onanistic.

In *All About Eve*, and in other Mankiewicz films, erotic scenes often involve a solitary character. The only time we see Bill and Margo in bed they're 3,000 miles apart, talking on the phone. (Later, at the Curran Theatre, they play half of an unerotic fight on a bed onstage.) Eve's initial seduction attempt—clandestine letters to Bill while he's away—involves only her.

Even when a sex scene is played *à deux*, passion is subordinate to speech. Whether we believe her or not, Eve claims that the first night she and Lloyd Richards spent together they "talked all night."

Put another way, orgasm in a Mankiewicz movie is deferred, sometimes forever. In *The Ghost and Mrs. Muir* Gene Tierney is sex-proof in her prolonged affair with the phantom, Rex Harrison. Only at her death does the honeymoon begin. Then there's Addie Ross, the insinuating, invisible narrator of *A Letter to Three Wives*. The movie is structured on her epistolary seduction of the husband of one of the wives, yet she doesn't get him after all. (Celeste Holm, narrating the voice-over role of Addie, makes her as vivid a character as anyone we do see.) In *The Barefoot Contessa* Rossano Brazzi tells Ava Gardner on their wedding night that his body was blown apart in the war. Though he bears no visible scars, we're to understand that his penis is permanently dysfunctional.

To return to the hotel scene with Addison DeWitt and Eve Harrington—what a feat of directing Mankiewicz brought off: He coaxed fire from Sanders, once he woke the actor up. From Baxter, smoldering and ready to go off, he got fireworks. Scenes like this one, less famous than the "fasten your seat belts" set pieces, didn't necessarily win Mankiewicz his Oscars. But they do show his genius.

Chapter 12

A New Word for Happiness

*A*t the time of *All About Eve*, Bette Davis's screen persona bordered on the sadistic, owing to her punishing portrayals in such films as *Of Human Bondage, The Letter, The Little Foxes*, and *Beyond the Forest*. (Her sadistic apotheosis was still twelve years in the future, when she teamed up with the perfect movie masochist, Joan Crawford, for *What Ever Happened to Baby Jane?*) Bette had a cruel streak off-screen as well, as an incident in San Francisco unfortunately shows.

One morning, a week into shooting at the Curran Theatre, Davis and Baxter had just finished being made up for the dressing-room scene when Karen Richards introduces Eve Harrington to Margo and friends. "See you on the set, Bette," Anne called as she whisked by.

Celeste Holm, early on the set as usual, had finished her makeup and was already in place, chatting with Gary Merrill and Hugh Marlowe. Thelma Ritter studied herself in a nearby mirror to make sure she looked dowdy enough for the scene.

A stagehand rushed up with a telegram addressed to Bette, and just then the assistant called out, "Everybody on the set, please."

Bette tore open the yellow Western Union envelope, ran her eyes over the message, and grimaced. Moments later she strode onto the set with lips pursed. Her expression indicated grim pleasure.

The telegram was from William Sherry. His message pleaded with Bette to call off the divorce and try yet another reconciliation. Bette proceeded to read the telegram, with sarcastic emphasis and loud laughter, to everyone within earshot. Gary laughed loudest. Hugh Marlowe chuckled. Celeste lowered her eyes and pretended to pick a speck of lint off her skirt. Since she and Bette weren't speaking, it's doubtful she would have laughed even if she had found Bette's performance hilarious. Anne concentrated on her lines—this was a very important scene for her—and pretended not to hear.

In the words of Marion Richards, little B.D.'s nanny, the telegram was "beautiful, tender, sweet." Nurse Richards claimed that "Finally everyone was howling. The only one who didn't go along with ridiculing it was Anne Baxter. She was offended by the whole thing. As was I."

Marion Richards no doubt remembered precisely what happened that day on the set. She had a vested interest, for not long after Bette's merciless reading of the telegram, William Sherry began writing letters to her. Bette was later to claim that Sherry had fallen in love with the young nanny before he and Bette split up. This Richards and Sherry denied.

But she did marry him. On August 6, 1950, not long after *All About Eve* was in the can, Marion Richards, in a seamless shift from nursemaid to stepmother, became Mrs. William Grant Sherry.

"Suddenly," according to Bette's biographer Barbara Leaming, "it was being said about town that in the innocent-seeming young nursemaid with 'the face of an angel' Bette Davis had discovered her real-life Eve Harrington. There was also speculation that Sherry's involvement with the twenty-two-year-old had been going on for some time and that Davis's affair with Gary Merrill was nothing more than a cover-up for her shame over having been abandoned for the much younger woman."

If Bette's affair with Gary was a mere cover-up, she enjoyed it to the full. Her spirits had lifted as soon as filming began. She played records on the set, between takes, and danced the Charleston for the entertainment of cast members. (We can guess which ones were amused.) In fact, the filming of *All About Eve* turned into perhaps the happiest professional experience of Bette's life. The script helped, and Mankiewicz, of course, but so did love.

Celeste Holm excepted, Bette laughed and talked with her colleagues, which surprised Olivia de Havilland when she heard about it. For Bette usually avoided conversations on the set. According to de Havilland, "She would say good morning, but not a lot more. She was saving her energy." Another co-star, Geraldine Fitzgerald, said, "Perhaps people got the impression that she was being testy because of her habit of repeating what you said after you said it. I think that was simply because she wanted to be sure she had gotten what you had said to her. I remember that once she was asked by Edmund Goulding, the director of *Dark Victory*, to stand "over there." She retorted with "*Over there?*" And then she went over there and stood like she was asked to do."

Bette told Anne Baxter, "I thought I was through at forty-one. Then along came Margo Channing."

A few years earlier, Bette had said at the end of *Now, Voyager*, "Don't let's ask for the moon—when we have the stars." But now Bette had the moon as well, for in addition to playing Margo, Gary was her new lover. Every day, when work ended, she and Merrill went out to dinner, sometimes with others in the cast, sometimes alone. Anne Baxter recalled the "big martinis" they drank.

Bette, at this time, might well have borrowed a line from Eve Harrington: "There should be a new word for happiness." At last Bette had work, and love, and plenty to drink. It's a truism that life goes better when you're getting laid, and Bette and Gary, after the martinis, spent every night together. Marion Richards, who shared a room with little B.D. directly under Bette's suite, claimed she heard Bette's bed "going up and down" all night, even though good hotels are constructed to minimize such sounds. And this was the Fairmont, a good hotel in San Francisco, where nervous fault lines mandate especial care in building.

Bette herself said of this period, "There is a near-perfect time in a person's life, just past forty, when you have outgrown most of the wildness, either the work is going well or you have adjusted your sights, and you are at peace with your private self. The time may come only once, and this was mine."

As filming in San Francisco drew to a close, Bette and Gary realized their affair had become serious.

The other man in Bette's life was Joe Mankiewicz. Was it true, as Anne Baxter claimed, that their director knew so much about women that "we're all just glass to him, and he sees everything that makes us tick"? If Mankiewicz "saw through" Bette Davis like a crystal clock, he no doubt perceived her enormous gratitude for a first-rate script and a sure-footed director with a polished style.

Still, he had been more than a little apprehensive about working with such an obstreperous diva, for Bette's reputation was no secret. As soon as *Variety* and the other trade papers announced that Bette was replacing Claudette Colbert, Mankiewicz got several cautionary phone calls from directors who had worked with her in the past. (Along with one congratulation: William Wyler, who had directed Bette in *Jezebel* [1938], *The Letter* [1940], and *The Little Foxes* [1941], phoned to tell Mankiewicz that working with Bette would be a ball.)

The most explicit warning came from Edmund Goulding, a friend of Mankiewicz's who had directed Bette in four films: *That Certain Woman* (1937), *Dark Victory* (1939), *The Old Maid* (1939), and *The Great Lie* (1941). On the last film it is a Hollywood legend that Bette and her co-star, Mary Astor, rewrote the script daily. "Dear boy," moaned Goulding in a Noël Coward accent, "have you gone mad? This woman will destroy you, she will grind you down to a fine powder and blow you away. You are a writer, dear boy. She will come to the stage with a thick pad of long yellow paper. And pencils. She will write. And then she, not you, will direct. Mark my words."

Mankiewicz, girding his loins, prepared for the worst—"Always a good thing to prepare for, among theatre-folk," he said. Goulding's forecast proved inaccurate. In place of squalls came halcyon days. "Stormy Weather" occurred but once, briefly on-screen in a few bars of piano music at Margo's cocktail party.

Long after *All About Eve*, Mankiewicz brimmed with compliments for his leading lady: "Barring grand opera, I can think of nothing beyond her range." And Bette brimmed back: "Mankiewicz is a genius—the man responsible for the greatest role of my career. He resurrected me from the dead."

Toward the end of their smooth sojourn in San Francisco, Mankiewicz decided to tell Bette about Goulding's call. (Goulding had said, "And you may quote me, dear boy.") One afternoon, as they sat around between camera setups, Mankiewicz put it to her. "After those warnings, I expected you to be Lady Macbeth—and instead you're Portia." Whereupon he began reciting Portia famous speech, "The quality of mercy is not strain'd, it droppeth as the gentle rain from heaven. . . ."

Bette stopped him with a snort. "That inimitable Davis snort," Mankiewicz called it; "then she laughed. Her snort and her laugh should both be protected by copyright."

She said, "I am neither Lady Macbeth nor Portia. But yes, I suppose my reputation is pretty much as advertised."

"Why haven't I seen any sign of it?" Mankiewicz asked.

"Look, Joe," she said, "you know as well as I that there is nothing more important to an actress than a well-written part—and a director who knows what he wants and knows how to ask for it." She thumped the *Eve* script. "*This* is heaven," she said, "but as often as not the script has been a compromise of some sort. And the director can't make up his mind whether we're to stand, sit, run, enter, or exit; he hasn't the foggiest notion of what the scene is all about or whether, in fact, it's a scene at all."

The point she's making here is neatly summed up by one of Bette's friends, Roy Moseley: "How she behaved depended on whether she liked and respected the people she was working with. If she thought they were idiots she would do everything in her power to get rid of them. If that failed she would try to do their jobs for them. But if she liked and respected them she would do anything for them."

Moseley buttresses this coget assessment of Davis's demanding professionalism when he describes one way she apparently did others' jobs for them. "At home she had copies of her scripts bound in red leather, some of them covered in masses of handwritten notes. I was interested to see that the screenplay which had the fewest notes was *All About Eve*."

It's almost a disappointment to discover how few annotations Bette actually made in the script. When I examined her copy of it at Boston University, I found that most of her penciled comments occur in the dressing-room scene when Margo Channing first encounters Eve Harrington. She wrote the word "Drink" some half-dozen times. Beside Margo's line, "It was Fort Sumter they fired on—" she wrote "One eyelash" and a few lines later on she inserted a carat and wrote, "Next eyelash." There follow such mundane notes to herself as, "Start cold cream," "Finish cold cream," "Start to turn back to table," "Start Kleenex with cold cream," and "Light cigarette."

More beguiling than Bette's jotted reminders are the various stains throughout her copy of the script. On the title page I found two large splotches of ink. In a Rorschach test they would resemble blue irises beginning to wilt, as Bette's career had wilted before *All About Eve*.

On page 26 I noticed a few brown coffee stains, one the size of a half-dollar, the others no larger than a penny.

Turning the page, I came across more brown stains, along with a tiny reddish smudge no bigger than a lentil. Lipstick, or a drop of blood? And if so, whose? A purely fanciful explanation would be that the blood was scratched from Celeste Holm after one "Good morning" too many.

On page 165 I stumbled on unmistakable lipstick, this time the faint outline of a kiss, as though Bette loves what Addison has just done to Eve: He has slapped her. And Bette kissed the page! Of course. Caught up in this bitchy brawl, wouldn't she just? For, reading the script that first time, Bette was already Margo Channing. (Besides, she had a very *physical* relationship with her mementos. One of Bette's scrapbooks has a picture of Joan Crawford with her teeth blacked out.)

Two pages later, more lipstick, as Addison reveals to Eve what he has learned about her sordid past.

Pages 170, 171, and 173: The red reappears, then trails away. I take it as Margo's farewell kiss, since it's Bette's exit from the film. Her parting lines are calculated to leave 'em cheering: "Nice speech, Eve. But I wouldn't worry too much about your heart. You can always put that award where your heart ought to be."

Chapter 13

A Little Taking In Here and Letting Out There

*M*ankiewicz soon realized that two weeks in the Curran The-atre wasn't enough time. Production fell behind one day the first week. The second week, another day and a half.

Word came that Zanuck was getting upset. Thus began a rat-tat-tat of memoranda, phone calls, and wires. The subliminal message was always the same: "Catch up—or else." (For Mankiewicz the "else" implied no more than the risk of strategic scenes hurriedly whacked from the movie. For directors held in less regard it could mean subsequent blacklisting as financially irresponsible, or even removal from the film.)

Whatever pressure Mankiewicz was under to speed up, it didn't affect the way he handled actors. No one who worked on *All About Eve* ever suggested anything else. Bette Davis herself, a sensitive barometer of moviemaking pressures, registered Mankiewicz's aplomb with this comment: "It was, for the most part, a happy and charmed set."

It was also unusually quiet. Tom Mankiewicz, Joe's son, recently described the hush that fell on his father's sets. "Dad had the quietest sets in the business. Over the years I've worked as a writer, a director, an assistant director, and a producer, and so I've been on hundreds of soundstages in many different productions. Dad's were the quietest. You walked on his set and you thought you had stumbled into a *take*. But then you noticed that the red light wasn't on."

Since Tom Mankiewicz was only eight years old when *All About Eve* was filmed, he didn't observe the shooting of his father's most famous film. He believes, however, that this set would have been as controlled and subdued as the Joseph L. Mankiewicz sets he visited later. (Father and son worked together on a film once, when Tom was second assistant director on *Cleopatra*.)

"Even the crew worked quietly," Tom says. "Dad couldn't stand screamers. Everything was under his control, and I believe that's an important part of his best movies. They're terribly controlled and precise. And yet there was a lot of humor on his sets."

Everyone had a laugh the day Bette Davis took her bows. In the film, the only time we see Margo Channing before an audience is when she comes out for curtain calls after a performance of *Aged in Wood*. Shooting this scene required Bette, in hoop skirts and a dark wig, to bow again and again until every detail was perfect. But what actress can endure bowing to no applause? Bette's performance in the Curran Theatre that day was witnessed only by a handful of the cast and crew.

After a dozen bows greeted by silence, Bette straighted up, walked to the edge of the stage, peered into the darkness, and shouted, "I want to tell you all that you have been a most abominable audience!"

At last she got her applause.

The day they shot the rain scene—the one that precedes Celeste Holm's initial meeting with Anne Baxter in the alley—the sun was shining in San Francisco. Mankiewicz notified the cast and crew that he wanted rain outside the Curran Theatre at five o'clock that afternoon. Workmen set up hoses and sprinklers, and at the appointed hour everything was ready. "Okay, let's have the rain," Joe called out. Before the hoses could be turned on, however, clouds moved in and a chilly drizzle started to fall. Anne Baxter turned to Bette Davis and said, "Even God has heard of Joe's two Oscars."

At the end of two weeks plus in San Francisco, *All About Eve* moved to Los Angeles for more than a month of solid work.

Each day since the start of filming, the dailies—i.e., the unedited film shot on a given day, also called "rushes"—had been sent airmail to Los

Angeles where, the following afternoon, Zanuck would gauge the progress of *Eve*. He watched the dailies immediately after lunch, usually in the company of his executive assistant, the head of the production department, and various other cronies. When the dailies were screened, Barbara McLean, head of the editing department, was always there in the projection room in the basement of the studio's administration building.

On a typical day Zanuck, McLean, and company would settle in for an hour or so of watching the rushes from *Eve* and other films in production. "What have we got today, Bobbie?" Zanuck would ask, pressing the buzzer that notified the projectionist to begin.

Barbara McLean, a pad on her lap for taking notes, might say, "We start with Bette Davis raising hell when she learns about her understudy," or whatever the particular scene involved.

"At the end of filming in San Francisco," said Gary Merrill, "I got Bette's permission to drive back to her house for the weekend, along with Bette's sister, Bobby, and B.D., with the bodyguard in tow." April had dissolved into early May. After spending the weekend with Bette at her house in Laguna Beach, Gary went home to Malibu. His wife, Barbara Leeds, seems not to have smelled a rat. A few days later the Merrills attended a dinner party where Gary, in an "alcohol haze" as he phrased it, started talking to some of the other guests about Bette Davis. What had it been like working with her, they wanted to know, and was she really the termagant that some people claimed?

"I'd marry Bette Davis in a heartbeat if she'd have me," Gary announced. It's easy to imagine the looks on faces around the dinner table. Later Merrill confessed that his statement was "not exactly the sort of thing to say in front of one's own wife." When Gary and Barbara Merrill returned home that night, "the dishes began to fly. Amongst the ruins of the china, we decided to get a divorce."

A few weeks later Barbara Leeds Merrill, testifying in the divorce proceedings, intimated that "twenty-seven-year-old Anne Baxter had been Gary's first choice for an affair in San Francisco." But, she added, since Baxter was madly in love with her husband, John Hodiak, Gary had settled for Bette Davis, who was forty-two. To quote Bill Sampson in the movie, "It sounds like something out of an old Clyde Fitch play."

On-screen and off, half of Hollywood seemed out to get Bette Davis. Was it, she must have wondered, because she was a middle-aged woman determined not to act her age?

On top of everything else, her cocktail dress didn't fit. This dress, which Edith Head designed for Bette to wear in the party sequence, was everything it should be: tight-bodiced, wasp-waisted, full-skirted, shoulder-baring, ankle-skimming. Edith's original sketch had a square neckline. The designer said she had high hopes for Bette's dress because the fabric, brown *gros de Londres* (a heavy silk) photographs magnificently in black and white. And, to make the dress even more opulent, Edith trimmed it in sable.

While the cast was in San Francisco for two weeks, Edith had been working on the cocktail dress and other outfits that Bette would need for scenes to be shot at the studio in Los Angeles. Bette's eleventh-hour casting as Margo Channing had left Edith and her staff in a tizzy, and so, because of their tight schedule, the dress wasn't made up until the night before Bette was to wear it in the big scene.

Edith arrived at the studio early to make sure the dress was pressed and camera-ready. "There was Bette," Edith recalled, "already in the dress, looking quizzically at her own reflection in the mirror. I was horrified. The dress didn't fit at all. The top of the three-quarter-length sleeves had a fullness created by pleats, but someone had miscalculated and the entire bodice and neckline were too big. There was no time to save anything, and a change would delay the shooting."

Edith told Bette not to worry about it. She, the designer, would take full responsibility for the snafu. But she dreaded the hassle. Edith walked to the door on jelly legs, turned the knob, and—

"No, wait," Bette said. "Turn around and look, Edith."

Edith took one look and her eyes brightened, even behind the tinted glasses that had become her trademark.

"Don't you like it better like this, anyway?" Bette asked as Edith retraced her steps.

Bette had pulled the neckline off her shoulders and as Edith approached she wiggled one bare shoulder. "I could have hugged her," Edith said later. "In fact, I think I did." With a few simple stitches Edith secured the neckline in place, and Bette hurried off to the set. As Edith watched Bette sashay out, she realized that the dress—its form, color, fit, even its magnificent female susurration—swept along in exact rhythm with Bette. It contained her like a glamorous second layer of skin. The dress was exactly right.

It's a shame Mankiewicz wasn't there to record this scene, since one of his motifs is women's clothes getting remade. Eve Harrington retailors a suit of Margo's and in *A Letter to Three Wives* Ann Sothern attempts an impromptu makeover of Jeanne Crain's tacky party dress. A variation on this theme takes place in Mankiewicz's earlier film, *The Late George Apley* (1946). Peggy Cummins tries on the wedding gown handed down by her fiancé's grandmother. It's not her style, so she rushes off to New York to buy a modern one. In these scenes Mankiewicz was perhaps alluding to his mother, whom he described as "a very talented dressmaker."

Celeste Holm, who only heard the story of Bette's ill-fitting outfit long after the fact, observed that "Bette's dress did just the right thing for her character. Margo had a terrible sense of being old. That dress made her all the more eager to show off her shoulders and be voluptuous" when Bill Sampson gets waylaid downstairs by younger, fresher Eve Harrington at Margo's welcome-home party for him.

Charles LeMaire and Edith Head both won Oscars for their *All About Eve* costumes. Edith, however, always regretted that she started work on the picture too late to dress Marilyn Monroe. In fact, Edith never dressed Marilyn for a movie—surely a great lacuna in both careers. "I met Marilyn socially several times," Edith said, "and we always talked about clothes. She was extremely knowledgeable about fit and fabric, which surprised me. I never thought she looked especially comfortable in what she wore. Every designer who worked with her cinched her and harnessed her. Marilyn was a free spirit who should have been dressed in such a way that she would be able to forget about her clothes. When a woman is sexy, she knows it and she doesn't need clothes that constantly remind her."

Chapter 14

A Career All Females Have in Common

ilming of the party scene, that first day on the studio set in Los Angeles, involved almost everyone in the cast. When Bette arrived, magnificent in her Edith Head gown and proud of her own improvements to it, not a thing was going on. People were standing, sitting, milling around, talking, yawning. "Why?" Bette asked.

She headed toward Gary Merrill and Hugh Marlowe, who were playing poker. "The new girl," Gary informed her. "Marilyn Monroe. She's almost an hour late."

Just then Harrison Carroll, a veteran reporter for the *Los Angeles Herald Express*, strolled over to Gregory Ratoff and said hello.

"Ees that all I'm getting, a leetle hello?" Ratoff demanded in his blustery voice. Everyone liked to tease Ratoff, probably because he resembled his *All About Eve* character: "dear, sentimental, generous, courageous Max Fabian" from Eve Harrington's point of view, a "sly puss" from Margo Channing's. Ratoff's accent and his shaggy-dog personality made him irresistible.

Born in 1897 in St. Petersburg, Russia (also the birthplace of George Sanders), Ratoff produced, directed, and acted in New York before going to Hollywood in the early 1930s. There he was often cast as eccentric directors and producers with ludicrous accents, like the one he plays in *Eve*. But Ratoff eventually directed more pictures than he appeared in, thanks to Darryl Zanuck.

The effusive and flamboyant Ratoff seems to have been as entertaining off-screen as on. Anne Baxter noted in her memoirs that "Grisha," as he was affectionately known, "was a close friend of Darryl and Virginia Zanuck's, a sort of court jester" who "spent most weekends with them at their home."

Zanuck biographer Mel Gussow recounts a slapstick anecdote about the friendship. A picture directed by Ratoff proved to be a fiasco at a preview. As he and Zanuck drove back to the studio afterwards, Ratoff wept all the way. "How could I haff done this to you, Derrill? What a tragedy," lamented the disgraced director. As they approached the gate of 20th Century-Fox, Ratoff flung open the car door and declared, "I'm going to kill myself!" Whereupon he jumped out and began running. "For Christ's sake, stop him," Zanuck yelled. Then he shouted after Ratoff, "Don't worry, I'll recut it. I'll fix it. Come on to the house." Ratoff slunk back into the car and at the Zanuck home he was put to bed in an upstairs guest room. Zanuck went downstairs, and when a long time had passed and he didn't hear anything, he decided to tiptoe back upstairs. He peeked in. Ratoff was sound asleep. Zanuck shook him awake and yelled, "You son of a bitch! How the fuck can you sleep?"

Anne Baxter also had stories about Ratoff. She had known him in every sense of the word. Here's an anecdote from her book, *Intermission*.

One Sunday in 1946, so Grisha described, Darryl was pacing around the pool in his bikini, swinging his polo mallet and cursing the problem of casting Sophie in *The Razor's Edge*. Grisha spoke up: "Darryl, darling, what about Anne Baxter?"

"Nah!" Zanuck snarled disgustedly. "She's a cold potato."

With that, my pal Grisha went into action. "Darryl," he growled with an evil leer, "please, darling, I have had it—it's marvelous."

"You're kidding, Grisha!"

"That's right, Darryl. Marvelous!"

Monday morning my agent got a call. Could I dine with Edmund Goulding, the man who would direct *The Razor's Edge*, and test Tuesday?

The role won her an Oscar.

Harrison Carroll, the *Herald-Express* reporter, asked Ratoff a few questions for the paper before moving on to Bette Davis.

"Your throaty voice, Bette—are you doing a takeoff on Tallulah Bankhead?" he asked innocently.

"That throaty voice you refer to," Bette answered, "is because I suffered a broken blood vessel on my last picture. Which reminds me, why didn't you come to RKO and do a story on me then?"

Not letting her change the subject, the reporter continued, "Then the character is not in any way modeled after Tallulah?"

Bette threw back her head and laughed a baritone laugh. At that moment she would have reminded anyone of Bankhead. "No, it positively and specifically is not a takeoff on Tallulah." Then she added, this time sounding more like Bette Davis, "Do you think we want to get sued?"

Just then Marilyn rushed in, out of breath as though she had run several blocks. Or just left the arms of a lover. "I'm so sorry," she whispered to everyone and no one.

Mankiewicz talked with her quietly for a few minutes and then asked everyone to take their places. Gregory Ratoff gushed to Celeste Holm, "She ees going verrry far, thees dame, you wait and see."

"Why?" Celeste snapped back. "Because she's kept us all waiting an hour? I think it takes more than that." Celeste arched an eyebrow and considered the irritating starlet, who looked rather lost. "Besides—she's dressed ridiculously in that *tit*ular number. We're filming a cocktail party. No one else is in an evening gown."

Charles LeMaire had, of course, designed Marilyn's *tit*ular gown, as Celeste slyly dubbed it, precisely as such. The first time he saw the Monroe figure he knew that Marilyn and décolletage went together like gin and vermouth. (Twenty years later, a picture of her in a low-cut gown was chosen to illustrate the entry "décolletage" in the first edition of *The American Heritage Dictionary of the English Language*. For reasons of political punctilio the photo was dropped from later editions.)

Did LeMaire know how the camera would worship Marilyn during the brief time she's on-screen? She steals her first scene with Bette Davis even while trying, apparently, *not* to steal it. Marilyn stands, barely moving except for her natural shimmer, and the viewer's eye is glued to her long after she's spoken her two or three lines. The strapless white gown helps, but the costume was incidental to her allure. Already, in the lobby scene filmed in San Francisco, the camera had devoured her and there she didn't even wear the white gown. For that scene "she chose (with the approval of Zanuck and Mankiewicz) an item from her own wardrobe, a tightly woven sweater-dress that also showed her figure to good advantage in *The Fireball* and *Home Town Story*."

It was just about this time that Constance Bennett, spotting the unknown but lovely young Marilyn Monroe at a Hollywood party, reportedly drawled, "Now there's a broad with her future behind her." And seeing Marilyn in *All About Eve*, you know it's true, even without the hindsight.

For this party sequence, which runs for more than thirty pages in the script, LeMaire designed for Anne Baxter a rather mousy cocktail dress that alludes to Margo's flashily glamorous one. The drabness is appropriate, since at this point in the story Eve is still vastly overshadowed by Margo. Perhaps we're supposed to guess that Eve's dress is one of Margo's hand-me-downs. Earlier in the film Eve has altered one of Margo's suits—"a little taking in here and letting out there"—which had become too "seventeenish" for Margo's advancing maturity. Dressing Eve in her mentor's outmoded clothes reinforces sartorially Birdie's warning that Eve is studying Margo "like a play or a book or a set of blueprints."

Zsa Zsa Gabor, a frequent visitor to the set, seems to have studied first one, then another, of the actresses who played scenes with her husband. Was she, like Eve Harrington, motivated by Thespis, or was she just on the lookout for rivals? Later she blithely wrote, "I liked Bette Davis and admired her acting." Bette, in her own memoirs, didn't exactly return the compliment, though she did recount an incident that took place one day at the studio.

Zsa Zsa (who, like Miss Caswell, might have passed for a graduate of the Copacabana School of Dramatic Art, but was not) clicked onto the set in ultra-high heels and matching outfit. Spotting Mankiewicz, she fluttered over to him and said, "Joe, dahlink, I must take my husband avay from you."

Mankiewicz slowly removed the pipe from his mouth, smiled, and said, "How are you, Zsa Zsa? I believe George is in his dressing room, taking a nap."

"Ve haff to go shopping," she cooed. "Dahlink, I promise to giff him back tomorrow."

"Just a minute, honey," Joe said with a frosty smile. "Just one thing. We're making a fucking picture!" Suavely he took her arm, turned her toward the exit, and sent her on her way.

Perhaps the inopportune visit was merely a ruse on Zsa Zsa's part, for she felt "wretched during the shooting because, whenever George made love on the screen, I was sick with jealousy." Not that he kissed Marilyn on-screen, but someone reported to Zsa Zsa that the two lunched together in the studio commissary every day.

Irate, Zsa Zsa confronted George with this damning evidence. But her husband merely stared. For a long moment he didn't speak. Then, with compassion in his voice, he said, "But the commissary is so crowded, the only place the poor girl can sit is with me. So I make room for her. And you know," he added with admiration, "she writes quite good poetry."

Zsa Zsa, caught off guard, was speechless for the only time in her life. "*Poetry!*" she thought. "How can I fight her poetry?"

But there wasn't time to say anything, because at that very moment George Sanders grabbed his wife and made violent love to her. "Normally," Zsa Zsa revealed later, "violent love wasn't George's style and, almost without thinking, I said, 'George, I bet you were fantasizing about Marilyn all the time we were—' "

Livid despite his exertion, George picked up the former Miss Hungary and the future Queen of Outer Space, carried her bodily through the French doors and into the garden, and tossed her, squealing and kicking, into the swimming pool. After which he went upstairs for a long siesta.

The foregoing is told from Zsa Zsa's point of view. But everyone in

Hollywood remembers the past in highly idiosyncratic tableaux. This is Marilyn's own flashback, from _My Story_, to that warm spring day in Los Angeles in May 1950:

I was sitting in the studio commissary having lunch with Mr. George Sanders. We had sat down at the same table more or less by accident, having entered the commissary together, also by accident. The whole thing was an accident. Mr. Sanders was just beginning to eat his chicken salad when the cashier's assistant came to the table and told him he was wanted on the telephone.

About five minutes later Mr. Sanders returned to our table, called for the waitress, and paid his check.

"If you'll pardon me, I must go now," he said to me.

"But you haven't had your lunch yet," I said.

"I'm not hungry," said Mr. Sanders.

"You said you were terribly hungry when you sat down," I said, "and would have to be careful not to overeat. Why don't you just have a bite so you'll have some strength for your big scene this afternoon."

Mr. Sanders looked so pale that I was really worried.

"Unless you're sick," I said.

"I'm in perfect health," said Mr. Sanders, "and I must leave now."

"I'll drive you over to the stage," I said. "I came in my car, and I noticed you walked."

"Oh no, thank you very much," said Mr. Sanders. "I don't want to bother you."

"It's no bother at all," I said. "I've finished my lunch. It's a shame for you to walk all that distance on an empty stomach."

I stood up and started to leave the commissary with Mr. Sanders, but he pulled briskly away from me and I couldn't have kept up with him unless I broke into a trot. So I walked out slowly alone wondering what I had done to make Mr. Sanders rush away from my company.

On the set ten minutes later, Mr. Sanders' stand-in, who was almost as charming and polite as the star himself, came to me and said, "Mr. Sanders has asked me to request of you that hereafter when you say good morning or good-bye to him, you will make those salutations from afar."

I turned red at being insulted like this but I suddenly realized what had happened. Mr. Sanders' wife, Zsa Zsa Gabor, obviously had a spy on the set, and this spy had flashed the news to her that he was sitting at a table with me, and Miss Gabor had telephoned him immediately and given him a full list of instructions.

What They Said About Zsa Zsa and What Zsa Zsa Said About Herself

Oscar Levant: "Zsa Zsa Gabor has discovered the secret of perpetual middle age."

Zsa Zsa: "After a certain age, dahlink, it's either the face or the fanny."

Oscar Levant: "Zsa Zsa not only worships the Golden Calf, she barbecues it for lunch. And she's the only woman who ever left the Iron Curtain wearing it."

Interviewer: "Zsa Zsa, how many husbands have you had?"

Zsa Zsa: "Do you mean apart from my own?"

Oscar Levant: "Zsa Zsa does social work among the rich."

Zsa Zsa: "I don't know anything about sex. I was always married."

When someone complimented Zsa Zsa on the relatively modest jewelry she was wearing in a TV studio, she said, "Dahlink, these are just my working diamonds!"

Zsa Zsa: "The best way to attract a man is to have a magnificent bosom and a half-size brain and let both of them show."

It's curious that Marilyn didn't use her memoirs to settle a score with Bette Davis. According to rumors that have circulated for nearly a half-century, Marilyn had to run away and vomit after filming her two scenes with Bette. Since Marilyn's character, Miss Caswell, dashes to the ladies' room to be sick after her audition, it's possible that this rumor merges life with art.

But Gregory Ratoff, six years after *All About Eve*, told an interviewer that Bette went out of her way to make nasty remarks to Marilyn. One such, according to Ratoff, was this: "I know and you know and everyone knows that kitten voice of yours is goddamned lousy—and it's lousy because you never trained it as a *real* actress does!" Ratoff claimed that Marilyn, after Bette's broadside, went away to cry as well as to vomit.

Celeste and Bette had a big scene coming up. The party sequence had taken nearly a week. Four days were spent filming the Sarah Siddons Awards banquet and finally, with supper in the Cub Room of the Stork Club completed after several full days, all the big scenes involving five, six, seven, eight cast members and more were at last done. Now Mankiewicz concentrated on scenes that required two and three people.

And so, on one of the hottest days of spring, while searing lights burned down on them, Bette and Celeste bundled up in fur coats and played their car scene. Lloyd Richards and Karen are driving Margo to the station to catch a train back to New York for her evening performance when the car sputters to a halt on a snowy road. Footage of the surrounding wintry landscape, which the film's second unit had shot several months earlier in upstate New York, was projected on a process screen behind the specially prepared car.

The scene gains momentum slowly. At first the dialogue is all about what time it is, when the train leaves, and how far it is to the nearest farmhouse. Then, when Lloyd leaves to seek help, the exchange between Margo and Karen becomes one of feminine intimacy. In musical terms, it's a duet. The action stops while Margo bares her soul to Karen. The duet builds to Margo's confessional climax, one of her most famous "arias." It begins famously, "Funny business, a woman's career" and goes on for several minutes, concluding with " Slow curtain. The end."

Later Bette called this "one of the most descriptive speeches about the problems of an actress growing older." She added that "the public, the critics, even friends, thought they saw glimpses of Bette Davis in these lines." But Bette denied it emphatically: "This speech did not apply to me. I was not Margo Channing, her kind of actress, her kind of glamorous lady."

Bette and Celeste played the scene like the finest of friends. The soundstage wasn't air-conditioned, and with overhead lights ablaze, the temperature inside the coupe soon reached 100 degrees. When it was over they, and Mankiewicz, realized what a good job they had done, despite the dispiriting heat. (Makeup artist Ben Nye mopped perspiration off their brows many times, and repaired their dampened makeup.)

In spite of the friction between them, Bette maintained that the scene wouldn't have been the same without Celeste. "She was perfect," Davis said generously.

Not once but twice, as it turned out. When Mankiewicz and Zanuck viewed the rushes, they discovered that a slight jiggle in the process film had spoiled several shots. And so once more the following day Lloyd Richards crawled out of the car to go for help, while Bette and Celeste sweltered in mink as the lights grew hotter and both women, between takes, drank water as though they were field hands and not actresses.

For those outside of show business, it's always surprising that actors who dislike each other can play scenes of affection, friendship, even love. Who would guess, watching Bette and Celeste in that car, that they had so little use for each other?

Just a few days earlier Bette had bruised Celeste's injured feelings once again. They were filming the Stork Club sequence, whose main focus is the table where Margo, Bill, Karen, and Lloyd are seated. Predictably, these four sat for hours at the table while the crew made lighting checks, adjusted camera setups, and fixed the many other technical details of filmmaking.

Celeste felt uncomfortable when silence descended on a social affair, even one that was purely make-believe. So, in an effort to be pleasant and to lighten the drudgery of movie work, she told her table companions, "Do you know that the man who manufacturers Pyrex, when he found out that people were using those Pyrex teapots to make martinis in—he stopped making them?"

The charming response would have been something like "Oh really? How interesting." But Bette was no specialist in charm. Besides, she had a husband she didn't want, a boyfriend who was married, a career that was on the skids unless *All About Eve* could dredge it up from the muck. And this mention of martinis, reminding her of all those she had drunk last night, made her crave another one right then.

Gary Merrill and Hugh Marlowe chuckled politely at Celeste's anecdote, one of them made a jovial retort, and Celeste herself laughed musically. When the mirth died down Bette glanced toward Celeste. Then she looked at Hugh, and finally turned her gaze to Gary. Lowering her eyelids for effect, she drawled: "I don't know *how* I've lived this long without knowing that."

The Wit and Wisdom of Dame Celeste Holm

In 1979 Celeste Holm, who is of Norwegian descent, was dubbed into knighthood by King Olav of Norway, thereby becoming Dame Celeste Holm. Prior to this honor, she was often quoted for her flippant and acerbic opinions. Following it, her statements took on a certain gravity. Herewith, a sampling:

"The life of an actress isn't a bed of mink."

—1946

"I have always, on some level, been aware of how cruel people are to each other. I have been so anxious to remind people of our imperative need for each other."

—1988

"I have never been interested in making love with a man whose child I wouldn't want to bear."

—1955

"The basic theme [of *All About Eve*] irritates me. The theatre is not the jungle and we are not out to kill each other, because

if we were we'd never get a show on. We are bonded to each other and must cooperate."
—1989
"Television is just like summer stock, except that winter never comes."
—1949
"My favorite show is always the one I am doing. All you have is now—do the best you can and enjoy it."
—1980

But everyone loved Thelma Ritter. "One of my favorite people in the whole world," Celeste Holm proclaimed years later. "She did life just right in this era of feminist crap. She was Catholic, she had been a leading woman in stock, she was a very good actress, she got married, she had children, then when the children were old enough she went back into the business. And that's just the way to do it." Celeste herself, married four times and always at work, didn't do it that way.

Gary Merrill called Thelma "a character actress with great common sense." The common sense shines through in every performance. How could she have played a woman who didn't have it? One reason she's perfect in *All About Eve* is that her character, Birdie, who abhors pretense and deception, is wise to Eve Harrington's machinations from the start.

Like Birdie, Thelma Ritter had been a vaudevillian. Thelma on the vaudeville stage may not have "closed the first half for eleven years" as Birdie haughtily claims to have done, but Mankiewicz treasured her "as a fiddler would a Stradivarius." He wrote the role of Birdie for her and no one else. "I adored her," he said.

He, along with Zanuck, helped start her out in movies. In 1946 the director George Seaton, under contract to 20th Century-Fox, went to New York in search of character actors for *Miracle on 34th Street*. Seaton's wife, a childhood friend of Thelma Ritter's, introduced them and Seaton gave Thelma a walk-on as a harried housewife who argues with Santa Claus during the Christmas rush at Macy's. Darryl Zanuck, after watching the rushes, ordered Thelma's role enlarged. She went to Hollywood for three days of extra shooting.

When *Miracle on 34th Street* was released, Thelma (born in Brooklyn but long a resident of Forest Hills, Queens) took her young son and daughter into Manhattan to see the picture in its first-run engagement at the Roxy. "We sat behind some housewives," she recalled, "and when I came on I heard one of them say, 'My God, look at the face on that one!' "

It was a face that America would soon recognize. And it matched her gravelly umpire's voice. After a bit part in *Call Northside 777*, Mankiewicz cast her as Sadie, Ann Sothern's maid in *A Letter to Three Wives*. Sadie, though instructed to announce that "Dinner is served," keeps right on saying it the old way: "Soup's on!" What could be more American than that? And Americans—at least those who love movies— have been on Thelma Ritter's side ever since.

A string of roles followed, each one played so indelibly that casting directors came to describe "a Thelma Ritter type" as the sort of character actress needed to play certain droll, gritty parts.

Thelma's husband, Joe Moran, was a vice-president at the advertising firm of Young & Rubicam. Together the couple eventually earned enough money to maintain several homes, but Thelma preferred to do her own housekeeping, even in a hotel suite. "When I was running three houses," she once said, "the place in Hollywood, the one in Forest Hills, and our summer place on Fire Island, I'd get a little confused. I'd reach for the mustard in Forest Hills and it wouldn't be there and I'd say, 'I bought some just yesterday.' And I had—but in California."

Thelma and Bette got along well together. One thing they had in common was reading. Although Bette's work often left her too exhausted to read, she kept a stack of books beside her bed. Thelma read a book a day, bulleting through novels, scripts, and plays at top speed. She loved Dickens and tried to reread his novels about once a year. (Thelma herself, and the roles she played, are like Dickens characters translated into the American comic idiom.)

"I like Bette and she likes me," Thelma said years after the two had worked together in *All About Eve*. "Maybe it's because I'm homely and she has always thought of herself as homely. When we worked on *Eve* there was so much humor between us, both in our lines and in our chemistry off-screen, that she relaxed with me. I never had a single rough word with her."

A few years later Bette returned the compliment as only she could. Playing a Bronx housewife in *The Catered Affair* (1956), she assumed the voice and accent of Thelma Ritter.

While Edith Head was staying up nights to complete Bette's wardrobe, Thelma decided to buy the kind of dress Birdie would wear. She searched the rack at Macy's, she looked at Gimbel's, then she went home to Queens and shopped around. Where were all those $1.98 dresses that would look right for her character? At last she gave up and called Charles LeMaire at Fox. He fixed her up with a $1.98 dress—but it cost him $200.00 to do it.

Thelma's maternal quality attracted Marilyn Monroe, and the year after *All About Eve* they worked together again, in *As Young As You Feel*. Ten years later they made their third film together, *The Misfits* (1961). Their relationship remained cordial, but by then even Thelma found Marilyn's erratic work habits and perpetual tardiness exasperating. She complained along with everyone else on the set. But afterwards, when Marilyn was dead, Thelma said, "I adored that girl from the moment we met."

Possibly the only criticism anyone ever leveled at Thelma is that she wasn't on-screen enough. In *All About Eve* she vanishes during the cocktail party and isn't seen again. She also disappears too soon from *The Misfits*, where she is one of the few actors who doesn't resemble, emotionally at least, a walking skeleton.

One reason Thelma Ritter is so well remembered in *Eve* is because it's her best role. Another is that, as she herself pointed out, "Birdie always says the thing people never can think of until it's too late."

Zanuck had no trouble getting Thelma Ritter to work for him at Fox. Celeste Holm was a different matter, and after he had lured her there he came to regret it.

Holm had the good fortune to play Ado Annie in *Oklahoma!*, which opened on Broadway on March 31, 1943. The reviews were ecstatic, and many of them singled her out for added praise (e.g., the *New York World-*

Telegram: "Celeste Holm tucked the show under her arm. . . . This is an astounding young woman."). Zanuck, ever alert to astounding young women, wanted to see more of her. He made several offers and finally Celeste, taking a break from the show in 1944, traveled to Hollywood to make a screen test.

Directed by Zanuck's comic henchman, Gregory Ratoff, the test became a production. It required three weeks of advance preparation, and cost $2,500 to produce, a bundle in those days. Holm was filmed in black-and-white and also in Technicolor. Not only did she have the services of a full-time director, she also had a supporting cast that included Sir Cedric Hardwicke, Vincent Price, Mischa Auer, and Dick Haymes. "She is not just good," shouted Gregory Ratoff when he saw Celeste on film for the first time. "She is zenzational!"

Zanuck, though less effusive than Ratoff, was nevertheless impressed by Holm's screen test. He offered her a part in *Where Do We Go From Here?* (directed by Ratoff) in 1945. Celeste turned it down. Her success in *Oklahoma!* had unleashed a flood of offers from Broadway as well as Hollywood. As for the splashy screen test, Holm considered it a vehicle not only to show Fox what she could do, but also to show her what Fox could do. "I liked the stage," she said. "I knew the stage. Pictures were an unknown quantity."

Zanuck kept after Celeste, but in the meantime she was playing the lead in another Broadway musical, *Bloomer Girl*. Eventually he signed her to a long-term contract, a deal that soon made both producer and actress unhappy and led the studio at one point to put her on suspension. Celeste made her Fox debut in a slight musical called *Three Little Girls in Blue* (1946). Critical consensus was that even in a minor role she stole the film from June Haver, Vivian Blaine, and Vera-Ellen. A New York theatre colleague, Fitzroy Davis, later wrote that "Celeste had acquired an early genius for handling the press, and succeeded in obliterating from attention the three presumed stars of that film."

Holm and Zanuck didn't get along. "I could never communicate with him," she admitted. "He loved girls, but he didn't like women. A girl would say, 'Yes, sir, whatever you say, sir.' A woman said, 'Wait a minute! This isn't going to work.' "

Nevertheless, he gave her the role of an intelligent professional woman in *Gentleman's Agreement* (1947), for which she won an Oscar. She was not badly used in any of the films she made at Fox during this period. The same cannot be said, however, of the unfortunate *Champagne for Caesar* (1950), which she made on loan to United Artists.

In the late forties, Celeste ran into Zanuck and his family at Sun Valley on a skiing trip. She liked the Zanuck children, and they seemed fond of her. She had also sung at an afternoon party in Hollywood, which the youngsters attended. It was only natural, then, that young Dickie Zanuck wanted to speak to the lovely young actress on the ski slopes. But his father warned him: "Don't tell her how good she is. She'll ask me for more money."

Perhaps Dickie Zanuck praised her too much, for a year or so later Celeste was well paid for her work in *All About Eve*. She never changed her opinion of Zanuck, however. Long after he was dead and she had grown old, Celeste sniffed, "I understand he bought me because he did not want Louis B. Mayer to get me."

Chapter 15

The General Atmosphere Is Very Macbethish

On the morning when Bette Davis, Gary Merrill, and Anne Baxter were to film the confrontational scene that lends Bill's coming-home party its "Macbethish" air, Bette was worried. This pivotal scene is Margo's awakening to the threat of Eve Harrington. The five pages of dialogue that Margo and Bill exchange in Margo's living room must not become static even for an instant. If it did, the audience might lose interest. That would be fatal, because this scene functions as the door leading into the rest of the film.

During rehearsal Bette said, "I don't understand how to play this. What can we do so that it's not just a talky scene?"

Mankiewicz puffed his pipe. Then he looked around the set. At last he said, "Do you see that candy jar on the piano?" He took Bette's arm and they walked over to it. The candy jar was empty. Mankiewicz called over the second prop master and said something to him.

Later, when it was time to play the scene, Bette recalled what Mankiewicz had told her: "The madder you get, the more you want a piece of candy."

Of course Margo craves a piece of candy. And of course she doesn't dare, because actresses are always on a diet. And Margo at forty is on a stricter diet because she now suspects that her svelte young protégée is after Bill.

The cameras rolled. At Margo's sarcastic line about Eve—"She's a girl of so many interests"—Bette jerked open the candy jar, picked up a piece of chocolate, brought it to her mouth and *almost* popped it in, then threw it back in the jar.

Just then Bette made a peculiar face. Mankiewicz halted the shooting. "What's wrong?" he asked.

"I'm sorry, Joe," Bette said meekly. "I didn't mean to, but I *loathe* eating chocolates in the morning."

Mankiewicz and Bette huddled for a conference. Another prop man was dispatched to the commissary, and when he came back he brought tiny squares of gingerbread to masquerade as chocolates.

Then the scene continued. Margo's anger builds; so does Bill's. Outraged at what he considers her unwarranted jealousy of Eve, Bill lectures: "You have to keep your teeth sharp. All right. But I will not have you sharpen them on me—or on Eve." Margo opens the candy jar again, quickly slams it shut, and snaps back: "What about her teeth? What about her fangs?"

Another angry lecture from Bill: "She hasn't cut them yet, and you know it! . . . Eve Harrington has never by word, look, thought, or suggestion indicated anything to me but her adoration for you and her happiness at our being in love!" At this, Margo opens the candy jar, grabs the seductive piece of "chocolate," throws it in her mouth, and chews furiously, eyes bulging as she swallows, seething all the while.

And that's how a scene that was already good on the page turned out brilliant thanks to the director's flourishes, and thanks also to an actress who knew what to do with "a genius piece of business," in Bette's words. (Ten years later Tony Perkins devised his own jittery candy-nibbling scene in *Psycho*. Was he thinking of Margo Channing at the Bates Motel?)

During the cocktail party we get a look at Margo's bed, which is piled high with minks and sables—$500,000 worth, in fact. To Birdie, the bed

looked like "a dead animal act." Dead or alive, Fox was taking no
chances. When the scene was shot, the studio posted special security
guards to protect the furs.

During a break after Bette's scene with the chocolates, Mankiewicz
grinned and said, "I'm still waiting for you to start directing the picture.
After all, Eddie Goulding said you would; he thinks you're 'a horrible
creature.' "

Again, Mankiewicz heard that Bette Davis snort, which he thought
deserved a copyright. "Mr. Goulding is a genius moviemaker," she said,
but was she sincere, or entirely ironic? It was hard to tell, even for
Mankiewicz. "But he was always drifting away from the story. He also
loved to act, so he would act out your part for you. And the way he acted
out a role many times did not suit the way I thought the character should
be. He *did* find me difficult, because I was very stubborn about the woman
I was playing—and I didn't think he could play her as well as I did."

Later that day Bette herself got the chance to make a brilliant contribution, when the time came for her to speak what was destined to become
an immortal line. Margo's cue comes from Karen, who says: "We know
you, we've seen you like this before. Is it over—or is it just beginning?"

Margo, instead of retorting immediately as indicated in the script, drains
her martini, walks toward the stairs with a shoulder-rolling, hip-swinging
swagger. She halts, swerves, regards Karen, Lloyd, and Bill with a scowl,
then lets it rip: "Fasten your seat belts, it's going to be a bumpy night!"

But Mankiewicz didn't come up with this timing. It was Bette's own.
She said: "Those are things you should be able to do as an actress that a
director wouldn't think of telling you. When Margo holds back like that
it lets you know she's collecting more venom."

(Twenty-five years later Bette was flying to Australia to do her one-
woman "Bette Davis Show," a retrospective of her life and career replete
with film clips, reminiscences, questions from the audience, and tart
remarks about former co-stars. As the distant lights of Sydney twinkled
into view, the captain announced on the intercom that Miss Davis was
invited to come forward and visit the cockpit. From there she would
have a spectacular view of the city at night as the plane landed. As Bette
went through the cockpit door she heard a roar of laughter from the

cabin. Turning, slightly puzzled, she saw passengers pointing up to the illuminated sign that had just flashed on. It said, Fasten Seat Belts.)

In the "Fasten your seat belts" scene, Hugh Marlowe, as the playwright Lloyd Richards, is the least exciting actor on-screen. But Marlowe is that way throughout the movie, conforming to Hollywood's image of writers. (This drab stereotype perhaps sprang from the low self-esteem of scriptwriters, who were bottom feeders in the studio pecking order. Irving Thalberg called them "jerks with Underwoods.") But the cards are stacked against any actor who portrays a writer. Even Bette, playing a novelist-playwright in *Old Acquaintance* (1943), is rather sluggish. Like it or not, we recall not Bette but her co-star, the fidgety Miriam Hopkins.

Hugh Marlowe has no bravura scenes in *All About Eve*, or elsewhere in his career. ("He was a stick," Mankiewicz said bluntly.) In fact, he's one of those slow-burning, carbohydrate actors who all look like versions of Gregory Peck. (Such actors always resemble high-school principals.) But at least Hugh Marlowe, in *Eve*, gives good support. As unexciting Lloyd Richards he's as firm as a new mattress.

Hugh Marlowe had three strikes against him from the start: his real name—it was Hugh Herbert Hipple. Born in Philadelphia in 1911, he grew up in the Midwest, started his career as a radio announcer at WHO in Des Moines, Iowa, and when he left the station his old job was given to another would-be actor named Ronald Reagan.

From Iowa, Marlowe headed for Hollywood but made a four-year stopover at the Pasadena Playhouse, a celebrated movie-actors' training ground in those days. He made a film in 1936, two the following year, and eventually left town to appear on Broadway in 1942 with Gertrude Lawrence in Moss Hart's *Lady in the Dark*, with music by Kurt Weill and lyrics by Ira Gershwin.

In the forties Marlowe was twice under contract to MGM, and twice dropped, before moving to 20th Century-Fox in 1948. There he played standard second leads: a songwriter in *Come to the Stable* (1949) with nuns Loretta Young and Celeste Holm, a fighter pilot in *Twelve O'Clock High* the same year, and a sculptor in *Night and the City* (1950).

Marlowe married and divorced several times. One wife was the actress Edith Atwater. Another was actress K. T. Stevens, the daughter of director Sam Wood. Marlowe spent the last thirteen years of his life appearing in the NBC soap opera *Another World*. He died in 1982.

Racier than any of his on-screen roles was an incident that took place when Marlowe was starring in *Anniversary Waltz* at the Alcazar Theatre in San Francisco in 1956. His co-star was Marjorie Lord, best remembered as the wife of Danny Thomas in the TV show *Make Room for Daddy*. A few seconds after the curtain went down on the second act, Lord slapped his face and sent him reeling. And Marlowe slapped her back.

The tabloids loved it. HE KISSES, SHE SLAPS, HE'S FIRED, headlined the *New York Journal-American*. In the *New York Post* the headline ran, HE WHO GOT SLAPPED GETS THE GATE. (Why didn't some clever headline writer call the story A BUMPY NIGHT?)

Versions of the incident differed. The feud had started a week or so earlier when Marjorie Lord objected that Marlowe was "overly ardent in the love scenes." She accused him of inventing "some quite violent embraces that weren't in the script at all." Different ways of playing the little family comedy were never quite resolved, and so, on a Thursday evening, something happened to provoke the fight.

Newspapers, even the louder ones, were circumspect at the time, so we don't know precisely what Hugh Marlowe did. The *Journal-American*, quoting Marjorie Lord, titillates with ellipses: "Frequently he . . . well, some things just weren't in the script." Did his tongue wander, or was it perhaps that he goosed his co-star?

According to the gentleman himself, "I had just kicked the TV set at the end of the second act. I'm off balance. She swats me on the side of the face. So I slapped her right back in the heat of emotion. Miss Lord is a charming girl but new to the business."

Marjorie Lord made her stage debut in 1936.

After the exchange of blows, the actors finished the performance. The following night, however, when Marlowe showed up at the stage door, it was barred to him. The theatre management had hired special policemen to keep down a row, and the actor was informed that his contract had been terminated.

To paraphrase Lloyd Richards, "The general atmosphere was very

Macbethish." More so, surely, than anywhere in those plays Lloyd kept writing for Margo: *Remembrance, Aged in Wood, Footsteps on the Ceiling.* Though we never see Margo perform in them, we can guess that Lloyd Richards writes quite conventional plays. As portrayed by Hugh Marlowe, how could Lloyd be more than a well-made playwright?

Chapter 16

I Call Myself Phoebe

 always followed my cock, not my head, with the ladies," Gary Merrill said. He didn't make that blunt comment to Hedda Hopper, however, nor to Louella Parsons, both of whom were in a scramble for details of his romance with Bette Davis. Their pursuit seemed to go on around the clock now that *All About Eve* was finishing up and Gary and Bette had dropped even the trappings of propriety. They were living in sin!

One Monday, after Bette, B.D., and Nurse Richards had spent the weekend at Gary's house, the phone rang. (That was the day Bette and Celeste filmed their 100-degree automobile scene, so Gary hadn't been called to the studio.) Hedda Hopper jumped right in: "I know Bette spent the weekend with you!" She prattled on about what a great person Bette was and how much pain men had caused her. "And if you treat her badly," Hedda warned, "you'll be in a lot of trouble." Meaning, of course, from the damage Hedda would inflict in her column.

Gary, half-playing Bill Sampson, turned on the sexy boyish charm. Hedda liked him, despite what her spies had reported: that he was a slob who didn't make his bed and left stacks of dirty dishes in the sink.

A couple of hours later the phone rang again and it was Louella Parsons. "Is it true you have asked Bette to marry you?" Louella pried. If I can handle Bette Davis, Gary must have told himself, I can certainly deal with Louella Parsons, so he told her about the poodle he and Bette had bought that weekend for little B.D.

"But Gary," Louella gasped, "poodles have to be clipped and combed. Don't you dare neglect that animal! I've heard that you live in a messy place where the beds aren't even—"

"I plan to let the poodle become a bum, like me," Gary drawled.

Louella loved it, and next day she reported their conversation in her column, adding that "Gary looks like a beachcomber. He lives in dungarees and a plaid shirt, and he has the blackest beard in history." Hedda picked it up later that week, rewording the shaggy-dog story only slightly.

From then on, Gary got good press from both ladies. One of them wrote a bit later (and the other soon wrote more or less the same): "I know a couple of Bette's previous husbands quite well and they tell me Bette and Margo are one—the same unpredictable type of person, complete with the flinging around of mink coats and staccato excitability. Plus the genuine warmth and intelligence and sense of humor that Margo had. Margo, Bette—it's all the same, and if you liked Margo, you'll love Bette. Gary Merrill did and does, both ways."

Toward the end of shooting at the studio, Bette and Gary played the scene where Bill rushes in to comfort Margo after Addison DeWitt's devastating column. There was no need for the makeup man to supply glycerin tears, because Mankiewicz directed Bette to turn her back to the camera for Margo's paroxysm of weeping. ("One's back can describe an emotion," Bette wrote in *The Lonely Life*.)

Margo's body, from behind, heaves with sobs. She's like an abandoned waif. Suddenly, at the door, there's Bill, who runs to Margo, takes her in his arms and holds her. He says, "Bill's here, baby. Everything's all right, now." Karen quietly exits, the scene ends, at least on-screen, but on the set that day it didn't end quite like that. In fact, the embrace heated up, with passionate kisses added after the camera had stopped. At that point Mankiewicz called out, "Cut! Cut! This is not swing and sway with Sammy Kaye." Bette raked her fingers through her hair. She and Gary repaired to her dressing room and didn't return for three-quarters of an hour. ("All love scenes started on the set are continued in the dressing room after the day's shooting. *Without exception*," said Alfred Hitchcock. But in this case, five o'clock was too long to wait.)

As the end of May 1950 approached, completion of *All About Eve* was at hand. One important piece of work remained: retakes of the Stork Club scene. Bette, the first time, had offended Celeste with an unkind remark. Now Celeste had the last laugh.

The climax of this scene comes when Margo announces that she doesn't want to star in Lloyd's new play, and Karen breaks into peals of relieved laughter. Solved are everyone's problems, particularly Karen's— she has escaped Eve's blackmail. Celeste's laughter—first a husky cackle, then a tinkling bell—dissolves in silvery circles on the air.

Bette thought it was the damnedest thing: Celeste could laugh on cue, like Shirley Temple crying real tears. Bette herself was capable of almost everything else, but a few seconds of laughter left her winded and she had to start over.

"Cut," Mankiewicz called. He had the shots he wanted.

"I can't do that," Bette grumbled. For the first time in weeks she addressed Celeste when the camera wasn't on. "How do you do that?"

"It's easy," Celeste answered.

"Well, *I* can't do it," Bette repeated.

Mankiewicz (who, according to Celeste, enjoyed showing Bette that there were other actors in the picture) said, "Would you like to do it again, Celeste?" And she seized the chance to giggle on and on until at last Mankiewicz, highly amused, puffed on his pipe and said, "Okay."

As a practical joke—or was it retaliation for her laughter?—Gary Merrill, now entirely in league with Bette, told Celeste about a new shampoo. For he had discovered that she had a hair-washing compulsion. Gary, along with a couple of others in the company, sent Celeste on a wild goose chase around Los Angeles in search of an extraordinary new hair product called F.A.G. The cockamamie acronym supposedly stood for "follicle aggrandizement gel," which was reputed to work wonders. So off went Celeste, to this pharmacy and that, asking brightly, "Do you have any F.A.G. shampoo?"

At the end of *All About Eve* a stagestruck teenager is about to loot Eve Harrington's life just as Eve had plundered Margo's. Although these final scenes in the movie were not literally the last ones Mankiewicz shot at 20th Century-Fox toward the end of May 1950, this is where we leave the set. Principal photography is over, the cast has worked long and brilliant hours, and a coherent film remains to be shaped out of thousands of celluloid images.

The *All About Eve* Network

Hollywood—both the geographical entity and the state of mind—has always been a small town where people know one another and work together. Here is a tabulation of instances when Mankiewicz directed *Eve*'s cast members in other films, and also when cast members (and the ubiquitous Zsa Zsa Gabor) worked together in earlier and later films.

Mankiewicz directed George Sanders in *The Ghost and Mrs. Muir* (1947), Thelma Ritter (and Celeste Holm, voice-over only) in *A Letter to Three Wives* (1949), Walter Hampden in *Five Fingers* (1952).

Bette Davis and Walter Hampden appeared in *All This, and Heaven Too* (1940). Davis and Barbara Bates were in *June Bride* (1948). Davis and Gary Merrill appeared in *Another Man's Poison* (1951) and *Phone Call From a Stranger* (1952).

Gary Merrill and Hugh Marlowe appeared in *Twelve O'clock High* (1949). Merrill and George Sanders appeared in *Witness to Murder* (1954). Sanders and Randy Stuart were in *I Can Get It for You Wholesale* (1951).

Sanders and Zsa Zsa Gabor co-starred as hard-boiled lovers

in *Death of a Scoundrel* (1956), but by then they had been divorced for several years. Gabor and Marilyn Monroe both had small parts in *We're Not Married* (1952).

Hugh Marlowe and Celeste Holm were in *Come to the Stable* (1949).

Anne Baxter and Marilyn Monroe appeared in *Ticket to Tomahawk* (1950). They were both in *O. Henry's Full House* (1952), and so was Gregory Ratoff.

Marilyn Monroe and Barbara Bates appeared in *Let's Make It Legal* (1951). Monroe and Hugh Marlowe were in *Monkey Business* (1952). Monroe and Thelma Ritter appeared in *As Young As You Feel* (1951) and *The Misfits* (1961). Ritter and Bess Flowers were in *Move Over, Darling* (1963).

Thelma Ritter and Hugh Marlowe were in *The Birdman of Alcatraz* (1962).

Barbara Bates, who plays Phoebe, the ambitious teenager that Eve Harrington will come to regret taking in, has become a Hollywood ghost. If you mention her as a cast member of *All About Eve* you're likely to hear, "Which one was she?" Everyone recalls that final shot of Phoebe bowing to herself—and to us—in front of Eve's triptych of mirrors, her image reflected to infinity. But who was Barbara Bates?

For one thing, she never took to Hollywood, though she eventually ended up in the pages of *Hollywood Babylon*. She was born in Denver in 1925, and her start in movies sounds like something invented by a press agent, as indeed it was, for the story was told by Barbara's first husband, who had worked as a Hollywood publicity man for some twenty years when he met Barbara in 1944.

His name was Cecil Coan and, according to his version, he was on a bond tour with several stars in the closing days of World War II. During an appearance in Denver, Coan and his stars—or were they really starlets?— noticed a lovely teenager who pressed forward to gather autographs. "You're a remarkably pretty girl," said Coan. "I suppose you know that?"

"I've heard," Barbara answered seriously and without a trace of flirtation. They chatted and Barbara revealed her dreams of being an actress. "Well," said the suave middle-aged publicist, "if you're ever in L.A. look me up." He gave her his card, as he had given it to many before. Later that year someone called on Cecil Coan. Who is it, he thought as his secretary ushered the girl warily into his office, I don't think I've ever laid eyes . . . "You remember me," Barbara said, and it was not a question but a statement, for she took people, quite literally, at their word.

Getting a studio contract wasn't so hard if you had connections, and when Barbara signed with Universal the Denver papers ran stories about her for weeks. She made her debut as one of Yvonne De Carlo's handmaidens in *Salome, Where She Danced* (1945).

Cheesecake. The word puckered Barbara's lips like a lemon, and yet she posed endlessly in shorts, swimsuits, tight sweaters, and Rosie-the-Riveter coveralls for photos intended to stimulate servicemen in the lapsing days of war. *Life* magazine put her on the cover, and that issue— May 28, 1945—reportedly sold more copies on Denver's newsstands than any other magazine had ever sold before.

"I was never the pin-up type," Barbara said wistfully some years later, long after she had married Cecil Coan and, having been dropped by Universal, had become a featured player at Warner, where she played the title role in *June Bride*, starring Bette Davis. But everyone eventually quarreled with Warner Bros., and Barbara, too, left after a blow-up. Depression, never far away, gripped her with icy fingers. Her despair was profound but somehow it seemed not totally related to reversals in her career.

By the end of 1949 life called to her, and she answered. Barbara and Cecil moved into a new house in Benedict Canyon, they spent weekends sailing their yawl in Pacific waters, and 20th Century-Fox, where Barbara had a new contract, cast her in *Cheaper by the Dozen*.

And then Joseph L. Mankiewicz structured his new screenplay so that a bit player monopolizes the screen at the end, and the final fade-out is hers rather than Anne Baxter's or Bette Davis's. A small part, yes, but it was Barbara Bates's most important one and the one for which she is remembered, if at all. *The Hollywood Reporter* said of her performance in *All About Eve*: "Barbara Bates comes on the screen in the last few moments to more or less sum up the whole action and point of the story. It's odd that a bit should count for so much, and in the hands of Miss Bates all the required points are fulfilled."

Later she appeared insignificantly in *The Secret of Convict Lake, Let's Make it Legal, Rhapsody*, and many other fifties films, until she and her husband moved to London in hopes of aggrandizing her career. Barbara made two pictures there. On two others she was replaced after filming had begun. It was rumored she had severe personal problems, but no one found out what they were.

The Coans returned to Hollywood and Barbara made her last movie, *Apache Territory*, in 1958. From time to time she managed to appear on a lone television show. She made two TV commercials, one for floor wax and another in which she appeared with Buster Keaton in praise of some product long forgotten.

While Cecil Coan suffered a decline from cancer, Barbara Bates trained to become a dental assistant and when her husband died in 1967 she returned to Denver, though without fanfare, for she had not fulfilled the hometown dreams. It was said that she could have been as famous as Linda Darnell, but look how she had let folks down.

She took a job in a hospital, where none of the patients dreamed that this middle-aged woman with the sad, weary face had once been a movie star. One day she ran into her childhood sweetheart from long ago, and they married. The marriage made the papers, though far from the front page. Barbara's mother, Eve Bates, told a reporter, "Barbara is finally at peace with herself." But Mrs. Bates's assessment was premature.

Three months after the marriage, on March 18, 1969, Barbara Bates, in a mood of sunless depression, turned on the gas and died by asphyxiation.

But what of that final scene, where Barbara Bates, as Phoebe, is trapped among endless reflections of herself, without companion? This is how Mankiewicz conceived the scene in his screenplay: "Slowly, she walks to a large three-mirrored cheval. With grace and infinite dignity she holds the award to her, and bows again and again . . . as if to the applause of a multitude."

A significant fact about Mankiewicz and his mirrors is that he borrowed the whole thing from Orson Welles, who had done it famously in *The Lady From Shanghai* (1948). Both directors flash these mirror sequences as a final virtuoso flourish, though in the Welles film noir Rita Hayworth shoots down her husband, Everett Sloane, and he shoots her, shattering the mirrors to bits. As both lie dying in the wreckage of splintered glass, Sloane says to Hayworth: "For a smart girl, you make a lot of mistakes."

This same line, though of course unspoken, is implicit in the mirror-ending of *All About Eve*. Ironically it is we, the audience, who "speak" the line, however silently or subliminally, to Eve Harrington. We gasp at her deadly error, which is the same one Margo made: The enemy was at the gate, and now the enemy is invited in . . . to devour. Mankiewicz implies, with his mirrored multiplicity of Phoebes, that the plague of Eves and Phoebes is unstoppable; cut down one and a hundred more spring up. If Mankiewicz is in any sense a visionary, his vision is this: that show business survives on the bloodsucking of its many Eves and Phoebes.

In less baroque terms, we might wonder why Mankiewicz added this ten-minute coda with Eve and the brazen intruder and that looking-glass into forever. It has been pointed out that formally, the story ends after Eve's speech at the Sarah Siddons banquet, when Margo speaks her final line: "You can always put that award where your heart ought to be." Richard Winnington's comment, in London's *News Chronicle* in 1950, is typical of those who find the ending unsatisfactory. He called it "an artistically unjustifiable would-be clever climax." The film critic Richard Corliss calls the ending of *All About Eve* "a totally redundant coda which blunts Mankiewicz's modestly ironic point."

Had the film ended with Margo's devastating little speech, we would have come full circle, back to the awards dinner where the picture opened. At that point, everything wise and witty having been said, we know all about Eve, Margo, Bill, Karen, Lloyd, and everyone else in the story. There's no real need to visit Eve's opulent new Park Avenue apartment. We can imagine her improved circumstances, as well as the lack of pleasure they'll bring.

Perhaps Mankiewicz felt that ending the movie with Margo's speech would smack of the well-made play. That kind of neat, final-curtain ending belongs to the theatre, not to the movies. And though Mankiewicz was often accused of making filmed plays rather than "cinematic" movies, in this looking-glass dénouement he followed his visual instinct.

It's unorthodox to introduce a new character to end a movie, but Mankiewicz, like all Hollywood moralists, didn't trust his audience to draw their own conclusions. (Although he might have, since *All About Eve* is a picture for grown-ups.) But even if he had, the censors hovered close by, insisting that evil be punished. And Eve's Sarah Siddons Award was hardly a punishment.

Tradition required that Hollywood fables, even shrewd and amusing Mankiewicz fables, must carry an unambiguous message at the end. (The fables of La Fontaine, pungent and witty, also follow this format. Each fable consists of a little play—the "body" as La Fontaine himself called it—to which a brief maxim or teaching—the "soul"—is often attached.)

The "body" of *All About Eve* is the main story, which begins and ends at the Sarah Siddons banquet. Actually, Margo's final line contains the law and gospel of the story. "You can always put that award where your heart ought to be" implies: Have a heart, love with your heart, use your heart for forgiveness, and never trade it for gold or high regard. (Unlike the Tin Man, Eve doesn't realize that she lacks a heart.)

But some commentators see the Eve-and-Phoebe sequence— Mankiewicz's "second" ending, as it were—as an ethical pop quiz pinned to the movie: "Did you pay attention? All right, question number one: What is Eve Harrington's punishment for all her nasty deeds? Two: True or false, we all get what we deserve in the end. . . ."

If we look for the difference, in movies, between art that reveals a new vision and craft that retools a familiar blueprint, that difference is perhaps this: that an artist—whether writer, director, actor, or even producer—allows the viewer room enough to create his own final ending, along with the meaning that ending implies, while others include a manufactured meaning with the ticket price.

All About Expenses

The filming of *All About Eve* was to have ended in May 1950, but since production ran over a few days, Mankiewicz didn't call a wrap until the first week of June. According to Fox records, the film was brought in for $1,400,000 ($500,000 of which went to cover cast salaries). The original estimate for total cost of the film had been $1,246,500.

Attached to the copy of Mankiewicz's treatment dated September 26, 1949—the copy that bears the original title, *Best Performance*—is a sheet headed "Planning Production Cost Estimate" for Story 309, which was the story number assigned to *All About Eve*. This itemized sheet shows, or should show, a breakdown of the original estimate of $1,246,500—the amount given as "Grand Total" at the end of the sheet. But the figures add up to $1,108,508.29. We can only wonder if the discrepancy was caused by math anxiety or creative bookkeeping.

Planning Production Cost Estimate

Story Rights and Expenses	3,500.00
Scenario	47,208.29
Cast	300,000.00
Production Dept. Service	278,385.00
Adm. Overhead	137,115.00
Art	16,000.00
Set Cost	55,000.00
Light Platforms	4,500.00
Strike Labor	9,500.00
Rerecording	10,000.00
Titles, inserts and fades	8,500.00

Talent tests	3,000.00
Editorial	5,000.00
Production and Dir. Secys.	3,000.00
Staff	15,000.00
Extras	20,000.00
Operating Labor and Management	25,000.00
Camera	22,000.00
Sound	12,000.00
Electrical	2,000.00
Mech. Effects and Snow Dressing	2,000.00
Set Dressing	23,000.00
Women's Wardrobe	16,000.00
Men's Wardrobe	6,000.00
Makeup and Hairdressing	7,000.00
Process	3,000.00
Spec. Effects and Scenic Art	3,500.00
Production Film	20,000.00
Stills	3,500.00
Location Exp.	23,000.00
Misc.	25,000.00
Grand Total:	1,246,500.00

Cast salaries, according to surviving figures compiled by casting director Bill Maybery, were as follows:

[NB: stock = under contract to 20th Century-Fox]

Anne Baxter—(stock) $4,000/wk to 3/25/50; then $5,000 wk
Bette Davis—$130,000 for 12 wks
Celeste Holm—$35,000 for 8 wks—pro rata thereafter
George Sanders—$6,000/wk 10 wks
Hugh Marlowe—$750/wk (stock)
Thelma Ritter—$1,750/wk 6 wks

Gregory Ratoff—[no figure given]
Barbara Bates—$250/wk (stock)
Leading Man—Craig Hill—$100/wk (stock)
Marilyn Monroe—$500/wk 1 wk guarantee
Doorman—Leland Harris—$175/wk, 1 wk
Walter Hampden—$2,500/wk—1 wk
Claude Stroud—$750/wk convrtd from $150 a day

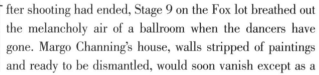

Chapter 17

The Time I Looked Through the Wrong End
of the Camera Finder

After shooting had ended, Stage 9 on the Fox lot breathed out the melancholy air of a ballroom when the dancers have gone. Margo Channing's house, walls stripped of paintings and ready to be dismantled, would soon vanish except as a celluloid image. Her big tropical plants had been carted away for a jungle picture, and her furniture and gewgaws, including the candy dish and the piano it sat on, had, after careful inventory, been packed up once more in a studio warehouse. The Stork Club, bare and deserted, resembled a loading dock. The dining hall of the Sarah Siddons Society was bare, the chandeliers and distinguished theatre portraits all dispersed. Gone were the tables from the banquet, and gone, too, were their white tablecloths; the flowers; the rich paneling of the ornate dining hall. Carpenters had already recycled the wood for another set.

Over at last. The cast and crew of *All About Eve* would never be together again. Even now they had scattered. Bette and Gary, inseparable, lived by the sea in her house in Laguna Beach. For variety, they sometimes drove up the coast to his place at Malibu. Marilyn retreated to her little apartment at 718 North Palm Drive, and Celeste and Thelma flew back to New York. George and Zsa Zsa continued to spar over his flirtations, real and imagined. And Joe Mankiewicz was the new president of the Screen Directors Guild. On May 31, a week before shooting ended, his peers had elected him to this prestigious post. He was nominated by Cecil B. DeMille. After such an eventful spring Mankiewicz needed a break, and in late June he took his family to Europe for a vacation in France and Italy.

Mankiewicz on Himself and Others

Mankiewicz on Cecil B. DeMille: "DeMille has his finger up the pulse of America."

On Katharine Hepburn: "The most experienced amateur actress in the world."

On *Keys of the Kingdom* (1944), starring Gregory Peck and produced by Mankiewicz: "217 minutes of high thought and low lighting."

On F. Scott Fitzgerald: "I wonder if Scott had looked more like Wallace Beery whether his reputation would be as great."

On Hemingway's dialogue: "Read it aloud and you start to giggle, it's so bad."

On being the younger brother of Herman Mankiewicz, who for a long time was more highly esteemed than Joe: "I know what they'll write on my tombstone: HERE LIES HERM—I MEAN JOE MANKIEWICZ."

During the frenzied filming of *Cleopatra*, Taylor and Burton dominated the world's headlines. When an Associated Press reporter, on the set in Rome, asked Mankiewicz *The Question*, the director said: "The real story is that Richard Burton and I are in love and Elizabeth Taylor is being used as our cover-up." Then Joe kissed Richard Burton on the mouth and walked off the set.

All About Eve was finished, but the movie still didn't exist. It was no more than an unwieldy batch of celluloid in metal cans, thousands upon thousands of tiny images. Those little frames of film formed an inchoate mass, like words in a dictionary that the storyteller must quarry and weigh and arrange for his tale.

In the case of Mankiewicz, that dictionary of images was abridged, for, unlike many directors, he edited his films, in a sense, while shooting them. This directorial trait has rarely been mentioned in commentary on Mankiewicz's work, but Celeste Holm says, "He's the only person I ever saw who cut while he shot. You'd be doing a scene and he'd put his hand over the camera and say, 'Cut to' this or that. He said, 'I'm not giving that cutter one frame that I don't want on the screen.'" (John Ford, Alfred Hitchcock, William Wyler, and other top directors also edited through the camera, so that, at least in theory, it would have been impossible to put their films together differently.)

Mankiewicz knew, of course, that the less surplus footage he provided for editors and producers to pick over, the tighter his own control of the picture would be. Such control lessened the chance of a film belonging aesthetically to someone else. Tom Mankiewicz, the director's son, corroborates Celeste Holm's assertion. "Like many directors, Dad protected himself that way. He wanted to shoot a film in his own style. So he'd film certain scenes the way he wanted them, with no coverage, and then if Zanuck said, 'That scene is too long,' Dad could say, 'Darryl, we've got what we've got. We can't cut it.'"

Many actors wouldn't notice this subtle director's ploy, but Celeste Holm had a keen interest in all aspects of moviemaking. In fact, she even learned basic cutting from Barbara McLean, the editor of *All About Eve* and many other famous films.

"You want to see how to cut a scene?" McLean asked Celeste one day on the Fox lot in 1946, while Celeste was at work on *Three Little Girls in Blue*.

"You bet," said Celeste.

McLean glanced around the editing room at a few million feet of film. "Who do you like best?"

"Vera-Ellen," Celeste replied, referring to one of her co-stars in the picture.

"All right," said Barbara McLean, "let's make this her scene." And the editor demonstrated how to "give" a scene to a particular player by cutting to her reaction.

"You see," said Celeste, "the director in the theatre shows the audience where to focus its attention through the movement of all the actors onstage. But motion pictures do it with cutting. So the movie audience just sits mindlessly, not making any choices."

As her remark indicates, Holm preferred stage acting to movies. She once said, "Hollywood is a good place to learn to eat a salad without smearing your lipstick." Whatever her caveats about the movies, however, Celeste Holm's admiration for Mankiewicz was enormous. "He was the most sophisticated director I ever worked with," she said.

Part of his sophistication was the belief that only he could shape his work. Other fingers, including editorial ones, would leave a sticky smudge. But if a picture must have an editor, Barbara McLean (1904–1996) was one of the best. Tom Mankiewicz emphasizes that his father wasn't afraid McLean would sabotage his picture: "He only worried about Zanuck."

Born Barbara Pollut in New Jersey, she married Gordon McLean, a projectionist, in 1924. They left immediately on the long trip to Hollywood, where, like thousands of movie-intoxicated youths, Barbara intended to become an actress. In photographs of the period she has dark hair, almond-shaped Egyptian eyes, and thinly plucked brows. Her resemblance to silent stars like Vilma Banky and Pola Negri was no doubt intentional.

Few aspirants made it to silent stardom, and Barbara McLean was not among the elect. But she did possess a Hollywood skill. As a girl she had worked in her father's film laboratory in Palisades Park, New Jersey. There she cut negatives and patched together release prints. "I learned all about the density of positive and negative film," she recalled many years later.

Her marriage broke up and she needed work. Because of her experience, she got a job at Fox's laboratory on Western Avenue in Los Angeles. (This was a few years before Fox Film Corporation merged with Twentieth Century.) In those days, editing frequently amounted to little more than simple cutting—trimming edges and splicing loose ends to arrange shots in elementary continuity. The term for those who performed such work was "cutter," a word still sometimes used in a faintly derogatory sense in place of the more high-end job description, "editor."

The first film McLean edited after her apprenticeship was *Coquette* (1929), Mary Pickford's first talkie. McLean didn't own a car, so America's Sweetheart, en route from Pickfair, stopped for her every morning and dropped her off at night. (It's unclear why *Coquette*, Pickford's United Artists film, was being worked on at Fox; by the late twenties UA had built its own studio.)

After Zanuck and Joseph M. Schenck formed 20th Century-Fox in 1935, "Bobbie" McLean, as she was known in the industry, went on to edit some of the studio's most prestigious productions, including *Alexander's Ragtime Band, The Song of Bernadette, Viva Zapata, Niagara*, and many more. Nominated seven times for Academy Awards, she won an Oscar for *Wilson* in 1944. In 1949 Zanuck promoted her to head of the studio's editing department, a post she held until her retirement twenty years later.

Described as "creative, imaginative, and expert in her art," McLean "repeatedly demonstrated a solid dramatic grasp, a knowledge of what could be done with film, and a keen awareness of story values."

Some studio directors wanted their editors on the set, while others considered an editor's presence a threat to their authority, and fierce arguments often resulted. Barbara McLean generally spent three or four hours on the set with every director she worked with, noting their approach, particularly during the first weeks of filming. In the case of *All About Eve*, she waited until production moved to Los Angeles before observing Mankiewicz at work.

In 1951 Barbara McLean married the director Robert D. Webb, who specialized in action-oriented films. Webb's most famous picture, however, is *Love Me Tender* (1956), a Civil War drama with ballads, which marked Elvis Presley's debut. McLean and Webb met and started dating when Susan Hayward, a Fox star, invited them to dinner at her home.

Barbara McLean once estimated that she studied half a million feet of film every year. "I see every picture that I cut more than a hundred times," she told a reporter. "I sit all day before a Moviola—half photograph and half loudspeaker—watching the action and listening to the dialogue." Her aim, like that of most good editors, was to make the final cut so seamless that it looked as if she had done nothing at all. McLean believed that women were better film cutters than men "because every woman is at heart a mother. A woman uses the scissors on a film like a mother would—with affection, understanding, and tolerance." In spite of her rather jarring metaphor, McLean did treat the films she edited with devotion and tenderness.

According to film historian Ephraim Katz, "Editing has traditionally been one of the few movie crafts wide open to women, most likely because the position involves little contact with the male-dominated technical crews, but also because it requires manual dexterity rather than brawn and an observant aesthetic eye." Another film historian, Martin Norden, speculates that "women very early got a foothold in editing because it was originally seen as a menial job, requiring only that they follow the orders of men as to the duration of a sequence or the order of the shots. By the time filmmakers began to discover that film could be rearranged, shuffled, and cut in ways that would make the final effect much more powerful for an audience, women were technical masters."

Dede Allen, considered one of the most creative American film editors, believes one reason the field has always been open to women is because "they are good at little details, like sewing." Margaret Booth, still another legendary editor, had a passion for detail; she recalled that before there were "edge numbers" on a film frame—those tiny numbers that identify a particular shot—she would sit for hours trying to determine whether Lillian Gish had her eyelids closed or open.

In Barbara McLean's unair-conditioned workroom, in June 1950, hung strips of celluloid, and on every flat surface were stacks of film cans. There was an inspection table where she and directors and producers could eyeball the goods, but the most important object was the Moviola, an editing device with a small viewing screen that showed film running at sound or slower speed. The Moviola could be stopped or started on individual frames, enabling an editor to examine scenes closely and to mark them for sound synchronization or optical effects.

Superficially, at least, the process of editing a film seems to run parallel with editing a book for publication. The manuscript arrives in what the author considers its final form. One or more editors at the publishing house then take over, making few changes if the manuscript is "clean" but sometimes totally reshaping one that's unwieldy. The author then approves or disapproves the changes and, necessary compromises having been reached by all concerned, the book is sent to the printer.

But such is not the case in editing a film. The main difference is that movies have usually been routinely edited as they are shot. There is no real equivalent in publishing, since writers don't ship off their work at the end of the day for assemblage. Film directors do.

This editing practice, not widely known outside the film industry, often surprises even those who are well versed in other aspects of the movies. For example Tom Stempel, a film historian who interviewed Barbara McLean in 1970, asked her: "Was this standard policy to cut the picture as it went along? I'd always had the impression that the films were cut after the shooting had stopped." McLean answered: "Oh no, you cut as you go along. Every studio does that. You'd be in a hell of a mess otherwise. What if you needed some stuff and the sets had already been torn down? By the time you got through with the whole picture, it was pretty nearly set. All you had to do was just add the whole bit up together."

Bitter quarrels often erupted over the final cut of a film. Would the release version please the director, or the producer? Rarely did they share the same vision.

All About Eve is the exception that proves the rule, for it seems to have pleased Mankiewicz, Zanuck, McLean, and all other interested parties. No one connected with it is on record as having complained about the film's ultimate arrangement. It's impossible to pin down the minutiae of editing *All About Eve*—who selected which shots, who suggested that others be dropped, and the like. Such records either were not kept or they have disappeared. But we do have clues.

The best indication of the film's integrity is that the story we see on-screen remains basically as Mankiewicz conceived it from treatment through shooting script. Second, in the words of Tom Mankiewicz, "Dad was riding high at the time. He was bouncing off *A Letter to Three Wives* and the two Oscars he won for that picture, so he was at the height of his power and control—the height of his artistic testosterone, if you will. Meaning he was able to win fights against Zanuck because he was the fair-haired boy of the studio." Third, although no director had final cut in the studio era, Mankiewicz, like most important directors, "was in the editing room all the time," according to his son. Yet his presence there didn't jar Barbara McLean. Later she said, "We were very good friends," and Tom Mankiewicz states that his father always spoke "very affectionately" of her. After they finished the picture, the director gave McLean a key chain with a gaggle of tiny Oscars attached to represent her own Academy Award and those of the other Oscar winners on the picture.

Goofs and Non Sequiturs

- Mankiewicz, Zanuck, and the editor, Barbara McLean, overlooked several minor blunders in the final cut. The first concerns a letter to Margo that comes out of nowhere and means nothing. In her dressing room, as Margo and Bill prepare to leave for the airport, he says, "Throw that dreary letter away, it bores me." She does so and that's that. It's possible that Mankiewicz had in mind a deceitful letter written by Eve Harrington in Mary Orr's story. In the movie, however, no such thing occurs.

  A more whimsical explanation is that this letter is an oblique reference to *A Letter to Three Wives*. Or, if Mankiewicz were able to read the future, a foreshadowing of Bette's notorious "I've Written a Letter to Daddy" in *What Ever Happened to Baby Jane?*

  Curiously, the same thing happens in *Hamlet*. In Act IV, scene VI, a messenger enters, giving Claudius a letter from Hamlet. "And this to the queen," says the messenger. But, as Hardin Craig notes in his edition of *The Complete Works of Shakespeare*, "One hears no more of the letter to the queen."

- A possible mistake occurs when we see Margo taking curtain calls after a performance of *Aged in Wood*. The curtain rises, and she looks completely surprised. "Who, me?" is the expression on her face. Is it a directorial error, as Charles Affron suggests in his book *Star Acting*, or is Margo feigning star humility?

- During Margo's fierce quarrel with Lloyd, she snarls this line: "I'm lied to, attacked behind my back, accused of reading your silly dialogue as if it were the Holy Gospel." In the heat of that scene, her line seems to make sense. But what Mankiewicz wrote was: ". . . accused of reading your silly dialogue inaccurately as if it were the Holy Gospel." And that's what Bette should have said. With the word "inaccurately" omitted, the line is absurd.

- When Barbara Bates, as Phoebe, flatters Eve with a mention of "the Eve Harrington Clubs they have in most of the girls' high schools" it sounds false. That's because it is. Fan clubs were for movie stars, and although Eve has already packed for Hollywood, she hasn't yet made a film. The Eve Harrington Clubs are as phony as the John Doe Clubs in Frank Capra's *Meet John Doe* (1941). (Was Mankiewicz perhaps poking fun at that off-center movie?)

- There's also a goof in the final credits. The name of Gary Merrill's character, Bill Sampson, is misspelled as "Bill *Simpson*."

Years later, after his retirement, Mankiewicz spoke to an interviewer about editing a film: "I get the best editor I can find and explain what I have in mind—what I want the scene to express. Then I leave the editor alone to do his work. I can profit from the editor's previous experience because he can give me ideas I wouldn't have come up with on my own. And I don't take a hands-on approach. Of course I know what a Steenbeck editing table is, and a Moviola, but I'd be totally incapable of using them myself."

To illustrate his relative indifference to the technical aspects of filmmaking, Mankiewicz talked about the time he—like Bill Sampson in *Eve*—looked through the wrong end of the camera finder. It happened while making *Dragonwyck* (1946), Mankiewicz's first film as a director. After the gaffe, Arthur Miller, the cinematographer, told the novice director, "Just leave it all to me." Mankiewicz did. From then on, he said, "Arthur handled the camera and I handled the actors. As far as I'm concerned, that's the only way to do it."

Mankiewicz took the same attitude toward a good editor like McLean. She, in consultation with Mankiewicz and Zanuck, "built" *All About Eve* from the ground up, using what Mankiewicz delivered. McLean paid attention chiefly to technical points of expertise and to rhythm and timing in the film. Mankiewicz, with his long takes, his even, cantering pace, and sparing use of fancy work, was an orderly filmmaker. With certain other directors, however, McLean found herself trying to figure out the beginning, middle, and end of a picture.

As her job neared completion, McLean knew that Zanuck was pleased. So pleased, in fact, that he decided not to preview *All About Eve*. At that time, previews often indicated uneasiness about a movie, or some part of it, such as the running time or the ending. In this case Zanuck was confident they had what it took.

McLean liked the picture, too, and that was important. Studio executives knew that when Zanuck prefaced a statement with, "Bobbie says . . ." he was not expressing an opinion but announcing a decision. If "Bobbie" hadn't liked it, she would have let him know. Whenever McLean and Zanuck disagreed, she stuck to her guns. "I don't care," she would tell the boss. "If you're not going to listen, then don't ask me. If you're going to ask me, then pay attention to what I say." Such uppity talk might have gotten her kicked out of other studios, but Zanuck knew her value. Besides, they had worked together so long that a certain gruff frankness had become their shorthand.

The unpolished version that McLean patched together during the filming of *All About Eve* was the assembly—that is, the initial joining together of shots in proper continuity. This involves a selection of takes, the elimination of unwanted footage, the trimming of scenes to a more or less desirable length, and the marking of transitions. A film's assembly is the stage just prior to the rough cut.

Soon after the final day of shooting, McLean and Mankiewicz completed the rough cut—i.e., the editing stage immediately before fine cut. A rough cut might be compared to the second or third draft in writing, which is often publishable even though it lacks the author's final burnish.

On Saturday, June 24, Mankiewicz delivered his rough cut to Zanuck. Zanuck, with McLean beside him, screened this cut two days later. We can extrapolate details of the ambience at their first viewing of the rough cut if we study a photograph of Zanuck and McLean taken in Zanuck's private screening room in 1952. This photo shows the two seated in oversized leather armchairs in the front row. Zanuck, in sports jacket, slacks, shirt, and tie, seems impatient for the screening to begin. McLean looks very much at ease in a light-colored skirt and blouse. Her face is alert, like someone poised to catch the slighest discrepancy between any two shots—and to correct them forthwith.

Since screenings and modifications of the edited work print usually took place at night in Zanuck's projection room at the studio, we can imagine him and McLean in a similar pose, and in similar attire, that Monday evening, June 26, 1950, as they sit down after dinner to finish off a long workday. Zanuck presses the buzzer to signal the projectionist, the lights dim, and this early version of *Eve* fills the screen.

"In the projection room," McLean said, "nobody made a sound. Even if you had a cigarette pack with that cellophane on it, you'd take it off before. Zanuck's powers of concentration were terrific. The editor sat next to him and when he didn't like something, he'd just touch you on the arm. I'd write in the dark."

At this rough-cut stage, of course, there was no 20th Century-Fox logo, no titles or credits, and no music. The abrupt start of the picture was either a long shot of the dining hall of the Sarah Siddons Society, which was Shot Number One in the shooting script; or a full close-up of the Sarah Siddons Award, which Mankiewicz had designated as Shot Number Two.

We don't know which shot came first in the rough cut, but we do know that the picture opens with the close-up of the award—"a gold statuette, about a foot high, of Sarah Siddons as 'the Tragic Muse,' " as Mankiewicz described it in the script. Did Mankiewicz decide on this as his opening shot while establishing the rough cut, or did Zanuck make the decision, perhaps in consultation with McLean? As production chief, Zanuck of course retained editing room privileges. In that editing room he personally supervised the cutting of many of the major Fox films.

Who Was Sarah Siddons and Why Did They Name Those Awards for Her?

Sarah Siddons encloses *All About Eve* like dramatic parentheses. The film's first shot is a close-up of the Sarah Siddons Award, and in the final shot Barbara Bates, as the conspiratorial young Phoebe, clasps this same statuette to her bosom. In addition, midway through the movie there's a close-up of the Siddons portrait that hangs at the top of Margo's staircase.

Considered one of the greatest actresses of the English stage, Siddons (1755–1831) was beautiful, talented, and shrewd. A great actress, yes, but also a celebrity in the modern sense, for she used her fame as a tool to manipulate her image. She promoted herself two centuries before the advent of press agents.

Her first entrance was inauspicious, for she was born at the Shoulder of Mutton public house in Brecon, Wales, where her parents were touring with a theatrical troupe. At age eleven she made her stage debut as Ariel in *The Tempest* with her father's company. Although her stage charisma was remarkable, she trod the usual uneven road to stardom. Success was not immediate, but eventually it made her the First Lady of the British Stage. She mesmerized audiences, then made them weep. Susceptible ladies fainted from the potency of a Siddons performance. Fans worshiped her, and in Scotland the word "Siddonimania" was coined to describe the hysterical adulation poured out by victims of "Siddons Fever." But fame is never cheap, and in Dublin they pelted her with apples and potatoes. More than once she was fired, thus becoming an early example of box office poison.

Siddons acted in many a play now forgotten, but earned her triumph in Shakespearean roles. Of these, it was Lady Macbeth that made the actress immortal. William Hazlitt, the English essayist and a contemporary of Siddons, described her in this role: "It was something above nature. It seemed almost as if a being of a superior order had dropped from a higher sphere to awe the world with the majesty of her appearance. Power was seated on her brow, passion emanated from her breast as from a shrine; she was tragedy personified." Charles Lamb, another contemporary, wrote that "we speak of Lady Macbeth while we are in reality thinking of Mrs. Siddons." Her first biographer, lucky enough to have attended a Siddons *Macbeth*, paid the supreme compliment: "It was an era in one's life to have seen her in it."

Mankiewicz understood such enthusiasm. He told an interviewer, "My passion is eighteenth-century theatre." He seems to have assessed the stars of two hundred years past as acutely as he scrutinized performances in Hollywood. Besides Sarah Siddons, Mankiewicz also admired Peg Woffington (ca. 1717–1760), a tempestuous Irish actress as theatrical off the stage as on. He said, "I think I've read everything written about her." Mankiewicz stated flatly that Woffington was *the* prototype of Margo Channing.

But he named his imaginary award for Sarah Siddons, perhaps because the name rings with glamour and authority. The award was indeed pure fiction at the time of *All About Eve*, but two years later life imitated art.

In 1952 several prominent Chicago ladies founded the Sarah Siddons Society to recognize the role of women in the theatre. One of the founders, and an early president of the group, was Mrs. Loyal Davis, mother of Nancy Reagan. Every year since then the society has presented its annual award to an actress for an outstanding performance in a Chicago theatrical production. The first winner, for the 1952–53 season, was Helen Hayes. Soon the Sarah Siddons Award became the most prestigious in the American theatre, after the Tony.

Celeste Holm won a Siddons in 1968 for *Mame*, Lauren Bacall in 1972 for *Applause* and again in 1985 for *Woman of the Year*. The 1973 award went to Bette Davis. It was a special recognition for *All About Eve* on the twentieth anniversary of the society's founding. The presenter was Anne Baxter. "I made an absolute fool of myself," Bette said later. "Anne went on and on about me and I cried. It was the first time that I've ever broken down in public."

Mankiewicz relished the sweet irony of all this, for he couldn't suppress a smirk when discussing the Siddons Award. After all, he had dreamed it up to poke fun at the Oscars, the Tonys, and all manner of plaques, globes, medals, and certificates in the entertainment industry. But no one else took it lightly. His mock award was regarded very seriously by those who gave it and by the honorees. He told an interviewer, "I know Celeste Holm wept and thought it was a terribly important award. She wrote me a letter scolding me for not recognizing the importance of it."

Perhaps her letter was superfluous. In 1991 an interviewer noticed Mankiewicz's various awards on the mantel of his home in Westchester County, New York. There were his four Oscars; an Edgar for *Sleuth*; a D. W. Griffith Special Achievement Award; and "seemingly in a place of honor amid all the other awards, the Sarah Siddons Award for Achievement in the Theatre." Made by a propman at Fox, it was the very one that opens *All About Eve*.

Sarah Siddons, meanwhile, has made a comeback. In the summer of 1999 a joint exhibition at the J. Paul Getty Museum in Los Angeles and the Huntington Library and Art Collections in nearby San Marino paid tribute to her. The centerpiece of the

Getty's exhibition was Sir Joshua Reynolds' portrait, *Sarah Siddons as the Tragic Muse*. (It's a copy of the Reynolds portrait that's used in the movie.) Owned by the Huntington since the early 1920s, it was loaned to the Getty to hang with other grandiose portraits of Siddons painted by Gainsborough, Romney, Fuseli, and Thomas Lawrence. In addition, several new books about Siddons have recently been published.

Bette Davis probably wouldn't be surprised to learn about the return of Sarah Siddons. In a way she almost predicted it. In 1957, while living in Laguna Beach, Bette took part in the town's annual Festival of Arts, one feature of which is the Pageant of the Masters—a series of tableaux vivants with townspeople posing in recreations of great works of art. Bette looks every inch the Queen of Theatre in her representation of *Sarah Siddons as the Tragic Muse*. Before she donned the elaborate costume of Mrs. Siddons, however, Bette performed a lesser act of volunteerism. She was given a brush and can of paint, then sent to paint numbers of the backs of seats.

Screenwriter Philip Dunne, who knew Zanuck well, wrote that the studio head "was happiest when he was sitting in his projection room alone with his cutter, molding the picture closer to his heart's desire."

Zanuck himself told his biographer, Mel Gussow, "I work hard on scripts, and I'm a good script editor. But I think if I have any talent at all, it's editing in the cutting room, more so even than editing a script." Anyone who reads Mankiewicz's *All About Eve* script and then compares it with the actual film is likely to agree.

Mankiewicz, for all his clever dialogue, sometimes didn't know when to stop. For instance, in the scene where Addison, Miss Caswell, Bill, Eve, Karen, and Lloyd sit on the stairs discussing the maladjustments of life in the theatre, the dialogue sparkles because Addison's self-importance ricochets off Bill's common sense, and their weighty lines are both in counterpoint with the half-absurdist Marx Brothers frivolity of befuddled Max Fabian and the dizzy fox, Miss Caswell. But here's the part of the scene that was cut, presumably by Zanuck, right after Max's line "Did she say sable—or Gable?"

ADDISON

It is senseless to insist that theatrical folk are no different from the good people of Des Moines, Chillicothe, or Liverpool. By and large we are concentrated gatherings of neurotics, egomaniacs, emotional misfits, and precocious children—

MAX

(*to Bill*)

Gable. Why a feller like that don't come East to do a play . . .

BILL

He must be miserable, the life he lives out there—

ADDISON

These so-called abnormalities—they're our stock in trade, they make us actors, writers, directors, et cetera, in the first place—

MAX

Answer me this. What makes a man become a producer?

ADDISON

What makes a man walk into a lion cage with nothing but a chair?

MAX

This answer satisfies me a hundred percent.

This chitchat, had it stayed in, would have weakened the scene.

After viewing Mankiewicz's rough cut, Zanuck asked for some structural changes. Besides reducing several overstuffed scenes, he also eliminated parts of the voice-over narration. The film, of course, is conceived as a story told from the points of view of its three narrators: Addison,

Karen, and Margo. Addison's voice is the first one we hear: "The Sarah Siddons Award for Distinguished Achievement is perhaps unknown to you . . ." It continues until the freeze-frame that ends this first part of the awards banquet, then Karen's voice takes over the narration: "When was it? How long? It seems a lifetime ago." Margo's narration is first heard as she and Eve leave the airport together after Bill boards the plane; she speaks in voice-over only once after that, as the party begins: "Bill's welcome-home birthday party—a night to go down in history."

Among the passages Zanuck deleted in the editing room was a portion of Margo's airport voice-over explaining that they sent for Eve's belongings that night and "she moved into the little guest room on the top floor." This part was retained; thrown out was the following line, one of peculiar badness: "She cried when she saw it—it was so like her little room back home in Wisconsin." (Had Mankiewicz temporarily forgotten that Margo detests cheap sentiment?)

Zanuck also discarded this purposeless voice-over passage of Karen's as she repairs her makeup at Margo's soirée: "It's always convenient at a party to know the hostess well enough to use her bedroom rather than go where all the others have to go."

And so on. The full catalogue of these cuts would require a variorum edition of the script, but even a sampling buttresses Zanuck's contention that he was astute at separating cream from whey.

It's not surprising that Mankiewicz strongly opposed Zanuck's elimination of some footage that established and maintained the three interrelated points of view. It is surprising, however, that Mankiewicz apparently expected Zanuck to keep hands off such a long rough cut: It ran close to three hours.

Zanuck said, "All pictures are invariably long. I found out that sometimes it's good to start with them too long. Then, in the cutting room you realize you've already expressed the same thought several times. I run a picture three times, stop after every reel, and ask, What does that tell us? That's why cutting sessions run so long at night."

Mankiewicz, of course, expected his original structure to remain as he filmed it. The story told from three points of view was reminiscent of *Citizen Kane* and therefore had not only cinematic but emotional resonance for Mankiewicz because of his brother's intimate connection with that film. What rankled Mankiewicz more than the trimming of his three voice-over narrators, however, was Zanuck's elimination of one scene that Mankiewicz had shot from two points of view.

This was Eve's speech, on Margo's staircase: "Why, if there's nothing else, there's applause. I've listened backstage to people applaud. It's like, like waves of love coming over the footlights." Mankiewicz wrote, and filmed, this speech as seen first by Margo and then by Karen. In the script, any distinction between these two scenes is murky and there is no clear reason for doing the same thing twice. (It's unlikely that Mankiewicz had seen *Rashomon*, since it wasn't released in this country until December 1951, although it's possible the Japanese film was screened privately in Hollywood before then. Or Mankiewicz might have read the two stories by Akutagawa that the film was based on.)

How the two versions of Eve Harrington's "Applause Aria" looked we cannot know, because Zanuck considered such a double-barreled view redundant. The point having been made, Zanuck scrapped the extra footage and retained Eve's speech so that it's seen from the point of view of anyone in earshot—including us, as it were.

Years later, when Mel Gussow interviewed Mankiewicz for the Zanuck biography, the director sneered: "Not bad for a little man. The essence of Darryl is also the essence of Napoleon." But he also conceded that "Zanuck was a talented man, although the longer he is concerned with something, the worse he is. Just like his cutting—peak to peak to peak. In the days when character was developed more deeply, he would break a director's heart and a writer's heart. He was impatient with anything cerebral."

Based on the available evidence—and it's unfortunately scant—a lot that Mankiewicz considered "cerebral" in *All About Eve* amounted to grandstanding. It's hard to believe the picture would have been better if Zanuck hadn't used his scissors. Just look what happened to Mankiewicz *after* Zanuck. In *The Barefoot Contessa*, which Mankiewicz produced, wrote, and directed, he finally had the freedom to film a scene from two points of view. When Rossano Brazzi slaps the South American playboy (Marius Goring) who has insulted Ava Gardner, we see it twice: first from

Brazzi's point of view, a bit later from Gardner's. It's showy and superfluous, it adds nothing to this leaden movie, and a few years later it seems to have given Godard and Truffaut—both admirers of Mankiewicz—some of their worst ideas. The notion for this flashy duplication goes back to _Citizen Kane_'s twice-repeated opening night at the opera and the shifting encounters between Kane and his first wife at the breakfast table.

Once free of Zanuck's control, Mankiewicz made three terrible films. After _The Barefoot Contessa_ came _Guys and Dolls_ and _Suddenly, Last Summer_, each one an artistic obituary. (And each one with its defenders.)

On the other hand, consider Zanuck's astute shaping of Mankiewicz's breakthrough picture, _A Letter to Three Wives_, the year before _All About Eve_. The film was based, like _Eve_, on a story in _Cosmopolitan_. The story, by John Klempner, bore the romantic title "One of Our Hearts." Later the author expanded it into a novel titled _A Letter to Five Wives_, which Zanuck purchased on the basis of a synopsis. The material traveled from hand to hand until it reached Mankiewicz, who wrote a script called _A Letter to Four Wives_. Zanuck liked the script but wrote Mankiewicz a long memo telling him to eliminate one of the couples from the story. In other words, said Zanuck, "Cut one wife." Afterwards even Mankiewicz conceded that he had made a better picture by following Zanuck's advice.

Along with substantive cuts to _All About Eve_, Zanuck seems to have eliminated a bit part that has been mentioned in several reference books over the years. The end credits list Eddie Fisher as stage manager. I assumed, along with others who noticed the name, that it referred to the singer Eddie Fisher, who would have been about twenty-one years old when the picture was made. This is not the case. Tom Mankiewicz says, "Dad never mentioned that to me, and as far as I know he met Eddie Fisher for the first time when Eddie was married to Elizabeth Taylor in the late fifties." Fisher's two autobiographies contain no references to _All About Eve_. We see the stage manager of _Aged in Wood_ when Margo is taking curtain calls, and we also see a stage manager at Eve's rehearsal for _Footsteps on the Ceiling_. Perhaps one of them was named Eddie Fisher.

The Leading Man with No Lines

We see Craig Hill (born 1927) in a fleeting shot or two midway through the movie, with Eve in rehearsal for *Footsteps on the Ceiling*, Lloyd's new play. Hill is presumably Eve's leading man, yet he speaks not a line.

Craig Hill was a contract player from the late forties through the mid-fifties (*Cheaper by the Dozen*, *Tammy and the Bachelor*). From 1957 to 1959, he appeared in *The Whirlybirds*, a syndicated TV adventure series concerning helicopter heroics. Eventually he left Hollywood and at last report he owned and operated a restaurant in Bagur, Spain.

A week or so after Zanuck's cuts, Barbara McLean had shaped and polished *All About Eve* to the point where it existed visually from beginning to end. But without a musical score it was like a page without punctuation—half naked, and in need of the aural part of its structure.

Chapter 18

And You, I Take It, Are the Paderewski Who Plays His Concerto on Me, the Piano?

ong before the advent of spoken dialogue in 1927, pictures had come to seem bare without music. Most major silent productions were released with an accompanying score, a practice that quickly became a tradition. Soon it was rare for a film to be released without at least a rudimentary score, and by 1950 studio brass had come to love background music. To them, a movie deprived of it was like an elevator without Muzak.

Alfred Newman, a top studio composer and head of Fox's music department, was assigned to do the score for *Eve*. Newman once said: "I'm terrified every time I undertake a new film score. I sit and stare at the blank manuscript paper, pondering the unfathomable depth of my dry well. Finally, in pure desperation, before I can run and hide, I reach out and jab a quarter note onto the page." Overcoming his usual creative anxiety, Newman soon set to work on *All About Eve*.

In a memorandum to Alfred Newman and to Zanuck, Mankiewicz stressed the importance of identifying each narrator—Addison, Karen, Margo—with a musical leitmotif, while reserving a separate theme for Eve. "The musical entity of our film," he wrote, "consists of a basic theme, Eve—and three variations on that theme."

Newman followed Mankiewicz's directive, though not literally. Instead of the suggested basic theme and variations related to certain characters, Newman composed instead what he designated the "Overture" but which might just as well be called the "Theatre Theme." Subordinate to this grand main theme are four separate, lesser ones: an identifying theme for Eve, and also one for each of the narrators of her story: Addison, Karen, and Margo.

Though *All About Eve* has sometimes been dubbed "All About Margo," musically it might be called "All About the Theatre," for the most recognizable tune in the score is the grandiose music which opens and closes the film. If ever you hum any part of the score, it will be this inflated, intentionally showy, grandiloquent melody. Page Cook, writing in *Films in Review* (August/September 1989) points out its resemblance to William Walton's "opening and closing fanfares in his 'Crown Imperial,' composed for the coronation of George VI" in 1936.

Significantly, the "Theatre Theme" starts up even before the first scene of the movie. This tripping music plays over the 20th Century-Fox logo, that most glamorous of Hollywood trademarks with its spotlights searching the sky above an Art Deco studioscape. (It was Alfred Newman who composed and recorded the fanfare that normally accompanied this logo and that came to be recognized as a symbol of Hollywood magic.)

The "Theatre Theme" flows into "Eve's Theme." This seamless transition is intentional, anticipating musically Eve's later declaration that the theatre "has given me all I have." It also suggests the paucity of her life offstage. "Eve's Theme" is not heard each time she's onscreen, nor is she always visible when it is heard. Instead, the Eve leitmotif is used according to the dramatic requirements of a given situation.

During the opening sequence, in the dining hall of the Sarah Siddons Society, we hear "Addison's Theme" for the first time. It is properly serpentine, like his name: adder, Addison. We hear only a few bars of this fluty, snake-charmer music, which might almost have been borrowed from a Maria Montez spectacle. We hear it again, more briefly still, when Addison, lurking outside the dressing room, overhears Eve's attempt to seduce Bill.

Next comes "Karen's Theme," wistful and sweet, with a hint of soap-opera sentimentality. We hear it when Addison introduces her at the banquet. Variations on this Karen motif are repeated frequently, e.g., when she first encounters Eve near the stage door; again as she and Lloyd leave Margo's dressing room; at the point when she decides to give Margo "a boot in the rear"; and while she's watching Eve rehearse the role of Cora in Lloyd's new play. Her theme also overlaps the scene following Eve in rehearsal, where Karen answers the late-night phone call from Eve's girlfriend at the rooming house.

"Margo's Theme"—and swirling variations on it—is considerably more subtle than Margo. It contains a musical nod to Liszt's "Liebestraum" as well as a Stephen Foster–ish southern-belle motif, à la Hollywood, which is reprised full force during Margo's curtain call and then backstage after her *Aged in Wood* performance. We first hear Margo's theme when Addison introduces Margo to us at the Sarah Siddons banquet. It's played again as Margo and Eve leave the airport after seeing Bill off, then it accompanies Margo's narration of "Bill's welcome home–birthday party, a night to go down in history." It's repeated as Margo arrives at the theatre for Miss Caswell's audition, and a final time when Bill arrives at Margo's house to comfort her after Addison's scurrilous attack in his column.

Roughly one-half hour of the 138-minute film has musical accompaniment. In addition to the music that Alfred Newman composed for *All About Eve*, the film contains a generous amount of source music—that is, non-underscore by other composers. We hear "Liebestraum" endlessly at Bill's welcome-home-birthday party. It comes at us again when the car stalls and Margo turns on the radio. She turns it off and snaps, "I detest cheap sentiment." A little later she turns the radio on again. This time, to everyone's relief, it's Debussy's "Beau Soir" that's playing.

The hapless pianist at Margo's party tries to escape the "Liebestraum" moroseness with "Thou Swell" and "How About You," but in vain; Margo won't hear of it. Eventually, when Margo leads Max Fabian to the pantry for bicarbonate, the pianist seizes the chance to play "Manhattan," "Blue Moon," and other jaunty tunes. As a sly commentary on Margo's quarrelsome mood, he plays a snatch of "Stormy Weather." Later, during the nightclub scene, the band plays several fox trots, including "That Old Black Magic" and "Linger Awhile."

Once Newman had managed to set down on paper his first tentative notes, the process accelerated. After two weeks of work with Edward Powell, his arranger, the score was finished. They prepared the orchestration for sixty pieces.

Sixty musicians were called for the first session on Stage 1, Fox's soundstage especially prepared for recording. First, they rehearsed the music without film. Then *All About Eve* was projected again and again on a screen in front of Newman—now in his capacity as conductor—until he coaxed from his orchestra the exact interpretation he wanted for every musical note. In the glass-enclosed monitor's booth the recording engineer manipulated the dials, controlling the different microphone levels until he got the right balance and blend of tones. Finally a recording of the first reel was made and played back for approval. Reel by reel this process continued, and the next day the printed recordings were sent to the music department for synchronization with the film.

When the music cutters had finished building the music tracks into the film, it was sent to Rerecording for the final operation in making a picture. With the arrival of these music tracks the highly skilled rerecorders now had some fourteen sound tracks covering dialogue, music, and sound effects to be electronically combined into the single master sound track. After seven days the rerecording was completed, and on August 15 the composite print of picture and sound was received from the laboratory, inspected by Mankiewicz, and approved by Zanuck.

Alfred Newman received an Oscar nomination for his scoring of *All About Eve*. The winner, however, was Franz Waxman for *Sunset Boulevard*. It's doubtful that Newman suffered greatly from the loss, since he had won four Oscars already, for *Alexander's Ragtime Band* (1938), *Tin Pan Alley* (1940), *The Song of Bernadette* (1943), and *Mother Wore Tights* (1947). He would win five more in the years to come, and during his long career he received several dozen nominations. (A reporter who interviewed Newman in 1960 referred to "the forest of Oscars and other awards which line the den of his home.")

Born in New Haven, Connecticut, in 1901, Newman was the eldest of ten children. In 1911 this vast family moved to New York, where little Al, already a seasoned prodigy, came to the attention of Paderewski, who gave him piano lessons. At sixteen, Al became musical director of the first *George White Scandals* on Broadway. He conducted several Gershwin shows before going to Hollywood in 1930. First he was music director for United Artists, then for Samuel Goldwyn. In 1939 he moved to Fox, where he headed the music department until 1960.

Newman once said, "If I want to write great music, I've no right to be in Hollywood. Good picture music must always be inspired by the picture of which it is a part and not by the desire of a composer to express himself." Still, he sometimes wondered why the critics overlooked his contributions. The public, however, was not indifferent. Although the composer's job was one of the most obscure in Hollywood, Newman, like other movie composers, received his share of fan mail. Not the usual kind asking for autographed pictures, but rather, in Newman's words, "a high-class, impersonal, even rather learned kind, requesting information or entire scores or perhaps merely conveying compliments."

Whatever its merits, Newman's score for *All About Eve* is not considered one of his best or most effective. It does, however, accomplish its purpose, which is to underline and to heighten the emotional aspects of the film. Whether Newman himself is responsible for the entire score would be extremely difficult to determine. Like many of his colleagues, he didn't write every note of the scores assigned and credited to him; as head of the department he could not be expected to. He wasn't afraid to delegate, and he surrounded himself with an expert staff he could rely on to write music compatible with his own style. Frequently, however, a film would engage his sympathies so deeply that he made himself responsible for every note in the score. This was certainly true of *Wuthering Heights, The Song of Bernadette*, and his other major scores.

As for Newman's musical idiom, it has been described as conforming, like most Hollywood film music, to a "traditional, late-nineteenth-century romantic rhetorical style, painting with broad colorful strokes on a large canvas." Away from the studio, however, an earlier repertoire claimed Newman's attention. Once or twice a month he took a busman's holiday from composing. On those occasions he ducked out early from 20th Century-Fox to join a select group of movie musicians at someone's house. There they would play chamber music by Bach, Mozart, and Beethoven until the wee hours, pausing only to toast the masters with tankards of the best imported German beer.

Claude Stroud, the pianist at Margo's party, had an elastic face like Joe E. Brown's and a slightly demented, vaguely effeminate, slapstick quaver in his voice, also like Brown. Stroud began his career as an acrobat in a tightwire team, the other half being his twin brother, Clarence. The Stroud Twins, as they billed themselves, played circus engagements, toured in vaudeville, and later appeared in such Broadway musicals as *A Night in Venice* and *The Music Box Revue*. Rudy Vallee introduced the twins to radio on his popular show.

When Margo lambastes Birdie Coonan as "a fifth-rate vaudevillian," she might have been referring to the sort of act that the Stroud Twins typified. Excerpts from a *Variety* review in 1939 convey the rather desperate seediness of their particular show-business ambience, redolent of Mama Rose and Gypsy, of Blanche and Baby Jane Hudson: "At the Orpheum in L.A., Sally Rand's 'World's Fair Glamour Girls' are given equal prominence with Clarence and Claude Stroud in current stage show, but hardly live up to the billing. Stroud Twins show much improvement in material and stage demeanor since last caught here, and aside from a few gags running perilously close to borderline of offensiveness, keep their auditors in constant uproar." (The tail end of this low-comedy tradition hung on until the final broadcast of *The Ed Sullivan Show*.)

During World War II Claude Stroud entertained the troops in the Army Air Force show "Winged Victory." Years later he took "The Claude Stroud Show," as his USO tour was grandly billed, to Vietnam.

At the time of Stroud's Vietnam performances, an eager-beaver USO press release described him as "a professional veteran with a droll, cigar-in-hand delivery . . . a stylized mixture of George Burns, Fred Allen, and Edgar Bergen." Also on the tour was an accordionist (bizarre for 1968, when these young soldiers were listening to acid rock and Janis Joplin). Whereas Bob Hope took along a bevy of starlets on his tours, "The Claude Stroud Show" had but one: Susan McGuire, billed as "a tall, blonde, and very attractive entertainer with the right blend of intimate rowdiness and lady-like detachment." It sounds more like stag night at the VFW than a show for virile youth.

When Claude Stroud died in 1986 at the age of seventy-eight, one of the few publications to run an obituary was *Variety*. It noted his radio career, his many TV appearances in the fifties and sixties, and his roles in such films as *Breakfast at Tiffany's* (1961) and *My Six Loves* (1963).

No mention was made of *All About Eve*, and yet that cameo appearance is Stroud's lasting toehold in celebrity. After all, Margo Channing sits beside him on the piano bench. Surely her proximity confers immortality of a sort. If you call the name "Claude Stroud" no one recognizes it, but explain that he's the one who plays "Liebestraum" in *All About Eve*, and when Margo orders him to "play it again" he whines, "But that was the fourth straight time"—then of course everyone remembers. One brief scene, but if you were compiling a list of famous piano men in movies, you'd have to include Stroud along with Dooley Wilson in *Casablanca*, Charles Aznavour in *Shoot the Piano Player*, and Richard Pryor in *Lady Sings the Blues*.

Claude Stroud may or may not have played "Liebestraum" as they filmed the party scene. It made no difference, for the piano accompaniment was later dubbed.

Victor Jory and Elisabeth Bergner in the 1943 Broadway hit, *The Two Mrs. Carrolls.* Offstage she was living the plot of *All About Eve.* (Photofest)

Mary Orr, ca. 1946, when "The Wisdom of Eve" was published in *Cosmopolitan.* (Rudy Behlmer Collection)

In 1949, the year before *All About Eve*, Bette was her daughter's keeper when they appeared together in *Payment on Demand*. (Photofest) 3A.

Walter Hampden as MacBeth. (Jerry Ohlinger's Movie Material Store)

A great actress and a great woman: Bette Davis as Margo Channing.
(Photofest)

Tallulah Bankhead on Bette Davis: "That bitch stole my best roles for films." (Jerry Ohlinger's Movie Material Store)

Susan Hayward lost Scarlett O' Hara, and later she lost Margo Channing. (Photofest)

Marlene Dietrich as
Margo Channing?
Think again, said
Mankiewicz.
(Photofest)

Joseph Mankiewicz
wanted the extrava-
gant Gertrude
Lawrence as Margo.
Did she even read the
script? (Photofest)

Bette in a costume
test, looking like a
"junkyard."
(Photofest)

Marilyn Monroe—
valedictorian of her
class at the
Copacabana School of
Dramatic Art.
(Photofest)

How many martinis does that make, Margo? Thelma Ritter, Bette Davis, and Claude Stroud. (Photofest)

"Aged in Wood": The set was built, but didn't make it into the film. (Photofest)

Joseph L. Mankiewicz, Hugh Marlowe, Gary Merrill, and Celeste Holm on the set. (Photofest)

Anne Baxter and George Sanders, portraying characters of ambiguous sexuality, form parentheses around two heterosexual goddesses. Notice the portrait of Sarah Siddons over Marilyn's shoulder. (Photofest)

Barbara Bates as Phoebe. Did she take the subway back to Brooklyn, or did she spend the night? (Photofest)

George Sanders and Zsa Zsa Gabor arrive at the glittering premiere of *All About Eve*, at Grauman's Chinese Theatre, November 9, 1950. (UPI/Corbis-Bettmann)

Barbara McLean and Darryl F. Zanuck in the Fox projection room, ca. 1952. (Rudy Behlmer Collection)

In 1957 Bette Davis portrays Sarah Siddons in a tableau vivant at the Laguna Beach Festival of the Arts. (Festival of Arts of Laguna Beach)

Edith Head as she appeared onscreen in *Lucy Gallant*, 1955. She dressed Betty Davis for *Eve*, but no one else in the cast. (Photofest)

When Lauren Bacall played Margo Channing in *Applause* in 1970, Bette sent her a cryptic telegram on opening night. (Photofest)

Lyle Wheeler, art director of *All About Eve*, was the only person ever to receive the same Oscar twice. (Photofest)

Anne Baxter replaced Lauren Bacall in *Applause* in 1971. Left to right: Lee Roy Reams, Baxter, and Penny Fuller. (Photofest)

Chicago, 1973: Anne Baxter has just presented the Sarah Siddons
Award to Bette Davis. (The Sarah Siddons Society, Chicago)

Mary Orr and Martina Lawrence at Sardi's, ca. 1991. (Harry Haun)

Chapter 19

Wherever There's Magic and Make-Believe and an Audience, There's Theatre

 yle Wheeler was one of the first craftsmen to set to work on *All About Eve*. George W. Davis shares art director credit, but since Wheeler was the powerful head of the Fox Art Department we must assume either that his was the greater contribution, or that his approval was needed for virtually every detail. In any event, it was standard Hollywood procedure that the supervisor of the studio art department be credited on major films whether he actually contributed or merely advised. Milton Krasner, who photographed *Eve*, later praised Davis, not Wheeler, as one of the very few art directors who always kept the cameraman's problems in mind when designing sets, indicating that George Davis was more immediately involved with the film than Wheeler was.

I've waited to discuss art direction because the work of an art director can only be judged by looking at the finished film. However inventive and spectacular a look he may wish for the picture, the camera winnows out much of his decorative artistry. For that reason, it makes sense to discuss *All About Eve*'s mise-en-scène as a post-production phenomenon.

When we see a play, the stage designer's work—including architectural elements and landscapes—is visible at all times until the scene changes or the act ends. (Special effects, such as fog and stage blood, of course appear fleetingly.) In films, on the other hand, the director and the editor select, in every frame, those elements of decor and setting that the audience will see. As Orson Welles said, "In the theatre there are 1,500 cameras rolling at the same time—in the cinema there is only one."

Broadly speaking, the art director is responsible for the film's total look as it's being shot: locations, sets, furnishings, bric-a-brac. Often he determines the size of rooms (high ceilings or low?) and their configuration (L-shaped, square, or oval?), as well as the contents of those rooms. He and his staff decorate offices, airports, theatres, virtually every interior and outdoor space seen in a given picture. Sometimes the art director also advises on costumes—they shouldn't war with the sets, of course—and lighting.

In _All About Eve_, a physical sense of place is not especially important. To every character in the film, only one place matters: the Theatre. Not a particular theatre, not the Curran in San Francisco or the Shubert in New York, but rather some abstract, platonic idea of a stage—it could be anywhere—that lets them reiterate their art, whether it's playwriting, acting, directing, or writing columns about such stagecraft. As Bill Sampson puts it: "What book of rules says the Theatre exists only within some ugly buildings crowded into one square mile of New York City? Or London, Paris or Vienna? Wherever there's magic and make-believe and an audience—there's Theatre."

Art direction, like film music, should italicize certain plot aspects, certain traits of the main characters. But how was Lyle Wheeler to underline something so vague, so idealized? Addison DeWitt speaks for the other characters when he says, "I have lived in the Theatre as a Trappist monk lives in his faith. I have no other world, no other life." The Mankiewicz script, rich in repartee, offered little inspiration for the physical world of Margo and Company. Margo's dressing room is described as "a medium-sized box, lined with hot-water pipes and cracked plaster." Mankiewicz located her living room "one floor above street level. A long narrow room smartly furnished." Lloyd and Karen's apartment is "one large room, a small foyer with a door to the corridor." And so on. (Rookie screenwriters are often instructed not to "direct" the director in their scripts. Mankiewicz, in his, refrained from directing the art director.)

Wheeler's solution to what he may or may not have considered a perplexing task was rather Zen-like. (A Zen apothegm runs, "In the beginner's mind are many possibilities, but in the expert's there are few.") Ultimately, Wheeler let language speak for itself. Put another way, he refrained from placing visual distractions between Mankiewicz's dialogue and us. This he accomplished by making the sets so unobtrusive that the viewer's eye never flirts with decor. Instead, we focus on verbal stylishness. Consequently, we're likely to remember *All About Eve* as having "almost no visual dimension," which was Pauline Kael's assessment of the film's look.

It certainly wasn't because Lyle Wheeler couldn't pack every frame with visual affluence. As art director of *Gone With the Wind*, working closely with production designer, William Cameron Menzies, he helped enrich the film with thousands of objects, from antimacassars to Atlanta's burning skyline. And most of us remember *GWTW* visually; unless we belong to the cult, what do our ears recall but half a dozen famous lines and Max Steiner's extravagant score?

All About Eve, on the other hand, would probably have worked without any art direction at all. We can imagine its being filmed on the austere stage set of *Our Town*. In this respect the film remains aurally true to its radio-drama ancestor, Mary Orr's "The Wisdom of Eve."

More to the point is the subtlety and restraint that Wheeler and George W. Davis, his assistant, used throughout. Beginning at the Sarah Siddons Awards, less is more—though our eyes never feel cheated. At the banquet we see the awards themselves, we see sixty oil portraits on the walls, dozens of theatre people seated at tables, and on those tables cigarettes, lighters, liquor bottles, and glasses. Just enough. What we recall, however, are not objects but the faces of Addison, Eve, Margo, Karen, and the others, all of whom we meet in the first five minutes.

Margo's dressing room, drab and utilitarian, looks like a thousand unglamorous dressing rooms in as many theatres. In it are plain chairs; a dressing-table with lighted mirror; notes and telegrams tacked on the wall; an old-fashioned floor lamp; a coffeepot, cups, and sugar bowl. The most interesting visual is a small caricature of Margo in *Aged in Wood*. Later, a large version of this drawing serves as a poster in the theatre lobby when Margo arrives to read with Miss Caswell.

Margo's brownstone, presumably on the East Side of Manhattan, is conventionally decorated. We are not shown the outside, but the rooms appear to have been done up by an interior decorator with no particular flair. Margo's living room has several Louis XV fauteuils among the contemporary sofas and armchairs. The piano is there, along with an ornate commode (there's another one upstairs), a long marble mantelpiece, a portrait by Toulouse-Lautrec that is half hidden by an overzealous floral arrangement.

Margo's bedroom is no star boudoir like Joan Crawford's in *Mommie Dearest*. It's downright plain compared to Norma Desmond's in *Sunset Boulevard*, a bedroom that functions as Norma's alter ego. (Lyle Wheeler and George W. Davis were nominated for Oscars, along with their set decorators Thomas Little and Walter M. Scott. The winners were Hans Dreier and John Meehan, the art directors of *Sunset Boulevard*, along with their set decorators.)

Appropriately, it's the theatre—stage set, lobby, auditorium, and backstage—that reflects the most detailed art direction in *All About Eve*. That's where we see the real glamour. Part of this elegance comes from the Curran Theatre's natural grandeur, its gilded spaciousness and curvilinear sweep. We understand Eve's captivation the first time she goes backstage, for its crannies resemble a curiosity shop. It's jammed with intriguing props, antebellum furniture, outmoded Victoriana, and a large packing crate for the harp used in *Aged in Wood*. On this wooden box is printed the oblique warning "Handle With Care," perhaps meant semiotically as "Handle *Eve* With Care"—a caveat that every character ignores. (Mankiewicz told an interviewer many years later that this warning sign was his idea, not the art director's.)

Though we glimpse only a curtain call at the end of a performance of *Aged in Wood*, we can extrapolate from the witty stage set the sort of play Lloyd Richards has written. There's a canopy bed to suggest genteel sex, the enormous harp (read "art" and "culture"), an odd sculptured dog— translation: "bitch." We glimpse a row of columns, which, added to

Margo's Scarlett O'Hara hoop skirt, implies a honeysuckled Old South melodrama of wayward loves, betrayal, and lengthy speeches.

Aged in Wood

Fans of *All About Eve* often ask, "What is *Aged in Wood* based on?" There isn't an answer, really. If Mankiewicz had a particular work in mind, he didn't reveal what it was. It's more likely that the title is a parody of every sentimental antebellum melodrama he had seen or read. Here are a few of the contenders.

Dion Boucicault's *The Octoroon; or, Life in Louisiana* (1859). According to Ethan Mordden in *The Fireside Companion to the Theatre*, this play "tells of Zoe, a mulatto beauty caught between heroic George Peyton and the vicious Jacob M'Closky, a plantation overseer born in the north. *The Octoroon* proved as successful with southern audiences as with those in the north. The two sections saw the same work from different angles; the northerners linked Zoe's personal tragedy (she takes poison) to the slavery system, while southerners delighted in hating M'Closky, a rat from Connecticut."

Mankiewicz may well have been thinking of such popular plays as David Belasco's Civil War romance, *The Heart of Maryland* (1895) and Edward Sheldon's *Romance* (1913), which Mordden calls an "alas, my darling, we must part" salon piece.

In 1929 Mankiewicz had written intertitles for the silent picture *River of Romance*, based on Booth Tarkington's play *Magnolia*. Both titles reek of hoop skirts and honeysuckle.

On the other hand, *Aged in Wood* may have been an in-joke referring to Bette's unsuccessful attempts to win the role of Scarlett O'Hara and her revenge on David O. Selznick when she won an Oscar for *Jezebel* the year before *Gone With the Wind* was a candidate for Academy Awards.

The term "aged in the wood" is used in whiskey making.

Nowhere in the various dwellings—Margo's house, Karen and Lloyd's apartment, Eve's seedy boardinghouse and her subsequent Park Avenue apartment, or the Taft Hotel suite in New Haven where Eve and Addison enact the film's climax—nowhere do we observe personal items such as books, family photos, a childhood toy or memento, much less a live pet. Their homes are impersonal. Whatever domestic warmth these characters enjoy is in the theatre.

Which is Lyle Wheeler's oblique and very fitting gloss on the Mankiewicz script. When Addison says, seated on the stairs at Margo's party, "We're a breed apart from the rest of humanity, we theatre folk," he speaks as Mankiewicz's mouthpiece. Throughout his life Mankiewicz scrutinized the theatre and its inhabitants. His obsessive fascination with the actor, the craft of acting, the actor's persistent drive for success, and the vacuum in which the actor exists when not acting—these themes recur in several Mankiewicz films and in every serious interview he gave. And the word "actor" always means "actress."

"Men are less complicated and less intriguing," he said. "I'm talking about *actresses*—women who, since their earliest awareness of themselves, have been *compelled* to act in order to *be*. Margo Channing is a woman whose need to act equates with her need to breathe. Who, when she isn't 'on'—just isn't, at all."

Mankiewicz took all the stage as his world. Using the theatre (and its offshoot, Hollywood) as his laboratory of life, he found it heartless, delusional, bloody. But for those who, like Addison, have "no other world, no other life," it also teemed with truth. For Mankiewicz, the theatre and its inmates disclosed humanity's low secrets and lofty virtues. "I often wonder," he said, "why serious students of the human psyche look to anything *but* theatre folk for most of the answers they seek."

Lyle Wheeler, like Mankiewicz, was also a psychologist. While

Mankiewicz excavated the souls of actresses, Wheeler translated abstract inner conflicts and desires into visible evocations of character. In *Laura*, he loaded every domestic interior to function as combined case history and diagnosis of its inhabitant. In *Rebecca*, Wheeler contrived an estate—Manderley—which, just as surely as the actors, gives a performance of dark precision.

In photographs taken of Lyle Wheeler in his prime, he resembles an almost-handsome, second-rank leading man of the Zachary Scott type. Wheeler's well-shaped head, his arching eyebrows over quizzical eyes, and his Gable mustache create an effect of rather fierce determination. In one photo from the thirties, Wheeler, dressed in light slacks, dark blazer, and striped necktie, holds continuity sketches for the burning of Atlanta. According to some accounts, this conflagration was Wheeler's idea. Certainly the fire solved one of the biggest scenic and special-effects problems of *Gone With the Wind*.

Lyle Wheeler supposedly conceived his brilliant plan one day while roaming the forty-acre backlot at Selznick International. Instead of tearing down the sets of *King Kong*, *The Garden of Allah*, and *The Last of the Mohicans*—all of them still standing at the time—why not torch them and use the footage in the new Selznick epic? Such a bonfire was cheaper than building a facsimile of Atlanta; it also served the studio as instant urban renewal.

Wheeler (1905–1990), a native of Massachusetts, studied architecture at the University of Southern California. It's doubtful he ever heard a lecture there on how to burn a city, but then most of his training was on the job. Like other art directors during the studio era, he quickly learned to improvise.

Finding architectural work scarce during the Depression, Wheeler took a job as sketch artist and draftsman at MGM in 1931. Later he became supervising art director for Selznick International. He worked for a time for Alexander Korda before moving to Fox in 1944. In 1947 Zanuck promoted Wheeler to head of the art department, a position he held until he turned freelance in 1962.

Wheeler worked on some 400 films during his long career. Nominated twenty-nine times for Oscars, he won five: for *Gone With the Wind*

(1939), *Anna and the King of Siam* (1946), *The Robe* (1953), *The King and I* (1956), and *The Diary of Anne Frank* (1959).

In 1989, a year before Wheeler's death, a poignant story appeared in the *Los Angeles Times* under the heading THE DIARY OF LYLE WHEELER'S OSCARS. A Southern California couple had unwittingly become the owners of all five of his Academy Awards. This couple, attending a sale at a storage facility that was auctioning the property of tenants with delinquent bills, bought several plain brown boxes for twenty dollars apiece.

Returning home to Long Beach, the man and woman opened the shabby cartons. They were dumbfounded to find, staring up at them through lidless eyes, five tarnished statuettes issued by the most famous Academy in the world. Fearing burglary or notoriety, the couple waited almost three years before revealing the Oscars, which they had purchased in 1986.

In the early 1980s Wheeler had lost a calamitous amount of his savings in a failed investment. These losses, coupled with age and infirmity, forced him to sell his home and many possessions and to deposit the rest, including his Academy Awards, at a storage company. Eventually, when he wished to reclaim his goods, he found that the storage bill, in excess of $30,000, was more than he could afford. So, many of his sketches, artworks, books, research materials—and the five Oscars—were left behind. Soon everything was crated up and sold off along with used appliances, scratched furniture, and photographs of faces long dead.

But Lyle Wheeler's work, if not his name, had become famous. As film assumed its place among the fine arts, coteries had grown up around art directors, cameramen, composers, editors—all those craftsmen who once were taken for granted on the Hollywood assembly line. When the story of his lost Oscars was printed in the paper, an outpouring of public sympathy came his way. Then, in a noble gesture right out of a Frank Capra film, an admirer of Wheeler's vast body of work stepped forward.

Bill Kaiser, forty-one-years-old, had once worked for a year as a film librarian. He was crazy about movies, always had been, and knew an astounding amount of Hollywood lore. But library pay was no good, so he earned a nursing degree and eventually became a hospital administrator in Tuxedo Park, New York, a small town about thirty miles northwest of New York City.

One night Kaiser, his wife, Joan, and their two children were eating dinner when they heard on the evening news that the Southern California couple planned to sell Lyle Wheeler's Oscars one by one, beginning with his last award, for *The Diary of Anne Frank*. The asking price was $21,250.

Joan Kaiser noticed that her husband had stopped chewing and his face had turned pale. She turned to Bill and asked, "Do you know who Lyle Wheeler is?"

"Know who he is?" Bill yelped. "Every other movie on television has his name on it!" Later, when Kaiser recalled the night of the newscast, he said, "I was angry, I was depressed, I was moved. I decided to do everything I could to restore those Oscars to Lyle."

Kaiser soon tracked down Malcolm Willits, an expert on Hollywood artifacts and owner of the Collector's Book Store, at Hollywood Boulevard and Vine Street. Willits planned to auction the *Anne Frank* Oscar on behalf of the couple who had discovered the cache at the storage-company sale.

But Kaiser had something else in mind. With Joan's approval, Bill dipped into their savings account, the one they had started when they married sixteen years earlier. The removal of $21,250 left the account close to depletion.

"No, I'm not at all upset over how he's spending the money," Joan told a reporter. "It's not as though we're taking food from the mouths of our children. We saved it for something important, and this Oscar is important."

The onrush of news almost overpowered Lyle Wheeler. At eighty-three, he was frail and worn out. A widower, he lived alone in a retirement home in Culver City on a fixed income of $1,000 a month. But now, suddenly, he was famous. Whether he was famous now, in the troubled present, or whether all the fuss was as distant as turning on the television and seeing a movie he had designed years and years ago, Lyle could not quite puzzle out. Too much good news is not so different from bad news, he must have thought as messengers of good fortune paraded through his bedroom.

He had just won another Oscar!

Or so it seemed, although with so many people telling him things it was difficult to sort it out. Someone had just announced to Lyle that in a few days he was to appear at a private awards ceremony in the Blossom Room of the Hollywood Roosevelt Hotel where, long ago, the first Oscars were presented to Janet Gaynor and Emil Jannings. That was before Lyle himself had worked on a picture, which seemed strange because he felt like the oldest man in Hollywood, now that so many of the stars were dead.

The subdued ceremony in the Blossom Room lacked the ballyhoo that had accreted to the Academy Awards over the years. Instead, a small group of friends, family, and reporters gathered to watch Wheeler accept the award for Best Art Direction for *The Diary of Anne Frank*— surely the first time anyone ever accepted the same Oscar twice.

The award was presented by Terry Moore, who used to be famous and who had worked in eight of Wheeler's films, including *Daddy Long Legs* (1955) and *Peyton Place* (1957). "It gives me great pleasure . . ." she said with an enormous smile as Lyle was helped onto the podium amidst warm applause and cheers.

"I didn't believe I was ever going to see even one of these again," the winner said, looking down at the prodigal Oscar, now safe in his arms. A tear rolled from Lyle's eye and dropped onto the little man's twenty-four-karat gold stomach. The statuette, worn and pitted by time, was as dear as a puppy or a kitten to the elderly man. He clutched it tightly in his trembling hands.

Afterward, a reporter asked Lyle what he planned to do with his restored treasure. He paused for a long moment and then said, "Well, I want to put it someplace where it won't be stolen."

Chapter 20

I'll Marry You If It Turns Out You Have
No Blood At All

anuck, having made his revisions on the rough cut of *All About Eve* in June 1950, saw no need for retakes. Mankiewicz and others at the studio took this as proof of the producer's confidence in the picture.

In the editing room, Barbara McLean incorporated Zanuck's changes. Then she "cut in" the main title, which, after several modifications in design, had now been approved by director, producer, and art director. The studio's legal department, after careful scrutiny, had also approved the credit titles, making sure that each one conformed to the rather fussy contractual stipulations of all concerned.

Redubbing was required for certain lines impaired by outside noises during shooting. One of those "loops" involved Bette Davis and George Sanders. Mankiewicz, ever protective of his work, at first declined Barbara McLean's offer to do the looping with the two actors. (In technical language, looping is the process of recording post-synchronized replacement dialogue, specifically by running loops of film through a projector and dubber, repeatedly recording the replacement dialogue until the performer achieves or approximates lip sync.)

"Back then I would sit and do all the loop lines," McLean recalled later. "I used to do it on all the actors. I told them how to read. But Mankiewicz said, 'I'm going to do my own.' I said, 'Well, Joe, why don't you let me do it? Bette is going away. If you don't like the way I do it, you can do them over again.' "

Bette and George read for Barbara, and she inserted their redubbed lines without a seam. "By golly," she said, "Joe never changed one word." With all such fine-tuning complete, the picture again went to Zanuck for inspection. He made a few minor adjustments and the next day the film was delivered to the Production Code Administration. A routine form letter, dated July 11, 1950, went out from Joseph I. Breen to Colonel Jason Joy at 20th Century-Fox, informing the studio that *All About Eve* had been given the necessary certificate of approval. Attached to the letter was Certificate No. 14544.

For each film reviewed by employees of the Production Code, a detailed summation page was drawn up that functioned as a de facto moral index of the film's content. In the case of *All About Eve*, this summation page tallies "much drinking." It also lists "happy ending, in sense that each achieved his or her goal," and in answer to the question, "Does picture end with promise of marriage or continued love?" the censors wrote "Yes."

Bette Davis and Gary Merrill must have wished occasionally during the 1950 midsummer that they were back at Fox, where their chief irritant was the disapproval of Celeste Holm. They exhausted themselves dodging reporters and denying rumors that they would marry as soon as they shed their respective spouses. These denials were calculated to keep the estranged Mrs. Merrill and Bette's estranged husband from gaining undue legal advantage in divorce proceedings. In addition, although Bette and Gary were living together, it was necessary to keep up the wholesome fiction that they were merely "dating."

Thanks to a quickie divorce granted in Juárez, Mexico, Bette Davis became a free woman on July 4, 1950. Back in Los Angeles, she assumed a distraught expression for waiting reporters at the airport. "No one is very happy, really, about a divorce," she confided to the press.

In a more straightforward vein, William Sherry told other reporters the same day, "I shall set off a great big firecracker in honor of my own independence."

On July 27, Barbara Leeds obtained an interlocutory decree in her divorce from Gary Merrill after testifying that he had said he no longer loved her, that he neglected their guests at parties, and that he once told her she "looked like a dog." Under a financial settlement signed July 26, he promised to pay her $1,000 a month until her death or remarriage.

But the interlocutory decree was a first step only. California law stipulated that the divorce would not become final for a year. And so Gary flew to Juárez, where he also obtained a quickie Mexican divorce early on the morning of July 28. That afternoon, he married Bette Davis.

The ceremony was performed at the home of divorce attorney José Amador y Trias by Judge Raúl Orozco. Bette wore a navy blue dress with white gloves. Gary wore a gabardine suit with a maroon tie. The service was performed in Spanish. After the marriage Bette refused to pose for a photograph kissing her new husband. She had done it before at one or two of her weddings and considered it bad luck.

A few weeks later, two fillers appeared in *The New Yorker*. Bette preserved both of the wry press slip-ups in a scrapbook:

Orozco, addressing Miss Davis, asked: "Usted, Bette Davis, toma Gary Merrill como su legitimo esposo?"
The attorney translated the question: "Do you, Bette Davis, take Gary Merrill for your lawfully wedded husband?"
"eYs," Miss Davis replied.
—Indianapolis Times
You won't catch Bette napping.

LIFE IN HOLLYWOOD DEPARTMENT
[Sheilah Graham in the *Mirror*]:
Bette Davis's new mate, Gary Merrill, expects his marriage to last five years.

Bette Davis: "An hour after I married him, I knew I had made a terrible mistake."
Gary Merrill: "The downfall of the marriage was Bette's stubborn

insistence on perfection. She would empty the ashtray before the cigarette was out, and she had the bed made before my feet hit the ground."

Bette Davis: "The joke was on both of us. I loved making a home for him, but he did not at all like that domestic side of me. He wanted me to be Margo Channing."

Gary Merrill: "The stars of *All About Eve* co-opted the movie and lived it out in their off-screen lives. They were already living out the script even before they were signed for the movie. Bette Davis played out the role in our marriage—and Gary Merrill went right along. She had shattered all his dreams with her disdain for everyone's feelings but her own, her insensitivity, and her humiliating insistence on having her own way. She did not care who was cut down with the sharp scythe of her tongue, she was self-righteous in her desire to be the queen."

Bette Davis: "Not long after our divorce in nineteen sixty, I ran into Joe Mankiewicz at a party. For years I had been asking him to write a sequel to *All About Eve*, telling what had happened to Margo and Bill. I said, 'You can forget about the sequel, Joe. Gary and I played it and it didn't work.'"

A Flash-Forward

The marriage of Bette Davis and Gary Merrill was tidy in only one respect: It lasted exactly a decade, from 1950 to 1960. Otherwise it was a parade of depressing floats: drunkenness, strife, abuse. We therefore fast-forward to the end, when Bette and Gary toured the country during 1959–60 in "The World of Carl Sandburg." *Life* reported late in 1959 that they had so far "brought the show to 21 cities . . . Using excerpts from the poet's stories, songs, verses, and jokes, the team puts on a breezy, poetic vaudeville." Pictures accompanying the feature show the two looking grim and aged beyond their years.

The marriage had ended long before, though the divorce was

yet to come. During the tour Gary and Bette scarcely spoke to each other off-stage. In San Francisco they stayed in separate rooms at the same hotel they had occupied during the making of *All About Eve*.

Even more dispiriting is the sad fact that professionally they had declined, in less than a decade, from the acidulous wit of Mankiewicz to the folksy pieties of Sandburg, the Norman Rockwell of American Literature. The pithiest comment on their endeavor came from an unlikely source.

Ethel Barrymore lay on her deathbed, drifting in and out of consciousness. A friend, uncertain whether she was even awake, tried to rouse her with light conversation. "And you know," he said, "Bette Davis and Gary Merrill are touring in 'The World of Carl Sandburg,' reading his poetry." Ethel's eyes flew open. "Thanks for the warning," she whispered.

Bette's career during the next three decades, until her death in 1989, includes few of the performances one wants or expects. The public never turned against her, however, and many of her fans dutifully attended the trashy movies and watched the tepid TV dramas in hopes of another comeback. The closest thing to it arrived in 1962, when Bette teamed up with Joan Crawford for the infamous *What Ever Happened to Baby Jane?* Whatever its shortcomings, it's fixed forever in the Davis canon. Just when she seemed most passé, she gave perhaps the strongest screen performance of the early sixties, a moribund time for old Hollywood but a final electroshock to Bette's legend.

Gary Merrill didn't have a legend, and so the countless movies and TV appearances he made after *All About Eve* are hardly remembered at all. One day about 1965, in a deep depression, he considered jumping from the terrace of his small New York apartment. But he lacked the energy and the courage. He had sunk to the bottom of his life. A few days later, when he turned on the television, he heard familiar voices. *All About Eve* was on the late show. "I sat and watched it unfold," Gary recalled in his memoirs. "I hadn't seen that movie since it first came out, fifteen years before."

By the time the movie ended, Gary realized that he would never quite know where Margo Channing and Bill Sampson ended and Bette Davis and Gary Merrill began. And it no longer mattered. To Gary, that night in front of the TV, the fault for what went wrong between them seemed mostly Bette's. "She had totally cut herself off from others. I finally understood why she had chosen *The Lonely Life* as the title of her book—and she was welcome to it. I began to laugh at the marvelous joke. I felt a sense of liberation when I realized that Bette had been as big a fool as I."

After their divorce the former lovers rarely crossed paths, though Gary publicly denied the accusations made against Bette by her daughter, B. D. Hyman, in *My Mother's Keeper*. Gary Merrill died of lung cancer on March 5, 1990, exactly five months after Bette.

Chapter 21

You'll Give the Performance of Your Life

anuck's confidence in *All About Eve* verging on enthusiasm, he saw no need for audience previews with their questionnaires and dubious suggestions for improving a film. The only screening was for members of the press from Hollywood and around Los Angeles.

All About Eve and Its Trailers

The studio produced four trailers, one way of signaling exhibitors that this was an important picture. As a signal to theatregoers, three of the four trailers included special material. For example, one opened with this title: "Scoop! Bette Davis Tells *Newsweek* Magazine *All About Eve*. Reporter Leonard Slater Interviews Famous Actress on the Set."

In a contrived interview conducted on a sofa, the stiff reporter says, "Miss Davis, may I have your opinion of her?"

Bette's answer, surprisingly, is entirely the words of Addison DeWitt: "The golden girl, the cover girl. The girl next door [etc.]." She winds up her animated speech with more of Addison's words: "A contempt for humanity and the inability to love or be loved . . . insatiable ambition and talent." (Bette's pronunciation of those two words, here and in her movies, always sounded like "luff" and "luffed.")

The one-minute interview is followed by half a dozen lively scenes from the picture, lasting about two minutes.

In a separate trailer, Anne Baxter is interviewed by a different reporter, and Celeste Holm by a third, who asks, "Miss Holm, what was your experience with Eve?" Her saucy reply: "Well, she never fooled me much—just too much. I recognized all her weapons of warfare a little too late. Her beauty—her heartlessness. She had the manners of an ambassador and the morals of a pirate."

The regular trailer was more formal, beginning with the title, "Ladies and Gentlemen, This Theatre Announces a Motion Picture So Unusual in Quality . . ."

These entertainment journalists no doubt arrived at the studio screening room expecting a fairly good picture. The more skeptical among them, however, recalling Bette's recent flops, weren't betting on the Davis future. Who could remember the last time she was really good?

The lights went down. Over two hours later, when they went on again, there was a moment of silence. And then it burst out—applause, more and more of it. They began to stand up, and an instant later the most influential movie audience in Southern California was on its feet. The tribute was to *All About Eve* and everyone responsible for it. But especially Bette Davis. Applause lasted until the room was half empty. By the time they got back to their typewriters, the press had forgotten all about Bette's last few movies. This new one proved how good she was. It had "Box Office Hit" written all over it.

Soon, the buzz in Hollywood was that *All About Eve* looked like a masterpiece and that Bette Davis had orchestrated the comeback of the year. Everyone in town was eager to see it, but first there was the New York opening. The Hollywood premiere would follow a few weeks later.

The picture opened at the 6,200-seat Roxy, on Seventh Avenue at Fiftieth Street in the Theatre District, on Friday, October 13. No actor would have opened a movie on such an unlucky day, but moguls and businessmen and theatre exhibitors don't depend on luck. They depend on cash, good reviews, word of mouth, weekend crowds. And fanfare.

The Roxy itself had enough decorative fanfare to upstage most films that played there. Built on a scale to rival Radio City Music Hall, the Roxy could have passed for a tarted-up branch of the Metropolitan Museum. The theatre featured a five-story rotunda large enough to hold 4,000 people, an architectural theme that grafted Renaissance details on Gothic forms with fanciful Moorish overtones, a music library, a set of twenty-one grand chimes weighing 10,000 pounds, fourteen Steinway pianos scattered throughout the theatre, an electrical plant sufficient to serve a town of 25,000, and washroom facilities for 10,000. The theatre's battalion of ushers, drilled by a former Marine, so impressed Cole Porter that he paid the young men a musical compliment. In "You're the Top," one of his witty superlatives is "You're the pants on a Roxy usher."

Having chosen this sumptuous setting, Fox attempted a prestigious road-show policy for *Eve*. Ads in the New York papers, allegedly placed by "the Men and Women of 20th Century-Fox," explained that "when we first saw *All About Eve*, we became aware that its utter fascination and charm were immeasurably due to the fact that we were seeing it the only way it should be seen—from the beginning." Patrons of the Roxy, therefore, would be admitted only at the start of scheduled showings—four a day. Prices started at $1.00 for a 10:30 A.M. weekday show and increased to $2.00 on weekends.

As sensible as it seems today, the innovative policy of seeing a movie from the beginning was ahead of its time in 1950. Cinephiles welcomed the absence of people climbing over their feet, but most moviegoers were confused. "Why are we standing on line outside in the cold when there are empty seats inside?" some complained. "Save the 'theatrical experience' for Broadway shows," grumbled others. The flood of telephone calls to the box office became so heavy that the management hired an extra operator to provide information.

And so a week later Fox and the Roxy abandoned their highfalutin plan. Back to the "grind" policy of continuous performances, with people arriving and leaving throughout the show. After the theatre reverted to a customary schedule, ticket sales increased 25 percent. *Variety* reported that "while the Roxy will probably gross a big $91,000 on the initial week ending tomorrow, a combination of favorable word-of-mouth and unanimous rave reviews indicated the figure would have gone much higher had *Eve* been playing on a straight exhibition policy."

The reviews were not unanimous raves. Bosley Crowther of the *New York Times* wrote that "Mr. Mankiewicz has been too full of fight—too full of cutlass-edged derision of Broadway's theatrical tribe. . . . Two hours and eighteen minutes have been taken by him to achieve the ripping apart of an illusion which might have been comfortably done in an hour and a half." Crowther never got around to telling a thing about the plot. Instead, he described the characters in monster-movie terms: "Eve, who would make a black-widow spider look like a ladybug" and Margo, "an aging, acid creature with a cankerous ego and a stinging tongue. . . . George Sanders is walking wormwood." (Crowther makes the movie sound like a documentary on lethal arthropods.)

More typical of the reviews is this one by Leo Mishkin in the *New York Morning Telegraph*: "*All About Eve* is probably the wittiest, the most devastating, the most adult and literate motion picture ever made that had anything to do with the New York stage . . . a crackling, sparkling, brilliantly written and magnificently acted commentary on the legitimate theatre. Bette Davis gives the finest performance she has ever played on the screen."

Hollywood braced for a hit. On November 6, three days before the West Coast premiere, Bette Davis finally pressed her hands and feet into wet cement in front of Grauman's Chinese Theatre. Why had Sid Grauman waited so long to immortalize her?

Two servicemen, S.Sgt. Jack Spencer and T.Sgt. Bert R. Nave, assisted Bette as she knelt down and then arose. Newsreel cameras recorded the belated initiation. Bette's mood was jovial. As she stepped over Betty Grable's legprints, she quipped, "Too bad there's no way to imprint my poached-egg eyes down there."

The cement had hardened by the night of the premiere. On Thursday, November 9, a thousand fans filled the specially erected bleachers in front of Grauman's before sundown. Thousands more lined Hollywood Boulevard. A headline that morning in the *Hollywood Citizen-News* had proclaimed, GALA PREMIERE TONIGHT FOR "EVE" AT CHINESE.

"The fans were treated to a glittering array of evening gowns," stated the *Hollywood Reporter*, "and to add to the lustre and significance of the evening, the Roosevelt Hotel across the street blacked out all letters on their big electric sign except the word EVE."

As the stars arrived by limousine, emcee Harry Crocker introduced them over a microphone. He was kept busy, for all of these attended: Lana Turner, Ava Gardner, Kirk Douglas, Linda Darnell, Van Heflin, Joan Bennett, Janet Leigh, Larry Parks and Betty Garrett, Tony Martin and Cyd Charisse, Richard Conte, Ezio Pinza, Charles Coburn, Mercedes McCambridge, Louis Jourdan, Paul Henreid, Janet Gaynor, Paul Douglas and Jan Sterling, Donald Crisp, Debra Paget, Jean Hersholt, Robert Cummings, Robert Mitchum, George Raft, Macdonald Carey, Hedy Lamarr, Danny Kaye, Dorothy McGuire, Gregory Peck, Franchot Tone, Van Johnson, Corinne Calvet, Victor McLaglen, Jeanne Crain, Glenn Ford and Eleanor Powell, Teresa Wright, and Greer Garson.

Marilyn Monroe arrived on the arm of her agent and protector, Johnny Hyde, the man who had landed her the part of Miss Caswell by twisting Zanuck's arm. A few of the fans recognized her; others asked "Who is she?" never guessing that even the initials "M.M." would someday be bigger than all the other names combined. Johnny looked bad. His face was ashen and he seemed to clutch Marilyn's arm for support. He died of a heart attack five and a half weeks later.

Anne Baxter and John Hodiak, so much in love, arrived together and chatted with the emcee. They were followed by George and Zsa Zsa, Mr. and Mrs. Hugh Marlowe, Darryl and Virginia Zanuck, and Mr. and Mrs. Joseph L. Mankiewicz.

Celeste Holm didn't attend, for she was starring on Broadway in

Affairs of State, written especially for her by the French playwright Louis Verneuil. Celeste was ecstatic, for Verneuil had also written Sarah Bernhardt's last two plays for her. "I'm afraid some of Verneuil's extremely French ideas on extra-marital relations have had to be revised for American audiences," Celeste coyly told a reporter.

Along with her new play, Celeste was singing nightly at the Plaza Hotel's Persian Room. She had turned her back on Hollywood and wouldn't return until 1955 for *The Tender Trap*. "It was a world of showing off and tennis playing and cars," she said. "I couldn't stand it." But Bette said, "I love Hollywood. The only reason anyone goes to Broadway is because they can't get work in movies."

In the forecourt of Grauman's, where her freshly pressed hand and footprints caused a stir, Bette was all smiles as she explained to reporters why she wasn't staying for the movie. "My husband, Gary Merrill, is in Germany making *Decision Before Dawn* and I promised him I would not see our picture until he returned."

Inside the theatre, *All About Eve* kept the audience laughing. There was perhaps the occasional wince, for some of those present surely wondered if Mankiewicz had targeted them in such lines as the one about "permitting mature actresses to continue playing roles requiring a youth and vigor of which they retain but a dim memory."

There was not only laughter but also sporadic applause. When Addison DeWitt slapped Eve and warned her, "Now remember as long as you live, never to laugh at me," the audience roared its approval not only for Eve's comeuppance, but for George and Anne's bravura acting.

And, when the movie ended, there was long and enthusiastic applause.

It was a night of Hollywood festivity. Dinner parties preceded the premiere, one hosted by Zanuck and another by Mankiewicz. After the film there were more parties, in homes and in nightclubs along the Sunset Strip.

The studio bash was held at Ciro's. Bette's "date" was her mother, Ruthie. A telephone was brought to their table and Bette placed an overseas call to Gary in Germany. "It was Bette's night of triumph," wrote Louella Parsons. "It was heartwarming to see the great and the near-great of Hollywood line up to pay her tribute."

Sitting in the front banquette of Ciro's, with Clifton Webb and Jane

Wyman close by, Bette heard a commotion at the front entrance. "I'm surprised they've got any flashbulbs left," she muttered to Ruthie. "Who'd arrive at this hour?" Turning her head, Bette saw another star framed in the doorway, wearing a red brocade gown under a full-length white mink coat. The star was posing for pictures.

Presently the new arrival, floating on glamour, made her regal way toward Bette. Under her breath Bette said, "Oh, Christ!" For her new admirer was Joan Crawford.

(Many years later, each time *All About Eve* was shown on television, Joan took her phone off the hook so that she wouldn't be interrupted. "She must have seen it ten times," said a friend. She pointedly told the same friend that she watched it "because of the *script* and the *director*." But Mankiewicz, Joan's former boyfriend, said, "She never told *me* she liked it.")

Bette was not delighted to see Joan that night, but even an unwelcome apparition couldn't dim her triumph. They kissed and exchanged warm words, these two who had both so recently been labeled "box office poison." Once again Bette Davis was a force to be reckoned with. From there, it was on to the Oscars.

Things I Promised Not to Tell

This phrase, which is neither seen nor heard in the film, occurs in the script. There, Mankiewicz designates it as the title of Addison's newspaper column the day he attacks Margo. But that's only one bit of minutiae connected with *All About Eve*. I hope some readers will find the following as irresistible as potato chips.

Several lines in *Eve* were not exactly new. Margo's retort to Karen, "I'm so happy you're happy," was heard in *Dragonwyck* (1946), the first film Mankiewicz directed. (He also wrote the script.)

- In *Bordertown* (1935), Bette Davis taunts Paul Muni: "You've an adding machine where your heart ought to be." In *Eve*, she tells Anne Baxter, "You can always put that award where your heart ought to be."

- In *Beauty for the Asking* (1939), starring Lucille Ball, there is a character named Eve Harrington. She's played by Leona Maricle in this obscure comedy revolving around cosmetics and hairdos.

- There are two allusions to Cole Porter songs in *All About Eve*. When Margo proclaims, "I hate men," she's quoting the title of a number from *Kiss Me, Kate*. Karen's query to Bill Sampson when he's comforting Margo after Addison's newspaper attack—"I guess at this point I'm what the French call de trop?"—comes from, and rhymes with, "You're the Top."

- In Mary Orr's story "The Wisdom of Eve," Margola (the prototype for Margo) lives in a "nest of forty rooms at Great Neck, Long Island, called Capulet's Cottage." Too bad Mankiewicz didn't use this name for a Margo Channing hideaway; it's the perfect retreat for a star who lives like an institution.

- Cora, the name of the heroine in Lloyd Richards' new play *Footsteps on the Ceiling*, is the name of the character played by Lana Turner in *The Postman Always Rings Twice* (1946).

- Kenneth Anger, in *Hollywood Babylon II*, refers to *Eve* as a "triple-suicide movie." His tasteless epithet is not entirely accurate. It's true that Barbara Bates and George Sanders killed themselves, but the death of Marilyn Monroe is best described as mysterious.

- Several members of the *All About Eve* cast wrote, or co-wrote, autobiographies. George Sanders was first, with *Memoirs of a Professional Cad* in 1960. The only one to write two autobiographies was Bette Davis: *The Lonely Life* in 1962 and *This 'N That* in 1987. Gary Merrill's 1988 memoir is *Bette, Rita, and the Rest of My Life*. Anne Baxter's autobiography, published in 1976, is titled *Intermission*. Marilyn Monroe perhaps dictated *My Story* to a journalist sometime in the 1950s; it was published in 1974.

- The only female character in the film who is not, and has never been, on the stage is Karen Richards, played by Celeste Holm.
- For die-hard trivia fans who also speak French: Match the line from *Eve* with its translation in the subtitled version shown in France.

1. Les esclaves ne sont pas encore syndiqués.

2. Quel beau sujet de pièce! Il ne manque que l'infâme séducteur!

3. Accrochez vos ceintures, la nuit va être agitée.

4. Partout où il y a de la magie, de l'illusion et un public, il y a le théâtre.

5. Que je vous désire m'apparaît subitement comme le comble de l'improbabilité.

A. Fasten your seat belts, it's going to be a bumpy night. (Davis)

B. I haven't got a union. I'm slave labor. (Ritter)

C. That I should want you at all suddenly strikes me as the height of improbability. (Sanders)

D. Wherever there's magic and make-believe and an audience, there's Theatre. (Merrill)

E. What a story! Everything but the bloodhounds snappin' at her rear end. (Ritter)

(Answers: 1-B; 2-E; 3-A; 4-D; 5-C)

Chapter 22

Those Awards Presented Annually by That Film Society

t the end of 1949, the San Francisco Drama Critics Council had named Bette "Worst Actress of the Year" for *Beyond the Forest*. At the end of 1950, the same group voted her Best Actress for *All About Eve*. Accolades arrived almost daily: Bette Davis, "Actress of the Year," *Look* magazine; "Best Actress," the French film industry; "Most Popular Actress," *Photoplay*. Bette shared the latter award with Joan Crawford.

Joan herself made several minor 1950 best-lists, for she had appeared in two Vincent Sherman pictures: *The Damned Don't Cry* and *Harriet Craig*. In January 1951, when both Joan and Bette made the *Photoplay* list, both agreed to attend the ceremony the following month to accept their gold medals.

February 12, the day of the *Photoplay* awards party. In the middle of the afternoon Bette's phone started ringing. "Haven't you heard? You're nominated! And *All About Eve* got more nominations than any other picture, ever."

Joan Crawford, who had expected an Academy Award nomination for one of her Vincent Sherman pictures, got none. She was shattered. Feel-

ing ill, she took to her bed and canceled her scheduled appearance at
the *Photoplay* awards dinner that night.

Bette, wearing a black cocktail dress and a flowered hat, swept into the
party with her arm locked in Gary's. She drank champagne. She accepted a
kiss from her former co-star Ronald Reagan and congratulations from his
fiancée, Nancy Davis. Jane Wyman and her new beau, Hollywood attorney
Greg Bautzer, seated beside Bette and Gary, congratulated her on her hon-
ors and wished them all the best as newlyweds.

The evening was well underway when Bette stretched across Greg
Bautzer to ask Jane Wyman a question. Waving her cigarette toward an
adjacent table, Bette whispered, "Who *is* that kid between Ann Blyth
and Elizabeth Taylor? He keeps staring in my face."

"Don't you know him? That's Joan Crawford's son, Christopher. He's
only nine years old, but he's accepting the award tonight for his mother."

"How *sweet*," said Bette. "And just where is Joan?"

"She's at home ill," Jane Wyman explained.

"Oh," replied Bette in a stage whisper. "Something *fatal*, I hope."

It was Anne Baxter's fault that Bette didn't win the Oscar. If Anne hadn't
insisted on running against Bette for Best Actress, Baxter herself might
well have gotten the Academy Award as Best Supporting Actress, and
Bette might have won another Oscar, her third, for her performance as
Margo Channing.

Although Baxter played the title role, and was on-screen as much as
Davis, the part of Eve Harrington seemed less important than the role of
Margo Channing. It still does. For one thing, Anne Baxter had the
ingenue role, while Bette played the star. Also, Eve was younger, while
Margo had reached her full-bodied zenith. And, using a purely intuitive
criterion to determine whose role is supporting and whose is not, everyone feels that the movie would survive without Anne Baxter, though not
without Bette Davis.

Baxter had already won an Oscar as Best Supporting Actress for *The
Razor's Edge* in 1946 but she considered *All About Eve* her breakthrough
picture. If she didn't qualify as Best Actress now, she never would.

And so she campaigned hard for a nomination in the Best Actress category. The thrust of her campaign took place within the walls of 20th Century-Fox, because the designation of each nomination was made by the studios, regardless of the role's billing or importance. It's hard to blame Baxter for convincing Zanuck to boost her into Best Actress. Besides, they all thought she had a good chance of winning. The competition—or so it looked early in 1951—shouldn't have been too hard to beat.

For starters, Bette Davis was unpopular all over town. Too many directors, producers, writers, and technicians knew, either firsthand or from rumors, what a monster she could be on the set. The long history of the Academy Awards proves that Oscars have often been given not as true rewards for professional excellence but rather as bouquets to persons the industry wishes to exalt. They have also been denied to those who didn't meet Hollywood norms. And so, with her reputation, and since *All About Eve* hadn't yet been validated as an Oscar classic, there seemed little chance that Bette Davis could win another Academy Award.

Gloria Swanson, who hadn't worked in years before *Sunset Boulevard*, was a contender, but how many Academy members would vote for her as that dotty old vamp who made Hollywood squirm? Judy Holliday in *Born Yesterday* looked like a flash in the pan; besides, she was considered a visitor from Broadway. Eleanor Parker, a nominee for *Caged*, seemed anything but a front runner. And so Anne Baxter started to look like a shoo-in.

Consequently, on February 12, 1951, when the Academy Award nominations were announced, Anne and Bette were neck-and-neck on the Best Actress list. They were the first two actresses ever nominated for starring roles in the same film. Later Mankiewicz said, "Bette lost *because* Annie was nominated. Annie lost *because* Bette Davis ditto. Celeste Holm lost because Thelma Ritter was nominated, and *she* lost *because* Celeste ditto."

Celeste and Thelma, of course, were nominated in the Best Supporting Actress category. *All About Eve* was nominated for a total of fourteen awards, the most nominations ever received up to then, and for many years to come. It held the record until February 1998, when *Titanic* tied it with fourteen nominations.

Eve was also nominated in the following categories: Best Picture;

George Sanders as Best Supporting Actor; Mankiewicz as Best Director and for Best Screenplay; Milton Krasner for Best Black-and-White Cinematography; Lyle Wheeler, et al. for Best Art Direction and Set Decoration in Black-and-White; 20th Century-Fox Sound Department for Best Sound Recording; Alfred Newman for Best Scoring of a Dramatic or Comedy Picture; Barbara McLean for Best Film Editing; Edith Head and Charles LeMaire for Best Costume Design for a Black-and-White Picture. *Eve* won in six of the nominated categories.

In later years the Academy Awards came to be described as "a symbol that captures the essence of American popular culture" and "the most visible prize in the world." But on the night in question—March 29, 1951—the Oscar ceremonies were visible only to those in attendance, for they were not televised until 1953. Even so, Oscar was perhaps the most *audible* prize in the world, for awards night had been broadcast complete on radio since 1945. (The Academy, with admirable foresight, filmed these pre-television Oscar events, and recently, at the Academy of Motion Picture Arts and Sciences, I watched the awards for 1950, as different in comportment from the present day as the court of Versailles is from Las Vegas.)

Then as now, Oscar fever raged for days before the event. Even airline passengers were susceptible. Sam Lesner, a film writer for the *Chicago Daily News*, reported on March 27 that "the beautiful sunset over Los Angeles didn't jibe with a movie poll taken among passengers on our plane as it approached the film capital. Ballots handed out by the plane's stewardesses showed Bette Davis, instead of Gloria Swanson of *Sunset Boulevard* fame, as the top actress of 1950."

Long before 8:00 P.M. on awards night the stars began arriving at the RKO Pantages Theatre on Hollywood Boulevard. Thousands of fans cheered the arrival of Elizabeth Taylor, Dean and Jeanne Martin, Louella Parsons, Ronald Reagan, Tony Curtis and Janet Leigh, Darryl Zanuck, Esther Williams and Fernando Lamas, and George Sanders with pre-blonde Zsa Zsa.

A limousine rolled past. On the windshield was a large sticker that bore a picture of the famous statuette. This sticker acted as laissez-passer for cars to cross police lines.

John Lund, star of *My Friend Irma* and *My Friend Irma Goes West*, was the radio commentator who detailed the glamorous events underway: "Outside the Pantages Theatre it's pandemonium. . . ."

Inside the Pantages Theatre the stage was dominated by a giant copy of the Oscar statuette, with rows of smaller copies arrayed on each side of it. Alfred Newman conducted the Academy Awards Orchestra in a medley, including "Mona Lisa" (nominated for Best Song) and "Baby, It's Cold Outside." Perhaps he chose the latter as a sly allusion to all the sable and mink in the theatre, and also to Karen's line in *Eve*: "Women with furs like that where it never even gets cold."

Charles Brackett, President of the Academy of Motion Picture Arts and Sciences and co-author of *Sunset Boulevard*, delivered the opening address. Seldom glancing up from his notes, he alluded to timely topics such as "the Russian land grab" and "young American blood spilled in Korea." His speech, resounding with pomp and noble solemnity, sounded like a high-school commencement address.

Fred Astaire, the suave emcee, also read from notecards. He said, "Tonight we present ten-inch statues worth forty-one dollars, but Caesar's legions did not fight harder for the treasures of Gaul."

The evening moved quickly because acceptance speeches were brief and there were no production numbers. There wasn't much hokum except for the nominated songs, which included one from *Wabash Avenue* that rhymed "noggin" with "Copenhagen," and "Mule Train," sung with shrill conviction by Frankie Laine, who made it famous. Whatever skullduggery might have taken place in the fight for these forty-one-dollar, twenty-four-karat gold-plated statuettes was temporarily forgotten, and no one used the evening to filibuster.

Jane Greer, Debra Paget, Coleen Gray, Jan Sterling, and David Wayne led off by presenting various technical awards. Lex Barker and Arlene Dahl, husband and wife at the time, presented the award for art direction, Phyllis Kirk the award for short subjects.

In the meantime Robert Merrill, Metropolitan Opera baritone, sang the second nominated song, "Mona Lisa." Merrill was photographed only in long shot until the end of the song, then in medium shot. He got no close-up, perhaps because he was not movie-star handsome.

Backstage, Marilyn Monroe was petrified as the time approached for her Academy Awards debut. She was wearing a black dress with a spidery tulle cape like a cowl. The color and the design of the dress were unflattering, and when she discovered that it was torn, she burst into tears. Fellow starlets Debra Paget, Jane Greer, and Gloria DeHaven rushed over and consoled her while a fashion attendant did some quick mending.

As Marilyn came onstage the orchestra played "Oh, You Beautiful Doll." And she did look beautiful, in spite of the unfortunate dress. Her voice was steady as she presented the award for Best Sound Recording. Like other presenters, she seldom glanced up from the podium while reading her notecards, though she displayed great poise and showed not a sign of the nerves that must have terrified her. But she never presented another Oscar.

Marilyn was followed by an improbable troupe of presenters: Debbie Reynolds, Marlene Dietrich, Gene Kelly, Ruth Chatterton. Using a lorgnette to read the nominees, Chatterton presented Joe Mankiewicz his first Oscar of the evening, for Best Screenplay. Next came Leo McCarey, who gave Mankiewicz his second Oscar, this one for Best Director. Mankiewicz gave no acceptance speech in either instance, although he had just entered the record books as the only person to win both the Director and Screenplay awards for two consecutive years.

Mercedes McCambridge, the next presenter, read the list of Supporting Actor nominees: "Jeff Chandler in *Broken Arrow*, Edmund Gwenn in *Mister 880*, Sam Jaffe in *The Asphalt Jungle*, George Sanders in *All About Eve*, and Erich von Stroheim in *Sunset Boulevard*. And the winner is George Sanders, *All About Eve*."

Since Sanders won the only acting award for *Eve*, and because his actions and emotions that evening are well documented, it's worth a pause to hear his version, with additional dialogue supplied by Zsa Zsa.

Sanders accepted his Oscar, bowed to the audience but made no speech, walked backstage, and started crying. Safely behind the curtain, he wept uncontrollably. "I can't help it," he sobbed. "This has unnerved me."

All tears were forgotten when, ten years later in his memoirs, Sanders described the evening in acerbic tones that echoed Addison DeWitt. His words can almost be read as "The Acceptance Speech They Wouldn't Let

Me Make": "It is generally imagined that after receiving an Academy Award one's salary shoots up. From personal experience I have to report that this is not so, and judging by the case histories of some of the winners, one is lucky still to receive any salary at all. Be that as it may, everyone wants an Oscar, and the handing out of these coveted trophies takes place at a highly emotional ceremony which makes strong men weak and turns egocentric actresses into weeping and blushing maidens. The correct procedure for winners is to disclaim all credit for their victory and to look stunned and transported with ecstatic disbelief and surprise. This is the moment when one draws to the limit of one's reservoir of histrionic skill."

It wasn't an entirely happy night for Zsa Zsa, who felt left out: "We heard, 'The winner—George Sanders.' I was wild with excitement. I threw my arms around George and kissed him. 'Oh George, I'm so proud, go up, go up!' Without looking at me he rose and walked to the stage. He said into the microphone 'Thank you,' and Oscar in hand, he vanished behind the curtain.

"I sat alone as the other awards were handed out. The ceremonies came to an end—and I sat there. People filed out, the auditorium became completely empty, and I sat there; a huge, naked electric bulb was switched on: ushers came down the aisles, turning back the seats. I sat alone in the empty, eerily lit auditorium. Somewhere behind the curtains before me, the winners were savoring the triumph of their careers—photographed, interviewed, congratulated—I could hear their laughter and merriment. My husband was there, part of the laughter and merriment. He had completely forgotten me.

"Finally, George remembered. An usher came and led me backstage. Nearly everyone had gone. At night, I would think: if I had a career . . ."

George himself paints a less poignant picture of his helpmate: "The night I got my Oscar I was accompanied to the ceremony by Zsa Zsa Gabor, to whom I was then married. The occasion for me was filled with such painful suspense that I never rose above a state of frozen stupefaction, in contrast to Zsa Zsa who was soaring and plunging between enough dizzy emotional heights and depths for both of us, first of all with delight at attending this top-flight Beano, secondly with triumph at being associated with the winning team, and thirdly with black indignation when it was tactfully explained to her that she had not won a prize herself. She was scarcely eligible by virtue of the fact that she had not as yet made any films, but this quirk of circumstance seemed irrelevant to her, and for some time afterwards she remained both hurt and insulted."

As the event neared its climax, Dean Jagger presented the Best Supporting Actress award to Josephine Hull for *Harvey*. Petite and rather feeble, she was helped onto the stage by several gentlemen. She grasped her Oscar and gave an endearing old-lady speech. She was so tiny, and her mink stole so large, that it seemed capable of asphyxiating her if it slipped so much as an inch.

Helen Hayes then appeared to announce the Best Actor Award. Looking somewhat like a flash-forward to Eve Harrington at age fifty, the First Lady of the American Stage played to the house: "I wish I could tell ya how good it is to be back here." She beamed as they responded to her cue for applause. Hayes accepted for the winner, José Ferrer, who then joined the proceedings by radio hookup from New York. "Hello, ladies and gentlemen, three thousand miles away, and hello Helen Hayes," he said.

Broderick Crawford announced that the winner of the Best Actress Award was Judy Holliday, who was also in New York. And then, rather incongruously, Dr. Ralph Bunche of the United Nations made a speech about responsibility and the necessity of the motion picture industry's always acting democratically. He stated that in the UN, as in Hollywood, there is drama, comedy, even ham. That said, he presented the award for Best Motion Picture of 1950—*All About Eve*—to Darryl F. Zanuck. (This was Zanuck's second honor of the evening. Earlier he had won the Irving G. Thalberg Memorial Award.)

Alfred Newman and the Academy Awards Orchestra played the *All About Eve* theme, and Zanuck concluded with "Thank you, Joe."

Fred Astaire closed the evening by saying, "It is a great privilege to serve you. Good night."

In New York, José Ferrer and Gloria Swanson were appearing together in a stage revival of *Twentieth Century*. Since they couldn't leave the show to attend the Academy Awards, Ferrer decided to combine an awards-night party with a celebration of Swanson's birthday (March 27, two days before). With so many potential Oscar winners in New York and attending the party at the Cafe La Zambra—Celeste Holm, Sam Jaffe, Thelma Ritter, George Cukor—the Academy arranged to install a radio hookup. Someone ran up to Sam Jaffe's table to tell him he had just lost to George Sanders. The press asked the remaining nominees to sit together at a table in the middle of the café. Judy Holliday and Gloria Swanson, meeting for the first time, shook hands. José Ferrer sat between them. George Cukor took the seat next to Gloria Swanson, and Celeste Holm sat on his other side.

With 280 guests, the party was in full swing when Ferrer was announced as Oscar winner for Best Actor. Judy Holliday and Gloria Swanson shrieked for joy, along with everyone else in the place. A few minutes later Judy Holliday, and not Gloria Swanson, was named Best Actress, and La Zambra went wild again. Gloria hugged Judy and said, "Darling, why couldn't you have waited till next year?" But the radio network forgot to pull a switch and Holliday didn't get to make a speech.

Gloria Swanson congratulated the winners and told reporters: "Well, this just means the old warhorse has got to go back to work."

Bette Davis attended neither the Academy Awards in Hollywood nor Oscar Night East in New York. She was somewhere on the Yorkshire moors filming a British movie called *Another Man's Poison* with Gary Merrill. (In it she retains the Margo Channing hairdo and the Margo Channing line readings—insofar as we can tell where Bette leaves off and Margo starts. But in every scene, Bette seems to realize what a lousy movie it is.)

In England, Bette and Gary, along with cast and crew of *Another Man's Poison*, were gathered at a wee-hours party around a radio to hear the winners announced from America. When Broderick Crawford began reading the Best Actress nominees, Bette stood up expectantly. Crawford opened the envelope and read, "The winner is Judy Holliday for *Born Yesterday*." Bette said to her assembled colleagues, "Good. A newcomer got it. I couldn't be more pleased." But she left the party early and returned to her hotel, where she informed the desk that she was not to be disturbed under any circumstances.

Years later Bette Davis said her two Oscars, for *Dangerous* (1935) and

Jezebel (1938), didn't mean much because they were for the wrong films. She felt she should have won for *The Letter* and especially for *All About Eve*.

Bette made no ungracious comments about Judy Holliday's surprise win. Rather, she contended that actors who have played roles on Broadway for a period of time, as Holliday had done in *Born Yesterday*, should be placed in a separate Academy Awards category from film actors who play a role for the first time on-screen. In support of her argument she cited the writing-award categories: original screenplay versus adaptation.

When an interviewer asked Bette in 1950 if she had seen Gloria Swanson's performance in *Sunset Boulevard*, she said: "Gary and I were on our way to Maine when we saw it advertised at a small-town theatre. We spent the night there just to see the picture. I think she gave a heavenly performance." Years later, in a 1982 *Playboy* interview, Bette's admiration was undiminished: "Swanson was up for an award that year, and if she'd won, I'd have shouted hooray. She was sensational, just fantastic, and she had never won."

Shortly before her death in 1985, Anne Baxter told an interviewer, "I've decided recently that I was wrong. I *should* have accepted another supporting Oscar and then Bette would have undoubtedly gotten hers." When Bette heard of Anne's statement, she replied without rancor, "Yeah, she should have."

Acclaim for *All About Eve* didn't stop with the Oscars. This is a partial list of the film's other awards and citations over the next couple of years:

Best Picture, New York Film Critics
Best Picture, San Francisco Drama Critics Council
Best Film, the British Film Academy
Second Best Picture of the Year, National Board of Review
One of the Ten Best Films of the Year, *Time* magazine
Special Jury Prize, Cannes Film Festival (1951)
Best Director, Mankiewicz, Directors Guild of America
Best Director, Mankiewicz, New York Film Critics

Best Writing in an American Comedy, Mankiewicz, Writers Guild of America
Golden Globe for Best Screenplay, Mankiewicz

On June 11, 1952, the French minister of commerce and industry, Jean-Marie Louvel, presented Bette Davis with an award as best actress of the year for her performance in *All About Eve.*

If some fiduciary academy had given awards for box-office success, *All About Eve* would have trailed any number of lesser lights. DeMille's *Samson and Delilah* was number one at the box office in 1950, with $11 million in North American rentals. *Cheaper by the Dozen* made $4.3 million, *Twelve O'Clock High* $3.2 million. *Eve* brought in a respectable but unspectacular $2.9 million in domestic rentals, eventually going on to make $4.2 million in rentals worldwide.

All such figures, however, are necessarily approximate. To quote Aubrey Solomon, Jr., in his book *Twentieth Century-Fox: A Corporate and Financial History*, "In the golden years of Hollywood, when Twentieth Century-Fox, as well as the other studios, owned its own theatre chains, the entire business was a closed circle. Only studio bookkeepers knew for certain whether a picture made or lost money and even then they were never sure. The more money a movie grossed, the more overhead a studio lopped off that gross. With such practices, most movies never showed more than meager profits."

Those unreliable studio account books need not detain us. Besides, even before profits were tallied, *All About Eve* was ready to assume a dual persona that no amount of box-office receipts could purchase. Like the improbable plot of some earlier Bette Davis movie—twin sisters living wildly unequal lives, or the fantastic metamorphosis of Charlotte Vale in *Now, Voyager*—this prestigious, award-winning movie was about to change. Starting out as a fine picture by almost any standard, it soon mutated into something more. This second personality had perhaps appeared as early as the premiere in 1950, and surely by Oscar night in 1951. For *All About Eve*, recognized immediately as a Hollywood classic, was soon to become a classic of camp.

Chapter 23

Waiting for Me to Crack That Little Gnome on the Noggin With a Bottle

 allulah Bankhead was mixed up in *All About Eve* from the start, though no one could discern precisely how. Perhaps it was only because the movie capitalized on her campy style: the disdainful Bankhead grimace followed by a ribald put-down, the androgynous basso voice, the boozy mannerisms and the cocaine rhythm of her life. Or did Tallulah seep into the movie more insidiously than that? Bankhead herself was convinced that she and Margo Channing were the same.

She was right, but not entirely. If Tallulah had not existed, it would *not* have been necessary to invent her, for there was already Bette Davis. But without Tallulah to copy, Bette wouldn't have excelled as the champion of high-camp theatrics. Without Mankiewicz, the Davis reputation might have expired like Rosa Moline at the end of *Beyond the Forest*— slumped on the wrong side of a tank-town railway track.

When *All About Eve* came out, there was no word to describe the aroma of Bette's performance in it. The word *camp* was a subculture verb meaning "to cut up and carry on outrageously behind closed doors." As a noun and adjective, it hadn't yet ascended, in aesthetics and journalism, to the privileged plateau of "comedy," "tragedy," and "tragicomedy," though it partook of all three. In the early fifties, even the euphemism "cult film" had no currency.

Those who responded to camp were initiates in the arcane lore of certain motion pictures that seemed loaded with startling subtexts—flamboyant alternative messages which the initiates alone seemed capable of deciphering. These cabalists cultivated devotion not only to such movies, but also to a certain brand of star. These revered stars—usually actresses—served as figureheads of a vast freemasonry, with its tacit fellowship and sympathy, its submerged rites and codes, its mysterious semiotics. One of the nicer names for this secret fraternity in those day was "homophile." To outsiders the word sounded genteel, evoking classical antiquity and neurasthenic "bachelor" poets.

But these moviegoing homophiles cheered for a raucous kind of upside-down gentility. They endorsed Margo Channing's sneering epithet for her best friend: "happy little housewife." They loved it when Tallulah, at the end of her radio program, sang "May the Good Lord Bless and Keep You" in such a low voice that her music director, Meredith Willson, intoned, "Thank you, Miss Bankhead, sir."

And they must have considered 1950 an annus mirabilis, for it brought not only *Sunset Boulevard* and *All About Eve*, but also the debut of that very radio show where Tallulah began her campaign to snatch Margo Channing away from Bette Davis. That show was the place that launched a thousand quips.

By 1950 Tallulah's acting career was virtually over. Too old for movies and too erratic for the theatre, Tallulah the Legend was now without an audience except for the friends, real and counterfeit, whom she regaled in supper clubs and at house parties. Already she was playing the one role that would last the rest of her life: Tallulah Bankhead. In a sense, that's the only one she had ever played. The role was frazzled, and it had limited appeal.

To make matters worse, Bette Davis had starred in movie versions of Tallulah's stage triumphs: *Dark Victory* (1939) and *The Little Foxes* (1941). A few years later, Bette and Tallulah both attended a party given by Jack Warner, Bette's boss. Here is Bette's account of their meeting: "Most of the guests had left. I was standing at the bar when up swept

Tallulah. I was a bit anxious about what her behavior would be. 'Dahling,' she said, 'you've played all the parts I've played, and I was so much better.' 'I agree with you, Miss Bankhead,' I said. She wafted quickly out of the room. She didn't get the fight she wanted."

Bette's soft answer chimes with other comments she made about Tallulah. For example, she always maintained that she didn't go after the role of Regina Giddens: "On *The Little Foxes* I begged the producer, Samuel Goldwyn, to let Tallulah Bankhead play Regina because Tallulah was magnificent on the stage. He wouldn't let her. He should have; I had to do that part exactly the way Tallulah did it, because that's the way Lillian Hellman wrote it. But I was always sad that Tallulah couldn't record Regina from the theatre, because she was marvelous."

Bette could afford to be generous. To millions of moviegoers, she played the Bankhead roles as though Tallulah had never performed them at all. Tallulah, on the other hand, had but one reason to stroke Bette Davis, and that was to draw blood. And publicity.

The timing of Tallulah Bankhead's *The Big Show* on NBC radio couldn't have been better. The first broadcast took place Sunday, November 5, 1950, at 6:00 P.M.—three weeks after *All About Eve* opened in New York, and four days before its Hollywood premiere. Tallulah's big-name guests that night were Jimmy Durante, José Ferrer, Frankie Laine, Ethel Merman, and Danny Thomas. Immediately the show was a hit.

A running gag on the program was the feud between Tallulah and Bette Davis. The idea was funny, and Tallulah made it funnier. She exaggerated all the hostility she'd ever felt toward Bette, and the audience ate it up. It's easy to imagine Tallulah's delight: Now she could take revenge every week.

Someone asked Tallulah on the air if she had seen *All About Eve*. "Every morning when I brush my teeth," she drawled. Later Tallulah growled, "Dahling, just wait till I get my hands on *that woman*. I'll pull out every hair in her mustache." Later still, she said, "If they ever make a film *All About Me*, I'll play it myself."

Away from the microphone, however, Tallulah wasn't amused. She was furious that Bette had copied her hairdo, her voice, her exaggerated mannerisms. It didn't help that *Time*, *Life*, and *Newsweek*, in their reviews of *All About Eve*, noted recognizable traces of Tallulah. *Life* stated flatly, "Bette Davis in the movie is obviously modeled on Tallulah Bankhead."

All of this riled her so much that she threatened legal action. Tallulah called up Darryl Zanuck to rant: "That bitch stole my best stage roles for films, and now she is holding me up to public ridicule with her imitations."

It's possible that Tallulah's threats worried Zanuck. He probably knew that in 1949 she had sued Procter and Gamble, NBC, CBS, and the Benton and Bowles advertising agency for the unauthorized use of her name in a jingle for Prell shampoo. The jingle went, "I'm Tallulah the tube of Prell / And I've got a little something to tell / Your hair can be radiant oh so easy / All you've got to do is take me home and squeeze me." (Bankhead settled out of court for $5,000.)

According to some reports, Bette—perhaps at Zanuck's behest—wrote letters, sent telegrams, even telephoned Tallulah to explain why her voice had sounded that way in the movie. But Tallulah was not mollified. "There was no intentional imitation of anyone," Bette assured a reporter. "I feel that in this picture I played myself more than in any part I played in the last ten years. Maybe Miss Bankhead and I are alike, you see. That could happen."

Spoken like a press agent. But Bette had a point. Meyer Berger, in a 1944 profile in the *New York Times*, might just as well have substituted the name "Bette" for "Tallulah":

Standing still, Tallulah somehow gives the impression she's at a destroyer's prow, knifing into a howler. Her long, tawny hair whips into her face with every gesture. She flips it back impatiently every few seconds with a motion almost as regular as breathing. Her speech is a racing torrent, the whisper-in-a-rain-barrel sound of it curiously hypnotic. She paces like something wild that's caged, chain smokes, drains off Cokes as fast as her maid snatches empties from under her restless fingers.

The rivalry was more than a decade old when Bankhead went on the air. Tallulah, knowing she had latched on to a good thing, wasn't about to turn loose. One night on her radio program, in the middle of a recitation of her career achievements, Tallulah paused.

Her sidekick asked, "What happened next?"

"Bette Davis," sighed Tallulah.

But once a week on radio wasn't enough. Tallulah took her "Big Show" on the road. She opened a national lecture tour in Dallas on December 5, 1950. The evening was called "Tallulah Tells All." The word *all* was no coincidence. Describing the evening in the *Dallas Times-Herald*, reviewer Clifford Sage captured Tallulah's obsessive wit:

> Someone in the audience wanted an imitation of Bette Davis. On the point of complying, Tallulah changed her mind. "Why should, I, dahling?" she asked. "She's been imitating me long enough." Then she gallantly took the curse off the comment with: "But really, it's been sheer coincidence that Bette's played the leading roles in such films as *Dark Victory*. I really admire her very much." She twisted her shoulders in mock, saccharin modesty, and all but winked. "After all," she added, putting back the curse, "where would Bette be without me—and where would I be without her, by the way!"

The *Dallas Morning News*, reviewing "Tallulah Tells All," ran a photo of Bankhead above a look-alike picture of Bette as Margo Channing. The caption was WHICH IS TALLULAH? John Rosenfield, in the accompanying article, wrote that "if Miss Bankhead's remarks are to be taken literally she hates Miss Davis's innards." He went on to note that "in *All About Eve* Bette Davis wears her hair as Tallulah does and shouldn't, sports an Alabama accent offstage, makes Tallulah faces, admits to forty, and composes the nastiest insults ever offered as social amenities."

The following year, for the new season's first broadcast of "The Big Show," Tallulah traveled to London. Convinced that the feud with Bette Davis was evergreen, Tallulah launched a fresh attack from overseas. "Don't think I don't know who's been spreading gossip about me and my temperament out in Hollywood, where *that film* was made: *All About Me.* And after all the nice things I've said about that *hag.*"

But the jokes, only slightly recast, had begun to pall. It takes two clever people to stoke a feud, and their timing must be exquisite. Bette, for the moment, was busy elsewhere, and so Tallulah's one-woman vendetta began to sound a little desperate.

The show, based on a scripted "comedy of insult" format, filled up with multitudinous references to Tallulah's advancing age and her sexual aggressiveness. To guest George Sanders, she said, "I've decided to grow old gracefully." To which he replied very dryly, "And have you?" Tallulah: "Whenever I'm in Hollywood I turn down dozens of offers." Sanders: "Any for pictures?" And so on.

The next year, 1952, Tallulah's autobiography was published. "Forced to vote for a Davis, I'll take Jefferson and give you Bette," she wrote on page 2. Farther on, she brought it up again. This time the cattiness was subdued right up to the last sentence, where she chose to insert the knife:

> The gossips and the gadabouts made a great to-do about Bette Davis' characterization of a truculent actress in *All About Eve*. These busybodies said Miss Davis had patterned her performance after me, had deliberately copied my haircut, my gestures, my bark and my bite. For comedy reasons this charge was fanned into a feud on my radio show. I was supposed to be seething with rage over the alleged larceny. In superficial aspects Miss Davis may have suggested a boiling Bankhead, but her over-all performance was her own. I had seen Miss Davis play Regina Giddens [in *The Little Foxes*] on the screen, and I knew I had nothing to worry about.

Later in 1952, Tallulah savored one of the most satisfying nights of her career. On Sunday evening, November 16, in a live radio broadcast from the Belasco Theatre in New York, NBC's *Theatre Guild on the Air* starred Tallulah Bankhead herself as Margo Channing in *All About Eve*.

This was a one-hour radio version of Mankiewicz's *All About Eve*. Such a stripped-down production strikes us today as bizarre. It's as strange as hearing *Jurassic Park* reenacted on drive-time radio. But from the thirties to the fifties it was common practice for top stars (and lesser ones) to perform in radio adaptations of recent movies, either their own or others'.

Bette Davis, for instance, did radio versions of *Dark Victory*, *Jezebel*, and *Now, Voyager*. (Her co-star in the latter, a presentation of *Lux Radio Theatre*, was Gregory Peck.) Hedy Lamarr and Alan Ladd once co-starred as Ilsa and Rick in a radio version of *Casablanca*.

November 16, 1952, was Tallulah's Night of a Hundred Stars, and she was every one of them. Full of herself, she introduced the radio play like this: "Good evening, dahlings. The play we're performing for you this evening on *Theatre Guild on the Air* is called—and I never could understand why [*audience laughter*]—*All About Eve*. True, there is an Eve in it, and what a part that is. There's also a glamorous and brilliant leading lady of the theatre, whose true identity has been kept a secret too long [*loud laughter*]. Tonight, dahlings . . . tonight baby intends to do something about that [*laughter*]. So to get on with it, we raise the curtain on *All About Eve*. Hah!"

This radio version was adapted from the Mankiewicz screenplay by Arthur Allen, who took many an unfortunate liberty with the material. Like the movie, the radio play opens with Addison's voice-over. But for radio the adapter used several lines that Mankiewicz, or Zanuck, had rejected. This is how the radio script begins: "Hello, permit me to introduce myself. My name is Addison DeWitt. I am a drama critic and columnist, which means I am essential to the theatre, as ants to a picnic or the boll weevil to a cotton field. The story properly begins one rainy night backstage at the Curran Theatre on Broadway [sic]."

Lines spoken by one character in the movie are distributed to other characters on radio. In the film, for example, when Karen says to Margo, "She worships you, it's like something out of a book," Lloyd retorts, "That book is out of print." Now it's Margo who speaks Lloyd's line.

And not very well. Listening to Tallulah as Margo Channing—punctuated with endless "dahlings"—you realize how completely and inalterably the role belongs to Bette Davis. Tallulah sounds overconfident and tentative at the same time. She's a little too drunk in the party scene, a little too strident throughout, and her Margo has none of the vulnerability of Bette's. Hearing this performance, it's easy to understand John Mason Brown's famous review of her acting in *Antony and Cleopatra*: "Tallulah Bankhead barged down the Nile last night as Cleopatra—and sank."

Others also suffer by comparison with the movie cast. Eve Harrington, played by Beatrice Pearson, has the dithery voice of an ingenue Edith Bunker. Kevin McCarthy as Lloyd, Alan Hewitt as Addison, and Don Briggs as Bill are interchangeable. As Birdie, Florence Robinson at least does a near-perfect imitation of Thelma Ritter. And Mary Orr, who invented Eve in the first place, plays Karen Richards.

Asked what it was like to work with Tallulah Bankhead, Mary Orr still shudders. "I think she was a very bitchy woman, really I do. When we did the broadcast, she came over to me and said, 'Dahling, I understand you wrote Margo Channing based on me?' I said, 'No, Miss Bankhead, she was based on Elisabeth Bergner.' When she heard that, she thundered: 'You didn't?' And she never spoke to me again!"

Bette continued to deny that she had Tallulah in mind while playing Margo. Asked by *Playboy* in 1982, "Was there any truth in the story that you were doing a bit of Bankhead shtick in *All About Eve?*" Bette responded, "No truth at all. We never even *thought* of her. Bankhead was *far* more eccentric than Margo Channing."

Mankiewicz, too, dismissed speculation that Margo Channing was a caricature of Tallulah. "It's nonsense," he said. "If Claudette Colbert had played the role, everyone would have said we were doing a take-off on llka Chase."

And yet the scent of Tallulah lingers. She's like the victim in an Agatha Christie plot, albeit a comic intrigue sans murder. Unless, as Tallulah insisted, *All About Eve* was some form of character assassination.

Bette Davis is not the only suspect.

Perhaps this is the time to recall Edith Head to the witness stand. "I steeped myself in Tallulah," she said, "and everything looked as if it was made for her, yet the clothes complimented Bette. What you must understand is that Bette was *becoming* Tallulah Bankhead or Margo Channing, or whoever the hell she was supposed to be."

Anne Baxter, too, had reason to want Tallulah read. Read, that is, as the vainglorious prototype for Margo Channing, a temperamental aging actress who deserved what she got at the hands of Eve Harrington. For Anne Baxter was a Tallulah survivor—in 1945 they had co-starred in *A Royal Scandal*.

"Tallulah had a multitude of reasons for hating Anne Baxter, who played her lady-in-waiting," said Bankhead's biographer, Lee Israel. "There was Anne Baxter's personality—which simply rubbed Tallulah the wrong way. There was her age, twenty-two—which simply rubbed Tallulah the wrong way. There was her politics—Republican—which simply rubbed Tallulah the wrong way. And there was the *deference* paid directly and indirectly to the younger actress, especially by Lubitsch, which was the most offensive phenomenon of all."

It didn't help that Anne Baxter's grandfather, Frank Lloyd Wright, visited the set and watched Tallulah at work. "Not bad for an old dame," he said loudly. Bankhead bristled. The next take required her to tap Baxter lightly with a slap. Instead she sent her reeling.

Ernst Lubitsch, who originally was to direct *A Royal Scandal*, suffered a heart attack and had to withdraw. His assistant, Otto Preminger, took over as director; Lubitsch stayed on as producer only. One day Lubitsch and Tallulah had a frightful row. She "reviled him with a barrage of scurrility that might have shocked Henry Miller" and stormed into her dressing room, where she ripped off her dress and hurled her wiglet across the room.

Did this perhaps inspire Anne Baxter's fury in the scene where Bill Sampson rejects Eve's advances? Scorned, Eve Harrington rips off her wig, bangs it onto her dressing table, snatches it up again, and tries to rip it apart. She seems about to destroy the room when Addison suddenly appears. If Tallulah recognized herself on-screen as the source of Eve's rage, she perhaps had one more reason to hate Anne Baxter.

After *All About Eve* came out, Tallulah claimed that Mankiewicz had visited the set of *A Royal Scandal* five years earlier to study her mannerisms. Mankiewicz countered with suave malice: "I visited the set, true. But I was studying Lubitsch, not Bankhead."

While we're rounding up the usual suspects, we must include Darryl Zanuck. According to Tom Mankiewicz, "Zanuck's choice for the role of Margo Channing after Claudette Colbert dropped out was Tallulah Bankhead. He and Dad had a big fight about the casting. That I know." This assertion contradicts the written records of Zanuck, Joe

Mankiewicz, and the Fox casting director. In fact, it's a rather amazing fillip—tantamount to the appearance of a surprise witness.

When Zanuck uttered the name "Tallulah Bankhead," Mankiewicz must have seen hell open up. Her presence would mean the end of his quiet, orderly sets. Tallulah would drink, she would snort. She would steal scenes and wreck the ensemble acting he had in mind for this film. And when Tallulah realized she was playing not only Margo Channing but Tallulah Bankhead as well, then what? Would she, like Bette Davis at Warner Bros., try to rewrite the script? Since Tallulah hated Anne Baxter, how would their scenes turn out, especially the early ones where Margo dotes on Eve?

We don't know whether Tallulah ever got wind of her near miss with *All About Eve*. If so, it was doubtless on her long list of grievances when she called up Zanuck to threaten a lawsuit.

Tom Mankiewicz stops short of saying that his father based Margo Channing on Tallulah. Rather, he explains, "What Dad tried so hard to do was to create a three-dimensional Margo. I think those scenes about what it means to be a woman, and Margo's relationship with Bill, are very un-Tallulah. Dad and Tallulah Bankhead didn't know each other very well, so I'm not sure how he could have patterned the role on her."

It's demeaning to writers to see their characters pinned wriggling to the wall above a neat label "based on" some real person. That's one reason Mankiewicz said later, when asked about the Margo–Tallulah connection, that the archetype for Margo Channing was the eighteenth-century English actress Peg Woffington. "I've always told the truth about that," Mankiewicz told an interviewer, "and nobody has ever quite believed me."

Mankiewicz undoubtedly directed Bette Davis to play certain scenes à la Tallulah. For instance, the one where Margo, arriving late for the audition, encounters Addison DeWitt in the theatre lobby. Addison says, "I refer to your new and unpregnant understudy, Miss Eve Harrington. . . . Didn't you know?" Margo answers quickly, "Of course I knew." But it's not a Bette Davis line reading. Rather, it sounds like a drag queen doing Tallulah. Bette's voice drops even lower; she seems to scoop the line up off the floor and throw it at George Sanders. And the words aren't articulated, they're carelessly poured out like bourbon at three o'clock in the morning. The line reading is intentionally undisciplined, and very effective. It's a sign of Mankiewicz's subtlety that he had Bette "do" Tallulah just this once, fast but with poisonous accuracy. In the writing, however, he used the Bankhead household as a paradigm.

If Margo Channing—how she walks, talks, sleeps, thinks, drinks—resembles not only Bankhead but a bevy of other actresses as well, certain details of Margo's living arrangements are less generic. After all, Mankiewicz knew the gossip. Actresses fascinated him, and so did the theatre. As a show-business insider and a connoisseur of scuttlebutt, there was little he didn't hear.

He would have known all about Edie, for instance. Edie Smith became a devoted fan when Tallulah first appeared on the London stage in the twenties. According to a Bankhead biographer, "When Tallulah decided that she needed a live-in right hand, she invited Edie to work for her. Edie agreed. In no time at all, Tallulah was totally dependent on her new friend and factotum." (In the script, Mankiewicz wrote: "That same night we sent for Eve's things, her few pitiful possessions. . . . Eve became my sister, lawyer, mother, friend, psychiatrist, and cop.")

Edie Smith, fortunately, had no designs on Tallulah's career. That's perhaps the reason she lasted some thirty years. "As scripts arrived, they were placed atop a monumental pile of similar entries which Tallulah never touched. Edie screened them and passed them on to Tallulah if they seemed suitable for her hybrid, hothouse talents." (Mankiewicz's script: "There's the script to go back to the Guild. . . . It seems I can't think of a thing you haven't thought of, Eve.")

If Edie Smith, devoted friend and handmaiden, served Tallulah as half Eve Harrington and half Birdie Coonan, Dola Cavendish was Bankhead's Birdie with a million bucks but without the sassy comebacks. According to another biographer, Dennis Brian, "Dola was a wealthy Canadian who behaved as though Tallulah was the Empress of the British Empire and she, Dola, a humble and adoring subject." (Margo Channing to Eve Harrington: "And please stop acting as if I were the Queen Mother.") Brian said, "Tallulah never traveled with a pocketbook—emulating the Queen of England—but had Dola trailing after her carrying the petty cash."

Dola, too, took a shine to Tallulah in London in the twenties. Too shy to wangle an invitation to meet her idol, Dola instead queried mutual acquaintances, "Can I help her in any way? Does she need any money?" It was Tallulah who finally insisted on an introduction to her mysterious benefactress. (Eve: "I'd like anything Miss Channing played in." Margo: "Would you, really? How sweet.")

Back in North America, Dola eventually moved into Tallulah's house. "She shopped, helped with the mail, traveled with Tallulah, ran Tallulah's morning tub, scrambled eggs for her at three o'clock in the morning, and listened adoringly when the actress, who was experiencing an increasing amount of difficulty falling asleep at night, wanted somebody to talk to until dawn." (Birdie: "I haven't got a union. I'm slave labor.")

Tallulah, famously pan-sexual, seemed content not to awaken Dola's dormant lesbianism. "I know what people think," she told a friend, "but I've never even seen Dola in a slip."

The household occasionally grew tense when Dola, or Edie, felt undermined by the other's attempt to take over functions that belonged to her. (Margo: "Birdie, you don't like Eve, do you?" Birdie: "You want an argument or an answer?")

Dola and Tallulah spent forty years together, separated eventually by Dola's death in 1966. Two years later Tallulah died.

Mankiewicz may also have borrowed from Tallulah to fashion Eve's career. Phoebe, the high-school girl who sneaks into Eve's apartment the night Eve wins the Sarah Siddons Award, tells her idol: "You know the Eve Harrington Clubs they have in most of the girls' high schools? Ours was the first. Erasmus Hall. I'm the president."

This strikes a false note to American ears, since fan clubs in the United States have always been devoted to film stars. But a similar, all-girl following sprang up around Tallulah in London. During the ten-month run of *The Dancers* in 1923, a fanatical claque of some two dozen Cockney girls, most of them in their late teens, cheered Tallulah's performances from the gallery. They attended every possible performance and waited for her as she entered and left the theatre. Tallulah, only a few years older than they, was soon on a first-name basis with the gallery girls.

According to Lee Israel, "By the time Tallulah opened in *Scotch Mist* in 1926, she had amassed a gallery following more loyal, fervid, and numerous than any star in London. There were now hundreds of these girls; tailoresses, laundresses, clerks. On an opening night of Tallulah's, they queued for blocks, waiting for their chance to crowd into the overheated gallery section, which comprised backless, hard tiers of pews."

Mankiewicz may have had these Tallulah groupies in mind when he made *All About Eve*. In populating the film, he perhaps drew not only on Elisabeth Bergner and her "terrible girl" but also on Tallulah and her seraglio. For isn't Margo's household, at the beginning of the movie and for some time thereafter, an all-female ménage where even Bill Sampson, as Margo sharply reminds him, is a guest and not a director? (Are we meant to infer that in her house he's also the erotic director only when she says so?)

Margo and Birdie live under the same roof in wisecracking domesticity. Margo's big life demands minions, of whom Birdie—formerly "a fifth-rate vaudevillian"—is chief and indeed the only visible one until the advent of Eve. The collapse of vaudeville seems to have washed Birdie onto the shores of Margo, where she ingratiated herself as dresser, sidekick, friend, and maid-of-all-work. The two women are together all the time—at home and at the theatre.

Maybe that's because Birdie is Margo's closest link with reality. Only she can deflate that star ego with impunity. Their arrangement echoes Tallulah and Estelle Winwood, whose friendship endured for decades. Winwood, twenty years older than Bankhead, was a disciplined character actress who possessed the common sense that Tallulah lacked. (She reportedly also flushed Tallulah's cocaine down the toilet every chance she got.) Although Winwood was married at various times during her long life, and Tallulah stayed married for a few years, they were often paired as lovers. Whether they were or not, Winwood moved in with Tallulah for several years during the forties.

Margo and Birdie, we assume, have been happily together for ages, since they know each other so well. Then Margo takes in Eve. Suddenly Margo's house turns into a ménage à trois. Or, more ambiguously, a marriage of actresses. Birdie mistrusts Eve from the first, and as Eve gains favor with Margo, Birdie's displeasure grows. Why doesn't Birdie move out?

Because dramatically this marriage of thespians—Birdie the has-been, Margo at the zenith but on her way down, the ascendant Eve—is Mankiewicz's triptych of the Three Ages of the Actress. It's also his parody of the Three Graces.

Such a matchup flings open all sorts of archetypal doors: Birdie, though female, assumes the role that Joseph Campbell labels "the Wise Old Man of myths and fairy tales, whose words assist the hero through the trials and terrors of the weird adventure." Part of Margo's weird adventure is turning forty. Meaning middle age, menopause, loss of ability to play Lloyd's characters like Cora, who is "still a girl of twenty." (Mankiewicz once referred to Margo's crisis as a "professional menopause.")

This is Margo Channing's Long Dark Cocktail Party of the Soul. Suddenly beset by doubt and danger, she must undergo harrowing rites of passage. In Campbell's words, these rites "occupy a prominent place in the life of a primitive society." What society—in the eyes of Mankiewicz—could be more primitive than the theatre?

Folk mythologies, we read in learned books, populate every wild and unsure spot outside the normal traffic of the village with destructive and deceitful presences. Meet Eve Harrington. "The figure of the Tyrant-Monster," to quote Joseph Campbell once more, is "self-terrorized, fear-haunted . . . the world's messenger of disaster . . . with uncontrollable impulses to acquisition." Eve, we recall, wreaks havoc in her drive for a part in a play.

But 20th Century-Fox in 1950 was hardly the right milieu for these Jungian snipe hunts. Mythic woolgathering never made a buck, and so perhaps it's best to discard such airy speculations. Or, to adapt a Freudian adage to the matter at hand, sometimes an understudy is just an understudy.

Archetypes to one side, it's true that Joe Mankiewicz had a way with actresses. Although George Cukor is Hollywood's most famous "women's director," Mankiewicz is certainly a contender for the title. In Mankiewicz films, actresses often give better performances than actors.

Starting with Gene Tierney in *The Ghost and Mrs. Muir*, through the distaff cast of *A Letter to Three Wives* and *Eve*, and including some of his worst movies—*The Barefoot Contessa, Suddenly Last Summer*—the women come out ahead. Ava Gardner is the only good thing in *The Barefoot Contessa*. Elizabeth Taylor and Katharine Hepburn, intentionally or not, achieve camp apotheosis at the hands of Mankiewicz in *Suddenly Last Summer*. In *Cleopatra*, he almost salvages Taylor. In fact, he comes close a number of times to salvaging the whole picture.

Apart from George Sanders in *Eve* and Brando, James Mason, and Gielgud in *Julius Caesar*, how many actors performed with great distinction in Mankiewicz films?

Asked by an interviewer whether, as a writer, he was more attracted to women and their problems, Mankiewicz answered, "I'm well-nigh besotted by them. Writing about men is so limited. Men react as they're taught to react. Women are, by comparison, as if assembled by the wind."

On the set of *All About Eve*, the editor Barbara McLean said to Mankiewicz, "You have a wonderful understanding of women. How do you know so much about them?" His answer: "What do you mean, how do I know so much about women? Because I live with them."

Chapter 24

I Could Watch You Play That Scene
a Thousand Times

*I*n 1950, when Mankiewicz made that statement, he was married to the Austrian actress Rosa Stradner, his second wife. (After her death in 1958, he would marry once more.) Mankiewicz had also "lived with" women via numerous love affairs. Among his ex-girlfriends were Joan Crawford, Judy Garland, and Linda Darnell. It's likely, though, that his answer to Barbara McLean also implied the women he lived with in literature.

"Literature" in this context includes movies, radio, and television, hit plays, magazines, and other forms of pop culture. Mankiewicz, as author of the *All About Eve* script and also as auteur of the film, was a practioner of literary craft in every sense of the word. His work, at its best, was worthy of comparison with that of leading novelists and playwrights of his time. He probably knew this, but in 1950 who would dare suggest what Brad Radnitz, president of the Writers Guild of America, West, stated so boldly in a 1997 interview: "The screenplay is the form of literature that has supplanted the novel in this century"?

Whether this new genre has really ousted the novel is open to long debate. Perhaps it's safer, if less theatrical, to say that screenplays, and the movies made from them, have fused the novel and the drama, mixing in opera, dance, the circus, commedia dell'arte, and various earlier entertainments. This gallimaufry began in the 1890s with the first tentative films. By 1950 that new genre, the screenplay, could claim a small library of excellent writing. At its best, a shapely and polished script might achieve as much as any other written text. In the hands of a brilliant few it brought glory to the screen.

Mankiewicz, with *All About Eve*, matched anything in the pantheon of classic screenplays: *Citizen Kane*, by Herman J. Mankiewicz and Orson Welles; *Casablanca*, by Julius and Philip Epstein and Howard Koch; the joint screenplays of Billy Wilder and his various collaborators. The list of such works is small, but they're so potent that they do indeed threaten to overwhelm the standard novel. And not only the novel, but plays and other traditional genres as well.

If we look for a movie masterpiece, we usually mean an entertaining story with memorable characters played by attractive or otherwise absorbing actors. It has a beginning, a middle, and an end. The story also has a point, which is not the same thing as a message or a moral. And the movie maintains the right rhythm for its material. When it's over, we feel as though we've seen a movie and not a movie-of-the-week.

All About Eve meets these criteria. What the film *isn't*, however, also counts. If we circle this movie as though viewing a piece of sculpture from behind, the changed angle privileges *Eve*'s negative properties. We see, so to speak, what isn't there.

This is not a family movie; it's strictly for grown-ups. Kids didn't go for it then and they still don't. It's not corny or titillating or obvious like so many movies of its time, nor does it contain moral uplift. It has a bit of cheap sentiment—"You're an improbable person, Eve, and so am I. . . . We deserve each other"—but not much. In no sense is *All About Eve* a mystery or a film noir, nor is it romantic except in the most astringent sense of that word. And it isn't political, unless we read Eve's treachery and deceit as a veiled allusion to conspiracies and witch-hunts of the time.

Thus the rear perspective. But in front, the normal viewing position, what do we find to account for this movie's freshness? It's one of the least dated films of the studio era. Even now, every time we watch it, we the audience tacitly repeat to the entire cast what Eve tells Margo early on: "I could watch you play that scene a thousand times."

Another criterion for a movie masterpiece is that it have not only a text, but also a subtext. Or, in the words of film scholar, Bernard Dick, "There is the film projected *on* the screen and the film projected *from* the screen. The first is the text—the collaboration between a director, a screenwriter, a cast, and a crew; the second is the subtext—the harmonization of the text and the associations it evokes in us." In other words, we locate the subtext somewhere between ourselves and the screen.

Movies have always been layered with meaning. A film's text—that is, its most obvious meaning and appeal—is often what reviewers and audiences respond to at first. Later on come explorations of the world below the surface, the subtextual tiers of a film's visual and verbal content.

First the text.

All About Eve opened to loud applause. Following its premiere at the Roxy Theatre all eight of New York's daily papers showered it with praise. *Newsweek* wrote that "Hollywood, in considering a theme so close to home, has maintained a highly literate and adult attitude." *Time* considered it "probably Hollywood's closest original approach to the bite, sheen, and wisdom of high comedy," while *Look* proclaimed it "the most literate film of the year."

Further afield, *Good Housekeeping* reviewed it from the rather poignant angle of America's powerless wives: "The story of how an older actress, in the autumn of her fame, is succeeded by a younger woman . . . *All About Eve* dramatizes with insight, humor, and a bitter kind of sympathy, the fear every woman has of a rival whose weapon is youth."

Christian Century, geared to mainstream Protestant readers, commended the film's "discerning view of human nature and the theatre." The review ended with this caveat: "Considerable drinking."

In the days before thumbs decided a new film's merit, newspapers across the country spread the excitement about *Eve*. But when it opened in Britain in December 1950, the reception was more restrained. Richard Winnington, for example, a critic for the *News Chronicle* in London, found *Eve* "disappointing" compared to *A Letter to Three Wives*. He noted, however, that the "stream of juicy epigrammatic wisecracks relating to the theatre had all the actors at the preview audience in fits."

The French title was simply *Eve*. According to François Truffaut, "the fashionable viewers" made it a hit in Paris. A few years later Truffaut heard these same fashionable audiences hiss at *La Comtesse aux pieds nus—The Barefoot Contessa*—on the Champs-Elysées. Jacques Doniol-Valcroze, writing in *Cahiers du Cinéma*, observed that "Mankiewicz only pretends to attack the theatre and its milieux, but it's really a lovers' quarrel."

Eve was honored at the Cannes Film Festival. Dubbed into various languages, it won prizes from Cuba to Japan. Back in Hollywood, Hedda Hopper summed up industry opinion when she headlined a Davis profile, COMEBACK IN "EVE" PROVES BETTE'S STILL FILM QUEEN.

For a while in the fifties, *All About Eve* was famous mainly as a star vehicle that put Davis back in her rightful place. It was noteworthy also as a film that got a bunch of nominations and won half a dozen Oscars, and as the picture that boosted Marilyn Monroe, although no reviewer at the time even mentioned her performance. In the movie industry, it was seen as fierce studio competition for television.

A Place Out of the Sun

The oldest member of the cast in *All About Eve* was the first to die. On June 9, 1955, Walter Hampden, the "Aged Actor" who presents Eve Harrington with the Sarah Siddons Award, suffered a stroke in a taxicab en route to MGM. He died two days later, at the age of seventy-five.

Born in Brooklyn, Hampden began his acting career in England in 1901 with a traveling repertory company. ("I went to England to get the Brooklyn out of my speech," he said many years later.) After mastering his craft in some seventy roles there, he returned to the United States and made his Broadway debut opposite Alla Nazimova in 1906 in a comedy called

Comtesse Coquette. Eventually he rose to prominence in Shakespearean roles; in all, he appeared in twenty-six of Shakespeare's plays, usually in the lead. He also gave more than 1,000 performances in *Cyrano de Bergerac* in the 1920s. A little later his dream of a New York playhouse of his own was realized when he opened Hampden's Theatre with a revival of *Hamlet.*

Hampden appeared in several silent movies. In 1939, after a twenty-two-year absence from the screen, he returned to Hollywood for *The Hunchback of Notre Dame.* The following year he appeared in *All This, And Heaven Too,* in which he delivers this admonition to Bette Davis: "Admit the sinful passion that led to this murder. Denounce this man who betrayed you."

Their paths had crossed before, as Bette reminded Hampden one day on the set of *All About Eve.* A very young girl had tried out for the part of a princess in a play that Hampden was casting in New England. When the aspiring actress walked onstage, Hampden took one look and said, "That homely little girl? Good heavens, no!" The homely little girl grew up to be Bette Davis.

A little later, *All About Eve* started to acquire a more solid reputation. It was variously described as "triumphantly literary in tone," "a true and savage indictment of the theatre," "an elegant comedy of manners," "théâtre filmé," suggesting a film whose sequences are acts and whose curtains are fade-outs; and "ersatz art of a very high grade, and one of the most enjoyable movies ever made."

All of this is true to some extent. But there is more. For a film to endure as a classic, its layers of meaning—we might almost call them its personalities, or selves—must somehow materialize so that later audiences discover more than the original audience found. For example, *The Wizard of Oz* (1939) didn't skyrocket until the fifties, when it was shown repeatedly on television and embraced by a new generation. *Casablanca,* released in 1942, languished with other war movies until 1957, when the Brattle Theatre in Cambridge, Massachusetts, across from Harvard, revived it forever. *Vertigo*, a disappointment to many Hitchcock cultists in 1958, seems still in the process of ripening for some insatiable future audience.

Before videocassettes made it possible to scrutinize a film frame by frame and line by line, only the most tenacious cinephile-scholars could explicate movies with the "close readings" available to critics of literary texts. Perhaps that's why *All About Eve*, and lots of other movies besides, remained largely unexplored, a rich Brazil of untapped resources.

"We tried to make a picture that would be practically a textbook on the old ways of making pictures." This statement comes from screenwriter Dudley Nichols, referring to his work with John Ford on *Stagecoach*. It might also have been said by Mankiewicz regarding *All About Eve*. That's because *Eve* is a textbook film that looks backward to the sophisticated comedies of the thirties, to the flashback structure of *Citizen Kane*, to a virtual chorus line of backstagers and romanticized accounts of show-biz tragedy and triumph. In the opposite direction, *All About Eve* predicts an improbable litter of movies strung out over the years, ranging from *The Bad and the Beautiful* (1952) and *Imitation of Life* (1959) to *Bullets Over Broadway* (1994) and Almodóvar's *All About My Mother* (1999).

The most textbookish technical device in *Eve* is the freeze-frame that Mankiewicz uses to stop the action when Eve Harrington reaches for her Sarah Siddons Award. This device goes all the way back to 1895, when Thomas A. Edison's *The Execution of Mary, Queen of Scots* used a freeze-frame to mark the decapitation. D. W. Griffith elaborated the freeze-frame in 1909 in *A Corner in Wheat*. To contrast the quick-moving rich with the slower-moving poor, Griffith formulated a *tableau vivant* where the movement of the poor becomes so slow that it stops altogether. It was Joseph L. Mankiewicz, however, who popularized the freeze-frame. It's used in *Fury* (1936), directed by Fritz Lang and produced by Mankiewicz. It's used again in *The Philadelphia Story* (1940), directed by George Cukor and produced by Mankiewicz, who claimed that the final freeze-frame of Cary Grant and Katharine Hepburn in a startled embrace was his inspiration and not Cukor's.

So the freeze-frame in *All About Eve* was not a Mankiewicz first, although he lived to see it become a cliché. Truffaut appropriated it for

The 400 Blows (1959), then the Czechs took it up, among them Milos Forman in *Black Peter* (1964) and Ivan Passer in *Intimate Lighting* (1965). Since the late sixties, when George Roy Hill froze the final frame of *Butch Cassidy and the Sundance Kid*, Hollywood has done it to death. Though Mankiewicz didn't invent the freeze-frame, he used it better than any director since. That's because he had a precise reason to stop the action as Eve Harrington reaches to accept her award. Having hooked the audience by presenting this young actress at her moment of triumph, and having shown a Greek chorus of sorts—Eve's sour-faced former friends at the Sarah Siddons banquet—Mankiewicz knows it's time to start over, this time at the beginning.

A more literal-minded director would have launched the film—where else?—at the start of the story. But an artist has other options. Mankiewicz began at the end, with Eve and her ill-gotten award, then doubled back to reveal the story from three different perspectives. Later directors often used the freeze-frame as nothing more than a chic, lazy conclusion to their films. Few of them had the imagination to vary the freeze-frame as Mankiewicz did, for rather than leaving the image frozen he injected visual rhythm by cutting to a close-up of George Sanders, then back to the static frame of Eve with outstretched arm.

Apart from this one innovative device, however, *All About Eve* is technically conservative. Bernard Dick, in his book on Mankiewicz, observed succinctly that "the camera moves when it should, and Mankiewicz cuts when he must." This observation is in line with Mankiewicz's own credo: "The best direction is where the viewer detects no camera movement and no effect of cinematic technique." And yet when Mankiewicz structured his film in flashbacks, narrating the story from three points of view— Addison's, Karen's, and Margo's—he used a tricky technique that requires a bravura command of film. Shifting point of view to come at a story from all angles via flashback is the grand method of Orson Welles in *Citizen Kane*, of Kurosawa in *Rashomon*. Billy Wilder adapted this structure for *Sunset Boulevard* (one long flashback from one point of view) and Preston Sturges used a variation of it in *Unfaithfully Yours*, where a wild series of fantasies running through Rex Harrison's mind functions both as imaginary flashbacks and "unreliable" flash-forwards.

In the wrong hands, however, multiple-narrator flashbacks are merely depressing. Two examples: Vincente Minnelli's *The Bad and the Beautiful* (1952), and Mankiewicz's own *The Barefoot Contessa*. In the Minnelli film, three drab narrators—Barry Sullivan, Lana Turner, and Dick Powell— unfold a moist melodrama about Hollywood sins: sex and drinking, divorce and treachery. Although it's more flashily "cinematic" than *Eve*, *The Bad and the Beautiful* proves you can't start a fire with damp matches. The dampest one of all is Kirk Douglas, abetted by a soggy script. The result is a shell of a movie, revealed from three vacuous viewpoints.

By 1954, and *The Barefoot Contessa*, Mankiewicz was mired in a smirking smugness that he apparently mistook for Shavian wit. Bogart, Edmond O'Brien, and Rossano Brazzi are the three narrators here. Their characters are not believable; they serve only as mouthpieces for Mankiewicz's gripes about Hollywood and the ravages of star-making. To his credit, the director soon realized his mistake. In 1960 Mankiewicz said, "I was angry at too many things; I tilted at too many windmills."

In structure, *Eve* is the offspring of *Citizen Kane*. Its comic style, how- ever, derives from the decade that ended in 1939. In fact, if you wanted to study comedies of the 1930s and couldn't find any, you could extrap- olate a lot just from watching *All About Eve*. Pauline Kael, discussing Herman Mankiewicz vis-à-vis thirties comedies in *The Citizen Kane Book*, characterizes the films of that decade: "They entertained you without trying to change your life. Many weren't even 'artistic' or 'visual' movies, which is why they look so good on television now. The writers [with their] toughness and cynicism and verbal skills had an almost aris- tocratic disdain for putting beliefs into words."

She might almost have been writing an abstract of *All About Eve*. Except that by 1950 Hollywood comedy had been tempered by the earnestness of war films, shaded by film noir, and chilled by the icy fin- gers of McCarthyism. And so *Eve* ends on a cautionary note: Look in those mirrors and see a bad girl's fate. Its "toughness and cynicism" are garnished with Freud, and there's a wee post-war sermon when Addison lectures Eve: "There was no Eddie—no pilot. You've never been mar- ried. That was not only a lie, it was an insult to dead heroes and the women who loved them."

Eve most resembles thirties movies in its fast-paced talkiness (think of *The Women*), its wisecracks and put-downs (*Stage Door*), even its whiff of the Marx Brothers' non sequitur ("Remind me to tell you about the time I looked into the heart of an artichoke"). The plot recalls *42nd Street* (1933): broken ankle throws star out of show, understudy goes on, next day understudy is new star.

In a few particulars *All About Eve* contains the seeds of a screwball comedy—one like *The Awful Truth* (1937), starring Cary Grant, Irene Dunne, and Ralph Bellamy. Both films are sex comedies played out in sophisticated milieux. Both have scenes in nightclubs, champagne toasts, and suggestive double entendres. There's a triangle in *The Awful Truth*, two in *Eve* (viz., Margo, Bill, Eve; and Karen, Lloyd, Eve). In both movies a couple breaks up and gets together again. The plot of *The Awful Truth* is set in motion when a car breaks down. This is echoed in *Eve* when Karen drains the gas tank to make Margo miss her performance so that Eve can go on, events that lead eventually to the film's resolution.

You could almost argue that John Barrymore, as the hammy, egomaniac producer Oscar Jaffee in *Twentieth Century* (1934), served as a distant prototype for Margo Channing. And what other ideas did Mankiewicz get from this Howard Hawks farce, where Carole Lombard plays a bitchy actress whom Barrymore discovers and casts in a terrible southern play? (Movie historian David Shipman has pointed out that "all dreadful plays in movies are set in the South.")

Certainly Mankiewicz drew on a comic tradition that depended on deft handling of actors, on the wit and timing of dialogue, and which used a minimum of cinematic trickiness. He learned his lessons well. So well, in fact, that *All About Eve* remains the definitive movie about backstage life, "backstage" being defined as everything in show business that the audience isn't supposed to see. But those who studied *Eve* as their primer were less adept. Most Mankiewicz followers were copycats.

Or perhaps it's more accurate to say that most Mankiewicz copycats were camp followers. That's true of imitative directors like Minnelli, and it's also true of a large segment of the audience. *All About Eve* flourished at the outset because it seemed obvious. It was backstage drama crossed with rollicking comedy, well played by a top-notch cast. And in 1950, all that seemed blatantly heterosexual.

Eve has endured precisely because of what wasn't obvious at first. The subtext has beguiled several generations of devotees, largely gay men, who have "read" the film as though it beamed a limelight into the closet of their hearts.

It's easy to reel off the reasons why *All About Eve* recruited such gay devotion. (I hope that readers will embrace these suggestions with an ironic skepticism, for all such explanations are open to loud debate.) First of all, the icon Bette Davis clones another icon right on-screen: Margo Channing. With her flamboyant body language, jaded sense of humor, and relentless irony, Margo caricatures every female impersonator—or is Margo a drag queen's impersonation of Bette Davis? Either way, she instantly found her target audience.

Mankiewicz never said it, but many a gay man might: "Margo Channing, *c'est moi.*" Margo lives the life a whole generation of gay men wanted to lead, at least in their dreams: a big-city life of money, prestige, and devotion, punctuated with wisecracks, bitch fights, late nights and breakfast in bed, and always getting in the last bon mot. In other words, gays like glamour. And wit. *All About Eve* is full of quotable lines with plenty of snap.

But more than anything, it's about women in conflict, and gays cheer for this theme (cf. Scarlett versus Melanie, Baby Jane versus Blanche, Veda and Mildred Pierce, Mommie Dearest and Christina). And *Eve* loads the dice. Here the battle is about age, for Eve Harrington's youth is her only real advantage. Gays identify with Margo's dread of aging. It's a fear that grips gay hearts, though it's less a defining trait now than it used to be.

Margo is also under siege. A younger woman, perceived as prettier, sexier, more feminine and more talented, tries to usurp her life. How many middle-aged gay men feel that young studs in the bars are grabbing what they themselves used to get? Paul Roen, in *High Camp: A Gay Guide to Camp and Cult Films*, puts it this way: "We are transfixed by Margo's beautiful face, which seems to be decaying right before our eyes. In its own way, *All About Eve* is as much a horror film as *What Ever*

Happened to Baby Jane? Here we have a middle-aged woman who, upon perceiving that her world is crumbling, expresses alarm and is promptly told that she's merely being paranoid."

Because she's getting older and because she's in jeopardy, Margo is the archetype of the Long-suffering Woman. Many gay men, like her, are in a sense terribly battered. They've been mistreated and rejected since childhood, by the world and often by their families. But Margo fits another archetype as well. Even before pop psych, she was rightly labeled a survivor. Who wouldn't admire her perseverence? In less reverent terms, she's a bitch with a heart of gold—gays have known many such. And Margo is an actress; that says it all. (What is it about a movie star on a staircase that makes gay men swoon?)

Gay men respond to other women in the cast: to Thelma Ritter's Birdie, a leather-lunged den mother who's the earthy voice of common sense; to Celeste Holm as the true friend who nevertheless commits a terribly disloyal act; to the daffy knowing innocence of Marilyn's Twinkie, Miss Caswell; and to Eve Harrington, played as a stalking predator who's closer to Lillith than to the original Eve. (The heterosexual Mankiewicz responded much the same to these females. "Male behavior is so elementary," he said, "that *All About Adam* could be done as a short.")

Savvy gays of course react to the camp aspect of George Sanders as Addison DeWitt, who seems so queeny yet is portrayed as lusting for females when the opposite must surely be the case. Mankiewicz confessed that Addison was "based essentially on me and what I think a theatre critic should be like—and on George Jean Nathan." With pronouncements like this, Mankiewicz comes across as a heterosexual trapped in a gay sensibility.

And so does *All About Eve*. When did so many Hollywood straights ever create such a gay entertainment? It is perfectly ripe. To misquote Shakespeare, ripeness is all (about Eve). Certainly *Eve* holds no monopoly here; most movies about show business are overblown, but not many have such a patina of real sophistication. That's because Mankiewicz was the Oscar Wilde of 20th Century-Fox.

Put another way, *Eve* transcends the usual vulgarity of Hollywood movies about actresses. Just contrast *Eve*'s chic milieu with the queasy goings-on at Norma Desmond's. The audience laughs with the characters in *Eve*, but it often laughs at those sad creatures in *Sunset Boulevard*. This observation is not a complaint; the unyielding bad taste of "actress movies" is exhilarating. Think of Joan Crawford in *Torch Song* (1953), Bette herself in *The Star* (1953), Judy Garland in *A Star Is Born* (1954), Lana Turner in *Imitation of Life* (1959), Geraldine Page in *Sweet Bird of Youth* (1962), Carroll Baker in *Harlow* (1965), Jean Hale in *The Oscar* (1966), Kim Novak in *The Legend of Lylah Clare* (1968), and many more.

Mankiewicz at his best wrote and directed with an operatic touch, and nowhere more than in *All About Eve*. Did some gays, even early on, perhaps view the movie in terms of opera, with the characters relating to one another as quartets, trios, duets? (The flashbacks evoke *Tales of Hoffman*, an older woman vying with a younger one recalls *Norma*, and Addison and Eve play their scene in the hotel room with the sexual frenzy of Scarpia and Tosca.)

Mankiewicz cleverly paced the speeches so that they come off musically. For example Eve, in Margo's dressing room, delivers a long recitative that starts out, "I guess it started back home. Wisconsin, that is . . ." Bill's lecture to Eve about the theatre—"Listen, Junior, and learn"—is a cavatina that's not sung but declaimed, though Bill flings out his arms as though he's about to sing it. Karen and Margo have a lovely duet in the stalled car, and the off-screen arrival and departure of movie stars at Margo's party recall the gypsies who show up in Act III of *La Traviata*. There's no Mad Scene, of course, but this is comic opera. Besides, how could Mankiewicz top Gloria Swanson's insane aria at the end of *Sunset Boulevard*?

It's instructive to speculate on the gay infatuation with *All About Eve*. But if you watch the movie with die-hard fans you'll find their admiration less schematic. More than politics, psychology, or camp, it's the vitality of the movie that keeps them hooked. After a showing of *All About Eve*, there's always something new to talk about. Here, for instance, is a typical audience gathered around a video monitor where the end credits have just scrolled by . . .

Glenn: "I don't have anything to say about the significance of *All*

About Eve, but when Margo is seeing Bill off at the airport and they walk past that sign, No Smoking Beyond This Point, I thought, This has to be the only time in the movie when she's not allowed to light up.'"

Sam: "Does she smoke as much in this one as in her other movies?"

Brian: "Cigarette consumption probably rose dramatically with each one of her films. No one smokes quite like Bette Davis."

Evan: "Bette's line in the dressing room, 'Lloyd, honey, be a playwright with guts. Write me one about a nice, normal woman who just shoots her husband'—Is this an in-joke about Bette in *The Letter*, where the movie opens with her doing precisely that—shooting her husband?"

Robert: "And the heated exchange between Bette Davis and Hugh Marlowe about actors having to rewrite and rethink the playwright's words to keep the audience from leaving the theatre—did Mankiewicz write that line with Bette herself in mind?"

Sam: "It could have been a sly Mankiewicz allusion to Bette's reputation for rewriting dialogue that didn't please her. But she never tried to rewrite Mankiewicz. He wouldn't have stood for it, and since she loved his script there was no reason to try."

Tim: "Margo, at the airport, wears only one earring because she was unable to locate the other one in her dressing room. That was thirty years before men—gay and straight—took up the earring fad."

Joe: "I like that scene in the bedroom where they're talking about fur coats. It's not vital to the movie but it conveys Broadway opinion of Hollywood success."

Evan: "Margo's crack about the movie actress who has just arrived— 'Shucks, and I sent my autograph book to the cleaners'—perhaps reflects her bitterness at being overlooked by the movie studios. Bill has just directed a film in Hollywood; Eve will soon get a flood of offers. But Margo not at all."

Gary: "For me the best part of the movie is when Bette Davis really becomes *Bette Davis*. At the cocktail party when she starts to get bitchy and nasty. That's when the movie takes off."

Glenn: "She played Margo Channing as a very complex character, while in many of her other movies she didn't bring in the nuances that we see here."

Robert: "Here she's vulnerable, unlike the Margo Channing you see portrayed by drag queens. They do her as a hard-edged bitch. They seize on that aspect of the character. But if you pay close attention to Bette's performance, Margo is more sinned against than sinning."

Evan: "In Hollywood, during the thirties, forties, and fifties, the easiest way to make a joke about a woman's age was to refer to the Civil War. For example, Bill says to Margo, 'I've always denied the legend that you were in *Our American Cousin* the night Lincoln was shot.' In *Dinner at Eight* there's a similar reference to Marie Dressler's advancing years."

Sam: "Is Eve Harrington too evil?"

Evan: "The thing that keeps her from being so is that she is obviously a talented actress."

Sam: "She's never seen onstage, so how do we know?"

Evan: "Because Eve's colleagues are astute observers of the theatre, right? You've got a playwright, a director, a critic—all three consider her a fine actress."

Steve: "Do you think Addison DeWitt compliments and flatters Eve just to get at Margo?"

Glenn: "Addison likes that crowd. Margo's crowd. He attends the cocktail party even though Margo says, 'I distinctly remember, Addison, crossing you off my guest list.' "

Sam: "One criticism often leveled at Mankiewicz is that the smart people in Margo's set would never have fallen for Eve's manipulation and deceit. They would have seen through her right away."

Glenn: "The audience is privy to her schemes before the other characters are."

Gary: "Her deception is very subtle at first. It rises to a crescendo later, but in the beginning she seems genuine."

Sam: "And theatre people can indeed be taken in by just the right kind of flattery. Think of Elisabeth Bergner."

Glenn: "When Margo says, 'Amen' as Addison and Eve stroll away together at the party, what does she mean?"

Evan: "The word *Amen* is used at the end of a prayer or a statement to express approval. Margo seems to mean, 'They are two of a kind; so be it. Let them scheme their evil schemes together.' "

Steve: "Just before that, when Addison sneers, 'Dear Margo, you were an unforgettable Peter Pan—you must play it again, soon.' What does he mean?"

Evan: "It's a dig about her age. Peter Pan was ever youthful; Margo isn't."

Robert: "Karen's remark about 'That boot in the rear to Margo. Heaven knows she had one coming. . . . We'd all felt those size-fives of hers often enough.' Just what is the literal meaning?"

Brian: " 'Size-fives' refers to Margo's shoe size. Meaning she had kicked all of them in the butt at one time or another. Or given them a 'boot in the rear,' to use Karen's genteel phrase."

Robert: "Does Eve have lesbian designs on Margo?"

Sam: "Wouldn't you, if you were a lesbian?"

Chapter 25

Tell That to Dr. Freud Along With the Rest of It

ve's designs on Margo, if that's what they are, never emerge, although the scene on the stairs hints that they exist.

> MARGO
>
> Put me to bed? Take my clothes off, hold my head, tuck me in, turn out the lights, and tiptoe out. . . . Eve would. Wouldn't you, Eve?

> EVE
>
> If you'd like.

> MARGO
>
> I wouldn't like!

If Eve's acceptance of Margo's "proposition" implies lesbianism, it's Margo, ironically, who plays it like a bull dyke. Her point is this: Leave me alone, sister; tonight it's Bill I'm after. When she's drunk, Margo turns into a dominatrix with a tongue like a whip.

Earlier, Margo was not so dismissive. Less than an hour after Bill's departure for California, she moved a stranger—Eve Harrington—into her house. "That same night, we sent for Eve's things. . . . The next three weeks were out of a fairy tale, and I was Cinderella in the last act. . . . The honeymoon was on."

This part of Margo's voice-over narration suggests a great deal. For one thing, this is not how you hire an assistant; it's how you start a love affair. Such haste, alas, leads to disaster, as it nearly did for Margo. But beginning that night, "the honeymoon was on," since Margo Channing, like Cinderella in the last act, had found her "prince." (And they lived happily for the next month or so, until Bill's picture wrapped and he returned to New York.) How could Mankiewicz *not* have meant us to read Margo's bisexuality from these clues? Maybe Bankhead's, too; maybe everybody's. After all, he had devoured Freud, and he lived in Hollywood.

Eve, of course, will sleep with anyone to boost her career. She beds both Addison and Lloyd, and makes a pass at Bill. Such expediency, however, doesn't necessarily make her bisexual. Away from the theatre, she chooses women. She has a girlfriend at the rooming house, and in the final sequence she takes in Phoebe, the devious young fan, for the night. Or so it's hinted. The lines, and the line readings, are suggestive. Eve says, "You won't get home till all hours," and Phoebe replies, "I don't care if I never get home."

Addison DeWitt—partially based on Mankiewicz, remember—is nobody's fool, least of all Eve's. Except for Birdie, he's the only one who never falls for Eve's deception. In these lines from the "Temporary Script" of March 1, 1950 (some later deleted—the deletions are shown in italics), Addison practically "outs" his protegée as they stroll down the street in New Haven:

ADDISON
Tomorrow morning, you will have your beachhead on the shores of Immortality.

EVE
Stop rehearsing your column.

ADDISON

I understand Eisenhower had a bad case of opening night jitters.

EVE

Isn't it strange, Addison. I thought I'd be panic-stricken. Run away or something.

ADDISON

Eisenhower isn't half the man you are.

These loaded references to General Eisenhower and the Normandy invasion are superfluous because Mankiewicz implies Eve's masculinity in a number of scenes. The first tip-off comes when she emerges from the shadows in the theatre alley and calls out to Karen Richards in a voice from her lowest register. It's almost a growl. Beginning with her next line, however, Eve speaks in a creamier, more feminine voice. From then on, she uses polished, actressy tones in the presence of her theatre friends. And she always speaks to Margo in her top register, her highest, most girlish pitch. Only in private—e.g., in her apartment in the final scenes—does Eve use her deeper "real" voice. Speaking to Phoebe, her young admirer, she sounds husky, rough-edged, aroused.

In a sense Anne Baxter read her lines as though she were singing opera: from lower register all the way to top notes. As Eve, she accomplished a diva's feat. Her voice rose from contralto, through mezzo, all the way to soprano, and at each step she colored it to express the character's deceit.

It was undoubtedly Mankiewicz who devised this vocal subtlety, since he loved opera as he loved all things theatrical. (The only time he ever directed for the stage was a 1952 production of *La Bohème* at the Metropolitan Opera, with Patrice Munsel, Richard Tucker, and Robert Merrill.) Our only real clue, however, to the source of Anne Baxter's vocal virtuosity in *Eve* comes from Tom Mankiewicz, the director's son. "One of Anne's greatest line readings," he says, "is only two words. It comes at the end, when Phoebe says to her, 'You're going to Hollywood, aren't you? From the trunks you're packing, you must be going to stay a long time.' And Eve answers, 'I might.' There is this thing in the way she says 'I might'—you just know she'll stay forever, that she's never coming back to the theatre, even though she said in her acceptance speech that her heart would remain there, on Broadway."

Tom Mankiewicz says he once discussed this line reading with Anne Baxter. She told him it was carefully rehearsed and completely intentional. Mankiewicz used a similar directorial device in *Sleuth*, his last film. He said, "I wanted Michael Caine to use his accent the way a violinist plays his instrument. Throughout the film I had him modulate his accent from upper crust to Cockney, according to the tension in a particular scene."

Besides vocal clues to her sexual preference, there is also the matter of Eve's costumes. In the theatre alley, where she accosts Karen Richards, Eve wears a drab outfit—as Margo puts it, she's "the mousy one with the trench coat and the funny hat." Some viewers see this get-up as boyish or tomboyish; others find it sexless. Vito Russo, in *The Celluloid Closet*, describes Eve in this early scene as "a sort of malevolent Huck Finn."

To viewers in 1950, it's likely that the trenchcoat and rain hat seemed natural. After all, it was a rainy night. (Some ladies in the audience, as well as furriers, might have pondered instead how Karen Richards would ever get her mink coat dry.)

And what about those bathrobes worn by Eve and her rooming house friend who makes the late-night call to Lloyd Richards? In Hollywood movies of the time, female boudoir apparel—nightgowns, robes, negligees—were used to bootleg a bit of sex and skin into a scene. (Celeste Holm is in a sheer nightie when she answers her bedside phone late at night.) But not here. Eve's bathrobe, and her friend's, reach to the neck, with no frills. In movie code of the time, such plainness would suggest an incomplete femininity. The scene's harsh lighting also suggests something "unnatural" about Eve.

After the phone call she beams at the girlfriend. The smile could signal either "Let's go to bed" or "Let's go back to bed." Whereupon Eve opens her arms in embrace, and they mount the stairs. But Lloyd Richards is on his way over. For Eve, it's a bustling night—as lesbian and as thespian.

Randy Stuart, as the girlfriend, played her brief role entirely in right profile. It's therefore surprising to see her full face in photos and in later movies such as *Room For One More* (1952) and *The Incredible Shrinking*

Man (1957). She had a Piper Laurie kind of cuteness, which helped her get a Fox contract in 1943, when she was nineteen. But she was a pro already, having grown up in a theatrical family.

In the forties she was a member of Jack Carson's radio show, appearing regularly as "The Hubba Hubba Girl." In the fifties she had a recurring role on TV in *Wyatt Earp* and a returning role as Harry Morgan's wife on *Dragnet*. She died in 1996 at the age of seventy-two, remembered, if at all, for her bit part in *All About Eve*. Was she photographed in profile because the camera favored one side of her face, or because, playing a crypto-Sapphist, she was seen as only half a woman?

From so many clues, vocal and visual, the audience was surely meant to infer something about lesbianism. Not the entire audience, of course, and not necessarily at a conscious level. But Mankiewicz the Freudian wrote, dressed, and directed Eve Harrington as more than just a "contemptible little worm"—Karen's epithet. To him, she qualified for the archetype of the Killer Lesbian. (Years later, Mankiewicz was still getting mail that asked whether Eve had lesbian tendencies. "Absolutely!" he told an interviewer in 1980.)

It's a grim joke that we learn "all about Eve" except who she really is. We're left to guess her psychological structure from the clues we're able to read. And many clues are homosexual, as they are with "that venomous fishwife, Addison DeWitt." What Mankiewicz does reveal—Eve the deadly lesbian—now strikes us as retrograde.

But we shouldn't judge Mankiewicz too severely. He was progressive even to encode the subject of homosexuality in the film. It's important to realize, too, that he handled Eve's lesbianism as neither funny nor shameful, nor frightening. We dislike her because she's "little Miss Evil." Whether that was intended as cause and effect—sexual deviance equals iniquity—is another matter, a subject for political debate. Mankiewicz, hewing to the psychoanalytic party line, half condemns and half bemoans the sad state of deviants via Addison's lecture: "You're an improbable person, Eve, and so am I. We have that in common. Also a contempt for humanity, an inability to love and be loved . . . We deserve each other." This view of homosexuality prevailed in medical and psychiatric textbooks of the time, and in books for the general reader.

But Mankiewicz broke with Hollywood tradition, and with American literary tradition, in one important way: The lesbian doesn't die at the end. By contrast, just two years earlier Gore Vidal, one of the boldest pre-Stonewall gay writers, had the homosexual protagonist of *The City and the Pillar* kill his lover. Death to deviants was everywhere de rigueur.

If Mankiewicz beamed a ray of enlightenment from the screen with *All About Eve*, he later regressed. In 1958, in league with Vidal and Tennessee Williams on *Suddenly, Last Summer*, he filmed one of the screen's most horrific gay deaths: Sebastian Venable killed and eaten by youths. Although Eve Harrington is about to be symbolically consumed by young Phoebe, the closest she comes to such literal devastation is when Margo threatens to "stuff that pathetic little lost lamb down Mr. DeWitt's ugly throat."

This is the most violent line in the film. As such, it vibrates with a kind of crude, brutal poetry. That's one reason it's disturbing. Another reason is that it suggests sexual violence by choking. We flash forward to Sebastian Venable's flesh crammed down young throats. Involuntarily we recall a grisly panorama out of *Hollywood Babylon*, including the fellatio death of F. W. Murnau and the murderous dildo shoved into Ramon Novarro's mouth by the hustlers who killed him. Margo's line could have been written for Dirty Harry.

The line is crude because it's so naked. It's also blunt and ungraceful. Why, then, is it poetic in any sense? Because of its contradictory layers of meaning: a lamb, the emblem of innocence, is equated with Eve, "little Miss Evil." Also because one of the dictionary definitions of "lamb" is "the flesh of a young sheep used as meat." The word *pathetic*, which has come to mean, among other things, "emotionally moving," originally had the stronger sense of "liable to suffer." And the phrase *ugly throat* connotes something grotesque and diseased. Suddenly Margo has turned into a bacchante, a flesh-tearing handmaiden of Bacchus. She has regressed from Lloyd Richards to Euripides.

Pushed to its limit, the line is full of venom. In fact, it's more punishing than anything written by Addison DeWitt in his column. After all, Addison surely told the truth about Margo and other "mature actresses" who continue playing youthful roles far longer than they should. Cruel, yes. But cruelty is part of a critic's job description.

Addison's column is reprehensible not for its candor but because of his motivation: he attacks Margo to boost Eve, his new trick. But how to explain Mankiewicz's severity in writing the line about "Mr. DeWitt's ugly throat"?

Mankiewicz himself might have explained it in Freudian terms. Having based Addison partially on himself, and writing the character as a foppish pseudo-fairy, the author must symbolically strangle his epicene creation. In other words, Addison étouffée. How? By stuffing a lesbian down his throat. But, to quote another sardonic line from Margo, "Tell that to Dr. Freud along with the rest of it!"

All of these slippery subtexts have some bearing on what Mankiewicz intended in *All About Eve*. But one reason it remains a fascinating film is that it eludes any one definitive reading. The more times you see it, the more loaded it seems with possible meanings. Conversely, it belies many of our projections. How can we not feel a bit foolish, poring over it as though it were Holy Writ?

Mankiewicz himself was dismissive of such endeavors. "I'm not prepared to say film is an art. I don't know any films that are going to be around two hundred years from now. In Hollywood of the forties and fifties we had no illusion about what we were doing: turning out entertainment for the public."

He was so right, at least the part about entertainment. *All About Eve* is indeed one of the most entertaining movies ever made, but to those long-ago gays who first elevated it to cult status it soared beyond entertainment. Watching it again and again, they began to venerate it. Not as a shrine to thwarted romance, like *Casablanca*, nor as a chapel erected to preserve vanished childhood, like *The Wizard of Oz*. Instead, *Eve* soon evolved into a rather raucous refuge from the anti-queer pogroms of cold-war America.

Its patroness was Saint Margo. Her very name comes from a Greek word meaning "pearl," and to the sexually disenfranchised she was, from the start, a pearl of great price. Cultured, yes, but like that grain of sand in the oyster, always an irritant.

The same could be said of Bette Davis, who had been a gay favorite since she became a star. It was natural that the success of *All About Eve* should converge with the Davis cult. Margo Channing might have been describing how Bette's fans viewed Bette when she summed up Eve's infatuation with the theatre: "All the religions in the world rolled into one, and we're gods and goddesses."

But gods and goddesses are remote. Even the commercial deities of Hollywood were elusive, since their newest picture often didn't stick around long even when it was a hit. Outside of large cities, a film like *All About Eve* might play for a week or less. Movies weren't shown on television until the mid-fifties, so those who wanted another crack at a certain picture had to chase it to neighborhood theatres or suburban drive-ins. Once the studio withdrew it from circulation, fans had nothing to rely on but memory. Cult followers of a movie really did need the drive and conviction of religionists.

There were ways, of course, to summon up fragments of the film. Stills gave many movies a lingering half-life, for they appeared not only in fan magazines but also in other national publications and often in local papers, thanks to Hollywood press-agentry. Devoted fans clipped and saved.

Before the concept of paperback "novelizations," one movie magazine, *Screen Stories*, retold in prose each month the scenario of five or six of the studios' biggest new productions. These retellings were illustrated with up to a dozen stills from the films, meaning that fans could revisit these movies provided they kept back issues of the magazine.

Bette Davis preserved the *Screen Stories* version of *All About Eve* in one of her scrapbooks. The adaptation covers a big chunk of the plot in this first galloping paragraph: "It was Karen Richards who found her, wide-eyed and tremulous, outside the stage door of the theatre where Margo Channing starred in Lloyd Richard's play, *Aged in Wood*. Karen took her backstage to meet Margo after Eve said she hadn't missed a performance since she came to New York. Stagestruck girls were a dime a dozen, but not girls like Eve. Eve was—different."

Missing from the magazine layout in that prose condensation of the

film is the still that would later become the most famous one from *All
About Eve* and also one of the most immediately recognizable stills from
the studio era. It's the one with Anne Baxter on the left, then Bette, then
Marilyn, and finally George Sanders on the far right. Although *Screen
Stories* didn't use this still in 1950 and other publications foregrounded
different ones, a few years later this particular one had become emblem-
atic of *All About Eve*. As a visual synecdoche, this photograph came to
stand for a complex set of codes and cultural assumptions.

Like the Mona Lisa, Whistler's Mother, and American Gothic, this
still has been reproduced so often that, on the surface at least, it has lost
some of its charge. But like those paintings, this image seduces the eye
because it's so many things at once: a fetching composition, an unforgettable portrait, an apparent fraction of something vast and meaningful.
And like those paintings, it has become the punch line of an in-joke that
not everyone gets.

According to Roland Barthes, "The still photo is not a sample but a
quotation." Meaning, presumably, that while a sample represents the
whole, a still picture is an autonomous image pulled arbitrarily from a
visual text.

Why did this particular image from *All About Eve* become the film's
virtual trademark? The easiest answer is that it's the best composed. Of
all the actor groupings in the dozens of stills from the movie, this has the
best balance. The still photographer on *Eve* took a lot of stiff photos—
the actors look posed; very little movement is implied. Perhaps this was
intentional, since the movie was seen as talky and theatrical.

This much-used still also lacks movement. All arms but Bette's are
pointed straight down. George Sanders' left hand is half-clenched, and
Marilyn clutches her dress. But an invisible word seems to hover in the
air, almost to jump from mouth to mouth like the marker on a TV sing-
along jingle. No one's mouth is open, yet the photograph resounds with
silent dialogue.

Provocative, too, is the angle of the actors' regard. George and Marilyn gaze at Anne Baxter. Why not at Bette? (Viewing this picture, don't
we assure ourselves that *we* would choose Bette for our focus?) Bette's
eyes cut toward Marilyn, as if to question her: "Why don't you look at

me?" Anne Baxter, in profile, is perhaps roving her eyes over them all in calculation.

Another possible reason this still became the film's quasi-official logo is because it "quotes" a crucial plot turn. "This must be, at long last, our formal introduction," says Addison to Eve just at this point in the film. Without this meeting, they might not have leagued against Margo.

From the way these four eyeball one another, we're certain they're having more than just a conversation. A jump from Hollywood all the way to the Italian Renaissance reveals this famous still as a profane parody of a genre—the "sacra conversazione," or holy conversation—popularized by such masters as Veneziano and Bellini. In a sacra conversazione, the Virgin and Child are flanked on either side by saints who may converse with her, with the beholder, or among themselves.

Our Fox studio master, lacking a virgin, a child, and saints, elected instead to depict in his devotional image three types of female beauty: the unripened, slightly masculine Eve; Margo, past the stage of full bloom; and Miss Caswell, a shimmering blonde bouquet. (Underlining her flowery status is the corsage at her waist. Over her shoulder, Muse-like, is the portrait of Sarah Siddons.) George Sanders is perhaps intended as an epicene nosegay. As ironic punctuation, he and Anne Baxter, portraying characters of ambiguous sexuality, enclose parenthetically the two heterosexual goddesses.

Chapter 26

Real Diamonds in a Wig

*A*s the cult spread, new converts demanded a vulgate that the masses could read. In 1951 Random House published the Mankiewicz shooting script. The author claimed, not quite accurately, that *All About Eve* was the first screenplay ever published in hardcover.

Even before publication, contraband copies of the script circulated from hand to hand. In New York and other stronghold cities, fans started acting out favorite scenes at cocktail parties. Some of the more zealous learned their lines as well as Bette and others in the actual cast had learned theirs. The difference was that these off-screen line readings added a second, even heavier, layer of camp.

The novelist, Joseph Hansen, born in the 1920s and a Bette Davis fan from youth, recalls that the movie "kept circulating to second-run, low-price theatres for at least a year after its first release, and probably even longer." Asked about gay attendance at these showings, Hansen says, "I suppose every gay guy with a passion for Bette felt wild enthusiasm for the picture from the very beginning. But we couldn't run out and buy videos in those days."

All About Eve appealed to other audiences as well. In April 1951, six months after its release, Darryl Zanuck mentioned the "large volume" of letters from habitual *non*-moviegoers. "Most of them are from people who say they had quit going to film theatres the past four or five years," he said. "They had seen so many bad pictures that they had lost faith in the quality of screen entertainment. *All About Eve* may not make as much money as certain other films, but it has reached an audience that has been neglected."

Not everyone wrote letters of praise, however. J. R. Moser, a member of the Fire Prevention Committee of Evansville, Indiana, was so distressed that he wrote to the National Fire Prevention Association, in Boston, about Bette's smoking in a particular scene. His letter, dated November 20, 1950, and preserved at the Academy of Motion Picture Arts and Sciences, reads in part:

> We have preached and preached not to smoke in bed, yet I viewed a movie last night where movie actors, under the influence of spirits, smoked in bed. This in my opinion encourages smoking in bed, as the public are quick to act on what they see done. I believe it is time we asked the cooperation of studios not to show actors smoking in bed. It is adult delinquency.

This letter reached Melvin Freeman, of the National Fire Protection Association, who in turn wrote to the New York office of the MPAA (i.e., the former Hays office, which by 1950 was known as the Johnston office): "The film that Mr. Moser has reference to is *All About Eve* with Bette Davis. Isn't there something we can do to see that producers eliminate such sequences in films?"

By January 1951 copies of these two letters had arrived on the desk of Joseph Breen, who replied to his New York colleagues:

> In the case of *All About Eve*, please have in mind that we have no authority, under the provisions of the Production Code, to withhold our approval of a picture because it contains a scene of a woman smoking in bed. When such eliminations are made, they are done voluntarily and willingly by the studio making the picture.

Bette herself probably never got wind of this little controversy. Years later, she talked about smoking as a characterization technique: "I discovered that for a performance a cigarette is a marvelous prop—sometimes for emphasis, sometimes for anger. For so many things. What emotions you can convey merely by putting one out! If I played a character who smoked, I didn't just take a puff or two in one scene only. I smoked all through the film, as any serious smoker would."

The Cigarette Scorecard

Although Bette Davis is Hollywood's most famous smoker, in *All About Eve* she meets her match. She smokes nine cigarettes, and Gary Merrill smokes an equal number. George Sanders smokes six, Hugh Marlowe three, Gregory Ratoff two, and Anne Baxter only one—at the end, when Eve makes herself comfortable with Phoebe. Apart from extras in a few scenes, no one else in the movie lights up.

Later in 1951 a very different kind of controversy was avoided through the vigilance of State Department officials in Washington. Fearful of offending a friendly South American dictator, they persuaded 20th Century-Fox not to enter *All About Eve* in the International Film Festival held in Montevideo, Uruguay. *Variety*, in an item titled "All About Little Eva?," revealed the reason why: "The story of a young film actress who is ruthless in her ambition and willing to step on necks of benefactors in order to get ahead in the theatre might be construed as paralleling the career of Eva Perón, wife of the president of Argentina. Latter lies just across the River Plate from Uruguay. Mme. Perón is a former actress."

When the film—dubbed in German—opened in Vienna in February, 1952, the studio found itself threatened with a lawsuit. Maria Zeppezauer, daughter of the Viennese playwright Marco Brociner, claimed that *All About Eve* was plagiarized in part from her late father's play *Behind the Curtain*, a local success when it was produced in 1909. The resemblances cited by the plaintiff—an aging female star, a youngster fighting to become famous, the involvement of a theatre critic—seem to have proved too flimsy for a judgment against 20th Century-Fox. *Variety* reported on March 5, 1952, that Mrs. Zeppezauer had "addressed a letter to the studio, pointing out similarities although she admits the film has differences in details from her father's work. She stated she will present detailed financial demands later." The lawsuit died on the vine. Fox's extant legal files are silent on the matter.

No Innuendos, Please—We're Anglo-Saxon

Censorship during the studio era was not limited to Will Hays and his heirs. Local censor boards, in the United States and abroad, made cuts in films as they wished. Here are a few examples from *All About Eve*.

- In Massachusetts the following bits of dialogue were eliminated:
  —"... rear end." (Ritter)
  —"something a girl could make sacrifices for" (Monroe)
  —"take my clothes off"; "I consider it highly unnatural ... unpregnant understudy"; and "I'm still not to be had for the price of a cocktail, like a salted peanut" (Davis)
- In Australia the following exchange was eliminated: Monroe: "Now there's something a girl could make sacrifices for." Merrill: "And probably has." Davis's line, "A fur coat over a nightgown," was also cut Down Under.

In Britain, the situation was reversed. A 1952 film called *It Started in Paradise*, featuring Kay Kendall, blatantly borrowed the central theme of *All About Eve* and applied it to the London fashion world. The movie failed, but Kendall's performance as a bitchy socialite gave her fledgling career a jump-start.

Hollywood, in the meantime, borrowed liberally from *Eve*, though subsequent fifties films contained no outright plagiarism. Besides, you can't copyright a party, and that's what caught the fancy of later filmmakers. Margo Channing's welcome-home/birthday party for Bill Sampson did for cocktails what Brando did for T-shirts and leather jackets—that is, established an institution.

The party, strictly speaking, is not a cocktail party. As far as we can tell from the movie, it begins long past the cocktail hour, usually defined as five to eight o'clock in the evening. But in the fifties a cocktail party had more cachet than similar social gatherings. (*Elsa Maxwell's Etiquette Book*, published in 1951, devotes separate sections to "The Tea Party," "Buffets," "Breakfast, Brunch, Luncheon," and "Cocktail Parties." As for Hollywood movies, the author might have omitted all but the latter.)

Before *All About Eve*, cocktail parties in the movies were amorphous. It was liquor that mattered, not the stylishness of its consumption. The camera might follow any actor around the room, not just the star, for the cocktail-party set piece hadn't yet evolved into a showcase for leading ladies. Near the end of *Now, Voyager* (1942), there's a brief, nondescript celebration where cocktails are served, but it's just that—predinner drinks. In *Smash-Up, the Story of a Woman* (1947), there's nothing distinctive about the boozy party scene. What we remember is Susan Hayward tossing them down. *Gentleman's Agreement*, also made in 1947, has a demure little gathering where Gregory Peck meets Dorothy McGuire for the first time. It's so subdued you expect them to sip Shirley Temples.

Mankiewicz might have borrowed two or three minor points from *The Velvet Touch* (1948), but How to Give a Party wasn't one of them. In this backstage crime drama Dan Tobin plays an intrusive, epicene gossip columnist who writes "Broadway Chatter"; Rosalind Russell kills her producer with a theatrical trophy named the Player's Award; and soon after its beginning the story dissolves into a long flashback. At the after-theatre party for great-lady-of-the-stage, Rosalind Russell, other members of the cast—Claire Trevor, Leon Ames, Leo Genn—get an equal share of camera attention. At this party, the drinks are barely visible.

But the pattern changed around 1950, when on-screen drinking became more prominent and more sophisticated. No doubt *All About Eve* helped engineer the shift: Margo's famous party became a convenient blueprint for movie cocktail parties for the next decade or so.

In 1952 *The Bad and the Beautiful* copied not only *Eve*'s flashback structure but Margo's party sequence as well. If the Minnelli cocktail party mimics *All About Eve*, so does the rest of the movie—in spirit, if not visually. And certainly not in wit.

Ironically, Mankiewicz's next soiree—in *The Barefoot Contessa*—has none of the style and wit of Margo's party. This later one is a hysterical psychodrama, a Come-Dressed-as-the-Sick-Soul-of-Hollywood party. It takes place in an expensively ugly Los Angeles house. Among the guests are a self-proclaimed "tramp," a rather self-righteous director (Bogart), and his "good" fiancée, Elizabeth Sellars, whose look of tight self-approval makes you root for the bad girl. Also on hand are a villainous producer (Warren Stevens) and a South American playboy (Marius Goring) who end up in a shouting match that has some of the lamest dialogue Mankiewicz ever wrote. Apart from its dispiriting badness, the worst thing about this party is that it shows no trace of borrowing from *All About Eve*. While everyone else in Hollywood was copying him, the only thing Mankiewicz borrowed from *Eve* was the name of a character. When Ava Gardner, as movie queen Maria Damata, stars in a film called *Black Dawn*, we see a shot of the marquee at the premiere. Her co-star is named "Lloyd Richards." (This kind of coy in-joke, rampant in the *nouvelle vague*, helped endear *The Barefoot Contessa* to Truffaut and Godard.)

Even a little throwaway movie like *Serenade* (1956), with Mario Lanza and Joan Fontaine, contains a more stylish cocktail party than *The Barefoot Contessa*. Directed by Anthony Mann, *Serenade* is another

backstage picture: Mario Lanza rises from the vineyards to operatic success but has romantic trouble when he marries Sarita Montiel (the Spanish Bette Davis) while trying to forget Joan Fontaine. At this Macbethish
cocktail party, Fontaine wears a dress that's a lot like Margo Channing's.
Vincent Price, playing a corrupt half gigolo, half homo derived from
Addison DeWitt, filches an Addison line to fling at man-eater Fontaine:
"We deserve each other."

By 1959, when *Imitation of Life* was released, *All About Eve* had
become the Queen Mother of backstage movies. In Douglas Sirk's camp
masterpiece, Lana Turner—ambitious, seductive, besotted by "the Theatre"—plays Lora Meredith, star of such Broadway hits as *Summer
Madness*, *No Greater Glory*, *Always Laughter*, and *Happiness*. (Did Lloyd
Richards come up with these titles? They're every bit as fruity as *Aged
in Wood* and *Footsteps on the Ceiling*. The difference is that
Mankiewicz's titles are blatantly tongue-in-cheek.)

The *Imitation of Life* screenplay (by Eleanore Griffin and Allan Scott)
echoes *Eve* in several scenes. For example, Lana, a widow, telling
boyfriend John Gavin about her theatrical beginnings: "My husband was
in the theatre, too—a director—a good director. Everything I know, I
owe to him. It was a small town, and a little theatre—but professional.
When he died, I had to make a living doing something else. I never
really wanted anything but the stage. . . . It took me five years to save
enough money to come to New York." (Eve Harrington, in Margo's dressing room: "There was a little theatre group there . . . like a drop of rain
on a desert. That's where I met Eddie. . . . We played *Liliom* for three
performances.")

Robert Alda, as theatrical agent Allen Loomis, lecturing Lana on how
to succeed in the theatre: "If the Dramatists' Club wants to eat and sleep
with you, you will eat and sleep with them. If some producer with a hand
as cold as a toad wants to do a painting of you in the nude, you'll accommodate him, for a very small part." In this scene it's not the lines that
recall *All About Eve* but rather the line readings, for Alda's phrasing and
inflections are a pastiche of Bill Sampson's speech to Eve that begins,
"The Theatuh, the Theatuh."

Lana, at rehearsal in an empty theatre, tells off the agent and also the playwright, though not so memorably as Margo chewing out Lloyd, Bill, and Max when she discovers that Eve is her new understudy. Later on, Lana at her dressing-room table is photographed from the same angle as Margo at hers.

Someone connected with *Imitation of Life* must have been a die-hard devotee of *All About Eve*, for there's even a scene where Lana treats her mink coat like a poncho—as though acting out literally Mankiewicz's witty dinner-table characterization of Margo Channing the first time he discussed the role with Bette. To round out the string of *hommages*, there are the inevitable parties—in this case, rather bloodless opening-night affairs where Lana and Company await reviews. It's *"Imitation of Eve,"* all right, but Lana as Lora Meredith never wins a Sarah Siddons Award. Even Universal-International and Douglas Sirk couldn't stretch a point that far.

The Queen of the Extras

Who is Bess Flowers? Why, Bess is famous in her fashion, at least among connoisseurs of obscure actors and seekers of the recherché. For her brief role in *All About Eve*, credit is due but none is given. You find her name not on the screen but rather in scholarly lists compiled by passionate cinephiles.

Bess Flowers speaks one line, near the end of the picture when she congratulates the latest winner of the Sarah Siddons Award: "I'm so happy for you, Eve." (She also appears in two other scenes: We see her on Walter Hampden's right at the opening awards ceremony, and we glimpse her at Margo's party.)

Bess Flowers (1900–1984) had a phantom career, for she appeared in hundreds of films and yet in a sense no one really saw her. That's because she specialized in bit parts and walk-ons. And yet, according to John Springer and Jack Hamilton in *They Had Faces Then*, she attracted "a cult of her own in the forties and fifties." If they ever make a film about *her* it will surely be called "Queen of the Extras," for that is Flowers' sobriquet among sharp-eyed film buffs. She appeared, perhaps not so coincidentally, in two fifties movies that owe much to *All About Eve: The Bad and the Beautiful* and *Imitation of Life*.

All About Eve seems to have impressed any number of later dramatists, filmmakers, novelists, critics, cartoonists, drag queens, advertising copywriters, and merchants. Some of those who paid homage—like Gary Carey, author of the 1972 book *More About "All Above Eve"*—saw it in theatres when it came out. "I was a kid," Carey recalls, "and I loved the theatre. *All About Eve* had an enormous impact on me."

James Baldwin probably wouldn't have used the phrase "enormous impact," but he did incorporate a faint echo of *Eve*. In his best-selling novel *Another Country* (published in 1962) a character named Jane quarrels with her boyfriend, Vivaldo. Exasperated, Vivaldo says, "You say another word, baby, and I'm going to knock your teeth, both of them, right down your throat." Baldwin continues: "This profoundly delighted her. She became Bette Davis at once, and shouted at the top of her voice, "Are you threatening me?" (In the movie, Margo shouts from the stage, "Are you threatening me with legal action, Mr. Fabian?") And Baldwin's novel, soon after the opening, goes into a long flashback à la Mankiewicz.

How much do Edward Albee's best plays owe to *All About Eve*? "Fasten your seat belts" hovers as a potent but unstated epigraph to *Who's Afraid of Virginia Woolf?*; surely there was never a bumpier night than George and Martha's. Albee's nod to Bette Davis in that play, however, is not to *Eve* but rather to *Beyond the Forest*: One of Martha's first lines is "What a dump!" Even so, Albee's polished dialogue and poisonous wit point Evewards, not only in this early work but also across the decades from *A Delicate Balance* up to his latest success, *Three Tall Women*.

Who's Afraid parallels *All About Eve* in several particulars. For example, the setting of Albee's play is a drunken party. What's more, George is younger than Martha and he taunts her about it. ("I'm six years younger than you are. I always have been and I always will be.") Bill Sampson, of course, is eight years younger than Margo. More specifically, Albee's play has at least half a dozen lines that match up with the Mankiewicz script either verbatim or in paraphrase, and certainly in tone and rhythm. Tabulated, they look like this:

1. Albee—MARTHA: "His wife's a mousy little type. . . ."
   Mankiewicz—MARGO: "Oh, the mousy one with the trenchcoat and the funny hat?"
2. Albee—MARTHA: "What do you take me for?"
   Mankiewicz—ADDISON: "What do you take me for?"
3. Albee—GEORGE: "Don't you condescend to me!"
   Mankiewicz—MARGO: "Don't be condescending!"
4. Albee—GEORGE: "Shucks!"
   Mankiewicz—MARGO: "Shucks. And I sent my autograph book to the cleaners."
5. Albee—GEORGE: "In my mind, Martha, you're buried in cement, right up to your neck."
   Mankiewicz—MARGO: "It is my last wish to be buried sitting up."
6. Albee—GEORGE: "I will not be made mock of!"
   Mankiewicz—MARGO: "I will not calm down! . . . I will not be tolerated. And I will not be plotted against!"
7. Albee—GEORGE: "You're spoiled, self-indulgent, dirty-minded, liquor-ridden. . . ."
   Mankiewicz—ADDISON: "You're maudlin and full of self-pity."

What does all of this prove? Only that one of Broadway's best playwrights was well acquainted with the work of one of Hollywood's best screenwriters. And that Albee had a keen ear for movie dialogue.

Although there's not a shred of evidence, it's beguiling to speculate: What if Albee intended George and Martha as Bill Sampson and Margo Channing after they've been married for years? Or, if not that, the play might be taken as a typical evening—raucous and alcoholic—with Mr. and Mrs. Gary Merrill.

If Albee pays elliptical tribute to *All About Eve*, Mart Crowley's *The Boys in the Band*, produced in 1968, throws the movie a nosegay in Act I and another in Act II. Michael, one of the main characters, subverts Margo's camp line "I detest cheap sentiment" with his ultra-camp version of it: "I *adore* cheap sentiment." Later, Michael describes another character this way: "Emory. . . . dislikes artificial fruit and flowers and coffee grinders made into lamps—and he likes Mabel Mercer, poodles, and *All About Eve*—the screenplay of which he will recite verbatim." (The fictitious Emory was based on those real "boys in the band" who memorized chunks of the screenplay and recited it at parties, especially in New York.)

One could argue that *Boys in the Band* and other plays of its ilk, by and about gays, owe more to *All About Eve* than mere passing allusions. Various dramas by Edward Albee, Mart Crowley, Terrence McNally, and other playwrights seem not only stylistically but also thematically indebted to *Eve*. Similarities of style and language are obvious: Many of these plays attempt crisp, bitchy dialogue drawn from real-life gay repartee and filtered through old Hollywood movies. Epigrams, put-downs, good and bad jokes—such talk existed in gay life before Mankiewicz, of course, though *Eve* was a rich lode that helped crystallize and institutionalize it in later works.

In such Eve-ish dramas, a flamboyant queen—male or female—resembling Margo Channing is set upon by various enemies who may or may not be defeated. For example, Martha in *Who's Afraid*; Emory and others in *Boys in the Band*; the lesbian "George" in *The Killing of Sister George*; even Maria Callas in McNally's *Master Class*.

These works are highly theatrical and often succeed because of their very staginess. They're usually well-made plays in which originality is subordinate to the pungent camp, general "Macbethishness," and, sometimes, lavish sentimentality. The end of *Boys in the Band*, for instance, is downright maudlin: Michael heads off to "a midnight mass at St. Malachy's that all the show people go to."

Charles Ludlam, founder of New York's Ridiculous Theatrical Company and author of such plays as *When Queens Collide, Stage Blood,* and *Camille,* must have subsumed *All About Eve* along with his other influences: costume dramas, grand opera, penny dreadfuls, the glossy kitsch of pop culture, and especially the movies of Maria Montez. As playwright and actor (often in drag), Ludlam always seemed on the verge of outdoing every diva in history. A critic once wrote that Ludlam's voice was "an amalgam of Gloria Swanson, Bette Davis, and Tallulah Bankhead on a wet day." Ludlam himself—who, like Mankiewicz, drew upon Oscar Wilde—uttered this epigram to an interviewer: "It's not easy to play a woman. I often think it must be hard for a woman to play a woman." Margo Channing couldn't have said it better.

In the early 1960s *Eve* started to turn up on television. Soon it was a *Late Show* staple. It became a revival house favorite as well, and by the 1970s a Siamese-twin double bill of *All About Eve* and *Sunset Boulevard* played frequently at the Carnegie Hall Cinema and Theatre 80 Saint Marks in New York and in similar movie houses in San Francisco and Los Angeles. All those fans who had memorized the script flocked to these revival theatres again and again, where they recited dialogue in sync with the characters on-screen. They acted—or acted up—right along with Bette. They even upstaged her, for their performances grew so unrestrained you couldn't hear anything else during long stretches of the movie.

Mankiewicz himself joined in the fun. His last film, *Sleuth* (1972) has a cast of two: Laurence Olivier and Michael Caine. Seven names appear in the credits, however; one of the false cast members is "Eve Channing." This in-joke is rather arch. Wittier was Mankiewicz's statement, when Olivier and Caine both ended up in the Oscar race, that he was the only director ever to have his entire cast nominated for Academy Awards.

It was also in 1972 that Mankiewicz tried, rather ignobly, to tamper with another writer's work. The book in question is *More About "All About Eve."* It has the peculiar subtitle *A Colloquy by Gary Carey with Joseph L. Mankiewicz, Together With His Screenplay "All About Eve."* The odd thing about that subtitle is that it conceals so much—e.g., who the author really is and what the book is about. But in view of the muddle that beset the project, that gauche subtitle (dreamed up by Mankiewicz) seems a fair compromise. I recently asked Gary Carey about it, and this is what he said:

"The plan was to publish a series of important film scripts with introductions, annotations, and the like. The publisher wanted Mankiewicz to write the introduction to *All About Eve*, but he preferred having another writer interview him. His first choice was Mart Crowley, but Crowley wasn't interested. I'm not sure why. One reason they approached me was because, a year earlier, for Pauline Kael's *The Citizen Kane Book*, I had prepared five pages of notes on the shooting script of *Citizen Kane*. So the editor recommended me as the interviewer and Mankiewicz agreed.

"The publisher wanted the introductory interview fairly brief, about twenty-five or thirty pages. So I took the train up to Pound Ridge, New York, interviewed Joe, and found him charming. I asked my questions, and he answered them. I wrote it up and it ran to about thirty pages.

"I turned it in and the editor was happy with it. He sent it to Mankiewicz to check. When it came back to me it was at least twice as long, maybe longer. That's when I realized that he probably didn't know how to structure this kind of nonfiction. So what I had done was provide the structure. At which point he began to rewrite the dialogue. Specifically, he rewrote his own stuff. He expanded it, changed things around, and the result was that it lost all spontaneity.

"I didn't object to his rewriting his own statements. Okay, I thought, if that's the way he wants it—but he had also rewritten mine. And this is where the trouble started.

"Because he had edited the transcript so that I was saying things like, '*All About Eve* is the greatest comedy of manners since *School for Scandal*.' I didn't believe that, and I didn't want to go on record as saying it. So I made some noise to the editor. He passed along my objections to Mankiewicz, at which point Joe became outraged. He told the editor. 'If he's so upset about the whole thing, I'll take his name off it.' My response was, 'Fine, let him have the discussion with himself!'

"What eventually took place was this: A meeting was arranged with

Joe, his agent Robert Lantz, and me. It was a breakfast meeting at one of those hotels near Fifth Avenue and Fifty-ninth Street, maybe the Sherry Netherland, although I'm not sure after all these years.

"It turned out to be pleasant and civilized. Joe was kind of pissed that I wouldn't go along with what *he* thought I thought about the movie. But he agreed finally to reinstate my material—to put back what I had originally said in the way I had said it. And that's all I cared about. I didn't want to come out looking like a horse's ass. The restorations were made, which was all I had demanded. Ultimately, I felt that Mankiewicz treated me fairly, though he did everything he could to keep my name out of any publicity about the book. That was fine, too, because I was paid a flat fee and therefore got no royalties. And the book didn't do very well anyway.

"I ran into Joe a few times in later years at critics' parties and screenings, and our meetings were cordial. In the end, I came to be amused by the book episode. I learned a lot from it. One of the things it taught me was that I wanted nothing to do with Hollywood."

And Carey did avoid Hollywood, though in later years he wrote biographies of some of its leading citizens, including Katharine Hepburn, Marlon Brando, Judy Holliday, and Louis B. Mayer.

When the book was published, Mankiewicz told a reporter, "I'm a pain in the ass with interviewers. Because too often they take it upon themselves to rephrase me, and if you make your living writing you don't like to be rewritten in midair, so to speak." He said he found his own quotes in the first draft "simplistic, skimpy, uninteresting," and had therefore rewritten them.

Whether one accepts Mankiewicz's version or Carey's, the "colloquy" between them speaks for itself. (The word *colloquy*, chosen by Mankiewicz, is defined by some dictionaries as a conversation that is "formal or mannered.") In this instance, Mankiewicz's side of the conversation is not only mannered, it's baroque. His comments on *All About Eve*, and his account of the rest of his career, are sometimes fascinating. His lengthy digressions, however, are maddening, and though the book is ostensibly a "biography" of *Eve*, it's only through Carey's clear journalism that the reader gets any of the "who, what, when, and where." Mankiewicz supplies the "why," but too often it's turgid and meandering.

Mankiewicz at his worst, however, was less turgid than Rainer Werner Fassbinder, the German director who paid him a dubious compliment in *The Bitter Tears of Petra Von Kant* (1972). One could go mad watching Fassbinder's films, and madder still trying to locate his "meanings." And so a brief pause only, to note the letter that lesbian fashion designer Petra Von Kant dictates to her mute secretary, Marlene. The letter is directed to a moneylender named Joseph Mankiewicz. In her silky "professional" voice Petra dictates, "Dear Mankiewicz, dear friend," then leaves the rest of her message to Marlene's discretion.

Is this allusion perhaps faintly anti-Semitic—pairing Mankiewicz's name with an occupation once reserved for Jews, who were in turn condemned for their "sin" of usury? More likely, Fassbinder intended an abstruse compliment.

In 1977 the Canadian film *Outrageous!* starred chubby Craig Russell as a hairdresser whose night job is impersonating Garland, Streisand, Bankhead, et al., onstage at gay bars. For his first club date Russell wears a scarlet version of Margo Channing's off-the-shoulders gown. But instead of "Fasten your seat belts" he starts off with "What a dump!" and from there lapses into Bette-and-Joan shtick from *Baby Jane*. Surprisingly, his Bette Davis/Margo number is the weakest in his repertoire. He's much funnier as the other Channing—Carol.

About the same time, but light-years from such drag monkeyshines, Films Inc. (a company that supplied classic movies to various nonprofit groups) put out an *All About Eve* discussion guide for use by schools, church groups, and cinema clubs. The brochure, written by a professor at Southern Methodist University in Dallas, was entitled *Dialogue With the World*. A brief introduction of the film ends with forced theological insight: "One of the things we say in the Church about the Crucifixion is that it unmasked evil and showed it for what it really was. In a similar manner, the gradual 'crucifixion' of Margo reveals to us the true complexion and inner workings of the evil that makes a god of selfish ambition." (The closest Margo comes to such deep thoughts is when she likens Eve's love of the theatre to "all the religions in the world rolled into one, and we're gods and goddesses.")

On the last page of its last issue of the 1970s, *Esquire* in December 1979 ran a full-page caricature of the *All About Eve* cast, drawn by Edward Sorel. Three cast members were conspicuous by their absence from the cartoon: Thelma Ritter, Hugh Marlowe, and Celeste Holm.

With each new decade, *All About Eve* became an increasingly recognizable American—and international—institution. Its characters and its dialogue were so familiar that they began to function as touchstones in the media and as shorthand in the marketplace.

In *Evil Under the Sun* (1982) Roddy McDowell played Rex Brewster, a prissy gossip columnist who reminded some reviewers of Addison DeWitt.

Not long after that, when Joan Collins was guest of honor on Dean Martin's televised *Celebrity Roast*, Anne Baxter appeared not so much to skewer Joan as to contribute a note of civility to an evening of cruel put-downs. Baxter pointed out that Alexis Carrington, whom Collins portrayed on *Dynasty*, had learned some lessons in villainy from Eve Harrington. Baxter added that the two characters' names even echoed each other.

Alan Rudolph's 1984 film *Choose Me* is sprinkled with sly allusions to *Eve*. The first shot in the movie is a neon sign of "Eve's Lounge," owned and operated by Eve (Lesley Ann Warren.) A bit later, Warren utters an "Oh, brother" with a Thelma Ritter inflection; there is a character named Max; and in Rae Dawn Chong's apartment the camera pans posters from many movies, including *All About Eve*. Scraps of dialogue seem to have mutated from the Mankiewicz script, as when Chong says to Warren, "I'm telling you, Eve—woman to woman." (Addison DeWitt and Eve Harrington talk "champion to champion" and "killer to killer.") Geneviève Bujold says she has never loved anyone. (Addison to Eve: "We have . . . an inability to love and be loved.") Bujold, as radio sex therapist Dr. Nancy Love, speaks in a much lower, sexier voice when she's on the air, indicating that Anne Baxter's upper and lower registers in *Eve* may have given her the idea.

In 1985 a group of British singers formed a gothic rock group called All About Eve. They are often referred to as "the Eves." From their songs and from information on their two Web sites, they must have chosen their name only because it struck them as euphonious, not because they felt any connection to the movie. It's quite possible that "the Eves" have never seen *Eve*.

The 1987 movie, *Anna*, is like a deconstruction of *All About Eve*, for in it we see the grunge and not the glamour of life in the theatre. The movie is about the humiliation of over-the-hill actors who are out of work and desperate for any job at all. Sally Kirkland plays the middle-aged refugee Anna Radkova, a former film star in Czechoslovakia who can't find a niche in America. Paulina Porizkova plays Kristina, also a Czech refugee, but a young, pretty one—an ambitious ingenue.

In a melodramatic variation on Eve Harrington, Kristina arrives penniless in New York and faints from hunger at the feet of ex–movie star Kirkland, who takes her in. Soon Kristina learns English and lands a Hollywood contract.

If you want to see a movie about an aging actress with everything but the bloodhounds snappin' at her rear end, this is the one to see. Anna, in a self-pitying Margo Channing mode, tells the ingenue: "You can borrow my life. Do whatever you want with it." "Thank you," says the younger woman. And she takes Anna literally. She appropriates Anna's life story—imprisonment, escape from the Iron Curtain, loss of career and family, etc.—and recounts it as her own on a TV interview show. Whereupon Anna throws Kristina's possessions out the window into the street.

Many years earlier, Margo Channing only threatened to "stuff that pathetic little lost lamb down Mr. DeWitt's ugly throat." But Anna doesn't stop at threats: She shoots the young usurper, then suffers a nervous breakdown. Kristina, recovered and back on the set, supplies the voice-over denouement of this low-camp trinket by informing us that she has paid for a face-lift for her benefactress so that Anna can restart her career in Hollywood.

The year *Anna* came out, a theatre in New York held a Seven Deadly Sins Festival. The sins were represented by the following pictures:

Greed by Erich von Stroheim's *Greed* (1924); Lust by F. W. Murnau's *Sunrise* (1927); Envy by *All About Eve*; Gluttony by Percy Adlon's *Sugarbaby* (1985); Sloth by Nikita Mikhalkov's *Oblomov* (1979); Pride by Orson Welles's *The Magnificent Ambersons* (1942); and Anger by Fritz Lang's *Fury* (1936).

In 1988 Bette Davis made a commercial for Equal sweetener. Bette isn't seen; instead, a little girl of ten or so lip-syncs her distinctive voice. The little girl wears a Margo Channing hairdo and gown. A pint-size grande dame, the child sits at a restaurant table while the contrived little vignette plays itself out. The commercial itself is no better and no worse than most. What's interesting, though, is the advertiser's assumption that millions of TV viewers will not only recognize Davis's voice but will also get the Margo Channing allusion.

Merchandising efforts using various cast members from *All About Eve* started even before the film was released. The exhibitor's manual, prepared by 20th Century-Fox for theatre owners, shows Anne Baxter and Hugh Marlowe in print ads for Black & Decker's electric tool kits. From the *Saturday Evening Post*, November 1950: "Take a Tip from Anne Baxter: Put Home-Utility on Your Christmas Gift List!"

Elsewhere in the exhibitor's manual: "To add momentum to your campaign for *All About Eve*, a giant nationwide promotion has been set up in conjunction with the distributors of Sortilège, the famed French perfume. Special window displays, poster art, etc., will be used setting off this distinguished promotion. In addition, scene stills from the film will be used showing stars Bette Davis, Anne Baxter, George Sanders, and Celeste Holm seated in the famous Stork Club where Sortilège has become a noted table favor."

Even then, merchants found Marilyn's image irresistible. From the same page of the manual: "Starlet, Marilyn Monroe, featured in *All About Eve*, lends her beauty to an endorsement of Sortilège that will be included in this exciting promotion package. Her picture will appear wherever the perfume is sold." The list of stores included Neiman Marcus and Jordan Marsh.

By the 1990s, when Marilyn Monroe was as famous as God, her name and signature, now registered trademarks, were used as often as permission could be secured from Roger Richman, the lawyer in command of her estate. Often they were merchanted in tandem with *All About Eve* as well as with her starring vehicles. Foley's Department Store in 1997 ran ads for "The Marilyn Monroe Collection (20% Off Entire Stock)." Among the items on sale were an "All About Eve Leopard Print Underwire Bra" at $25, with "Coordinating Bikini" for $12 more. Other undergarment choices included the "Gentlemen Prefer Blondes Molded Foam Slip" and a "Niagara Bra and Lace Skirt with Thong." Smart shoppers were also offered the opportunity to "join Foley's Bra and Panty Clubs." Those who did so were promised one free bra after purchasing six, or one free pair of panties after buying twelve.

Moving from underwear to formal wear, we come to the nineteen-inch hand-painted porcelain doll from the Franklin Mint in Pennsylvania. The full-page ad shows a small picture of Marilyn (cropped at the waist) in evening-gown costume from *Eve*. Beside her is the full-length doll in "shimmering white jacquard and softest faux fur. The waist of her gown is accented with silken roses, and she holds a satin evening purse in one hand. Elbow length sculptured white gloves, hand-painted shoes, and sparkling crystal drop earrings complete this memorable costume." At the top of the page, above the images, we read: "The movie was called *All About Eve* but in the end it was all about Marilyn." Which isn't true at all, but it sounds good when you're marketing dolls at $195 each, "payable in convenient monthly installments."

Margo Channing dolls, created so far by hobbyists rather than manufacturers, appear regularly in such publications as *Barbie Bazaar* and *Fashion Doll Makeovers*. Bradford Samuel, creator of a recent one, adheres to painstaking craftsmanship. For his Bette-Davis-as-Margo-Channing doll, he attached to her tiny cigarette an even tinier puff of smoke.

Although Celeste Holm appeared in some stills from *All About Eve* that helped sell Sortilège perfume, she wasn't called upon to endorse other products via her *Eve* connection.

In later years two members of the cast reached such legendary heights that contests were held to find persons resembling them. In New York, in the 1980s, there were Marilyn Monroe look-alike contests. In 1994 two plays about Bette Davis opened off-Broadway: *P. S. Bette Davis*, by Randy Allen, and *Me and Jezebel*, by Elizabeth Fuller. As a promotional gimmick for the latter, a Bette Davis look-alike contest was held in New York. The winner was James Beaman, who "seemed to know *All About Eve* by heart," according to *The New York Times*.

Woody Allen's *Bullets Over Broadway* also came out in 1994, with Dianne Wiest as an over-the-hill and over-the-top actress who deftly bypasses Margo Channing. Playing hard-boiled Helen Sinclair, she's half Norma Desmond and half Eve Harrington. Wiest even looks like an overripe middle-aged version of Eve. The resemblance is perhaps intentional, for *All About Eve* seems to loiter on the outskirts of this picture. *Eve*'s presence is veiled, however, except for one visual-and-aural quotation. That's when Helen Sinclair throws a cocktail party. Her house is full of people, the atmosphere is vivacious, and the pianist is shot from the same angle as Claude Stroud, Margo's piano player. Like Stroud, this one also plays a few bars of "Thou Swell." Allen, as director and co-writer, gives an ironic final nod to *Eve*: The understudy goes on when the star, a gangster moll, gets bumped off by a hit man because she's a lousy actress.

John Rechy, like many writers before and since, seems in thrall to *All About Eve*. In his 1988 novel, *Marilyn's Daughter*, characters from the movie appear several times side by side with actual film stars. For example: "It was one of those affairs that everyone in Hollywood attends. On a veranda, Jane Russell waved . . . and blew them a kiss. With extreme formality, Marlon Brando was introducing everyone to Movita, his new wife. John Derek at her side, Louella Parsons sat like a toad on a peacock chair. Everyone ignored Eve Harrington and her companion, Phoebe." Later, in a montage of salacious stories from *Confidential*, Rechy captures the spirit of that fifties scandal mag with zingers like UPPERS, DOWNERS, AND JUDY! and EVE HARRINGTON'S GIRL. Echoing a line from the Mankiewicz script, he writes, docudrama style, that "Jane Russell stood and applauded, champion to champion."

At some point—was it in the turbulent eighties?— Margo's most famous line widened from movie quote to American idiom. "Fasten your seat belts" is often used, on-screen and off, as a cool way of saying "Look out," "Don't mess with me," "Hold on to your hat."

In *Pretty Woman* (1990), when Richard Gere lets Julia Roberts drive his fancy car, she jumps in with the cry, "Fasten your seat belts." Dixie Carter, in an episode of *Designing Women*, drawls as she sets out to right a wrong, "Fasten your seat belts, it's going to be a bumpy night." In the March 1991 issue of *Torso*, a gay skin magazine, a four-page, XXX-rated cartoon sequence called "Heated Encounters" concludes with a sodomitic panel whose dialogue balloon is this: "Fasten your seat belts, it's going to be a bumpy evening." (One hopes the speaker's romantic aim is better than his quotesmanship.) *Fasten Your Seat Belts* is also the title of a 1990 Bette Davis biography, written by Lawrence J. Quirk.

You'll even hear it from the pulpit. At the world's largest Metropolitan Community Church, in Dallas, on Pentecost Sunday in 1999, the Reverend Delores Berry, a dynamic African-American preacher and gospel singer, was introduced like this: "Fasten your seat belts, it's going to be a rousing sermon."

Less famous phrases from the movie turn up all over the place. In an ad for a new lesbian bar, the caption is "Where the Elite Meet." *Publishers Weekly*, in an article on gay publishing trends, runs this subhead: "Is the Party Over, or Just Beginning?" The review of a mystery novel is headed, "Killer to Killer." A television documentary on Bette Davis is, predictably, "The Bumpy Ride to Stardom." These nods to *Eve* are not new. In *Touch of Evil* (1958), Janet Leigh says to Charlton Heston, "I'm very glad you're very glad"—Welles's (probably intentional) allusion to Margo's line, "I'm so happy you're happy."

The name Eve Harrington is also ubiquitous. When Ron Leibman missed several performances of *Angels in America* on Broadway, a writer for *The New York Times* stated that his understudy, Matthew Sussman, was "hardly a reprise of Eve Harrington." Leonard Maltin's *Movie and*

278 ■ *All About* "All About Eve"

Video Guide mentions an "Eve Harrington-like characterization." When Deborah Norville replaced Jane Pauley on the *Today* show, *New York* magazine likened Norville to Eve Harrington. Earlier, when Pauley replaced Barbara Walters, she too had been compared to Eve.

A made-for-TV movie on CBS in 1990 seems based on such network gossip. In *Her Wicked Ways*, Barbara Eden plays a respected television news correspondent who is stabbed in the back by ruthless newcomer Heather Locklear.

In *Sisterhood Betrayed: Women in the Workplace and the All About Eve Complex*, a 1991 self-help book aimed at career women, authors Jill Barber and Rita Watson devote chapters to both Eve and Margo: "The Eves in Our Midst," "Don't Be a Margo," "Eves at the Top," "How Margos Deal With Betrayal," and so on. In their introduction, the authors promise that the book will "teach you how to recognize the telltale signs of an Eve in others as well as in yourself" and "how to overcome betrayal anxiety." Later, in a grotesque jump from backstage conflict to current pop-psych, they explain that "Margo and Eve were in a codependency situation."

Fans of *All About Eve* continue to write about the movie, to talk about it in interviews, to exploit it commercially. In my own novel, *MMII: The Return of Marilyn Monroe* (1991), Marilyn's Miss Caswell appears in a fantasy scene. A character in Kurt Vonnegut's *Timequake* (1997) says, "The greatest movie ever, as anybody with half a brain knows, is *My Life as a Dog*. The second-greatest movie ever is *All About Eve*."

In 1998, the American Film Institute was more restrained than Vonnegut when it compiled a list of the top 100 American films. The selection was made by members of the film industry, including screenwriters, directors, actors, editors, cinematographers, executives, and historians. They ranked *All About Eve* number sixteen. Later that year *TV Guide* included *Eve* in its list of the fifty best movies to watch on television, describing it as "a smooth sip of champagne with a sprinkle of arsenic."

Director, William Friedkin, whose work includes *Boys in the Band* and *The French Connection*, first saw *All About Eve* in Chicago as a kid of twelve when it came out. He told an interviewer, "Over the years I've seen it probably twenty-five more times, and I've come to realize how brilliant it is. It gets richer and deeper for me. It really is a classic piece of American screenwriting and direction."

Isaac Mizrahi, the fashion designer, claimed with convincing extravagance that *All About Eve* taught him "the meaning of life." Specifically, Mizrahi pointed out the scene "when Celeste Holm is coming in from the alley on Broadway. She's got this mink coat on and when she takes it off, she's wearing this fantastic gray flannel jersey dress with matching gray flannel gloves. I always think, 'Isn't that so great that everything matches?'"

Paul Brown, a comedian on Comedy Central, gives "Seven Bad Reasons for Gays to Get Married." Reason Number Five: "Both of you name *All About Eve* as your favorite movie of all time." And here's Margo Channing, paired with Mildred Pierce, both in caricature, on the front of a greeting card. They're frowning at each other and holding a cake with many candles. "Happy Birthday" is the greeting. You open it and read, "From one Bitch Goddess to another."

Less amusing is a 1993 neo-disco song called "All About Eve," recorded by the group Fem 2 Fem. It's no fun; it's not even very danceable. The unfocused lyric mixes cinematic metaphors: The song starts out, "All about Eve, all about Eve, she devil, she devil, Wicked witch of the west—Hollywood, that is."

In 1999, the novelist E. Lynn Harris said in a *Publishers Weekly* interview, "I have an idea for a book: A writer is outdone by his protégé, someone who learned everything about the business from the older writer, who poured his heart out to the upstart." The interviewer asked Harris if he was planning an African-American *All About Eve*. "That's right," answered Harris. "That movie was something special."

It was bound to happen: Adult entertainment meets *All About Eve*, with more mixing of cinematic metaphors. Gay filmmaker, Marc Huestis, said, "I used to work in a video store and people would rent *All About Eve* and they would also rent *All About Steve*." Later there was *All About Yves*, and of course the inevitable "Fasten your seat belts, it's going to be a *humpy* night," spoken by George Payne in the gay skin flick *Kiss*

Today Goodbye (1980). (The prediction, of course, comes true.) *Fun Down There* (1990), a tepid turn-on with pretentions to plot, has supporting players who recite scenes from *All About Eve* and *Valley of the Dolls*.

A heterosexual turn-on with the cheesy title *The Budding of Brie*, said to follow closely the plot of *Eve*, is now extremely difficult to locate, even though it won the erotic movie equivalent of an Oscar in 1981.

Showgirls (1995) won no awards, though it would surely qualify in the category of world-class vulgarity. If Eve Harrington had hitchhiked to Broadway in tight jeans and leather jacket, she would have been a lot like Elizabeth Berkley's character, Nomi, in this hard-hearted howler. Nomi, a Las Vegas topless-and-bottomless dancer, will do anything to become the understudy of an aging headliner named Cristal.

Throughout the movie there are boneheaded winks in the direction of *All About Eve*. Nomi looks hungrily at a glitzy seminude casino revue, like Eve Harrington the first time she's backstage. Cristal, the Margo Channing figure, says, "I haven't missed a show in eight years." (Karen to Eve: "Margo just doesn't miss performances.") The first time Cristal sees her future replacement, it's when she looks up from her dressing-room table and the bold Nomi is standing in the door. Also like Eve, Nomi has an unsavory past. And when Cristal nixes her as understudy, Nomi pushes her down a flight of stairs. *Showgirls* is a good title; it's the best thing about the movie if you don't count such lines as "I chipped my tooth on a Quaalude." But it could also have been called "All About Naked Understudies."

Treacherous ingenues were around in movies long before *All About Eve*, of course. So were aging actresses, backstage melodramas, and satirical-sentimental tales about the pathos and glory of show business. Not until *Eve*, however, did any film shape all these motifs into a more or less realistic and believable account of unstoppable ambition, granite egos, and the politics of vanity. And Mankiewicz, like Molière, presented his dark drama in the form of chic comedy. It's so light on its feet that many viewers mistake it for a testimonial to playacting. That's Mankiewicz's left-handed compliment to the theatre. With his right hand—the one he wrote with—he denoted a dangerous and dishonest milieu underneath the greasepaint.

Since 1950, few movies about show biz have been untouched by *All About Eve*. Its impact was so strong—a Hollywood big bang—that moviemakers and moviegoers couldn't resist the Mankiewicz archetypes. That's why we can't watch *The Bad and the Beautiful, Imitation of Life, Anna, Bullets Over Broadway*, or a host of others without making the inevitable comparisons. The genetic code is there. Even when it's dormant, or absent—as is probably is from *The Rose* (1979), *Frances* (1982), and *The Dresser* (1983)—we look for it anyway.

Chapter 27

Why, If There's Nothing Else, There's Applause

*T*he ultimate tribute to *All About Eve* wasn't in the movies but on the Broadway stage: the hit musical *Applause*, which opened in 1970.

Although Cole Porter, in 1957, toyed with a proposal that he write the score for a musical to be made of the film, Bette Davis herself seems to have been the first person to seriously conceive such a show. In a 1964 taped conversation later heard by Davis biographer James Spada, Bette was asked, "Would you ever go back to Broadway?" She snapped, "I *hate* theatre." Mercurial as ever, a moment later she reconsidered: "But you know, I may. I'd love to do a musical version of *All About Eve*. It would be one of the great musicals of all time!"

But the obstacles, for Bette or anyone else, were formidable. For one thing, 20th Century-Fox wouldn't release the rights. In addition, by the mid-sixties *All About Eve* was considered not a classic but simply another "old" movie. Lacking political thrust and not hip enough to interest those under thirty, the film seemed irrelevant to that *engagé* decade. Most damning of all, however, in the eyes of over-thirty producers, the story lacked the crowd-pleasing schmaltz of such shows as *Man of La Mancha*, a Broadway hit in 1965, and *The Sound of Music*, which was born again as a film that same year.

Charles Strouse, the composer of *Applause*, found out all of this when he went looking for backers for a musical based on *All About Eve*. Strouse, born in 1928, had seen the film when it came out in 1950. Years later, after he and lyricist Lee Adams had formed a songwriting partnership for such Broadway shows as *Bye Bye Birdie* in 1962 and *Golden Boy* two years later, Strouse got the idea of adapting *Eve* for the musical stage.

"I had a tremendous feeling for the movie," Strouse recalls, "but I couldn't get anybody else interested in it. I approached a famous producer/director with the idea. When I told him what I had in mind—the story of Margo Channing and Eve Harrington, to be played by Ethel Merman and Carol Lawrence—he looked at me and said, 'No one is interested in the emotional problems of actors.' That was Harold Prince, by the way. I spoke to a lot of other people about the idea, and no one cared."

Strouse says these abortive conversations took place "sometime after *Golden Boy* and maybe even after *It's a Bird It's a Plane It's Superman* [1966]." His idea took further battering when *Hair* opened in late 1967 and soon became a smash hit. "Reviewers proclaimed that from then on every show would be a rock musical. And they were right—for a time," Strouse says. "During the next couple of years everybody was producing rock shows, and they were all failing. Then *Applause* opened and it was a dynamic success."

The road to vindication, however, was long and winding. The Charles Strouse–Lee Adams musical *It's a Bird It's a Plane It's Superman* closed after a disappointing run of 129 performances. It was their last show for four years.

In the meantime, Strouse went to Hollywood in 1967 to compose the music for *Bonnie and Clyde*. His office at Warner Bros. was near the office of Sidney Michaels, a playwright whose biggest hit on Broadway was *Dylan* (1964), with Alec Guinness in the role of the bibulous Welsh poet. Michaels, who had come to Hollywood to write screenplays, was in an office across the hall from Warren Beatty's. It was at Warner Bros. that he met Strouse.

Sidney Michaels recalls, "I was working on a script that never got filmed. They wanted some kind of follow-up to *Rebel Without a Cause*, so I went to San Francisco and looked around at the flower children. I came back thrilled and reported what I had seen. Jack Warner was horrified! But it didn't matter anyway, because a few days later he sold the studio to Seven Arts, so that was the end of my screenplay."

Michaels, who was born in 1927, had written a number of television dramas in the 1950s. In 1960 he wrote the script for the film *Key Witness*, directed by Phil Karlson, and in 1968 he collaborated with Arnold Schulman and Norman Lear on the script of William Friedkin's *The Night They Raided Minsky's*.

It was during their hectic months at Warner Bros. in the early part of 1967 that Charles Strouse approached Sidney Michaels with his idea for a musical based on *All About Eve*. At that point the show was still no more than a good idea. Michaels recalls that Strouse and Adams had not yet started the music when they asked if he would be interested in writing the book. Like everyone else in show business, Michaels had seen the movie in 1950. "I thought it was magnificent," he says. "So of course I was excited about the idea of a musical based on *All About Eve*." But first he told the eager composers, "Let's get the Mankiewicz screenplay."

They couldn't. Twentieth Century-Fox refused them permission to use any part of the script, and Mankiewicz himself was out of the loop. As the studio's employee, he had of course relinquished all rights to his work.

By mid-1967 Charles Strouse had finished composing the music for *Bonnie and Clyde*. Sidney Michaels had ceased work on the abortive flower-child script, and both had returned to New York. That's when *Applause* first began to take shape. Week by week Strouse and Adams wrote songs and lyrics, which they sometimes kept but also often tossed out. Work went faster now that the problem of the libretto had been solved.

Since they couldn't use *All About Eve*, they did the next best thing: They bought rights to Mary Orr's story, "The Wisdom of Eve." Or rather, Lawrence Kasha and Joseph Kipness bought the rights, for they had become producers of the nascent musical. In the late forties, when Mary

Orr and her agent sold the story to Fox, they had retained stage rights, scarcely imagining the day when those rights might actually earn money. But that day had finally arrived. "This time, at least, I was one up on 20th Century-Fox," crowed Mary Orr many years later.

Lawrence Kasha (1933–1990), a Brooklyn native, worked in regional theatre as a producer and director before coming to Broadway in 1963 as co-producer of *She Loves Me*. In 1964 he was associate director of *Funny Girl*, and two years later he staged a revival of *Show Boat* for the opening of the New York State Theatre at Lincoln Center.

Joseph Kipness (1911–1982), a Russian immigrant who came to this country at the age of twelve, made and lost several fortunes during his lifetime. In 1929 he started a freight company in the Manhattan garment district with one horse and one wagon. He expanded into the trucking business and the manufacture of women's clothes, and later owned several restaurants, including Dinty Moore's and the Stagedoor Canteen. His first big success as a Broadway producer was *High Button Shoes*, which opened in 1947 and ran for 727 performances. He produced some thirty plays in all, mostly musicals. Many were flops, but no matter how much money he lost, he was always stagestruck. He once told an interviewer, "The theatre has given me more happiness than I ever received in my life from anything else."

Once Kasha and Kipness had secured rights to the Mary Orr story, Sidney Michaels forged ahead. He recalls working on the libretto by himself, then meeting Strouse and Adams periodically. "We worked together the way you always do," he says. "You write something, you read it to each other, you play songs, you keep some things and reject others, you discuss and discuss and then you go back to work again."

At that point the show was called *Welcome to the Theatre*, a title that was later transferred to one of its most memorable songs. According to Lee Adams, *Make Believe* served briefly as the title, then it was called *Applause, Applause* and finally shortened.

As the show took shape, its producers tried to interest Anne Bancroft in playing Margo Channing. She, however, refused to sign a minimum one-year contract, fearing that boredom would set in after so many performances of the same role.

Asked if he had anyone in mind for the show while writing his early drafts, Michaels says, "Lauren Bacall was under consideration from the outset. I was strongly in favor of her. In fact, I believe I was the first to suggest her."

What happened next, at least the way Sidney Michaels remembers it, might be a scene from a movie—or from *Applause* itself. "I went to the theatre one night with my wife and we sat next to Jason Robards and Lauren Bacall, who were married at that time. I knew him, but not her. I explained to Jason that I was working on a musical based on *All About Eve* and asked if I could show him the script—intended for his wife, of course. I happened to have it with me that night. Jason said, 'Fine.' He took it and handed it to her. That's how she got it, right there in a seat in the theatre. She read it and said she'd love to do it."

Bacall, in her autobiography *By Myself*, is less specific. She writes, "I was approached about a musical version of *All About Eve*. The book was being written; nothing else was set." A possible reason for the star's vagueness is that, as the show moved forward, there were some bumpy nights. Before need arose to fasten seat belts, however, a director had to be found. It wasn't easy.

According to Sidney Michaels, "We went to Ron Field after going to almost every director we could think of. We knew he was very talented, so we took it to him but he didn't like it much."

Ron Field (1934–1989) was born in Queens and began his career across the river in Manhattan as a child actor in the original production of *Lady in the Dark* (1941). He danced in such musicals as *Gentlemen Prefer Blondes* (1949) and *The Boy Friend* (1954). In 1962 he choreographed the off-Broadway revival of *Anything Goes*. This soon led to jobs as a Broadway choreographer.

Field had never directed a Broadway show when the team from *Applause* went to see him. Some choreographers would have jumped at the chance; Field was cautious. No doubt he wanted his directorial debut to be auspicious. He also realized the danger of trying to remake *All About Eve* for the stage. "I was bucking a movie of great renown," he said.

When Ron Field demurred, Sidney Michaels told his colleagues, "Listen, I think we're going to keep on giving this play to directors and they're going to keep on turning us down. I'd better readdress the libretto, because there's obviously something wrong with it." So he did. "I sat down for the next two weeks, rewrote the entire book, and this time when Ron Field read it he flipped. He said, 'I'll do it.' And the next thing I knew they were asking me to leave!"

We have several very different versions of why the producers fired Sidney Michaels. According to Michaels himself, it was because of producer Lawrence Kasha. (The other producer, Joseph Kipness, was an old friend of Michaels. In fact, Michaels claims to have been instrumental in getting Kipness to co-produce.)

"Larry Kasha had a desire to direct the play," says Michaels, seemingly without rancor some three decades after the event. "He invited me to his apartment one night and said, 'I'm going to tell you my plans. We'll use Ron Field and then when we get out of town I will take over the direction of the show.' I said, 'Oh, I don't think so. I don't think that's such a great idea, Larry.' And he said, 'Oh really? Well, we'll see.' And the next thing I knew I was informed that I was out because they didn't like my book."

No one else connected with the show concedes such skullduggery. Lee Adams says, "My recollection is that we parted company because we didn't think Sidney was writing the same show we were." Both producers are now deceased. Kasha, however, told an interviewer in 1977: "I hired Strouse and Adams because I liked their work. At that time a writer named Sidney Michaels did the first couple of drafts of the script. And although I thought it was good, it wasn't good enough and I didn't believe that his script could work, and early on I had to ask him to leave. So we let him go and made a settlement with him and I hired Betty Comden and Adolph Green to do the book."

Charles Strouse insists that Sidney Michaels' book was rejected for a different reason. This is his version of events: "What happened on the road to Oz, so to speak, is that at a certain point in our work Lee Adams and I played the score for Lauren Bacall. She really liked it. Although she wasn't yet ready to commit herself, she said she wanted to play the role of Margo Channing.

"The show wasn't yet complete, however, at least not in her view. We got to know her better, we worked with her on some of the songs, but official rehearsals hadn't begun. As we went further along, she said she couldn't play Sidney's book.

"She was the linchpin, of course, the one who was making the show happen. Since she was so positive about the songs—Lee's and my work—we had to pursue what she wanted to pursue. And what she wanted was to bring in Comden and Green to write a new book."

Lauren Bacall, in her published account, is once again vague. Her deft use of the passive voice omits details: "A settlement had to be made with the first writer—the decision had been made to replace him. The powers that be asked how I felt about Betty Comden and Adolph Green taking over."

Sidney Michaels speculates that Bacall might have been averse to his book because "it had an equally large male lead opposite her. I heard she was upset over that; she refused even to answer her phone."

Certainly at this point everyone involved in the show was at a disadvantage, the main reason being that they wanted to do a musical version of *All About Eve*, a property that simply wasn't available to them. Mary Orr's "The Wisdom of Eve" contains the juicy kernel of the film, but the story is slight and contrived. It lacks the witty Mankiewicz dialogue and also the breadth of his cynicism about the theatre and those in it. Although the story's three main characters—Margola Cranston, Eve Harrington, and the playwright's wife, who narrates—are cleverly delineated, they are all female. In other words, the Orr story lacks a leading man. A further handicap is that it has none of those unforgettable supporting characters who helped make the movie so enjoyable.

As dissatisfaction with Michaels' book increased, Lawrence Kasha, through his lawyers, continued negotiations with 20th Century-Fox for rights to the Mankiewicz screenplay. In the 1977 interview quoted above, he detailed the process: "I went to David Brown, who's now a partner of Dick Zanuck of Zanuck and Brown. He was then in charge of East Coast operations for Fox. I knew David and we talked about the project. I told him what I wanted to do and he said, 'Well, contact the legal department and go through all that and I'll tell them of your interest and the things you've produced.' With his help and a little bit of persistence on my part I acquired the rights from Fox."

It's impossible to construct a precise chronology of *Applause* as it lurched from the Michaels libretto toward the new one by Comden and Green. A Charles Strouse aphorism seems especially relevant to those days of creativity and creative differences: "You'll find in the theatre that everybody remembers something quite different."

From Sidney Michaels' recollections, however, it appears that the producers waited to fire him until they had his replacements lined up. This is his account of the coup de grâce: "A meeting was called in Charlie Strouse's living room. Everybody was there—Joe Kipness, Larry Kasha, Strouse and Adams, Ron Field. We all sat down and it was Larry Kasha who said they weren't happy with the book I had written, except for Ron Field, who always said he loved it. They informed me that they wanted something entirely different. When I left I said, 'I don't want you to use a word of my script. So now you've got the Mankiewicz script, terrific. Use it.' They did ask if they could keep the structure I had created, the scenes in the restaurant and the subplot stuff, and I said yes. So they kept that."

Unlike an MGM musical with Judy Garland and Mickey Rooney, a real show is fraught with maddening setbacks. For whatever ornery or perverse reasons, 20th Century-Fox *did* and *didn't* grant rights to the Mankiewicz screenplay.

In May 1969, when Betty Comden and Adolph Green were called in by the producers to write a new libretto, Lawrence Kasha had not yet secured any rights at all from Fox. Soon, however, through the efforts of the producers' lawyers, the studio granted its oddly incongruous permission for the writers to use "a limited amount" of material from the film. "Only we didn't know what 'a limited amount' meant," Betty Comden said. "It can be very dangerous guessing about the meaning of such things." Adolph Green added, "We were also prohibited from using any character that wasn't in the original Orr story. That meant the part of the critic, played in the movie by George Sanders, had to go."

During the summer of 1969, Comden and Green completed two rewrites of the show, in which they developed their own characters. By the second rewrite, these characters—including Margo Channing, Bill Sampson, and Eve Harrington—had evolved rather far from those of the Orr story as well as from those in *All About Eve*. For example, the

Margo of *Applause* started her career in the movies and then moved to Broadway, à la Lauren Bacall. Among a host of other changes, the character of Addison DeWitt was split into two unequal parts: that of the producer, Howard Benedict (played by Robert Mandan), and the smaller part of a cheap Broadway columnist, Stan Harding (played by Ray Becker).

Suddenly, in a late-summer beau geste, Fox granted full rights to the movie script, possibly because Lauren Bacall had been officially announced as the star. She had just signed a run-of-the-play contract for ten thousand dollars a week. By then, however, the creative team of *Applause* had solved most of its problems and no longer required studio largesse. "Actually, we used very little of the movie script," said Adolph Green. In the published version there are roughly a dozen lines taken verbatim from *All About Eve*.

The decision to incorporate less rather than more of the Mankiewicz screenplay was made in view of artistic demands, as Comden and Green later explained: "*All About Eve* is made up of almost two-and-a-half hours of brilliant dialogue and situations which had to be adapted into a show that could contain no more than an hour-and-a-quarter of dialogue to allow for at least an equal amount of music and dance—and which could emerge on its own with a new and vital identity. And of course the film had to be metamorphosed into musical theatre that would be less 'all about Eve' and more 'all about Margo.' "

At the outset, Comden and Green had been reluctant to take the assignment, the main reason being that in all their successful years together they had never done *only* the book to a musical. They had always written the lyrics as well. But Strouse the composer and Adams the lyricist had already completed much of the score by the time Comden and Green were hired.

It was a difficult decision. Not only were they unable, initially, to use the Mankiewicz script, they were also reluctant to tamper with a classic movie that so many people knew almost by heart. A further disadvantage was not being asked to write the lyrics and, in Betty Comden's words, "Sometimes when you work with an old friend things don't turn out well." The old friend was Lauren Bacall.

Bacall had met Comden and Green years earlier in Hollywood. The three became close friends, and Bacall says she was as nervous about working together as they were. Despite her hesitation, however, Charles Strouse recalls that she was the one who demanded Comden and Green. Betty Comden herself, when asked "Was it Lauren Bacall who suggested to the producers that they bring in you and Adolph Green to write a new book?" answered elliptically, "I've heard that."

If Bacall engineered Sidney Michaels' replacement, she surely had sound artistic reasons for doing so. She also had too much at stake professionally to go after any talent but the best, friendship or no. Comden and Green must have struck her as the best possible team for *Applause*, since they had written the scripts for such popular backstage satires as *The Barkleys of Broadway* (1949), *Singin' in the Rain* (1952), and *The Band Wagon* (1953). Highly regarded by both Broadway and Hollywood, Comden and Green commanded more fame, prestige, and box-office draw than Strouse and Adams. More, in fact, than anyone in the show except Bacall herself.

As it turned out, working together placed no strain on the friendship. Comden says, "This was a perfectly professional relationship all the way. In other words, the work was the work and if we saw each other for dinner, that was a separate thing. There was no running to talk to her without consulting the director. We were the authors, she was the star, and everything went through the director, as it should. We came out of it close friends. I have happy memories of that show." When the libretto was published in 1971, Comden and Green dedicated it to Bacall.

Reading that libretto now, it's easy to find fault. Inevitably, the greatest temptation is to criticize it for what it isn't; and it isn't *All About Eve*. Rather, it reads like a paraphrase of Mankiewicz, minus censorship. In place of his psychological insight, his shrewd view of why fulfillment in the theatre is, for many, worth all the risks, Comden and Green supply mainly a PR notion of life on the stage. In their libretto even the suffering and betrayal are whittled down to rueful one-liners. A typical example of psychology replaced by shtick is this exchange from Scene Two of *Applause*:

MARGO

That line reminds me, *and* the audience, I'm playing someone considerably younger than myself.

BILL

You're sick, Margo.

MARGO

No—I'm forty.

In places, the libretto evokes an early-seventies sitcom: Margo to Bill as he leaves for Rome: "Hey, don't eat too much pasta. I want to be able to get my arms around you when you come back."

On the other hand, a libretto is not intended to stand alone. It's one piece of machinery in the vast spectacle of a musical show. Looked at from another angle, the Comden and Green libretto is the foundation of a stylish edifice constructed to encase the talents of Lauren Bacall and a number of other show people. Their work wasn't intended to compete with *All About Eve*. It was written as a deft variation on the Mankiewicz theme.

Aaron Frankel, who taught workshops in musical-theatre writing at the New School for Social Research in New York, describes the process of musical adaptations: "It is necessary to move *completely* from one medium with its conditions to another with very different conditions. The spirit of the source material is what must be cleaved to, and the letter forsaken. The aim of an adaptation is to exist as a clearly new experience."

The new experience in question started to rev up early in November of 1969. There was a reading of *Applause* at Ron Field's home on West Fourth Street in Greenwich Village, with actors, authors, and composers present. This meeting was of course full of excitement and promise. It was also politely tentative and, for a gathering of show people, somewhat reserved. Bacall explains why: "This was the first meeting of actors who were going to work together for a long time to come. Along with the others, I was quite self-conscious at first, then I had to rise above who and what the rest of the company thought I was. The main problem for me was that they all came in with their minds made up."

By the end of the evening, however, those present felt that the ice was broken. The general impression among younger cast members was that Bacall wasn't expecting star treatment. In Ron Field's living room she seemed more like Brooklyn's Betty Perske (her real name) than Hollywood's Lauren Bacall. After the read-through, Field served drinks, and by the end of the evening the consensus was that *Applause* was off to a good start.

The following week the cast went into formal rehearsal for two months. Bacall had started voice lessons in September. These continued. She also enrolled in a gym, and took dance classes with Ron Field's assistant, Tommy Rolla.

Although Bacall had always wanted to do a musical, when the time came she was scared. And understandably so, because she had never sung or danced professionally. She was also forty-five years old and had made only a handful of films since Bogart's death in 1957. No one would come right out and say it, but Lauren Bacall had evolved into a legendary bystander. She was the most famous widow in Hollywood.

Back in New York, her hometown, she had done two earlier plays. *Goodbye Charlie* opened in 1959 and lasted for only 109 performances. *Cactus Flower*, which opened in 1965, was a hit. Bacall played it for two years.

The lead in *Applause*, however, was bigger than anything yet. It could turn her into a new kind of star. Or finish her off. Later, in her book *Now*, she put into words the emotions she felt at the time.

> The Margo Channing of *Applause* and myself were ideally suited. She was approaching middle age; so was I. She was insecure; so was I. She was being forced to face the fact that her career would have to move into another phase as younger women came along to play younger parts; so was I. And she constantly felt that the man she was in love with was going to go off with someone else, of course someone younger, and I, too, had had those feelings. So Margo and I had a great deal in common.

Bacall was actually in a deeper crisis than Margo Channing. Margo, a star in great demand, must learn to act her age, onstage and off. She must also battle a younger rival while trying to calm her paranoiac fears that Bill is about to desert her. Bacall, on the other hand, wasn't getting any film offers, she had just divorced Jason Robards after an eight-year marriage, and her mother's recent death had left her devastated. She had every reason to work harder than she had ever worked before. If *Applause* didn't work, Lauren Bacall might soon be the name of a Hollywood remnant.

Facing the challenge and the risks of the show, she bulldozed ahead with a gutsy pronouncement that might have come from a Bogart-Bacall movie: "I've made an ass of myself before."

The first day of rehearsal started off with the press. Reporters and photographers milled around. Ron Field and Bacall performed a couple of dance steps from Margo's big number. Flashbulbs and questions: "How do you feel about doing a musical, Miss Bacall?" Then the press left and hard work began.

Len Cariou played Bill Sampson. In the play Bill is eight years younger than Margo; in reality Cariou was fifteen years junior to Bacall. Born in Canada in 1939, he had acted primarily at the Stratford Shakespeare Festival in Ontario and at the Guthrie Theatre in Minneapolis before making his Broadway debut in *The House of Atreus* in 1968. As a newcomer to the New York stage, Cariou of course had much to gain from *Applause*. Musically he had an advantage, since he possessed a smooth, creamy singing voice that recalled Gordon MacRae's. The fortuitous romance that blazed up between Cariou and Bacall during tryouts in Baltimore also proved an aesthetic asset onstage. Like Bette Davis and Gary Merrill twenty years earlier, *this* Margo and Bill saw to it that life imitated art.

In the process of translating *All About Eve* to the stage and updating it for the 1969–70 Broadway season, Comden and Green gave Birdie Coonan, the Thelma Ritter character, a sex change. In *Applause* Birdie is replaced by Duane Fox, Margo's hairdresser and confidant.

Ron Field spotted an actor in the movie *Star!* who he thought might be just the one to play Duane. The actor was tall, handsome Garrett Lewis. In the 1968 picture, starring Julie Andrews as Gertrude Lawrence, Lewis played actor-producer-director Jack Buchanan, one of

Lawrence's colleagues in the London theatre. Lewis seemed to have it all: looks, a singing voice, experience as a dancer, and a Broadway résumé that included *My Fair Lady* and *Hello, Dolly.*

In Los Angeles, Garrett Lewis got a call from his agent asking him to fly to New York to audition for *Applause.* "I talked with Ron for a long time about the show," Lewis recalls. "He had a particular interpretation in mind for the role of Duane. The character was a gay guy but Ron said, 'I don't want him to come across as a gay stereotype. For once, if there's a homosexual onstage I'd like him *not* to be effeminate.' "

When Garrett Lewis auditioned for the part of Duane Fox in the fall of 1969, homosexuality was just officially out of the closet, even in New York. The Stonewall riots had erupted a few months earlier, in June. Up to then, even the most "advanced" portrayals of gays on stage and screen were largely stereotypical, as in *The Boys in the Band.* So the character of Duane Fox as written by Comden and Green, and as envisioned by Ron Field, was a departure from the usual stock portrayals.

"It was tricky for males in show business at that time," Garrett Lewis says. "And being a dancer certainly had an onus. I had built up a non-stereotypical image in my work, and I wasn't interested in ruining it. The part of Duane seemed 'safe,' so I took it."

Lewis signed a run-of-the-play contract. He flew back to Los Angeles to pack, then moved into a big apartment in Manhattan expecting to be there for a while. "I had heard horror stories about Lauren Bacall," he laughs, "but I didn't experience anything like that."

At rehearsals, Lewis seemed to stick out because of his height. He's six foot three. The first time Bacall saw him she exclaimed, "My God, he's so *big!*" He towered over Len Cariou, who said at the audition, "I don't know if I can be on the same stage with him."

After several weeks of rehearsals, Lewis and his agent felt that some of those connected with the show—Comden and Green, or perhaps Strouse and Adams, or maybe the producers—wanted more of a certain kind of humor in his portrayal of Duane Fox. Lewis also perceived a certain dissatisfaction with the fact that he and Cariou were, in a sense, both leading men. It was all very unspecific, according to Lewis, but someone seemed to want a more recognizably homosexual interpretation of Duane, Margo's hairdresser. Was Garrett Lewis too butch? The question hovered at every rehearsal, unasked and unanswered.

In Act I, Scene Two, shortly after the initial encounter of Margo and Eve, Margo asks Duane to escort her and her new friend out on the town. "I've got a date," he says. "Bring him along," says Margo, which is the libretto's only explicit reference to Duane's homosexuality. Margo's matter-of-fact line—and Bacall's delivery of it—were commendably nonstereotypical. Indeed, *Applause* was a minor landmark as the first Broadway musical to present a gay character as having a viable sexual identity. Previously such characters were written and played as fops and fairies.

Feeling pressure to make Duane a shade more effeminate, Lewis decided to give them what they seemed to want. One day at rehearsal, when Bacall said, "Bring him along," Lewis swished. "I camped it up," he recalls, "and they all laughed hysterically. I suddenly realized I had made a terrible mistake."

Lewis had played the stereotype too well. In a sense, he emasculated the character—and himself. At that moment the powers that be spotted a cliché portrayal that would grab a cheap laugh. If it had been a movie they would have yelled, "Cut! Print it."

Instead, there were "long conversations," as Lewis puts it. He won't specify who said what, but the upshot was, "That's how Duane's got to be; he has to be nellier." Lewis was immensely uncomfortable. "I got crazy," he says. "I thought, I don't want to do this!" He turned it over to his agent, who held discussions. The issue couldn't be resolved, there were hard feelings, and Garrett Lewis quit the show.

It would be a mistake to assume that Lewis's departure was in protest at the offensive depiction of a gay character. His decision was personal, not political. He left the show because he wanted to maintain his straight-arrow image in order to continue working in movies. Then as now, Hollywood got the jitters over actors who were perceived as gay—unless they would settle for prissy Franklin Pangborn roles.

"I didn't want to play a character who was instantly recognizable to the audience as gay," Lewis says. "That's the way I live my life, but it's certainly not something I flaunt. Besides, it's a very different world in

California from the Broadway stage, and the West Coast was where I wanted to work."

Another person who was there at the time tells a radically different story. According to that source, "Garrett Lewis was *replaced*. The problem was that he was extremely good-looking, like a *GQ* model. Len Cariou, the leading man, lacked traditional leading-man handsomeness. The original casting didn't work right because the second male lead, played by Garrett, was stunning and Cariou wasn't. The humor just wasn't right."

The anonymous source betrays no maliciousness in recounting this. Indeed, the person is still indignant at the way Garrett Lewis was dismissed: "He was given his notice at the New Year's Eve party, just about like this: 'Happy New Year, you're fired.' "

Lee Roy Reams, who had auditioned for the role of Duane Fox but had lost to Lewis, was called in a short time later. He has a lot to say about *Applause,* but first a flash-forward to the subsequent careers of Garrett Lewis.

As it turned out, Lewis didn't continue for long in front of the cameras. By the time he appeared in *Funny Lady* in 1975, musicals were rare and other genres didn't interest him as much. Just then a friend of his, agent Sue Mengers, bought Zsa Zsa Gabor's house in Bel Air. Mengers and her husband liked the way Lewis had done his own home, so they asked him to redesign their new acquisition. Mengers said, "If it's good—and it had better be—you'll get lots of business. I've got the biggest mouth in Hollywood."

First Lewis removed the lemon-yellow shag carpet that Zsa Zsa had put down in abundance, along with her waterfall in the den. When the house was stripped to its bones he designed new carpets, new furniture, and tailored the place to the pleasure of its new chatelaine.

Garrett Lewis's second career was under way. Word of mouth from Mengers led to commissions from Barbra Streisand, Barry Diller, Herbert Ross, and many others. Then, in the late seventies when Ross was directing *The Turning Point,* he called Lewis in to decorate a couple of the sets.

A bit later Ross called again. He was at work on *California Suite* and not entirely pleased with some of the art direction. Lewis became a visual consultant on that picture. Career number three took off. As set decorator—"That means I do everything but the walls"—Garrett Lewis has received four Academy Award nominations, for *Beaches, Glory, Hook,* and *Bram Stoker's Dracula.*

Singer-dancer-actor Lee Roy Reams, raised in Kentucky, came to New York in the mid-sixties. He appeared in *Sweet Charity,* a Lincoln Center revival of *Oklahoma!,* and on television he danced on all the variety shows.

When Garrett Lewis left *Applause,* Reams stepped in to play Duane Fox. Shortly after Margo invites Duane to escort her and Eve on the town and to "bring him along" (i.e., his date), there's a scene in a gay bar in Greenwich Village. Reams describes Ron Field's original concept: "We walked into the bar and there was the date I was meeting. Margo, Eve, and I went up to him. Then he and I kissed, a little peck, not a big deal. It seemed perfectly natural to all of us.

"Then, during tryouts in Baltimore, when we did the gay-bar scene there was a *gasp* from the audience because two men had done a little kiss like you might give your father, for God's sake. It actually cast a pall; the show didn't play well that night.

"Next day we came into rehearsal and Ron said, 'Lee Roy—and I said, 'Don't tell me—you want to cut the kiss.' And we did. Ron replaced it with a hug."

Reams adds that Comden and Green had originally intended his character to be not only gay but black. "They were aware of the shortage of roles for black actors, and that's one reason they considered making Duane Fox African-American," he says. But the idea was dropped. Perhaps a double-barreled minority character struck the producers as too volatile. A same-sex interracial date might have caused a riot in Baltimore, and elsewhere.

Reams, a quick study and a polished pro, soon absorbed the shock of Garrett Lewis's departure. Now the cast seemed permanent: Bacall, Cariou, Reams, Brandon Maggart as the playwright Buzz Richards and Ann Williams as Karen, his wife. Diane McAfee, a twenty-one-year-old singer and dancer, was Eve Harrington. Another young performer, the energetic Bonnie Franklin, along with her fellow chorus gypsies, performed the show's title song as though it were the first show-stopping number in theatre history.

A second major change would soon cause another shock, but not until after the gypsy run-through.

Lauren Bacall had never been to a gypsy run-through before. In fact, she claims she didn't know what one was. But she liked the *Applause* gypsies—"the kids in the dance corps," as she calls them.

Here is Bacall's take on a gypsy run-through: "You do the show—no costumes or sets or orchestra, only a piano—in a theatre filled with the casts and gypsies from other shows running on Broadway."

Ron Field had scheduled the gypsy run-through of *Applause* on the Sunday before the cast left for Baltimore. Bacall remembers the nerves and the exuberance: "The date was January 18, 1970, the place the Lunt-Fontanne Theatre. I was dressed in slacks and turtleneck sweater. The theatre started to fill up. There was no curtain. The actors were shaking in the wings, the gypsies warming up way upstage in corners, using pipes as barres.

"Finally it was time. Ron, as is customary, walked downstage to explain the set, time, and place. As I heard 'Margo Channing' I made my first entrance. The applause was tumultuous. With no sets or costumes, the audience must use its imagination. They're privy to a new birth, the first unveiling of a creation. At the last curtain call the stage became flooded with every musical director, producer, writer I'd known—and actors, all bursting with enthusiasm."

Diane McAfee, playing Eve, recalls the gypsy run-through for its "wonderful screaming acceptance that was so overblown."

Lee Roy Reams remembers Bacall in the wings that day, waiting to go on, and her hands shaking quite visibly. "I clasped her hands in mine. I said, 'My career's on the line today as well as yours.' She laughed. We did not let go of one another's hands until the announcer said, 'Ladies and gentlemen, Margo Channing.' "

Reams felt sure after that performance that the show would be a hit, the main reason being its star. "She had this walk, and this voice, and that tossing of the hair—and it had nothing to do with Bette Davis," he says. "Besides that, she wears clothes like nobody else."

The first night in Baltimore, Lauren Bacall and Len Cariou, at the start of a flourishing romance, walked out of the theatre en route to a nightcap. They glanced at the marquee and did a double take. Their names were up in lights, but his was misspelled: "Ben Cariou."

Guys Like Us, We Had It Made

The most famous song by Charles Strouse and Lee Adams was not sung by Lauren Bacall or anyone else in a Broadway show. It's a tune almost as familiar as "Happy Birthday," yet of the millions who know it, few could name the composer or lyricist. It was made popular in the early 1970s by Archie and Edith Bunker, for it's the theme song of *All in the Family*.

According to Strouse, the Bunker music came about because he and Norman Lear, producer of *All in the Family*, became friends while working on *The Night They Raided Minsky's*. Strouse composed the music for that film, and Lear was co-writer. A little later, Lear showed Strouse several *All in the Family* scripts, and asked him and Adams to write a song. Strouse doubted that such controversial material would make it to television.

The number of people hearing the Strouse–Adams theme song in any broadcast of the sitcom was vastly greater than the number who have heard all their show music in every performance since their first collaboration, including the ubiquitous "Tomorrow," from their 1977 hit, *Annie*.

The Baltimore reviews of *Applause* were lukewarm. Lee Roy Reams recalls one notice that summed up the show as "a lot of homo ho-hum." The cast was depressed, the producers verged on panic. They had eight weeks ahead to improve—or else. "The pressure was constant," Bacall remembers. "Rehearse all day—scenes, songs, dances; performance at night; drinks at the hotel, sleep, breakfast, and start all over again."

A couple of weeks after the Baltimore opening Ron Field went to Bacall's dressing room before the Saturday matinee. He looked dour. Bacall guessed that the rumors were true: A cast member was to be replaced.

"Don't you think it's that out-of-town panic?" she asked. "The minute something isn't quite right, an actor is fired."

Field asked, "Do you like Diane?"

"Yes, I do," Bacall answered.

He said, "But you shouldn't; that's the problem. As Eve Harrington, she should present a threat to you. That's why the show isn't working the way it should. She doesn't come across as all those things Eve Harrington must be."

Sometime later Brandon Maggart, who played Buzz Richards in the show, knocked on Diane's dressing-room door. He said, "I have to tell you something."

She looked at him with sympathy. From his tone of voice, he must have gotten bad news.

"What's the worst news you can think of?" Brandon asked.

Diane gasped. "You got fired!"

He paused. Suspense built; he didn't answer. He might have been playing a climactic scene onstage. But the drama was real. Diane ran to Brandon and embraced him, for in recent weeks they had started to fall in love. "Brandon, I can't believe it! You got fired."

The pause ended. "No," he said. "You did."

It was probably the worst shock of Diane McAfee's young life. She could only stammer, "Why?"

Ron Field, Charles Strouse, and Lee Adams all gave her the same reason: "You're too young and rosy to scare Margo Channing, especially Lauren Bacall's Margo Channing."

According to McAfee, Ron Field felt so terrible about replacing her in the Broadway *Applause* that he immediately hired her to play Eve

Harrington in the show's bus-and-truck tour. Specifying the difference between the national tour and the one she did, McAfee explains: "The national is the A-class tour—the one that Lauren Bacall eventually took on the road. That one tends to stay longer in each place, and they fly you to it. The bus-and-truck tour, on the other hand, is exactly what it sounds like. You give one or two performances and you travel by bus. My contract at least stipulated that I got a double seat. I bought beads at Kmart for that seat, and a little plant to hang in the window, and a wine rack for the overhead luggage bin."

For ten months the bus rolled across the Midwest, to Arizona and New Mexico, up and down the coast of California. The various bus-and-truck Margo Channings included Patrice Munsel and Alexis Smith.

When her tour ended, Diane McAfee returned to New York and lived for many years with Brandon Maggart. They have two daughters, the youngest of whom is the singer and songwriter Fiona Apple.

Three decades later, Diane McAfee betrays no bitterness. She says, "It's nice to dream that I might have had a glamorous career, but perhaps that would have preluded my having children. And that I can't imagine. Yes, it's hard finding the right direction for my life right now, because there's nothing I really like to do except perform. I tried about five years ago to go back into musicals, but I discovered a different world. It wasn't the theatre I had left."

The Saturday after Ron Field told Bacall that Diane McAfee was to be replaced, he came to Bacall's dressing room again. The matinee was ready to start; why was the director's gaze pinned to the floor? When Bacall asked what the hell was eating him, Field intoned: "Just look in the fourth row center this afternoon. You'll see Gower Champion sitting there."

"So what?" replied the puzzled leading lady.

"So I'm being replaced," he muttered.

"What?" Bacall screamed. "Over my dead body!"

Gower Champion, sometime star of Hollywood musicals, was now a theatrical éminence grise, for he had gained a reputation as a doctor of shows ailing in tryouts. To Bacall, he might have been Doctor Death. If ever there was a perfect moment for a fasten-your-seat-belts scene, this was it. And Bacall was magnificent. If the critics could have seen her backstage!

"Come to my hotel after the performance," she ordered Field. Margo Channing, at that matinee, flamed with added fire and music.

Len Cariou joined Bacall and Field in her hotel suite. She phoned Joseph Kipness, one of their producers, and let him have it. "If the ship sails without him, it sails without me!" she thundered. Ron Field made frantic signals across the room. With the evening performance coming up, he was afraid she'd damage her voice.

Kipness tried to placate her. "Gower just came down to visit, he's passing through, we're old friends. As a matter of fact, he's meeting me in the bar in a little while."

"Oh he is, is he?" Bacall growled.

She hung up and called her agent. "If Ron goes, I go. Make it clear to Kippy!"

Bacall was livid. She grabbed Cariou with one hand and Field with the other. "Let's go to the bar and say hello to Mr. Champion," she drawled, and the acid in her mouth could have etched metal.

Just before entering the bar she linked arms with her two men and in they marched. She smiled ravenously at Kippy and Gower.

"Great show," said Champion, as Joe Kipness squirmed.

Bacall patted Ron Field's shoulder. "It's all because of him," she purred. "I don't know what I'd do without my director," she added with satiny significance.

And that's how Bacall showed them what a "difficult" star she could be. Years later, as an afterthought, she laughed about her scene in the hotel bar. "I did everything but flutter my eyelashes," she crooned.

Diane McAfee's replacement as Eve Harrington was Penny Fuller, who had previously auditioned for the part but couldn't shake her misgivings about the show.

Toward the end of 1969 Harold Prince summoned Fuller from Los Angeles to audition for his production of the new Sondheim musical, *Company*. Fuller, many years later, recounts the story of her lucky breaks as though she were telling the plot of a Ginger Rogers movie: "After the audition for *Company* I was walking out of the stage door when this guy called my name. He said, 'Oh, you're here. We were going to fly you in but they wouldn't pay for it.' "

Fuller looked at him in amazement, but before she could speak the man blurted out, "I'm the stage manager of *Applause*. I'm sure Ron Field will want to see you."

"Fine," she said, still taken aback.

How did this man know who she was and what she could do? Fuller's nonchalant reply: "I don't know, darlin'. I guess I was *somebody*." Perhaps the stage manager had seen her in *Barefoot in the Park*, her first Broadway show. Or in *Cabaret*. In it, as Jill Haworth's understudy, Fuller went on more than a hundred times. ("I developed an Eve Harrington reputation," she says, "because I was the understudy who kept taking over. But unlike Eve, I was a nice person— as far as I knew, anyway.") Besides her stage work, Fuller had appeared on television in *The Edge of Night* and other programs in the sixties.

She auditioned for Ron Field without having read all of the script of *Applause*. Everything was rushed because she had to catch a plane back to Los Angeles to do a pilot for a comedy series. She read the script on the plane. Her reaction: "I thought, Oh God, don't let me get this because I don't have the nerve to turn it down but I don't think it's very good."

While shooting the comedy pilot Fuller got a call from a friend, a theatrical agent who had attended the gypsy run-through of *Applause*. He told her, "The show is fabulous, but the girl playing Eve—don't think she's there yet." Penny was relieved. At least she had escaped the agonizing decision of whether to take the role or turn it down.

A few weeks later she was at the hairdresser's. "My head was in the sink and they were rinsing out the soap," she says, sounding like Ginger Rogers again. "Someone told me I had a call from my manager. They handed me the phone while my head was still in the sink. My manager announced, 'They want you to fly to Baltimore tonight to consider replacing McAfee in *Applause*.' "

With her hair still damp she dashed home and threw clothes into a suitcase. In Baltimore, Larry Kasha's secretary gave her a ticket for the next performance. Penny jumped when she saw the location. "You can't put me in the second row. Those gypsies will see me and they'll know why I'm here!" The secretary suggested, "Can't you tell them you're visiting an aunt in Baltimore?"

"Not with my reputation as Miss Replacement," Fuller exclaimed. But it was the only seat left in the house. "So I go in, sit down, and of course the very first thing, one of the gypsies does a pirouette, sees me, and I could *see* him see me, and I could just *feel* him telling everybody backstage, 'Penny Fuller's in the audience!' "

When the performance was over Penny knew exactly what was wrong. "My job was literally to be the villain. As yet, Margo wasn't really threatened."

Next day, a Sunday, Penny agreed to replace McAfee. She met Lauren Bacall. On Monday she had a music rehearsal, Tuesday a rehearsal with understudies, Wednesday she learned a new dance from Diane McAfee, Thursday she rehearsed with the actual cast, Friday there was a dress rehearsal with orchestra and lights, and at some weary hour of the afternoon Larry Kasha brought her a sandwich. Groggy from fatigue, Penny said to herself, "This is the pinnacle, honey. It doesn't get any bigger than this, when the producer brings you a tuna salad on rye."

Penny Fuller seldom gets the jitters. That Friday night, however, waiting to go on, she panicked: "I'm about to play to a theatre full of people, in a show that I've had two rehearsals for." Her next thought was more drastic: "If I get up right now and leave, nobody can stop me." But the next moment it was too late. She heard the announcement: "Ladies and gentlemen, at this performance the part of Eve Harrington will be played by Penny Fuller."

At that instant she had a flashback to childhood. "When I was a little girl in Lumberton, North Carolina, *Photoplay* magazine ran a contest called 'Come to Hollywood.' I didn't win. But I remembered that the magazine had three speeches for contest finalists. One was Ann Blyth's thing from *Our Very Own*, which was about being adopted. I don't remember what the second one was, but the third was Anne Baxter's 'Eddie and the Brewery' scene from *All About Eve*. I had worked on that speech upstairs in my bedroom when I was ten years old. And now here I was, about to go onstage and play 'Eddie and the Brewery,' even though in *Applause* Eve's boyfriend is no longer called Eddie and he's not a soldier in World War II but in Vietnam."

Penny Fuller vows it was the flashback that kept her from running out that night. "I said, 'I gotta see if I can do this.'"

And she gave the performance of her life—in Diane McAfee's clothes. "But Diane's shoes didn't fit me so I put a pair of gloves in them to keep them on. One of them flew off during a big number, so I just kicked the other one off and made it a theatrical moment."

Next day all agreed: Penny Fuller was silicone injected into a sagging show. Lee Roy Reams says, "Diane McAfee and Penny Fuller are both friends of mine, but I have to say that changing the actress who played Eve made a big difference. Penny played the role as a *woman*. Diane played it as a girl. And a girl was no competition for someone of Bacall's stature."

No doubt Fuller was a more convincing Eve Harrington because, at age thirty, she was older than twenty-one-year-old Diane McAfee. She was also a more experienced actress.

Knowing that her portrayal of Eve must be unlike Anne Baxter's in the film, Penny set herself a difficult task in the role. "I wanted to fool the audience at first, make them believe they didn't remember the story right. I wanted them to think, Why, Eve really *is* a sweet girl."

After Baltimore, the show moved to Detroit for a couple of weeks. There the reviews were much better. Next stop was New York for previews. And then March 30, 1970: opening night.

Perhaps a line from the Judy Garland song ran through Lauren Bacall's head as that evening approached: "Until you've played the Palace, you haven't played at all." She had been in show business most of her life, her film work had made her famous, her dreams had come true—and yet how often Lauren Bacall had wondered whether she might end up like Bette Davis and so many other ladies in decline, doing third-rate pictures and tepid TV adaptations of schlocky best-sellers.

The Palace Theatre, at Broadway and Forty-seventh Street, was sold out. But were they coming to praise *Applause* or to bury it? After all, as one commentator pointed out, "It was the tenth musical of a long and dismal season, the year of one-word titles—*Coco* and *Jimmy* and *Purlie* and *Georgy* and *Gantry*." Perhaps the show's prospects were actually raised by such lackluster arrivals. The same commentator asserted that "it looked especially good at the end of a dreary week that brought both *Minnie's Boys* and *Look to the Lilies*." And *Applause* had time to establish itself as a smash before *Company*, that other one-word hit of the season, opened a month later.

Opening night was everything they hoped for. The show unfolded without a hitch. Curiously, no one connected with *Applause* remembers exactly who attended, though Betty Comden neatly evokes the splash: "Whoever first-nighters are, they came. Many famous people, many famous names."

When Lauren Bacall made her entrance the applause was unstoppable.

At intermission Ron Field dared to be optimistic. He was a worrier, but—the show was actually going very well. No one forgot a lyric, flubbed a dance step, or missed a cue. Set changes glided with perfect precision; nothing stuck. If Ron superstitiously anticipated disaster in Act II, he was off. Nothing untoward took place. Then at last, the finale.

Field staged the curtain calls like a musical number. First the company took their calls, then stood in a V formation with arms outstretched toward Bacall, who was upstage center, at the apex of the V. Her back was to the audience. On cue she swirled around, flung her arms high in the air, and headed downstage. The audience adored her, loved her performance, loved her bow. She and all the others came back for repeated curtain calls.

Backstage—a mob scene. Bacall's dressing room was jammed with photographers and well-wishers. Other dressing rooms bulged as well. It seemed that every co-star, agent, producer, and college roommate had packed in to embrace Penny Fuller, Lee Roy Reams, Ron Field, and everyone else in the show.

Seen in the lobby after the curtain rang down was Sidney Michaels.

Various people who knew of his dismissal came to him and gushed, "You're being really marvelous, really terrific about the whole thing, Sidney." To which he replied, "Listen. I kept half of my royalties as part of the settlement. They've pulled off a hit and made me a lot of dough. Thank you, producers, and thank you, cast."

At length the performers managed to change into street clothes for the trip to Sardi's. Then there was the opening-night party at Tavern on the Green, in Central Park, hosted by Larry Kasha and Joe Kipness. Sometime after midnight they got hold of an early copy of the _Times_. A hush fell over the restaurant as Ron Field read aloud the review by Clive Barnes: "Whatever it is Miss Lauren Bacall possesses she throws it around most beautifully, most exquisitely, and most excitingly in a musical called _Applause_. . . . Miss Bacall is a sensation. . . . She sings with all the misty beauty of an in-tune foghorn. . . . Len Cariou is a bluff, tough delight. . . . As Eve, Penny Fuller has all the brassy, pushy, belty quality a young girl needs to make good."

The following Sunday, Walter Kerr, the _Times_'s other theatre critic, headlined his piece, BACALL TAKES YOUR BREATH AWAY. Reviews were equally ecstatic in the _Daily News, Women's Wear Daily_, and a host of other papers. A week later _Time_ and _Newsweek_ reviewed the show for the nation.

A notable dissenter, however, was Larry Cohen in _The Hollywood Reporter_. To him, _Applause_ was "a splashy bitch of a show that reeks of calculation and unconscious perversity. At the same time _Applause_ is sticking up its middle finger at show business, it is congratulating itself for its own insolence of spirit. It is a phony, oh-so-precious, aren't-we-cute hatchet job. Miss Bacall can't really sing or dance and the acting as opposed to the energy demands made upon her are minimal. What we are watching is the movie stripped of its guts."

But New York was solidly behind _Applause_. Three weeks after opening night the show won four Tony Awards. It was named Best Musical, and Bacall Best Actress in a Musical. Ron Field won two Tonys, one for Best Direction and another for Best Choreography.

Bette Davis wasn't about to give *Applause* any awards. But who would expect her to? After all, this was a pastiche of her best performance—but without her. In a *Playboy* interview years later she said, "I always imagined singing that song called "Fasten Your Seat Belts"—that would've been incredible. Then, when I saw it, Bacall didn't even get a *laugh* on that line in the show, just banged a guitar and finished. I couldn't believe my ears—one of the most famous lines!" Despite her misgivings, however, Bette saw the show not once but two times.

She didn't attend opening night, though she did send Lauren Bacall a telegram with the gnomic message: "The years have gone and now you are me."

Bette Davis and Betty Perske had met for the first time in 1939, long before the fifteen-year-old Perske ever dreamed she was destined for fame as Lauren Bacall. Their first encounter resembled a Lucy-and-Ethel escapade.

To begin with, it involved two Bettys and one Bette: Betty Perske, her friend Betty Kalb, and La Davis. Through a complicated network of family connections, the teenaged Bettys wangled an invitation to visit movie-star Bette while she was in New York. On a Saturday afternoon at teatime the two nervous, giggly girls arrived at the Gotham Hotel to pay a call on the Queen of Films.

Bette Davis was a study in graciousness. She offered her visitors tea, but they were too terrified to drink it; their hands were so shaky they couldn't hold cup and saucer. Predictably, both girls told the star that they had seen all her pictures, loved every one of them, and how they too wanted to act in movies. Rather than tossing off a sardonic Margo Channing–like quip, Bette was patient and kind, giving the usual advice about learning one's craft, jobs in summer stock, and the like.

Eventually there came a long pause. Betty Kalb gave Betty Perske a meaningful look: time to go. They gushed, "Thank you so much, Miss Davis," "We're thrilled to meet you," and so on. They all shook hands and the girls walked into the corridor. They took a few steps down the hall toward the elevator and—Betty Kalb fainted! The girls were mortified, but apparently Miss Davis had closed her door already and so knew nothing of the ignominious collapse.

They rushed to a nearby drugstore for restoratives, and a few days later both girls wrote florid letters of thanks to their idol. And Bette Davis wrote back. Her letter to the future Lauren Bacall included the words, "I hope we meet again sometime."

Bacall included this anecdote in her 1979 autobiography, *By Myself*. When Bette Davis read it, she chortled, "What Miss Bacall leaves out is that she fell into a dead faint and had to be carried back into the apartment again."

Did she faint, or didn't she? With so many Bettys in the same hotel suite, it's easy to understand the confusion over exactly who passed out and who administered first aid.

Davis and Bacall crossed paths once or twice at Warner Bros. in the forties, but they never became well acquainted. So Lauren Bacall was almost as nervous when Bette Davis paid her a backstage visit in 1970 as she had been that Saturday afternoon in 1939.

One night at intermission the *Applause* cast got word that Bette Davis was in the audience. When the play ended she knocked on Bacall's dressing-room door. "She sat on a chair, not on the love seat, which might have indicated she would stay awhile," said Bacall, who remembers her as reserved and polite but not effusive. Nervously making conversation, Bacall indicated that she felt ridiculous playing Bette's part.

After a short time, Bette rose to leave. At the door she told Bacall, "No one but you could have played this part—and you know I mean that."

Following her guest out of the dressing room, Bacall introduced others in the cast to Bette. According to Lee Roy Reams, "Bette Davis was professional in her demeanor that night. Not the friendliest or warmest of people, but professional." She did sign his *Applause* poster, however, which became a treasured memento.

Joe Mankiewicz, like Bette Davis, was irritated by the transformation of *All About Eve* into *Applause*. His son recalls a telephone invitation to Mankiewicz from Lauren Bacall: "Joe, you have to come down opening night." Explaining that his father and Bacall had been friends for years,

Tom Mankiewicz quotes his father as saying, "Betty, I don't think I'm ever gonna see it. I think it was a pretty good movie and I don't understand why you have to stop it fourteen times for songs."

Mankiewicz did see the show eventually, and afterwards he and his wife, Rosemary, went to dinner with Lauren Bacall. According to her, "He was happy to see how much of his work had been kept in our show and liked it better than he had anticipated." Or was he just being kind?

Charles Strouse heard, through mutual friends, that Mankiewicz was hurt by the omission of his name from the playbill and from the Tony Awards ceremony. "I don't blame him at all," says Strouse. "If I had been asked to speak at the Tonys, I would have said 'First of all let's thank Joe Mankiewicz for writing this masterpiece.' " Had he given that speech, Strouse no doubt would have thanked Mankiewicz also for suggesting one of the show's best songs. It came about like this.

In the summer of 1969 Mankiewicz was finishing his penultimate film, *There Was a Crooked Man*. Strouse, already at work on *Applause*, was hired to compose the film's score. As he and Mankiewicz grew better acquainted, Strouse filled him in on details of the musical. Mankiewicz said, "You know that the most famous line from *All About Eve* is 'Fasten your seat belts, it's going to be a bumpy night.' "

"Yes," said Strouse.

"If you don't turn that line into a song, you're crazy," said Mankiewicz.

And so "Fasten Your Seat Belts" became one of only two memorable songs from the show. (The other is "Welcome to the Theatre.") Significantly, it's Bacall's first big let-'er-rip number, with a bossa nova beat whose catchy rhythms emphasize Margo's high-voltage petulance. Most important, despite this song's evocation of Bette Davis in *All About Eve*, it's one of the places in the show where Bacall seizes Margo Channing and makes the character her own.

On May 4, 1970, exactly five weeks after opening night, four students were killed at Kent State University in Ohio when National Guardsmen opened fire during an anti-war protest. At her curtain call that night, Lauren Bacall waited for the applause to die down, then she made this announcement: "Ladies and gentlemen, could we have a moment of silence for the students who were killed today at Kent State." Silence descended on the house, except for a handful of playgoers who hissed and booed. Such reactions were not rare, even in "liberal" New York, at the height of the Vietnam War. Penny Fuller recalls a sign the stage-hands posted backstage: AMERICA—LOVE IT OR LEAVE IT.

Bacall stayed with the show in New York almost eighteen months. In 1971 she left Broadway for the national tour, after which she did the London production of *Applause*. Bacall's replacement on Broadway was Anne Baxter. The irony was exquisite: Eve the victimizer had lapsed into her victim.

But Rita Hayworth, not Anne Baxter, had been the producers' original choice as Bacall's replacement. Several months prior to Bacall's departure, Ron Field flew to California for a meeting with Hayworth. Although she had not yet been diagnosed as suffering from Alzheimer's disease, Field guessed immediately that she wouldn't be able to perform in the show. He later revealed that during their interview she could scarcely remember what she had said a moment earlier.

The producers, however, liked the idea of a marquee that read RITA HAYWORTH IN APPLAUSE. So she came to New York. In preparation for the role she went to a vocal coach, the dance captain gave her exercises, and Ron Field put her on a daily regime from ten o'clock to six. Sadly, after a month and a half of work, Rita Hayworth couldn't remember any of her lines. She declared to columnist Joyce Haber that she bowed out because she wouldn't have had enough time to rehearse the role. She also insisted that after weeks in New York she still hadn't met Ron Field.

Haber interviewed Anne Baxter shortly after the Rita Hayworth debacle. "It has put a helluva lot of pressure on me," Baxter said, "step-ping in at the last minute. I'm tired of stepping in for people. I did that for fourteen bloody years at Fox. Anytime anybody didn't want to do something, I had to take over."

Ron Field was relieved that Baxter consented to step in once more. Later, however, describing her performance, he paid her a left-handed tribute: "After a couple of weeks she began to play it like a film actress pretending to be in a stage play in a movie. In other words, when people in movies pretend they're on the stage: (very overdone) *How are you?* You know, it is all like pseudo–stage acting. The audiences didn't mind, however. By that time, a year and a half into the show, you don't get sophisticated playgoers. It's mostly tourists. But she had enormous energy and the crowds kept coming, so I thought I'd just let her be."

Baxter's colleagues from the cast are more charitable. Penny Fuller describes Bacall's performances as "platinum and silver" while Anne Baxter as Margo was like "burgundy and chocolate." She considers Bacall "a movie star/actress" and Baxter "an actress/movie star." Fuller adds, "It was Bacall's charisma and her persona that carried the show when she was in it. And that's not to belittle her acting. It was Anne Baxter's acting, on the other hand, and not charisma, that defined her performance."

Lee Roy Reams points out that both actresses "were very musical, and both understood the sense of the music." One reason their performances were so different, he explains, is that physically Anne Baxter was "a smaller presence" while Bacall was "a long-legged lioness."

Shortly after Anne Baxter joined the show, Reams's mother died. Preparing to go home for the funeral, he found on his dressing-room table an airline ticket and a sum of money. Anne wouldn't admit they were from her, but Lee Roy was convinced they were.

Penny Fuller and Anne Baxter also formed a friendship. Sensing, during Baxter's rehearsals, some of the new star's difficulties, and well aware herself of the problems of being a replacement, Penny went shopping at Tiffany's for a gift, "a little silver apple, the kind you use for saccharine or sugar pellets or some such." On it she had engraved: *Good-bye Eve, Hello Margo. Love AB from PF*. When Penny left the show Anne gave her a similar amulet, engraved: *Good-bye Eve, Hooray Penny. Love PF from AB*.

On Penny's last matinee in the show, she got a big surprise. "The theatre was very crowded that day, not because it was my last performance but because the show was still packing 'em in. During my early scenes I heard a peculiar sound offstage. I couldn't imagine what the hell it was: jingle, jingle, jingle.

"It kept on, and out of the corner of my eye I saw a small figure in the wings. On the arms of that small figure, gold bracelets were jangling like wind chimes. A little later, when I was about to make another entrance, I saw who *that* was: *That* was Bette Davis, standing there watching me, and jangling." Anne Baxter had invited Bette especially to see her and Penny Fuller together in the roles Baxter and Davis had once played. Since there wasn't a seat out front, even for Bette Davis, Anne brought her backstage and Bette watched the entire performance from the wings.

By then, Ann Williams had left the show. Her replacement in the role of Karen Richards was Gwyda DonHowe, who, according to Lee Roy Reams, "did one of the best Bette Davis imitations you've ever heard." The night Bette watched from the wings, everyone in the cast felt they were under a microscope. The Davis scrutiny made Gwyda DonHowe especially nervous, so that her line readings began taking on rather inappropriate Bette Davis inflections. "It was all very strange that night," Lee Roy Reams recalls.

Bette lingered after the show, since she and Anne Baxter were good friends. Chatting with Lee Roy, Davis said, "I hate what they did with your character. No harm in the way you played it. I just don't like them changing that wonderful character, Birdie."

Gwyda DonHowe and her husband, producer Norman Kean, spent their lives in the theatre, from the time they met while working in summer stock in 1957 until a January day in 1988 when he murdered her as she lay sleeping and then jumped to his death from the roof of their apartment building.

Penny Fuller elected not to do the national tour of *Applause*. She felt she had played Eve Harrington long enough. "It was a hard part to do," she says, "so much bitter anger in the character." But she did consent to appear in the show for six weeks in California. In San Francisco, she and Bacall played Eve and Margo at the Curran Theatre where, two decades earlier, Mankiewicz had filmed the theatre scenes of *All About Eve*. (Many years later, Penny Fuller and Lauren Bacall did a benefit together. They hadn't seen each other in ages. Penny knocked on the door of Bacall's dressing room and in a sweet, girlish voice, said, "Miss Channing?" Bacall raced to the door and the two howled with laughter.)

When Bacall left the national tour she was succeeded by Eleanor Parker. In London, Bacall played Margo Channing for a year at Her Majesty's Theatre with Angela Richards co-starring as Eve Harrington. A filmed version of the London production was telecast on CBS in 1973.

Meanwhile, back on Broadway, Anne Baxter left the cast of *Applause* at the end of April 1972, after some ten months as Margo Channing. Her replacement was Arlene Dahl, a leading lady in Hollywood movies of the fifties who later became a businesswoman and an expert in the art of staying beautiful long past youth.

Before Arlene Dahl knew she would join the cast, she saw Bacall in the show, and later she saw Anne Baxter. After both performances she went backstage to greet her old friends from Hollywood. Dahl recalls that "Anne showed me a calendar on which she was X-ing off the days until she could end this run. You see, she was frightened every time she did the dance numbers. In one number she was tossed from dancer to dancer, and she was afraid they were going to drop her. She had had a dream about it."

Then Arlene Dahl was named as Baxter's replacement and there was a spat. It mystified Dahl, because she considered Baxter her friend. She says, "When I came for rehearsals I was hoping, and had been told, that I was to use Anne Baxter's dressing room. But that did not happen. She wouldn't let me share it. I don't know why, but I used the leading man's dressing room instead. Which was unfair."

Although she had signed a six-month contract, Arlene Dahl stayed in the show for a much shorter period. According to her, Hitchcock's new film *Frenzy* was booked for the Palace, forcing *Applause* to close earlier than planned. Ron Field told a different version. When an interviewer asked him about Arlene Dahl, he said, "Oh my God, I didn't even pay attention. Larry Kasha put her in and the show closed two weeks later." (In fact, Arlene Dahl's first performance was on May 1, 1972, and she stayed with the show until it closed three and a half weeks later, on May 27. *Frenzy* opened in June at the Palace; according to *Variety*, "House taking summer off from legit.")

Of all the stars who played Margo in regional productions of *Applause*—Nanette Fabray, Eva Gabor, Patrice Munsel, Stefanie Powers—surely the most startling choice was Charles Pierce (1926–1999). When Pierce opened in what *Variety* dubbed "a lavender *Applause*" in San Francisco in May 1974, he got a rousing welcome from "the swish community" (another unfortunate *Variety* phrase) and an enthusiastic review from the *Chronicle*. Anyone who had seen his nightclub act would probably agree that Pierce, who built his career on impersonations of Bette Davis and other camp goddesses, was a prime candidate for Margo Channing.

On the other hand, neither *Applause* nor any other show could quite contain him. Where was the playwright funny enough to top Pierce's own material, that raucous nightclub act of imitations and witty one-liners? A typical show would start with a flashy introduction: "And now, ladies and gentlemen, the Ballroom in New York City is proud to present that master of disguises, that mistress of mayhem, the blonde that Hollywood forgot . . ."

During the evening Pierce would switch from Carol Channing to Barbara Stanwyck to Joan Collins, while dwelling, of course, on legends from every drag queen's pantheon: Marlene Dietrich ("I'm going to do a few numbers I did during the war. Some are in the audience tonight."); Joan Crawford ("Your bathwater is ready, Christina. I've been boiling it for two hours."); Mae West ("I feel like a million tonight, but I'll take one or two at a time."). But in looks, voice, and temperament, Pierce was always at his best as Bette Davis: "I'd like to do a scene for you—from all of my films!" (That "scene" was usually from *What Ever Happened to Baby Jane?* or from *Eve*. If the latter, Pierce would innocently acknowledge Bette's lofty co-star, "Celestial" Holm.)

Charles Pierce playing Bette Davis playing Margo Channing—it's exhilarating, it's camp art of the grandest kind. But surely we can be glad that Bette herself never got a crack at the musical. She was no singer (remember "I've Written a Letter to Daddy"), and while the same could be said of Lauren Bacall, the difference is that Bacall creates the *illusion* that she's singing. And Bette was no dancer, although as a young girl she studied briefly with Martha Graham. Graham's tutelage, however, taught Bette the art of *movement* rather than the art of dance. (Bette said, "Every time I climbed a flight of stairs in films—and I spent half my life on them—it was Graham step by step.")

The worst prospect of all, however, is that Bette would have wrecked the show, turning it into a drunken shambles by quarreling with everyone in sight. Which is what she had done during the 1961–62 Broadway season when she appeared in Tennessee Williams' *The Night of the Iguana*. The same thing happened in 1974, when Bette took the title role of *Miss Moffat*. That time, however, the agony was shorter, since the play closed out of town.

Applause was too full of ghosts, which Bette could not have endured. And being something less than magnificent, the show depended for its life on a star who could command and enlarge it, namely Bacall. She was absolutely right for singing-and-dancing Margo, just as Bette had been perfect in the film. Bacall's refusal to be anything but a star would convince just about anyone.

But time has been kinder to Bette. Watching a tape of Bacall in *Applause*, you admire her and give her her due. You believe every word of praise lavished on her, and still you look beyond Bacall to the black-and-white pentimento that emerges through the color and the songs. You even ask, and feel remorse for asking: Is this the real Margo Channing, or only the mock? For that earlier image burning into view will always be Bette Davis. How could it be otherwise? For *Applause* itself—whether in 1970 or today—amounts to little more than an adjunct to *All About Eve*, like an espresso bar in the basement of Bloomingdale's.

Another title for the show might have been *Forbidden Broadway*—because of the hubris of trying to improve *All About Eve*, and also for the standard-issue music that resulted from that attempt. Did you ever know someone who would break into spontaneous parodies of generic Broadway show tunes? If so, then you've heard a good bit of *Applause*, even if you've never listened to the cast recording. All not-so-great musicals sound rather alike, and this one has plenty of clichéd tunes and lyrics.

Detracting even more from the show is the book, which pushes the worn-out theme "Isn't it wonderful, the theatre is awful but we're putting on a show."

Surely the most concise assessment of *Applause*—and the greatest compliment to *All About Eve*—came from Billy Wilder. Leaving the theatre, he quipped: "You know, this show would make a wonderful movie."

postscript: *tell us about it, eve*

T he book was finished. As far as possible I had unified the
contradictory narratives and random gossip into an authen-
tic account of *All About Eve* and all those connected with it.
Except for one person.

Being privy to remarkable depictions of Martina Lawrence from Mary
Orr and Harry Haun, I tried early on to track her down. I looked up her
name in the Venice telephone directory, but it wasn't there. I checked
with an overseas operator. No listing. I wondered if she had moved, vanished. Died.

A couple of years went by. On a later trip to New York, I saw Harry
Haun again. This time he played the tape he had made at Sardi's the day
he invited Mary Orr and Martina Lawrence to tea. The voice, at last.

My first reaction was surprise. Martina Lawrence's theatricality on
the tape went beyond great-lady caricature. Her conversation was a performance, and the accent, which might pass for stage British to some
ears, was still in place. For all of its transparency, the accent nevertheless created a certain enchantment. To hear the woman speak reminded
me of precocious children wrapped up in fanciful games.

According to her rapid-fire autobiography on that tape, the life of Martina Lawrence was crowded with incident. Born in Chicago in 1921, she was named Ruth Maxine Hirsch. She spent a grim childhood, much of it in midwestern orphanages. At the age of eight she was brought to New York, and more orphanages. She said she acquired her accent from the movies.

In her early twenties she married a Viennese émigré Jew named Hans who, like Eve Harrington's Eddie, served in World War II. She spoke at length about Elisabeth Bergner and Paul Czinner.

Mary Orr didn't say very much, one reason being that her antagonist dominated the conversation. Unwilling to relinquish the past, Lawrence taunted Orr during one of several heated exchanges at the tea table: "You made quite a career mixing up fact and fiction." The dispute grew so boisterous that Harry Haun intervened with, "Girls, girls, there's no need for this."

At the end of the party, Mary Orr said, "Anyway, Martina, I hope you're happy now." And as though to ring down the curtain, Martina paused, drew breath, and replied, "I am."

The goneness of those long-ago events is all we can ever know for certain. At least that was my thought as I left Harry Haun that day. But he had dug up Martina Lawrence's address in Venice, and when I returned home I wrote to her asking for an interview by mail or by phone. I received no answer.

Then one day, a month after my visit to Haun, he called with some news. He started out, "She's baaack." Indeed, she was in town. Harry had just spoken with Martina. He told me where she was staying and I telephoned her. During that first conversation she was chatty and coquettish. She told me she had received my letter before leaving Venice. "I have little interest in *All About Eve*," she declaimed, "but people won't let me escape it."

I had no ready reply, nor did I need one. Suddenly she was wound up, telling me any number of things about herself and people she had known, friends and transgressors. Eventually I asked, "What brings you to New York?"

"I came to see Diveny, of course. You know we lost each other for all those years, and now she's in a play. It's not a frightfully large part, no, but you see, I wanted to give her my support. Diveny is a dear friend from long ago. The part is actually small, but important even though it's a nonspeaking role, you know. Sian Phillips is the star, and the play is called *Marlene*. I found certain things in it that are quite inaccurate, as when she says something unflattering about my idol—Garbo. Oh, Garbo was the one I always loved most, and of course Elisabeth knew Dietrich, but no one was like Garbo. And by the way, *you* wrote in an article that Elisabeth Bergner was known as 'the Garbo of the stage.' Never! That's not true at all! She was called 'die zaubere Bergner,' magical Bergner. I don't mean she never had anything to do with Garbo, because in her book—she was in Hollywood and there is a scene where she says that Garbo made a pass at her. Sometime at a party. One was not sure of Bergner's memory, either. In her autobiography there are lies, inaccuracies there, too."

At last I put in that I'd like to hear the story from her, in person. She laughed musically and said, "I am not good at making a long story short." Then, after some slightly flirtatious hesitation, she consented to an interview on condition that I accurately report her side of the story. "I want to clear my name," she declared. A few days later, I flew to New York and spent an afternoon with Martina Lawrence at the Pickwick Arms Hotel on East Fifty-first Street.

She is about five feet tall, and very thin. Her sharp features and lined face reminded me of Ruth Gordon in her later years. Martina—for we were soon using first names—was wearing a blue cardigan over a black turtleneck jersey, and black-and-white dotted slacks with large pantaloon legs.

On the day of our visit she was less ebullient than she had been on the phone. Sounding distressed, she asked, "How much time is it going to take? I mean, I'm an old lady and I might grow weary."

I told her to let me know if she felt tired. The next thing she said was, "All of them have lied, starting with Mary Orr. And also Harry Haun, who said things that Mankiewicz was supposed to say that are not true. I never corresponded with Mankiewicz. He was the guest of honor in Venice at an event, and the big deal was *All About Eve*. I decided I was going to call up just for the fun of it. His wife said that he was on his way out the door, he was already late, the boat was waiting for him. I said, 'This is Eve.' And oh, she called him back. He wanted to know if I could send him something, the proof of who I was. And I left it off at the front desk of the Cipriani Hotel."

I asked about Mankiewicz's assertion that she sent him a copy of Elisabeth Bergner's autobiography.

Martina said, "There were only four pages or so about me. I don't recall whether I sent him anything else. And I never heard from him. Harry Haun also wrote that I am a librarian. Ridiculous! When I sent the material to Mr. Mankiewicz, there was a bookshop called the Libreria San Giorgio. And my godchild—she will inherit my flat and anything that I have—she was working there at the time, and she gave me a large manila envelope that had Libreria San Giorgio stamped on it. 'Libreria' for someone who doesn't know Italian looks like 'library,' and it's not. 'Biblioteca' means a library."

(Rosemary Mankiewicz, the director's widow, confirmed that she answered the phone in the Cipriani Hotel when Martina Lawrence telephoned. She also noted the date: April 9, 1987.)

Martina mentioned living at the Rehearsal Club around the time of the Elisabeth Bergner episode, so I asked her to tell me about it.

Those memories seemed happy ones, for she smiled and her voice relaxed. "It was a theatrical boardinghouse," she said. "The Rehearsal Club was for aspiring actresses, singers, and dancers, at Forty-seven West Fifty-third Street. Anna Russell was there when I was. Two old brownstones were connected, and of course the play *Stage Door* by Edna Ferber and George S. Kaufman, and later the movie, were based on life at the Rehearsal Club.

"Anyway, one afternoon in June nineteen forty-six, the director, Kay Carlton, called me to her sitting room to show me the May nineteen forty-six issue of *Cosmopolitan*. A story in it, called 'The Wisdom of Eve,' had been brought to Miss Carlton's attention by one of the older girls in the club who knew vaguely of my association with Elisabeth Bergner. I read the story and was flattered and fascinated, but shocked by its slant, by its erroneous point of view. There was so much that was true—people, incidents, attitudes, entire conversations—that it was impossible for a stranger to know where truth ended and fiction took over. The story branded the girl a clever, phony, scheming, unscrupulous bitch.

"After reading it in Miss Carlton's office, I immediately went to see Mary Orr, the author. At first she denied any truth or coincidence of the story and accused me of being highly emotional and wrought up, of reading things into the story that were purely fictitious and created by her. I was angry now at her twisting things around and by her aggressivity. When I pointed out some obvious similarities, she changed her manner and told me how she had come to write the story and where she had gotten the facts. But the slant of it, of the girl's motives, came, she said, only from Bergner.

"Now, if I had been the girl Elisabeth Bergner judged me to be, having been 'seen through' by her would have been only a temporary setback. 'Eve' would have known how to use the incident to good advantage. She would have exploited it to get herself publicity and attention, as she does in the story. But where had it gotten me?

"All I wanted from Mary Orr was her admission that the best parts of the story were true, based on fact; that the two protagonists were Elisabeth Bergner and me; and that seeing any resemblance to actual happenings was not some 'figment of my imagination,' as she had first said. When she realized that I probably would not follow up my visit with legal action, her sharp, aggressive manner became almost cordial. She seemed relieved. As though she had sized me up rightly—and so she had!—as an odd, offbeat, inexperienced girl who wouldn't take the matter any further."

I was perplexed at such naiveté. Martina's anger seemed directed at the genre of fiction. Her gnawing unhappiness apparently fed on the plain fact that Mary Orr wrote a short story and not a literal account of certain events in the life of Martina Lawrence. My follow-up questions did not lead far.

She went on, "Most of the events were true. But to make up things, out of the top of one's head, that's wrong. That's immoral, that's unethical. You see, I've never liked fiction, Sam. Fiction, you can write anything you want."

I changed direction by referring to a statement from Harry Haun's tape: "You told Harry that you met Elisabeth Bergner and her husband by catching cabs. Will you elaborate?"

The oddity of such an encounter didn't strike Martina as odd, or if so she didn't let on. In fact, she took the phrase "catching cabs" almost as her madeleine to release the locked-up glories of her past. Her voice grew lyrical when she uttered the phrase.

"My husband was in the war, and I was staying at the Laura Spelman YWCA on October fourteenth, nineteen forty-four, my birthday. I was twenty-three that day. The institutional gloom of the place depressed me, and so I bought a ticket for standing room to see *The Two Mrs. Carrolls* at the Booth Theatre. However, that first time I saw Elisabeth Bergner on a stage bothered me. I was disappointed. I preferred her in the movies. I couldn't hear her very well and thought she must be ill. After the performance I saw Dr. Czinner. Smelling to high heaven with eau de cologne. Anyway, I recognized him from magazines and things, and I mentioned something about how was Miss Bergner. He said, 'Oh, you know Miss Bergner?' I said, 'No, I've only seen her in movies.' He said she wasn't well and had a cold and fever.

"After that first chat with Miss Bergner's husband, I came to the Booth Theatre every evening. It seemed so wonderful and strange to me that someone I admired and identified with on celluloid made far away in other countries was here and accessible.

"I was quite surprised that Elisabeth Bergner didn't have a car or a hired cab to take her home. I began to help Dr. Czinner flag down cabs. I always stayed in the shadows of the Booth Theatre in the alley to wait for Miss Bergner to arrive and leave the theatre. I never attempted to speak to her.

"After a month of flagging cabs and never missing her arrival and departure, my reward came. One afternoon after the matinee, Miss Bergner took me home with her, to Fourteen East Seventy-fifth Street. Dr. Czinner had told her I was more successful than he in catching cabs, and she thanked me. I told her I thought she should get home quickly on matinee days, to rest between performances. I felt protective towards her although we were very alike physically. I was a bit taller, with bigger feet. I wore her clothes but never the shoes she wanted to give me.

"Bergner didn't eat anything that first day she brought me home. She heated up five frankfurters, set them alone on a plate before me, and sat opposite me while I ate them—staring with those enormous eyes of hers. I didn't want to hurt her feelings and maybe never again be brought home. So I ate them and drank sweet, thick Turkish coffee brewed in its individual long-handled metal cup. That was the first of many visits to her duplex apartment on East Seventy-fifth Street.

"In the first weeks I knew Bergner she scarcely talked to me. She would exit from the stage door, come to where I waited, put her arm through mine, and take me with her to the waiting taxi. In the cab, she sat drawn up small and remote in her corner, smiling shyly, grateful to me, I thought, for not pressing her into conversation. Sometimes she seemed puzzled. She must have had questions she never asked me. I felt it in her frequent staring—quizzical, curious.

"I became her secretary. I remember my amazement and dismay when I found quantities of unopened mail in several large manila envelopes. Letters dating back many months, some even a year. Miss Bergner gave instructions that I was to be allowed out front whenever I wanted to see the show, even though its success had made it standing room only. I came just about every evening to the theatre. It made me less lonely to have some fixed place to go.

"I also began to work in the office for Dr. Czinner and Robert Reud, the co-producer of the play.

"The time came when the actress playing the role of the first wife in *The Two Mrs. Carrolls* gave her notice; she was leaving the show. The casting call went out and actresses now began to stream in to the office to try out for the part. Dr. Czinner asked me to read the scene with them. The woman who was finally chosen used to come in the office when I was there alone and rehearse with me. Her name was Alice Buchanan.

"Then the day arrived when she was to rehearse on the stage. She was to have her only run-through with Miss Bergner that evening after the performance. It was a Tuesday. Miss Buchanan was to make her debut the next day, Wednesday, at the matinee. She was frightened and nervous. The idea of playing with an actress of Bergner's stature and reputation awed and intimidated her.

"The stage manager called up Dr. Czinner's office and asked for another script to be brought over to the theatre. I took it over, and when I arrived they were breaking for lunch. Since Alice Buchanan and I had done the scene together in the office, she begged me to stay and rehearse with her while the others were at lunch. I had memorized Miss Bergner's part, so I did. It was fun having a stage to move around on. It was exciting to imagine an audience back in the last rows or up in the balcony and to know that we were projecting to them. When the scene was finished Dr. Czinner surprised us by appearing out of the first rows of the darkened theatre. He came onto the stage. He walked to me, past the actress, took both my hands in his and looked at me, smiled at me. He seemed very moved, very proud.

"That night, after the performance, I brought sandwiches and drinks backstage for Miss Bergner and Dr. Czinner. Then Alice asked me to go over the scene with her until Miss Bergner was ready for the run-through, and so we got started.

"At the high point of the scene, coming down the stairs, I had the strange feeling of being watched. I was without my glasses but I felt eyes on me. It was a tense moment in the play and I was too caught up in it to stop. When I got to the footlights—there was Miss Bergner!

"Several other people were around, on the stage and elsewhere. They were all watching Bergner. Those eyes I had felt fixed on me were hers. Only hers. I'm sure of that.

"I expected her to smile. To be rather amused at how well I was imitating her. Oh, but she continued to stare. She said nothing. My excitement, my joy, departed. I was miserable. Suddenly I had the flash of knowledge: I had done something terrible. Something wrong and horrible, and it had displeased her.

"Out front, towards the back of the theatre, a stagehand was replacing a bulb in the chandelier. He must have asked a question. We onstage didn't hear it, but we did hear another stagehand call out an answer: 'It's that kid that's always hanging around out front. She's as good as Bergner and what's more ya can hear her!'

"The silence was cold and deadly. Finally Dr. Czinner broke the dreadful impasse. He said that now Miss Bergner would take over.

"But Bergner, in a hoarse, tight voice, said, 'No.' She said that I was to continue in the scene so that she could watch 'the other one,' meaning Alice Buchanan.

"Later I was told that I should not have continued the scene. A couple of those present said that Bergner never took her eyes from me but watched as though hypnotized, fascinated, unbelieving, to see someone else do everything she did—subtle, personal, intimate gestures assimilated after weeks of keen observation. Of course she had some acting tricks. She had some coy, Mittel Europa mannerisms that could seem affected and cute. But imitation is the highest form of admiration, and that's all I had shown Bergner. Admiration, and unconscious empathy.

"The next day—Wednesday, as I said—Alice Buchanan made her debut in the play at the matinee performance. At the intermission, I went downstairs to the ladies' lounge to chat with Mrs. Moran, the attendant. I told her about the day before, how I was 'discovered' by Dr. Czinner at noon, and then by Miss Bergner that night. I was ecstatic, and still soaring.

"Three or four days later, in my capacity as secretary, I opened a letter addressed to Miss Bergner. But the letter was all about me! A fan letter to the great actress, but devoted to a girl that she, the writer, had watched and listened to in the ladies' lounge at the Wednesday matinee. I shall always remember the well-meant but tactless lines than annoyed Bergner so: 'Sometimes, Miss Bergner, we fail to see talent right under our very nose. This girl seems to work in some capacity around the theatre. She has all the markings of another Ingrid Bergman or, better still, Elisabeth Bergner.'

"Later, my cousin, Mildred Brody, a psychologist, said to me, 'What kind of person writes fan letters like this? Let's call her up and find out.' The woman was named Bea Elkin and she lived in the Bronx. She told us she liked Bergner although she wasn't really a fan. She said she had been very impressed by the girl and thought that by writing the letter she could help her in some way. For you see, she had overheard me telling Mrs. Moran about my 'discovery.' I remembered afterwards (with Mrs. Moran's help) that during the intermission a woman had pretended to comb her hair there in the ladies' lounge. But in reality, she was watching us in the mirrors that covered two or three walls.

"I took the letter to Dr. Czinner. I asked him if I might keep it without showing it to Miss Bergner. He said no, the letter was addressed to her; it was hers, she must see it.

"So I left it with her other letters. Several days passed. She said nothing about the letter. I began to wonder if it had ended up unread in those manila envelopes where she stuffed unopened mail. I was eager to know her reaction. And I wanted the letter for myself. It couldn't mean much to her, I thought, but everything to me.

"Finally I could wait no longer. Ten days later I asked Dr. Czinner about the letter. For the first time ever he was cool and abrupt. He said Miss Bergner had read it. He said she didn't need a third party to point out my talent. She recognized it, and so did he.

"I felt everything rushing to an end, and I wanted the letter as the one tangible proof that I hadn't dreamed this whole episode.

"I went to Miss Bergner's home while she was away. Thelma, her maid, told me she had seen Miss Bergner reading the letter, dwelling on it, and that she had taken it with her to the theatre. I returned to the Booth. Cordette, Miss Bergner's theatre maid, whispered that the letter was in the pocket of Miss Bergner's fur jacket. I said, 'Look, Cordette, I'm taking this letter. I want it, and she'll only tear it up anyway.'

"After the performance that Saturday night Cordette informed me that I was to wait in the greenroom for Miss Bergner. That night, it seemed she took longer than usual to remove her makeup and change into street clothes. At last she walked in. She told me she had read the letter.

"Then it began. She told me how hard she had worked on her voice, and how she had labored to learn stage movement, and there I was, without training or experience, doing the same things with such ease. '*That*,' she said, 'is talent.' She said those words sadly, not with anger or bitterness. I tried to explain that it was only because I had studied her performances so closely that I could imitate her.

"She was so cold! Never before had I felt such a chill. I realized at once that, knowing *the actress* Bergner quite well, Elisabeth the human being was a stranger to me.

"Her next command was the thunderclap: I was banished from the theatre. She could no longer trust me; I had taken property that was hers. She did say I could continue working for Dr. Czinner and his co-producer in their office.

"She left me alone and I wept for a long time. Then she came back, ready now to leave the theatre and go home. Alone, without me. 'Don't feel so bad. You have talent,' she said. She added that it had happened before; in Europe, clever young women had sought to use her to advance their careers. 'You're a better actress than they were,' she stated. 'I believed in your sincerity and your simplicity.' (In Mary Orr's story, the Bergner figure suspects that Eve wrote the letter herself. That leads to the split.)

"I was out of her life. To prove it even further, she told me I was not to accompany her and Dr. Czinner for the weekend to Lakehurst, New Jersey, where the *Hindenburg* had crashed and burned in nineteen thirty-seven. She never spoke to me again until we met twenty-seven years later.

"For several weeks after that terrible night, I waited in the alley six days a week, before and after every show, six evening performances and two matinees, hoping she would relent and speak to me. You see, I had a little part-time job, so I would come to the theatre in time for her arrival, then go about my business and come back when the play was over. But Bergner was unmoved. She ignored me.

"That's where Mary Orr first saw me. She came to the theatre with her husband, Reginald Denham, the director of *The Two Mrs. Carrolls*.

"I kept on working for Dr. Czinner. One day he told me that the John Golden auditions for new talent would be held soon and he wanted me to enter. I told him I had no interest in becoming an actress and that the loss of Miss Bergner's friendship was a high price to have paid for something I never wanted. Eventually I reconsidered, went to the public library, found my material—a scene from *Anna Christie*—and entered the competition. At the finals, I was one of four winners of the John Golden Awards, Anne Jackson was another. Then I left for Hollywood. It was May or June of nineteen forty-five. Miss Bergner's play was no longer running at the Booth Theatre, having closed a few months earlier, on February third.

"At that time I had changed my name from Ruth Hirsch to Ruth Attlee-Stewart. You see, my husband was Hans Gideon Stein, but to sound more American he changed it to John Gideon Stewart. By taking part of his name and adding Attlee, I became Ruth Attlee-Stewart, with a hyphen. No, no, Clement Attlee was not yet the prime minister of Great Britain, that was only after the war, in nineteen forty-five. Anyway, after I won the Golden Award, Bergner sent word by Mady Christians, the actress I was studying with, that I should take a professional name. She said that if I took the name Martina Lawrence, she would know it's not a real name and she would be able to follow my career. Big deal! Here she wouldn't speak to me, but she was interested in my career."

Facing Martina Lawrence at the end of this strange recital, I must have betrayed a look of panicked consternation. Martina snapped, "I have a feeling you are going to compound some more lies."

That was too much. I was exasperated. "Please!" I said. "Why would I travel to New York to see you if I didn't want the truth? I could write lies at home."

Her bullying ceased. "I don't expect other people, on the fringes of something, to remember all these things, but it happened to me, so of course I remember."

We were friends again. And we had come to the end of our interview. "I'm afraid I've tired you with so many questions," I said. "Let's end on a positive note. About you. Are you happy?"

"Yes," Martina said without a pause. "I have lived my life. I own a little flat. No one can ever raise the rent or take it away from me. I live in a city that is considered by many a very beautiful city, it's a walking city and I'm a walker, I'm interested in art and architecture and history. I have the best of it, I would say."

I turned off the tape recorder, and Martina walked me to the elevator. She rode with me to the lobby, talking all the while and intriguing our fellow passengers with her flair and her melodious, chiseled enunciation. Her vivacious presence signaled that she was out of place in an inexpensive tourist hotel. Those spectators in the lift, as Martina called it, seemed to wonder how she had strayed from the realm of opening nights and clumps of flowers in dressing rooms. We shook hands, and I walked out into East Fifty-first Street.

I felt as if I had awakened from a fever dream to reenter the reality of the city.

I confess that my final question was simply tossed out to help speed my departure. It was, of course, an echo of Mary Orr's statement on Harry Haun's tape, telling Martina, "I hope you are happy now."

Martina's cadenced answer to my question, however, vibrated in my head. It was sweet; it was poignant. And final. A playwright might have invented it to ring down the curtain, or a novelist to end a tale. Or was it yet another fork in the Borgesian path?

Walking around Manhattan that late afternoon, I felt that Martina had raised many more questions than she had answered. The main one being, Who on earth *is* Martina Lawrence? The New York setting produced this surreal image: She's an invention of Damon Runyon . . . in collaboration with Truman Capote, for Martina Lawrence is Holly Golightly grown old. She's also Kay Thompson's Eloise, now a geriatric enfant terrible.

Why had she devoted her life to this mulish campaign of setting the record straight? Her own version differs mainly in particulars, not substantively, from Mary Orr's story. And even though it stings to find yourself unflatteringly fictionalized, how could anyone stew for five decades over a second-rate story in a forgotten magazine? So what if she pinched a letter from a fur jacket? And "stalked" Elisabeth Bergner in some innocuous, juvenile way? There's nothing so terrible about any of it.

In my fanatical mapping of the evolution of Eve Harrington, I had at last found the missing link: Martina Lawrence, who had spawned all subsequent Eves. I determined to dig deeper into the fossil remains of that eventful Broadway season in the mid-forties, looking for bones or even a petrified footprint.

I found instead Mary Diveny, who isn't at all petrified and whose memory for detail rivals Martina's own. She is "Diveny," the friend Martina mentioned in our initial telephone conversation. I went to see her in *Marlene*, at the Cort Theatre on West Forty-eighth Street. Backstage after the play, I encountered an alert, kindly woman, a veteran actor who seemed as sensible and down-to-earth as everyone's favorite aunt. She was rushing to the Port Authority terminal to catch a bus to her home far north of the city, and so we arranged to speak later by phone.

"I came to New York to study at the American Academy of Dramatic Arts, and I lived at the Rehearsal Club from, I believe nineteen forty-five to nineteen forty-nine," Mary Diveny said. "Early in nineteen forty-six I got a job in a USO touring company. We went overseas, and I returned to New York, and the Rehearsal Club, in August of 1946. That's when I met Martina. She had lots of people interested in her for different reasons. That's because she was intriguing. She knew Guthrie McClintic, for example, who was married to Katherine Cornell. He was casting *The Playboy of the Western World* with Burgess Meredith. One of the young women in the cast wasn't working out, so McClintic called Martina. She read for the part, but she wasn't right for an Irish peasant girl. She told him, however, that she knew someone who would be perfect for it. He said, 'Call her,' and Martina did. 'Come right down,' she said. So I did, and I read for him and got the part."

Martina had told me at one point about her aspirations to act, then later she disavowed them. I wanted to know whether she had been in pursuit of a theatrical career back then.

Mary Diveny said, "She would try everything. But without being able to stick to it. She probably thought she was going to be an actress but she just never knew how to go about it the right way."

And did she have other jobs at the same time? "Oh, always," her friend said. "She never had any money. So it was always a waitress job or whatever came along to support herself. We were all like that. I worked at the Russian Tea Room as a hatcheck girl and cashier."

I asked if she knew Martina at the time of her involvement with Elisabeth Bergner. "No," Miss Diveny said. "All that had taken place shortly before we met. But we were all very much aware of it at the Rehearsal Club. Martina was unhappy because the story didn't reflect the way events turned out."

"Do you believe all the details of that incredible Bergner saga?" I ventured.

"Well," she answered, "really, I firmly believe it."

"What was Martina like in those days?" I asked.

"She was effervescent and full of energy. And volatile. She was a very intense person. Martina comes to town once or twice a year, and I always learn something new about her. Another phase of her life that I hadn't heard about before."

If Mary Diveny, who seems as wise and stable as Jane Wyatt in *Father*

Knows Best, doesn't question the veracity of Martina's adventures, then perhaps I shouldn't. But in the case of M. Lawrence vs. E. Bergner, M. Orr, et al., I still felt like a hung jury of one, so I decided to call a final witness.

After burrowing through old newspaper files and current phone directories, I located another alumna of the Rehearsal Club, a former Rockette who knew Martina while living there. This person agreed to speak only on condition of "everlasting anonymity," as she put it. Here is what she said.

"She was immature, unsophisticated, and naive. She'll tell you that herself, and it's true. She's still naive, even though she has traveled the world. She is a waif, a lone person. That mother of hers—oh, she was mentally ill. I remember her mother coming and yelling at her on the street. She was a harridan. She was very heavy, and that's why Martina is so thin. Because she would never, ever let herself be like her mother. She practically starved herself over the years trying to be as different as possible from that woman. She really did go to Hollywood, you know. After the John Golden thing. But the studio didn't work out. It was a big, big disappointment. People would be very interested in her for a while, that accent and all those gestures, but Martina lacked discipline. She took an acting course or something for a few weeks, but that doesn't do much for you, I'm afraid.

"And I can tell you something you don't know. Martina later latched on to Renata Tebaldi. I gather she also played Eve Harrington to her, except that this was the world of opera. Good luck finding out about it. You won't. Divas don't like to admit they've been had."

I found it curious that there was no sex in anyone's version. Paul Czinner was homosexual, and it seems that his marriage to Bergner was platonic. Unlikely, therefore, that he would seduce Martina or be seduced by her. Bergner was either lesbian or bisexual, but according to Martina she made no advances. And despite her mistrust of Martina, they rekindled the friendship, after a fashion.

In 1972 Bergner was appearing at a theatre in Mannheim, Germany, in Eugene O'Neill's *More Stately Mansions*, in German *Alle Reichtum der Welt*. Martina happened into town, looked up Bergner at her hotel, and they had a pleasant visit. But there's always a strange twist to Martina's tales, including this one. For Martina told me she wasn't sure that Bergner recognized her. "She seemed confused, and I'm not at all certain she realized who it was," Martina stated as though such vagueness were the norm.

They also corresponded. Martina showed me several letters from Bergner. The stationery bore the printed address 42, EATON SQUARE, LONDON. The letters, dated in the early 1970s, were pleasant but noncommittal, as though written to a young fan.

The categories to describe Martina Lawrence must exist in some diagnostic manual, but I don't care to look them up. I think it's in literature, not in psychology, where we find the better clues. During our interview I almost sensed two other people in the room, one elderly lady in conflict with another. The first was Ruth Maxine Hirsch, who never knew her father and whose illiterate, demented Polish-Jewish mother abused and hounded her. ("I was more afraid of her than of punishment in the orphanage," Martina said.) Later, as Ruth eked out a living, her mother always turned up to revile and taunt. The fights and harangues continued until the mother's death in 1981, when Martina was sixty years old. This aspect—the hardscrabble life of Ruth Hirsch—echoes the grimmest of Dickens and Zola.

The other side, Martina Lawrence, emerged from the orphanage to reinvent herself, only to lose the patronage of Bergner, her famous sponsor. It seems to have inflicted an unhealing wound. Then she glimpsed her reflection in the Orr story and the Mankiewicz film, and for half a century has nursed the quixotic obsession that she must correct the "errors" of fiction. Fiction, of course, is by definition incorrigible, and so her quest—years longer than Ahab's pursuit of the white whale—turned into a dry, rattling pastiche. Call it Moby Eve.

Is Martina Lawrence the doppelgänger of Ruth Hirsch, or vice versa? The question echoes such uncanny tales as Poe's "William Wilson" and Conrad's "The Secret Sharer." And the dual myth of Norma Jean versus Marilyn.

The most poignant parallel, however, is another Melville character, Bartleby the Scrivener. Once an employee of the Dead Letter Office, the passive-aggressive Bartleby clings to his idée fixe until it leads to grotesque and horrible inertia. The narrator ends the story with these resounding words: "Ah, Bartleby! Ah, humanity!"

When I think of Martina Lawrence, and of the eccentricity of her fifty-year crusade against a few contrived incidents in a magazine story, I don't know which is more apt: "Ah, Martina! Ah, humanity!" or the Margo Channing line, She's "a lamb loose in our big stone jungle."

Regarding the Martina Lawrence hieroglyphs, and attempting to translate them, I write in vanishing ink. Before I reach the predicate, the subject has dissolved. It cannot be real, the conclusion I have reached: that Martina, using her brief appearance in Mary Orr's story, inflated it to match the Mankiewicz script. In the depths of her mind she took up where the film faded out. And so it appears that Martina didn't have her identity stolen. Instead, she abducted Eve Harrington and has held her captive these many, many years—in the dimension of Time.

brief lives, etc.

All About Eve is sprinkled with theatrical allusions—actors, playwrights, critics, and the like. Many of these names were out of date even in 1950; today they're known only to cognoscenti. The same is true of certain topical references. The following list includes names and groups not discussed elsewhere in this book. Since it would be cumbersome to quote all lines in the script where these various references occur, I leave the matching-up to the reader.

NB: Two of the names, Poodles Hanneford and Paula Wessely, are spoken so quickly by Bill Sampson and Addison DeWitt, respectively, that they're quite hard to catch.

Beaumont and Fletcher: Francis Beaumont (1584–1616) and John Fletcher (1579–1625), English dramatists. Their names are always linked because of the plays they wrote together: *The Maid's Tragedy*, *The Scornful Lady*, etc. Fletcher wrote fifty-two plays in all, fifteen of them with Beaumont, sixteen by himself, and the rest in collaboration with other playwrights, including, perhaps, Shakespeare. Beaumont also wrote several plays alone. John Aubrey's seventeenth-century *Brief Lives* implies personal as well as professional intimacy: "They lived together on the Banke side, not far from the Playhouse, both bachelors; lay together; had one Wench in the house between them, which they did so admire; the same cloathes and cloake, &c; between them."

Byron: George Gordon, Lord Byron (1788–1824) is best known as one of the English Romantic poets. He also wrote plays. His dramas, all tragedies in blank verse, were aimed at the library and not the theatre. "I have had no view to the stage," Lord Byron announced in the preface to

Marino Faliero, Doge of Venice. And yet this play was staged in London in 1821. Most of his others received theatrical productions as well: *Werner, Sardanapalus, Manfred, The Two Foscari,* et al. A soupçon of Byronic dramaturgy: The Doge, Marino Faliero, about to be beheaded for treason, delivers a stream of the play's typically elaborate poetry:

> "Thou den of drunkards with the blood of princes!
> Gehenna of the water! thou sea Sodom!"

Eleanora Duse: Italian actress (1858–1924), one of the great tragedi-ennes of world theatre. She toured Russia in 1881, where Chekhov saw her as Cleopatra and was captivated by her art. It has been suggested that he had Duse in mind when he wrote *The Seagull.* In London in 1895 she and Sarah Bernhardt appeared together in Sudermann's *Magda.* Inevitably, the critics preferred one or the other. George Bernard Shaw preferred Duse. She disdained theatrical artifice, including the use of makeup on the stage, and was noted for her ability to blush or turn pale at will. Duse professed a Garboesque hatred of publicity, which of course insured press coverage of her every move.

Jeanne Eagels: American stage and film actress (1894–1929). Eagels was once described as "a striking blonde with haunted eyes that always seemed to be masking some hidden pain." In 1922, after eleven years on Broadway, she became a star "overnight" in Somerset Maugham's *Rain.* Addicted to alcohol and any number of drugs, she grew as erratic on stage as Marilyn Monroe would later become on film sets, and for similar reasons. In 1927, during a performance of *Her Cardboard Lover*, Eagels stopped the play abruptly and ordered Leslie Howard, her leading man, to fetch her a drink of water. When Howard made no move to do so, she walked off the stage herself to get the drink while the audience waited impatiently. One of her lovers was Libby Holman, the torch singer who later served as mentor and lover to Montgomery Clift. Eagels died of a heroin overdose just as the Jazz Age ended.

In 1957 Kim Novak starred in *The Jeanne Eagels Story.* An issue of *Screen Stories* that year emblazoned Novak on the cover in the Eagels persona of femme fatale. Wearing a halter made of pearls, Novak stretched her voluptuous body across the magazine like a slinky bejeweled cat.

Minnie Fiske: American actress (1865–1932) noted for replacing bravura performance with psychologically realistic portraiture. She starred in the plays of Ibsen and also in newer fare such as *Tess of the D'Urbervilles* and *Becky Sharp*. Married to a playwright-journalist, she billed herself as "Mrs. Fiske" and resisted the formation of Actors' Equity because she considered acting an honor, not a trade. An early animal-rights activist, she once had a man arrested for whipping his horse.

Clyde Fitch: American playwright (1865–1909) remembered for *Beau Brummel*, *The Girl With the Green Eyes*, and *The City*. When a character in the latter play learns that he has inadvertently married his sister, he brings down the second-act curtain shouting, "You're a goddamn liar!" The word *goddamn* was so shocking that it caused the drama critic of the *New York Sun* to faint. Today Fitch's plays hold little interest. Though they start out by creating conditions out of which a rigorous exploration of character and idea could develop, all degenerate into melodramatic devices and imposed happy endings. The denouement of *The Girl With the Green Eyes* tells enough:

JINNY (whispers faintly)

Dear Jack! You forgive *me*—all my beastly jealousy?

AUSTIN

There's one thing stronger even than jealousy, my Jinny. And that's love. That's *love!* (*He kisses her hands, and the curtain falls.*)

The Hairy Ape: An expressionistic drama (1922) by Eugene O'Neill. The hirsute title refers to Yank, the protagonist, and also to a literal ape who might be said to steal the show by crushing Yank.

Poodles Hanneford: Equestrian clown and acrobat (1891–1967), scion of a family spanning at least 150 years of circus history in Ireland and later in the United States. Buster Keaton spoke of Poodles as "the only trained acrobat I ever saw who could take a fall and make it look funny." Poodles made two-reel comedies in Hollywood. Then Fatty Arbuckle, ruined by scandal, hired him to appear under his direction. Part of Poodles's act can also be seen in the Shirley Temple movie *Our Little Girl* (1935). He was most famous for stepping off the back of a horse as if he were an animated cartoon character, giving the impression of being momentarily suspended in midair.

Helen Hayes: The First Lady of the American Theatre (1900–1993) needs no introduction. But her film performances make you wonder if she was really that great onstage. Bette Davis couldn't stand her. In 1984 they did a TV movie, *Murder With Mirrors*, at a time when Bette was already quite ill. Hayes said later, "She was imperious and very tough to get along with. I think we were all frightened by Bette."

The Hundred Neediest Cases: A holiday charity drive started long ago by The *New York Times*, seeking contributions each year from Thanksgiving through the end of December.

Liliom: Eve Harrington claims that she and Eddie gave three performances of this play in a little theatre production. Written in 1909 by the Hungarian playwright Ferenc Molnár, it was turned into the musical *Carousel* in 1944 by Rodgers and Hammerstein.

Lunt and Fontanne: Alfred Lunt (1892–1977) and Lynn Fontanne (1887–1983) were the First Couple of the American Stage during the early part of the twentieth century. They married in 1922. Two years later they had an enormous hit in Molnár's *The Guardsman*. From that point on they excelled in high comedy, and everyone called them the Lunts. Their good friend Noël Coward quipped that they were really the same person. Dedicated to the stage, the Lunts resisted Hollywood except for one unhappy venture, when they filmed *The Guardsman* in 1931. Upon their farewell in 1958, a Broadway theatre—the Lunt-Fontanne on West Forty-sixth Street—was named in their honor.

Richard Mansfield: American actor (1857–1907). On the eve of *A Parisian Romance* in 1882, Mansfield told some friends, "Tomorrow night I shall be famous. Come and see the play." On opening night the audience recalled him a dozen times for curtain calls. He had made his beachhead on the shores of immortality. A series of hits—*Doctor Jekyll and Mr. Hyde, Richard III, Cyrano de Bergerac, Beau Brummel* (especially written for him by Clyde Fitch)—established Mansfield as a leading American player. His 1894 *Arms and the Man* was the first Shaw production in the United States. Yankee audiences cheered his anti-royalist line in *Beau Brummel*. Out for a stroll, Beau meets a friend accompanied by the obese Prince of Wales, after Beau and the prince have quarreled. The protagonist inquires: "Who's your fat friend, Sherry?"

Arthur Miller: Born in 1915, Miller was considered one of America's three best living playwrights when his name popped up in *All About Eve*. The others were Tennessee Williams and Eugene O'Neill. Miller had been widely praised in 1947 for *All My Sons*, and in 1949 he had won the Pulitzer Prize for *Death of a Salesman*.

In December 1950, a month after the Hollywood premiere of *Eve*, Marilyn Monroe was walking toward the Fox commissary with Cameron Mitchell. Meeting two gentlemen, they stopped to chat. Mitchell introduced Marilyn to Elia Kazan and Arthur Miller. A correspondence sprang up between Monroe and Miller; they reportedly met from time to time during the early fifties. But Miller was already married, and Marilyn was hungry for stardom. By the time Monroe fled Hollywood for New York in 1955, the only roadblock to their romance was Miller's wife. A trip to Reno removed that obstacle. The Monroe-Miller nuptials, held in the summer of 1956, drew as much worldwide attention as the spectacular marriage of Grace Kelly to Prince Rainier of Monaco in April of that year.

Helena Mojeska: "The Polish Bernhardt" (1840–1909) maintained one of the largest repertoires in the Western world, from Shakespeare to Scribe, Racine's *Iphigénie* to the American melodrama *East Lynne*. She became an American citizen, but is buried in Krakow.

George Jean Nathan: American theatre critic (1882–1958) whose reviews from the 1920s to the 1950s elicited laughter and outrage, depending upon whether one was in the audience or on the stage. Perhaps he's mentioned in *All About Eve* to draw attention away from Addison DeWitt's resemblances to him. For example, both critics have vitriolic tongues, both are fastidious dressers with a liking for fur collars, both employ cigarette holders, and both enjoy the company of attractive young females who don't mind listening for long stretches of time. Nathan was often accused of hating every play he saw. In his autobiography, *Stars in My Hair*, director Reginald Denham, Mary Orr's husband and collaborator, had this to say about the man: "The rudest person to Mary and me among the Broadway critics was George Jean Nathan. He wrote that Orr and Denham were horticultural playwrights. Their first play was called *Wallflower*; the second [i.e., *Dark Hammock*] should have been called 'Stinkweed.' "

Our American Cousin: A comedy by Tom Taylor, first produced in 1858. It is remembered for one reason: Abraham Lincoln was watching it the night he was assassinated (April 14, 1865).

OWI: Eve, having done her homework, knows that Lloyd served in the OWI. During World War II, the Office of War Information was America's chief propaganda agency. The job of the OWI was to explain the war to the American people and their allies, to instill a will to win, and to be the government's liaison with radio, movies, and the press.

Ignace Jan Paderewski: Polish pianist, composer, and patriot (1860–1941). As a young man he drew the sort of hysterical following that would later attend the likes of Elvis Presley and Michael Jackson. Liberace, another pianist of Polish extraction, once displayed on television a miniature piano given to him by Paderewski. He caressed the little piano, fondled it, creating such a treacly scene that millions of fathers forbade their young sons ever to touch the piano again.

Peck's Bad Boy: When Lloyd accuses Margo of playing "Peck's Bad Boy," the allusion is to an 1884 play of that name by Charles Pidgin.

Young Hennery Peck, a juvenile lead, is the bane of his neighborhood, creating mayhem and making life a roaring hell for everyone around him. In 1891 George M. Cohan, age thirteen, played the pugnacious Peck in a road company.

Ada Rehan: American actress (1860–1916), born in Ireland. Using her real name, Ada Crehan, she made her debut in 1873 in a melodramatic potboiler written by her brother-in-law. Soon thereafter, a printer's error on a theatre program listed her as Ada Rehan, so she changed her name. She retired from the stage in 1905, when her brand of nineteenth-century acting was being replaced by a new naturalism.

Robert E. Sherwood: American playwright (1896–1955), author of serious-minded plays including *Idiot's Delight* and *There Shall Be No Night*. Perhaps his most famous is *The Petrified Forest*, produced on Broadway in 1935 and filmed the following year by Warner Bros. Humphrey Bogart and Bette Davis starred in the movie.

Stanislavski: Konstantin Stanislavski was the stage name of Konstantin Sergeyevich Alexeyev (1865–1938). Co-founder and director of the famous Moscow Art Theatre, Stanislavski is also known for his theories of acting. In America the Stanislavski system evolved into a technique known as "method acting," and was taught at the Actors' Studio in New York. Marlon Brando, Maureen Stapleton, Marilyn Monroe, and many other actors studied with Lee Strasberg at the Actors' Studio.

Svengali: A Hungarian musician in George du Maurier's novel *Trilby*. He controls Trilby's stage singing through his hypnotic power. A Svengali, therefore, is one who can exercise a sinister, mesmeric influence over another.

Thespis: A Greek poet and actor in the sixth century B.C., sometimes called the originator of tragic drama. When he stepped out of the chorus and spoke lines, an acting tradition was born. Long after his death, the word *thespian* became a synonym for "actor."

Paula Wessely: Addison mentions this name in the same breath as Jeanne Eagels and Helen Hayes, when he's telling Margo about Eve's audition. Although Wessely is not a legend of the caliber of Eagels and Hayes, she became famous in the German-speaking countries in the 1920s. Born in Vienna in 1907, she was first a stage star, then enormously successful in films. In 1934, she co-starred with Rosa Stradner, Mankiewicz's second wife, in *So Endete eine Liebe* ("Thus Ended a Love"). According to Cinzia Romani's book, *Tainted Goddesses: Female Film Stars of the Third Reich*, "the Nazi regime put to use Wessely's physical type—unglamorous, almost plain, the average middle-class German woman, someone whom audiences could easily identify with— by casting her in one of the most blatant of all German propaganda films, *Heimkehr* ('Homecoming'), 1941." Here are a couple of lines from the script: "Think of how it will be, just think! When everything around us will be German, and when we enter a store, we won't hear Yiddish or Polish being spoken, but only German!" According to an Austrian Web site, she was still alive as of 1998.

Alexander Woollcott: American drama critic and playwright (1887–1943). He is best remembered, however, as the prototype of Sheridan Whiteside in the Kaufman-Hart farce, *The Man Who Came to Dinner*. Woollcott himself was a fat, owlish man, very different in appearance from the distinguished Monty Woolley, who played Whiteside in the 1941 film version. (Bette Davis plays second fiddle to the imperious Woolley.)

As theatre critic for the *New York Times* and other papers, Woollcott was capricious in his judgments. He believed Charlie Chaplin "the greatest living actor" and called *The Skin of Our Teeth* "head and shoulders above anything else ever written for our stage." Both sharp-tongued and sentimental, he wrote nothing of enduring value. It was said of him that he had every aptitude for literature except a taste for the first-rate.

acknowledgments

My first explorations for this book were not encouraging. The main obstacle was the bleak fact of the moving-van fire that destroyed so much of Joseph L. Mankiewicz's material related to *All About Eve*. Mankiewicz himself was gone, and I didn't know whether his survivors would welcome my overtures.

Only one member of the cast was alive, and early on I telephoned Celeste Holm. Her peremptory dismissal of my project, recorded at the beginning of this book, added to my doubts about this quixotic pursuit. I followed the phone call with a letter, which received no answer.

I wrote another letter, this one to Mary Orr, and a few days later she telephoned me. Immediately I went to New York and spent a long afternoon with her. We have stayed in touch since then, and I hope she realizes how very grateful I am. Without her, a crucial early section of this book would have been no longer than a paragraph.

From that point, momentum built. I reached Tom Mankiewicz, the director's son, who extended every courtesy and spoke to me at length about his father's career. He put me in touch with Rosemary Mankiewicz, the director's widow, who was equally gracious.

These interviews, of course, had to be buttressed with all the thousands of facts and quotes and details available only in various print and electronic media. My search led literally across the country as I mined books, magazines, clipping files, cinema archives, and filmed documentaries for every conceivable embellishment to my "biography" of *All About Eve*.

At Boston University Libraries, where Bette Davis's papers are housed, Karen Mix assembled precisely what I needed from the Davis archives. At the Billy Rose Theatre Collection of the New York Public

Library for the Performing Arts, Christopher Frith was particularly valuable. He pointed me in all the right directions and brightened my sometimes grueling task with his good humor.

Surely no one writing about the movies could survive without the endless expertise of the following specialists in Los Angeles: Ned Comstock, of the Cinema-Television Library of the University of Southern California; Brigitte J. Kueppers, of the Arts Library–Special Collections at UCLA; Gladys Irvis of the American Film Institute's Louis B. Mayer Library; and the army of experts at the Margaret Herrick Library of the Academy of Motion Picture Arts and Sciences. Among the latter, Scott Curtis and Faye Thompson gave me special help, and Ed Carter set up a special screening of the 1951 Academy Awards ceremonies.

At the Los Angeles Public Library I located materials not available elsewhere. At the Huntington Library in San Marino, Shelley Bennett and Jennifer Frias provided leads about Sarah Siddons. Robyn Asleson, also of the Huntington, started by helping me with Mrs. Siddons and went on to provide clues on any number of topics.

In Dallas, where I live, the DeGolyer Library at Southern Methodist University was another gold mine, and Ron Davis, of the SMU History Department, brought many unusual sources to my attention.

Of all the collections I used, however, my most frequent quarry was the Dallas Public Library, with its excellent general collection and its outstanding holdings on film and theatre. Only rarely did I fail to find on the shelf exactly what I required. Robert Eason, now retired, was my earliest champion there. I also single out for praise every staff member in Humanities and in Fine Arts: Frances Bell, Rebecca Brumley, Roger Carroll, Yolanda Davis, John Elfers, Ruth Games, Tom Hannigan, Steven Housewright, Kate Jarboe, Kevin Jennings, Lisa Lipton, Ludmila Popelova, Ann Shelton, and Julie Travis.

Richard Kaufman, Principal Pops Conductor of the Dallas Symphony Orchestra, put me in touch with Patrick Russ, an orchestrator in Hollywood who read my pages on Alfred Newman and offered many helpful suggestions.

When the time came to write the chapter on *Applause*, I was fortunate in reaching many of those associated with the original production.

Charles Strouse, Lee Adams, Sidney Michaels, and Betty Comden conveyed a sense of how they created their respective parts of the show. Those who performed at various times in it—Penny Fuller, Lee Roy Reams, Diane McAfee, Garrett Lewis, and Arlene Dahl—surprised me with how much they recalled after thirty years.

The friends to whom this book is dedicated—Robert Sanchez, Glenn Russell, Evan Matthews, Steve Lambert, Tim Boss, Cary Birdwell, John Conway, Gary Schwartz, and Warren Butler—deserve pages of thanks for all they have done. I met them soon after I arrived in Dallas, and once a month we watch a movie together. The first time I played host, I of course screened *All About Eve*. The discussion afterwards was lively, and since then there have been many others. They have helped me during every phase of this book, often dropping everything to boost me over a hump. To quote Max Fabian in the movie, "It's friends that count. And I got friends."

The following persons, many of them close friends, others acquaintances or even strangers, all took time to talk with me about Hollywood circa 1950 or to discuss *All About Eve* in particular. They answered questions in person, by mail, and over the telephone, and never lost patience with my greedy quest for more information on the topic. (One person in this list predicted that in twenty years I'll still be prodding him for details as I complete Volume 18 of the *All About Eve Encyclopedia*, and he may be right.) I feel fortunate, personally as well as professionally, to have encountered each one: Donna Atwater, Brian Baldwin, Rudy Behlmer, Roderick L. Bladel, Gary Carey, Randy Carter, Diane Challis, Richard Challis, Mary Diveny, Roger Farabee, Kenneth Geist, Mel Gussow, Joseph Guy, Sarah Hamilton, Joseph Hansen, Aljean Harmetz, Joyce Saenz Harris, Tom Hatten, Harry Haun, Jeff Herrington, David Jones, Vernon Jordan, Pauline Kael, Gerry Kroll, David Lopes, Barry McBride, Pablo Navarro, Kenneth Neely, Lawrence J. Quirk, Nancy Davis Reagan, Lester Roque, Leigh W. Rutledge, Annie Stevens, and Virginia Tobiassen.

As I was finishing the book, *Vanity Fair* published a long excerpt from it. I wish for myself and for all writers the same editorial expertise and goodwill I encountered there. Those responsible for my happy experience are Graydon Carter, Wayne Lawson, Chris Garrett, James Buss, Ann Schneider, Michael Hogan, Pat Singer, Sharon Suh, and Mersini Fialo. And at the *VF* photo shoot: Brian Harness, Coby Markum, Yvonne Coan, and Katelin Burton.

My neighbors, Ed and Zeyphene McMackin, supplied everything from computer help to apple cobbler. My cats—Margo, Eve, Phoebe, and the anomalously christened Little Bit—did all the things that cats do, and I cheer them for it. St. Jude lived up to his reputation.

Several persons who requested anonymity are also hereby acknowledged in petto.

At the last moment, just as I was ready to send my manuscript to the publisher, Martina Lawrence made a surprise visit to this country. I extended my deadline in order to include her intriguing story. Her statements added color and texture, and I'm grateful to her.

Among those who lowered the stress of publication, I thank Alan Kaufman of Frankfurt Garbus Klein & Selz for legal advice; Karen Pilibosian Thompson for meticulous copyediting; and Michael Connor of St. Martin's Press for efficiency and good humor.

In the final spot of honor I salute my witty, perceptive, and enthusiastic editor, Elizabeth Beier, and my agent, Jim Donovan, whose love of books and movies makes him my ideal reader as well as my ideal agent.

selected bibliography

Two categories of books and periodicals are included in this bibliography: first, those that provided information on the many people connected with *All About Eve* and the Broadway musical, *Applause*, and second, books that in some way broadened my understanding of movies and those who make them. Some minor sources—books, newspaper and magazine articles, archival materials—are not listed below but are cited only in the notes section.

Acker, Ally. *Reel Women: Pioneers of the Cinema, 1896 to the Present.* New York: Continuum, 1991.

Affron, Charles. *Star Acting: Gish, Garbo, Davis.* New York: Dutton, 1977.

Aherne, Brian. *A Dreadful Man.* New York: Simon and Schuster, 1979.

Aldrich, Richard Stoddard. *Gertrude Lawrence As Mrs. A.: An Intimate Biography of the Great Star.* New York: Greystone Press, 1954.

Allen, Leigh. "The Filming of *All About Eve.*" *American Cinematographer*, January 1951.

Alpert, Hollis. *The Dreams and the Dreamers.* New York: Macmillan, 1962.

Andrew, Geoff. *The Film Handbook.* Boston: G. K. Hall, 1989.

Anger, Kenneth. *Hollywood Babylon II.* New York: Plume, 1984.

Anstey, Edgar. *Shots in the Dark.* New York: Garland, 1978.

Asleson, Robyn, ed. *A Passion for Performance: Sarah Siddons and Her Portraitists.* Los Angeles: The J. Paul Getty Museum, 1999.

Bacall, Lauren. *By Myself.* New York: Knopf, 1979.

———. *Now.* New York: Knopf, 1994.

Bankhead, Tallulah. *Tallulah: My Autobiography.* New York: Harper and Brothers, 1952.

Barber, Jill, and Rita Watson. *Sisterhood Betrayed: Women in the Workplace and the All About Eve Complex.* New York: St. Martin's, 1991.

Baxter, Anne. *Intermission.* New York: Putnam's, 1976.

Bayer, William. *The Great Movies.* New York: Grosset and Dunlap, 1973.

Behlmer, Rudy. *America's Favorite Movies: Behind the Scenes.* New York: Ungar, 1982.

———. *Memo From Darryl F. Zanuck.* New York: Grove, 1993.

Behlmer, Rudy, and Tony Thomas. *Hollywood's Hollywood: The Movies About the Movies.* Secaucus, N.J.: Citadel, 1975.

Bergner, Elisabeth. *Bewundert viel und viel gescholten: unordentliche Erinnerungen.* Munich: Goldmann, 1978.

Binh, N. T. *Mankiewicz.* Paris: Rivages, 1986.

Black, Gregory D. *Hollywood Censored: Morality Codes, Catholics, and the Movies.* Cambridge: Cambridge University Press, 1984.

Braudy, Leo. *The World in a Frame: What We See in Films.* New York: Doubleday, 1976.

Brian, Dennis. *Tallulah, Darling.* New York: Macmillan, 1980.

Brown, Gene. *Show Time: A Chronology of Broadway and the Theatre from Its Beginnings to the Present.* New York: Macmillan, 1997.

Burkhart, Jeff, and Bruce Stuart. *Hollywood's First Choices.* New York: Crown Trade Paperbacks, 1994.

Byrge, Duane. *Private Screenings: Insiders Share a Century of Great Movie Moments.* Atlanta: Turner Publishing, 1995.

Campbell, Joseph. *The Hero With a Thousand Faces.* Cleveland: World, 1956.

Carey, Gary. *More About All About Eve.* New York: Random House, 1972.

Carrier, Jeffrey L. *Tallulah Bankhead: A Bio-Bibliography.* Westport, Conn.: Greenwood Press, 1991.

Chierichetti, David. *Hollywood Costume Design.* New York: Harmony Books, 1976.

Ciment, Michel. *Passeport Pour Hollywood.* Paris: Editions du Seuil, 1987.

Collins, Joan. *Second Act.* New York: Doubleday, 1996.

Comden, Betty. *Off Stage.* New York: Simon and Schuster, 1995.

Comden, Betty, and Adolph Green. *Applause. Book by Betty Comden and Adolph Green. Music by Charles Strouse and Lee Adams.* New York: Random House, 1971.

Considine, Shaun. *Bette and Joan.* New York: Dell, 1990.

Conway, Michael, and Mark Ricci. *The Films of Marilyn Monroe.* Secaucus, N.J.: Citadel, 1964.

Corliss, Richard. *Talking Pictures: Screenwriters in the American Cinema.* New York: Penguin, 1975.

Coursodon, Jean-Pierre, and Pierre Sauvage. *American Directors*, vol. II. New York: McGraw-Hill, 1983.

Crist, Judith. *Take 22.* New York: Viking, 1984.

Custen, George F. *Twentieth Century's Fox: Darryl F. Zanuck and the Culture of Hollywood.* New York: Basic Books, 1997.

Davis, Bette. *The Lonely Life.* New York: Putnam's, 1962.

———. *This 'N That.* New York: Putnam's, 1987.

Davis, Ronald L. *The Glamour Factory: Inside Hollywood's Big Studio System.* Dallas: SMU Press, 1993.

Denham, Reginald. *Stars in My Hair.* New York: Crown, 1958.

Dick, Bernard. *Anatomy of Film.* New York: St. Martin's, 1978.

———. *Joseph L. Mankiewicz.* Boston: Twayne, 1983.

Dowdy, Andrew. *The Films of the Fifties.* New York: Morrow, 1975.

Dunne, John Gregory. *The Studio.* New York: Farrar, Straus, and Giroux, 1968.

Fischer, Lucy, ed. *Imitation of Life.* New Brunswick, N.J.: Rutgers University Press, 1991.

Fowler, Karin J. *Anne Baxter: A Bio-Bibliography.* Westport, Conn.: Greenwood Press, 1991.

Frankel, Aaron. *Writing the Broadway Musical*. New York: Drama Book Publishers, 1977.

French, Brandon. *On the Verge of Revolt: Women in American Films of the Fifties*. New York: Ungar, 1978.

Friedrich, Otto. *City of Nets: A Portrait of Hollywood in the 1940's*. New York: Harper and Row, 1986.

Gabor, Zsa Zsa. *My Story*. New York: Crest, 1961.

―――. *One Lifetime Is Not Enough*. New York: Delacorte, 1991.

Geist, Kenneth L. *Pictures Will Talk: The Life and Films of Joseph L. Mankiewicz*. New York: Scribner's, 1978.

Giannetti, Louis. *Masters of the American Cinema*. Englewood Cliffs, N.J.: Prentice-Hall, 1981.

Godard, Jean-Luc. *Godard on Godard*. New York: Viking, 1972.

Gow, Gordon. *Hollywood in the Fifties*. New York: Barnes and Co., 1971.

Greenberger, Howard. *Bogey's Baby*. New York: St. Martin's, 1976.

Gussow, Mel. *Don't Say Yes Until I Finish Talking: A Biography of Darryl F. Zanuck*. New York: Doubleday, 1971.

Haskell, Molly. *From Reverence to Rape: The Treatment of Women in the Movies*. New York: Holt, Rinehart and Winston, 1974.

Haun, Harry. "All About Eve." *Films in Review*, March/April 1991.

Hawkins, Harriett. *Classics and Trash: Traditions and Taboos in High Literature and Popular Modern Genres*. Toronto: University of Toronto Press, 1990.

Head, Edith, and Jane Kesner Ardmore. *The Dress Doctor*. Boston: Little, Brown, 1959.

Head, Edith, and Paddy Calistro. *Edith Head's Hollywood*. New York: Dutton, 1983.

Heisner, Beverly. *Hollywood Art: Art Direction in the Days of the Great Studios*. Jefferson, N.C.: McFarland and Co., 1990.

Higham, Charles. *Bette: The Life of Bette Davis*. New York: Macmillan, 1981.

―――. *The Films of Orson Welles*. Berkeley: University of California Press, 1970.

Higham, Charles, and Joel Greenberg. *Hollywood in the Forties*. London: A. Zwemmer Ltd., 1968.

Hochman, Stanley, ed. *American Film Directors: A Library of Criticism*. New York: Ungar, 1974.

Hummings, Neville March. *Film Censors and the Law*. London: George Allen and Unwin Ltd., 1967.

Inman, David. *The TV Encyclopedia*. New York: Perigee, 1991.

Israel, Lee. *Miss Tallulah Bankhead*. New York: Putnam's, 1972.

Kael, Pauline. *The Citizen Kane Book*. Boston: Atlantic, Little, Brown, 1971.

―――. *Kiss Kiss Bang Bang*. New York: Little, Brown, 1968.

Katz, Ephraim. *The Film Encyclopedia* (2nd Edition). New York: HarperCollins, 1994.

Kawin, Bruce F. *How Movies Work*. Berkeley: University of California Press, 1992.

Keylin, Arleen, and Christine Bent, eds. *The New York Times at the Movies*. New York: Arno, 1979.

Lambert, Gavin. *GWTW: The Making of Gone With the Wind*. Boston: Atlantic Monthly, 1973.

Lamparski, Richard. *Whatever Became of . . . ?* (Series 1). New York: Crown, 1967.

La Polla, Franco, ed. *L'Insospettabile Joseph L. Mankiewicz*. Venice: Edizioni La Biennale di Venezia, 1987.

Laufe, Abe. *Broadway's Greatest Musicals*. New York: Funk and Wagnalls, 1977.

Leaming, Barbara. *Bette Davis: A Biography*. New York: Summit, 1992.

Levy, Emanuel. *And the Winner Is: The History and Politics of the Oscar Awards*. New York: Ungar, 1987.

MacGowan, Kenneth. *Behind the Screen: The History and Technology of the Motion Picture*. New York: Dell, 1965.

McBride, Joseph, ed. *Filmmakers on Filmmaking*. Los Angeles: Tarcher, 1983.

McClelland, Doug. *Hollywood on Hollywood*. Boston: Faber and Faber, 1985.

———. *Starspeak: Hollywood on Everything*. Boston: Faber and Faber, 1987.

Mankiewicz, Joseph L. *All About Eve: A Screenplay*. New York, Random House, 1951.

Mast, Gerald. *A Short History of the Movies*. New York: Macmillan, 1986.

Mérigeau, Pascal. *Mankiewicz*. Paris: Editons Denoël, 1993.

Merrill, Gary. *Bette, Rita, and the Rest of My Life*. Augusta, Maine: Lance Tapley, 1988.

Meryman, Richard. *Mank: The Wit, World, and Life of Herman Mankiewicz*. New York: William Morrow, 1978.

Miller, Frank. *Censored Hollywood*. Atlanta: Turner Publishing, 1994.

Moley, Raymond. *The Hays Office*. New York: Bobbs-Merrill, 1945.

Monroe, Marilyn. *My Story*. New York: Stein and Day, 1974.

Moore, Louis, Donald Tait, and Julian Johnson. "The Truth About *All About Eve*." *Action*, December 1950.

Mordden, Ethan. *The American Theatre*. New York: Oxford University Press, 1981.

———. *Broadway Babies: The People Who Made the American Musical*. New York: Oxford University Press, 1983.

———. *The Fireside Companion to the Theatre*. New York: Fireside/Simon and Schuster, 1988.

———. *The Hollywood Studios: House Style in the Golden Age of the Movies*. New York: Knopf, 1988.

———. *Movie Star: A Look at the Women Who Made Hollywood*. New York: St. Martin's, 1983.

Moseley, Roy. *Bette Davis: An Intimate Memoir*. New York: Donald Fine, 1990.

Murray, Raymond. *Images in the Dark: An Encyclopedia of Gay and Lesbian Film and Video*. Philadelphia: TLA Publications, 1994.

Nathan, George Jean. *The Theatre Book of the Year, 1943–1944*. New York: Knopf, 1945.

Nickens, Christopher. *Bette Davis: A Biography in Photographs*. New York: Doubleday, 1985.

Orr, Mary, and Reginald Denham. *The Wisdom of Eve: A Play in Three Acts*. New York: Dramatists Play Service, 1964.

Osborne, Robert. *Academy Awards Illustrated*. La Habra, Cal.: ESE California, 1969.

Palmer, Christopher. *The Composer in Hollywood*. London: Marion Boyars, 1990.

Parish, James Robert. *Hollywood Character Actors*. New Rochelle, N.Y.: Arlington House, 1978.

———. *Hollywood Players: The Forties*. New Rochelle, N.Y.: Arlington House, 1976.

Parish, James Robert, et al. *Hollywood on Hollywood*. Metuchen, N.J.: Scarecrow, 1978.

Parish, James Robert, and Don E. Stanke. *The Leading Ladies.* New Rochelle, N.Y.: Arlington House, 1977.

Peary, Danny. *Cult Movies.* New York: Dell, 1981.

Quirk, Lawrence J. *Claudette Colbert.* New York: Crown, 1985.

———. *Fasten Your Seat Belts.* New York: William Morrow, 1990.

Richards, Stanley, ed. *Great Musicals of the American Theatre*, vol. 2. Radnor, PA: Chilton Book Co., 1976.

Riese, Randall. *All About Bette: Her Life From A to Z.* Chicago: Contemporary Books, 1993.

Riese, Randall, and Neal Hitchens. *The Unabridged Marilyn: Her Life From A to Z.* New York: Congdon and Weed, 1987.

Robertson, Patrick. *The Guinness Book of Movie Facts and Feats.* London: Guinness Publishing Ltd., 1988.

Roen, Paul. *High Camp: A Gay Guide to Camp and Cult Films.* San Francisco: Leyland Publications, 1994.

Rosen, Marjorie. *Popcorn Venus.* New York: Avon, 1974.

Roud, Richard, ed. *Cinema: A Critical Dictionary*, vol. 2. New York: Viking, 1980.

Russo, Vito. *The Celluloid Closet: Homosexuality in the Movies* (revised edition). New York: Harper and Row, 1987.

Sanders, George. *Memoirs of a Professional Cad.* New York: Putnam's, 1960.

Sarris, Andrew. "Mankiewicz of the Movies." *Show*, March 1970.

Shipman, David. *The Story of Cinema.* New York: St. Martin's, 1982.

Silverman, Stephen M. *The Fox That Got Away: The Last Days of the Zanuck Dynasty at Twentieth Century-Fox.* Secaucus, N.J.: Lyle Stuart, 1988.

Solomon, Aubrey, Jr. *Twentieth Century-Fox: A Corporate and Financial History.* Metuchen, N.J.: Scarecrow, 1988.

Spada, James. *More Than a Woman: An Intimate Biography of Bette Davis.* New York: Bantam, 1993.

Speck, Gregory. *Hollywood Royalty.* New York: Birch Lane, 1992.

Spoto, Donald. *Marilyn Monroe: The Biography.* New York: HarperCollins, 1993.

Stempel, Tom. "Interview With Barbara McLean" (unpublished). Conducted for the American Film Institute, Los Angeles, on August 4 and August 18, 1970.

Stine, Whitney. *I'd Love to Kiss You: Conversations With Bette Davis.* New York: Pocket Books, 1990.

———. *Mother Goddam.* New York: Hawthorn, 1974.

Stone, Peter. "All About Joe." *Interview*, August 1989.

Strouse, Charles, and Lee Adams. *Vocal Selections From "Applause."* New York: Strada Music, 1970.

Summers, Anthony. *Goddess: The Secret Life of Marilyn Monroe.* New York: Macmillan, 1985.

Suskin, Steven. *More Opening Nights on Broadway.* New York: Schirmer Books; 1997.

Swanson, Gloria. *Swanson on Swanson.* New York: Pocket Books, 1981.

Talbot, Daniel, ed. *Film: An Anthology.* Berkeley: University of California Press, 1969.

Taylor, John Russell. *Joseph L. Mankiewicz: An Index to His Work.* London: The British Film Institute, 1960.

Telotte, J. P., ed. *The Cult Film Experience.* Austin: University of Texas Press, 1991.

Thomas, Nicholas, ed. *International Dictionary of Films and Filmmakers. Vol. 1: Films*. Chicago and London: St. James Press, 1990.

Thomas, Tony. *Music for the Movies*. London: Tantivy Press, 1973.

VanDerBeets, Richard. *George Sanders: An Exhausted Life*. Lanham, Md.: Madison Books, 1990.

Vermilye, Jerry. *Bette Davis*. New York: Pyramid, 1973.

Wakeman, John, ed. *World Film Directors*, vol. 1. New York: H. W. Wilson, 1987.

Wheeler, David, ed. *No, But I Saw the Movie*. New York: Penguin, 1989.

Wiley, Mason, and Damien Bona. *Inside Oscar: The Unofficial History of the Academy Awards*. New York: Ballantine, 1988.

Williamson, Bruce. "Bette Davis Interview." *Playboy*, July 1982.

Winnington, Richard. *Film Criticism and Caricatures, 1943–53*. New York: Harper and Row, 1976.

Wood, Michael. *America in the Movies*. New York: Basic Books, 1975.

Zinman, David. *Fifty From the 50's: Vintage Films From America's Mid-Century*. New Rochelle, N.Y.: Arlington House, 1979.

notes

Certain minor sources not in the bibliography are included in these notes. Although I consulted several Web sites, I have not noted them here for two reasons: (1) the vicissitudes of the net and (2) the widespread unreliability of many such sites. All citations from Elisabeth Bergner, Michel Ciment, and Pascal Mérigeau are my translations. The following abbreviations are used:

PERSONS
Lee Adams—LA
Gary Carey—GC
Richard Challis—RC
Betty Comden—BC
Arlene Dahl—AD
Mary Diveny—MD
Penny Fuller—PF
Kenneth Geist—KG
Joseph Hansen—JH
Tom Hatten—TH
Harry Haun—HH
Celeste Holm—CH
Martina Lawrence—ML
Garrett Lewis—GL
Diane McAfee—DM
Rosemary Mankiewicz—RM
Tom Mankiewicz—TM
Sidney Michaels—SM
Mary Orr—MO
Nancy Davis Reagan—NDR
Lee Roy Reams—LRR
Charles Strouse—CS

INSTITUTIONS
New York Public Library for the Performing Arts, Lincoln Center—NYPL
Mugar Memorial Library, Boston University—BU

Margaret Herrick Library, Academy of Motion Picture Arts and Sciences—AMPAS
DeGolyer Library, Southern Methodist University, Dallas—SMU
American Film Institute, Los Angeles—AFI
Dallas Public Library—DPL

CHAPTER 1

p. 1—A terse headline—*Variety*, Sept. 27, 1951
p. 1—"Intellectual fog belt"—Geist, p. 218
p. 1—"Make my pitch"—unsourced clipping, NYPL
p. 2—"Why the hell"—CH to SS, Oct. 5, 1995
p. 2—"When you're"—KG to SS, Jan. 4, 1996
p. 3—"I'm not a dinosaur"—*LA Herald-Examiner*, June 4, 1976
p. 4—"Forgive me"—Carey, p. 100
p. 5–7—The scene between Gabor and Sanders is from Gabor, *My Story*; Gabor, *One Lifetime*; Sanders; VanDerBeets; and an anonymous source.
p. 8–9—Bette Davis–Darryl F. Zanuck conversation is amalgamated from Davis, *Lonely Life*, pp. 276–277 and unsourced clippings, Davis Scrapbook #50, BU
p. 10—"The film that ruined"—Mordden, *Movie Star*, p. 190
p. 10—"Betty Lynn recalled"—Spada, p. 267
p. 10—BOX: "might seem frivolous"—Spada, pp. 178–179
p. 12—Nancy Davis Reagan didn't know—NDR to SS, Mar. 19, 1998
p. 13–14—BOX: names are from Fox casting director's list, AMPAS

CHAPTER 2

p. 16—One reviewer—John Rosenfield, *Dallas Morning News*, Jan. 3, 1946
p. 16—"The way she"—ibid.
p. 17—"My husband, Reginald Denham" et seq.—MO to SS, Apr. 16, 1996
p. 21—"Based on Elisabeth Bergner"—Moseley, p. 167

CHAPTER 3

p. 29—"Would make an excellent"—Carey, p. 17
p. 31—BOX: "Margo Channing's career"—Haskell, p. 245; "Bette Davis's Margo"—Rosen, p. 266; "in the classic"—Hawkins, p. 28; "at one fell swoop"—Leaming, p. 225
p. 33—"Films about Hollywood"—Mordden, *Movie Star*, p. 63
p. 35—"The big problem"—TH to SS, May 1, 1999
p. 36—By comparison—Donald Spoto, *The Dark Side of Genius*, p. 341
p. 37—"In a memo"—Behlmer, *America's Favorite*, p. 211
p. 37—Mankiewicz discussed—Stone, *Interview*, Aug. 1989, pp. 71–75
p. 39—"And the author"—Bergner, pp. 218–219
p. 40—Haun sounded amused et seq.—HH to SS, Apr. 18, 1996
p. 41—Mary Orr remembers—MO to SS, Apr. 16, 1996
p. 41—In his article—Haun, *Films in Review*, March/April 1991, p. 83

CHAPTER 4

p. 43—"The memo recommended"—Behlmer, *America's Favorite*, pp. 202–203; Behlmer, *Memo*, p. 165

p. 44—"The picture was not"—Geist, p. 422

p. 44—"Between completing"—Geist, p. 167; Behlmer, *America's Favorite*, p. 203; Carey, pp. 18–19

p. 44—"I was alone"—Ciment, p. 197

p. 44—"Penned his scripts"—*Hollywood Reporter*, Oct. 21, 1975

p. 44—Mankiewicz said later—Carey, p. 19

p. 45—"Mutual trust"—Gussow p. 155

p. 46—"Difficult to swallow"—Behlmer, *Memo*, p. 166

p. 46—"Dull, obvious, dirty"—ibid.

p. 47—Mankiewicz delivered—Carey, p. 19

p. 47—Studio bookkeeping policy—ibid., p. 66

p. 47—"I have tried"—Behlmer, *America's Favorite*, p. 204

p. 49—"On page 32"—ibid.

p. 50—*BOX*: "I remember that"—Ciment, p. 210 (my translation); "I'd have had"—Geist, p. 18

p. 52—Pauline Kael says—Kael, *Kiss*, p. 393

p. 52—"Screenwriters and directors"—Kael, *Kane*, p. 89

p. 53—Colonel Joy was—Hunnings, p. 157

p. 53—"Some producers played"—Macgowan, p. 356

p. 53—He characterized the Jews—quoted in Black, p. 70

p. 54–57—Correspondence from Production Code files, AMPAS

CHAPTER 5

p. 59—"The hard-softness"—Affron, p. 7

p. 60—"I cried for days"—Quirk, *Fasten*, p. 332; Quirk, *Colbert*, p. 160

p. 60—"Fox couldn't"—Quirk, *Colbert*, p. 160

p. 60—"Joe's idea"—Quirk, *Colbert*, p. 161

p. 60—"Colbert would have"—*Films in Review*, Aug. 1991, p. 244

p. 60—"Question of aging"—Mérigeau, p. 131 (my translation)

p. 61—"Bette did"—Quirk, *Fasten*, p. 332

p. 61—"It wasn't my"—Quirk, *Colbert*, p. 3

p. 61—"I envy you"—Stine, *Mother*, p. 236

p. 61—"I say thank you"—Davis, *Lonely Life*, p. 278

p. 61—Later he explained—Carey, p. 69

p. 63—Mankiewicz claimed—Carey, p. 71

p. 63—"To this day"—ibid.

p. 63—"All scripts were"—ibid.

p. 64—"Approached her agent"—Aldrich, p. 333

p. 64—"When she refused"—Aldrich, p. 335

p. 64—"Who contracted"—ibid.

CHAPTER 6

p. 66—"He said she was"—Davis, *Lonely Life*, p. 277

p. 67—"Darryl Zanuck had"—Merrill, p. 88

p. 67—"I never tried"—Merrill, p. 162

p. 67—"On Sundays"—Merrill, p. 87

p. 68—"This was the first"—Davis, *Lonely Life*, p. 277

p. 68—"On that Sunday"—Merrill, p. 88

p. 68—"I had seen"—Davis, *Lonely Life*, p. 279

p. 68—"The makeup people"—Merrill, p. 89

p. 68—"Hollywood always"—Davis, *NY Times*, Mar. 10, 1968; quoted in McClelland, *Hollywood on Hollywood*

p. 68—"Bette had a few"—Merrill, p. 90

p. 68—"People get the"—to Hedda Hopper, unsourced clipping, Davis scrapbook #50, BU

p. 68—"Certainly wonderful" . . . "For this part"—This exchange from unsourced magazine article, Davis scrapbook, #50, BU

p. 68—"Never in the"—Considine, p. 247

p. 68—"Muscle-bound"—Leaming, p. 207

p. 68—"Decided to marry"—ibid.

p. 69—"In a suit"—Riese, *Bette*, p. 389

p. 69—"Screen tragedienne"—Riese, *Bette*, p. 199

p. 70—Surprise party—*LA Times*, Apr. 5, 1950

p. 70—*Winter Meeting* had been—Leaming, p. 212

p. 72—"Bitch virtuosity"—Carey, p. 70

CHAPTER 7

p. 73—"Bette Davis was"—Holm, SMU

p. 73—"So am I"—ibid.

p. 74—Easter sunrise service—*LA Times*, Apr. 10, 1950

p. 74—"I know one thing"—Holm, SMU

p. 76—"I was wearing"—Considine, p. 249

p. 76—"Fitz Fitzgerald"—Moore, *Action*, Dec. 1950

p. 76—"I had met"—Gabor, *One Lifetime*, p. 76

p. 77—"I saw she was"—Monroe, p. 58

p. 77—"There was just"—Crist, p. 46

p. 78—"That first night"—Holm, SMU

p. 78—"Later that evening"—Gabor, *One Lifetime*, p. 77

p. 78—"People had a habit"—Monroe, p. 142

p. 79—"Haven't you heard"—Spada, p. 270

p. 79—"Honey, we're going"—Considine, p. 249

p. 79—"Whiskey-throated voice"—Spada, p. 270

p. 79—"Bourbon contralto"—Carey, p. 73

p. 80—"Bette was letter-perfect"—Carey, p. 87

p. 80—"Early on"—Allen, *American Cinematographer*, Jan. 1951, pp. 10–11

p. 80—"Now an apprentice"—Moore, *Action*, Dec. 1950

p. 80—"Bette's professional attributes"—Carey, p. 88

p. 80—"The rehearsal period"—Crist, p. 39

p. 81—Shooting after midnight—Allen, *American Cinematographer*, Jan. 1951

p. 81—"Exteriors of the Shubert"—Moore, *Action*, Dec. 1951

CHAPTER 8
p. 82—"While other designers"—Head and Calistro, p. vii
p. 83—"Sure I would"—Head and Calistro, p. 92
p. 83—"Bette and I"—ibid.
p. 83—"She was wearing"—Head and Ardmore, pp. 94–95
p. 83—"Edith always took"—Head and Calistro, p. viii
p. 84—"I steeped myself"—Head and Calistro, pp. 93–94
p. 84—"She has a walk"—Head and Ardmore, pp. 94–95
p. 84—"We thought we had"—*Dallas Times Herald*, Aug. 8, 1978
p. 85—By seven o'clock—Moore, *Action*, Dec. 1950
p. 86—Clift's Redwood Room—*SF Chronicle*, Apr. 16, 1950
p. 86—"Miss Holm seemed"—ibid.
p. 86—"Miss Holm has developed"—ibid.
p. 87—"I'm glad you're"—*LA Herald Express*, May 20, 1950

CHAPTER 9
p. 88—Holm-Davis exchange from Holm, SMU
p. 88—"There is truth"—Merrill, p. 89
p. 88—"My first day"—Davis, *Lonely Life*, pp. 279–280
p. 89—"I don't think"—Merrill, p. 280
p. 89—"He's right"—*Collier's*, Dec. 9, 1955
p. 89—"I looked at"—Davis, *Lonely Life*, p. 280
p. 89—"Margo Channing waits"—Carey, p. 55
p. 89—"You're quite right"—Davis, *Lonely Life*, p. 280
p. 89—"At first"—Merrill, p. 89
p. 89—"The unholy mess"—Davis, *Lonely Life*, p. 280
p. 89—"Before long"—Merrill, p. 90
p. 89—"The last place"—Davis, *This 'N That*, p. 179
p. 89—"It was not"—Geist, p. 169
p. 89—"There was one"—ibid.
p. 89—"Would Miss Davis"—Considine, p. 251
p. 89—"I sensed in Gary"—Davis, *Lonely Life*, p. 281
p. 90—"I walked around"—Merrill, p. 90
p. 90—"I started falling"—Riese, *Bette*, p. 344
p. 90—"There was one bed"—Gabor, *One Lifetime*, p. 78
p. 90—"*That bed*"—Riese, *Bette*, p. 344
p. 90—"We only played"—Merrill to Louella Parsons, Jan. 14, 1951; unsourced clipping, Davis scrapbook #52, BU
p. 90—"I had fused"—Davis, *Lonely Life*, p. 280

CHAPTER 10
p. 91—"Considered her unphotogenic"—Monroe, pp. 61–62
p. 91—"Mr. Zanuck feels"—Monroe, p. 62
p. 91—"For the most part"—Carey, p. 75
p. 92—"There was a"—Carey, p. 77
p. 92—"He haunted"—ibid.
p. 92—"I wasn't about"—ibid.

p. 92—"On March 27"—Carey, pp. 77–78

p. 93—"And that poor"—Quirk, *Fasten*, p. 336

p. 93—"Even then"—Sanders, p. 70

p. 93—BOX: "politely but firmly"—VanDerBeets, pp. 110–111

p. 94—"That woman hates"—Collins, p. 79

p. 94—"I saw nothing"—Geist, p. 170

p. 94—"I always felt"—Holm, SMU

p. 94—"That girl's going"—McLean, AFI

p. 94—"About a year"—Baxter, pp. 296–297

p. 95—"Thees girl ees"—Geist, p. 170

p. 95—"Marilyn Monroe was seated"—Merrill, p. 90

p. 96—"Trivia fans remember"—Davis, *This 'N That*, p. 182

p. 96—"There has been"—Riese and Hitchens, *Marilyn*, p. 569

p. 96—"Mr. Zanuck has never"—Riese and Hitchens, *Marilyn*, p. 568

p. 96—"I disagreed and fought"—Riese and Hitchens, *Marilyn*, pp. 569–570

p. 97—"I thought of her"—Carey, p. 79

p. 97—Marilyn shook her head—Carey, pp. 78–79

p. 98—"A different sort of director"—Monroe, p. 95

p. 98—"It was the first"—Monroe, p. 95

p. 98—Lincoln Steffens trouble—Monroe, pp. 95–97

p. 100—The German actress—Summers, p. 50

CHAPTER 11

p. 101—On that Saturday night—Moore, *Action*, Dec. 1950

p. 101—"Every day was"—Baxter, p. 264

p. 102—"I was good"—Baxter, p. 263

p. 102—"Bette was really"—Stine, *Kiss*, p. 255

p. 102—Margo and Eve's—Stine, *Kiss*, p. 227

p. 102—"Nice to everybody"—Behlmer, *America's Favorite*, p. 212

p. 103—BOX: *Phantom of the Opera; The Actor's Nightmare*—Mordden, *Fireside*, p. 93

p. 103—Anne Baxter called—Baxter, 264

p. 103—"John Hodiak and I"—ibid.

p. 104—"We went to see"—Considine, p. 250

p. 104—"She was fine"—Holm, SMU

p. 104—"Our assistant"—Baxter, pp. 265–266

p. 105—"Mr. Mankiewicz insisted"—Holm, SMU

p. 105—"This cubbyhole"—Fox Exhibitor's Manual

p. 105—"Bette upstaged Anne"—Quirk, *Fasten*, p. 335

p. 105—Bette returned—Quirk, *Fasten*, p. 334

p. 106—"The nearest thing"—Sanders, p. 68

p. 106—"Vain, aging, flamboyant"—ibid.

p. 106—"Her lack of"—Quirk, *Fasten*, p. 335

p. 106—"George Sanders never"—Geist, p. 170

p. 106—BOX: "The kind of actor"—Sanders, p. 71

p. 107—"George slept soundly" et seq.—Baxter, pp. 264–266.

CHAPTER 12

p. 111—The telegram was from—Leaming, p. 223
p. 111—"Beautiful, tender, sweet"—Spada, p. 275
p. 111—"It was being said"—Leaming, p. 231
p. 111—She played records—Considine, p. 252
p. 112—According to de Havilland—Speck, p. 83
p. 112—Another co-star—Speck, p. 87
p. 112—Bette told Anne—Baxter, pp. 263–264
p. 112—"Big martinis"—Baxter, p. 264
p. 112—"Going up and down"—Leaming, p. 222
p. 112—"There is a"—Davis, *This 'N That*, p. 180
p. 113—"We're all just glass"—Geist, p. 171
p. 113—Cautionary phone calls—Davis, *Lonely Life*, p. 277
p. 113—On the last film—Carey, p. 86
p. 113—"Dear boy"—ibid.
p. 113—"Always a good thing"—ibid.
p. 113—"Barring grand opera"—Carey, p. 87
p. 113—"Mankiewicz is a genius"—Considine, p. 248
p. 113—"He resurrected me"—McBride, p. 108
p. 114—Goulding had said—Carey, p. 88
p. 114—"After those warnings"—ibid.
p. 114—"That inimitable Davis"—ibid.
p. 114—"Look, Joe"—Carey, pp. 88–90
p. 114—"How she behaved"—Moseley, p. 128
p. 114—"At home she had"—Moseley, p. 32

CHAPTER 13

p. 116—"For the most part"—Davis, *This 'N That*, p. 182
p. 116—"Dad had the quietest"—TM to SS, Aug. 21, 1997
p. 117—Everyone had a laugh—Fox Exhibitor's Manual
p. 117—"Let's have the rain"—ibid.
p. 117—At the end—Behlmer, *America's Favorite*, p. 207
p. 118—He watched the dailies—Dunne, pp. 65–66
p. 118—"I got Bette's permission"—Merrill, p. 91
p. 118—"I'd marry Bette"—ibid.
p. 118—Barbara Leeds Merrill—Leaming, p. 232
p. 119—Tight-bodiced—Head and Calistro, pp. 92–93
p. 119—"There was Bette"—Head and Calistro, p. 93
p. 120—"I could have hugged"—ibid.
p. 120—As Edith watched—Head and Ardmore, p. 96
p. 120—"A very talented"—Ciment, p. 173
p. 120—"Bette's dress"—Holm, interviewed on AMC "Hollywood Fashion" documentary, March 1996
p. 120—"I met Marilyn"—Head and Calistro, p. 106

CHAPTER 14
p. 122—"A close friend"—Baxter, p. 335
p. 122—"How could I"—Gussow, pp. 88–89
p. 122—"One Sunday in 1946"—Baxter, p. 335
p. 123—"Your throaty voice"—*LA Herald Express*, May 20, 1950
p. 124—"She chose"—Spoto, p. 207
p. 124—"I liked Bette"—Gabor, *One Lifetime*, p. 78
p. 125—"Just a minute"—Geist, 170; Davis, *This 'N That*, p. 182
p. 125—"Wretched during the shooting"—Gabor, *My Story*, p. 181
p. 125—"*Poetry!*"—Gabor, *My Story*, p. 182
p. 125—At that very moment—Gabor, *One Lifetime*, pp. 76–77
p. 126—"I was sitting"—Monroe, pp. 97–98
p. 128—"I know and you know"—Quirk, *Fasten*, p. 337
p. 128—Now Mankiewicz concentrated—Behlmer, *America's Favorite*, p. 207
p. 128—"One of the most"—Davis, *This 'N That*, p. 181
p. 129—"She was perfect"—Moseley, p. 119
p. 129—Slight jiggle—Behlmer, *America's Favorite*, 208
p. 129—"Do you know"—Holm, SMU
p. 130–31—BOX: "Life of an actress"—*Times Picayune*, June 23, 1946; "I have always"—Holm, SMU; "I have never"—McClelland, *Starspeak*; "The basic theme"—*Theatre Week*, Mar. 3, 1989; "Television is just like"—unsourced clipping, NYPL; "My favorite show"—unsourced clipping, DPL
p. 131—"One of my favorite"—Holm, SMU
p. 131—Gary Merrill called—Merrill, p. 89
p. 131—Mankiewicz treasured—Carey, p. 70
p. 132—"We sat behind"—*NY Times*, Feb. 6, 1969
p. 132—"When I was running"—ibid.
p. 132—She loved Dickens—*Current Biography*, 1957, p. 469
p. 132—"I like Bette"—Quirk, *Fasten*, p. 338
p. 133—Thelma decided to buy—Fox Exhibitor's Manual
p. 133—"I adored that girl"—McClelland, *Starspeak*, p. 2100
p. 133—"Birdie always says"—*Films in Review*, Nov. 1969, p. 553
p. 134—"She is not just"—*Films in Review*, Aug./Sept. 1974, p. 445
p. 134—"I liked the stage"—*LA Times*, Apr. 14, 1946
p. 134—"Celeste had acquired"—*Films in Review*, Aug./Sept. 1974, p. 445
p. 134—"I could never"—*NY Daily News*, July 2, 1990
p. 135—Liked the Zanuck children—Holm, SMU

CHAPTER 15
p. 136—"I don't understand"—McBride, p. 106
p. 137—"I'm sorry, Joe"—Riese, *Bette*, p. 11
p. 137—"Genius piece of business"—McBride, p. 106
p. 137—Tony Perkins devised—Stephen Rebello, *Alfred Hitchcock and the Making of Psycho*, p. 88
p. 138—Special security guards—Fox Exhibitor's Manual
p. 138—"I'm still waiting"—Crist, p. 40
p. 138—"A genius moviemaker"—ibid.
p. 138—"Those are things"—McBride, pp. 105–106

p. 138—Twenty-five years later—Davis, *This 'N That*, p. 93

p. 139—"He was a stick"—*Films in Review*, Aug. 1991, p. 240

p. 140—Feud had started—*Variety*, Apr. 18, 1956

p. 140—"Frequently he"—*NY Journal American*, Apr. 15, 1956

p. 140—"I had just kicked"—*NY Post*, Apr. 15, 1956; *NY Journal American*, Apr. 15, 1956

CHAPTER 16

p. 142—"I always followed"—Merrill, p. 198

p. 143—"But Gary"—Merrill, pp. 91–92

p. 143—"I know a couple"—unsourced clipping, Bette Davis scrapbook #52, BU

p. 143—"One's back"—Davis, *Lonely Life*, p. 240

p. 143—"Cut! Cut!"—Davis, *This 'N That*, p. 182; Geist, p. 169

p. 144—"I can't do that"—Geist, p. 169

p. 144—F.A.G. shampoo—ibid.

p. 146–48—Barbara Bates, who plays—details of Bates's life and career from *Film Fan Monthly*, Mar. 1970, pp. 15–20; Anger, *Hollywood Babylon II*, pp. 211–212

p. 149—"Artistically unjustifiable"—Winnington, p. 119

p. 149—"A totally redundant"—Corliss, p. 243

p. 151—BOX: According to Fox records—Carey, p. 66

CHAPTER 17

p. 155—On May 31—Geist, p. 173

p. 156—"I'm not giving"—Holm, SMU

p. 156—"Like many directors"—TM to SS, Aug. 21, 1997

p. 156—"You want to see"—Holm, SMU

p. 157—"Most sophisticated directors"—ibid.

p. 157—"He only worried"—TM to SS, Aug. 21, 1997

p. 157—"I learned all about"—Stempel, AFI

p. 157—In those days—Katz, *The Film Encyclopedia*, p. 406

p. 158—"Creative, imaginative"—Davis, *Glamour Factory*, p. 286

p. 158—Some studio directors—Davis, *Glamour Factory*, p. 289

p. 158—Barbara McLean generally spent—ibid.

p. 158—McLean and Webb met—*LA Times*, Apr. 2, 1996

p. 158—"I see every picture"—*Hollywood Citizen News*, Mar. 23, 1945

p. 159—"Because every woman"—Davis, *Glamour Factory*, p. 286

p. 159—"Editing has traditionally"—Katz, *Film Encyclopedia*, p. 407

p. 159—Another film historian—Acker, pp. 219–220

p. 159—Dede Allen—Acker, p. 220

p. 159—The Movieola could—Katz, *Film Encyclopedia*, p. 981

p. 160—"Was this standard policy"—Stempel, AFI

p. 160—"Dad was riding high"—TM to SS, Aug. 21, 1997

p. 161—"We were very good friends"—Stempel, AFI

p. 161—Tom Mankiewicz states—TM to SS, Aug. 21, 1997

p. 162—"I get the best"—Ciment, pp. 199–2100

p. 163—"Just leave it all"—Méigeau, p. 69

p. 163—Zanuck prefaced a statement—*NY Times*, Apr. 2, 1996

p. 163—"I don't care"—Acker, p. 235

p. 163—Selection of takes—Katz, *Film Encyclopedia*, p. 56

p. 164—On Saturday, June 24—Carey, p. 66

p. 164—Since screenings—Behlmer, *Memo*, p. xxi

p. 164—"In the projection room"—Stempel, AFI

p. 165—"In that editing room"—*Dallas Morning News,* Dec. 25, 1979

p. 165–68—BOX: He told an interviewer—Ciment, p. 223; "I think I've read"—Carey, p. 72; "an absolute fool"—Stine, *Kiss*, p. 102; "Celeste Holm wept"—*Interviw*, Nov. 1980; in 1991—*Films in Review*, Aug. 1991, p. 242

p. 168—"Was happiest when"—Behlmer, *Memo*, p. xix

p. 168—"I work hard"—Gussow, p. 88

p. 170—It's not surprising—Behlmer, *America's Favorite*, p. 209

p. 170—"All pictures are"—Gussow, p. 88

p. 171—"Not bad for"—Gussow, p. 156

p. 172—Later the author—Geist, p. 137

p. 172—"Cut one wife"—Gussow, p. 157

CHAPTER 18

p. 174—"I'm terrified"—Page Cook, liner notes for *Captain From Castile: The Classic Film Scores of Alfred Newman*, an LP recording

p. 174—"The musical entity"—Carey, p. 98

p. 175—"Opening and closing fanfares"—*Films in Review*, Aug./Sept. 1989

p. 177—After two weeks—Moore, *Action*, Dec. 1950

p. 177—Sixty musicians—ibid.

p. 177—When the music cutters—ibid.

p. 178—"If I want"—*NY Times*, Feb. 19, 1970

p. 178—"A high-class, impersonal"—*NY Times*, Mar. 21, 1937

p. 178—Wasn't afraid to delegate—Palmer, p. 71

p. 178—Newman's musical idiom—ibid.

CHAPTER 19

p. 183—"Almost no visual"—Kael, *Kiss*, p. 270

p. 184—Mankiewicz told an interviewer—Mérigeau, p. 35

p. 185—BOX: "tells of Zoe"—Mordden, *Fireside*, p. 15

p. 186—"Men are less"—Carey, p. 20

p. 186—"I often wonder"—Carey, p. 8

p. 187—Lyle Wheeler supposedly—Heisner, p. 109

p. 188—A poignant story—*LA Times*, Feb. 8 and Mar. 25, 1989

CHAPTER 20

p. 191—Zanuck, having made—Moore, *Action*, Dec. 1950

p. 191—Studio's legal department—ibid

p. 191—"Back then I would"—Stempel, AFI

p. 192—A routine form letter—Production Code Files, AMPAS

p. 192—For each film—ibid.

p. 192—"No one is very happy"—Leaming, p. 230

p. 192—"I shall set off"—ibid.

p. 193—"Looked like a dog"—*LA Times*, Aug. 23, 1951

p. 193—Ceremony was performed—Riese, *Bette*, p. 448

p. 193—"An hour after"—Leaming, p. 233

p. 193—"The downfall"—Riese, *Bette*, p. 297

p. 194—"The joke was"—Davis, *This 'N That*, p. 185

p. 194—"The stars of"—Merrill, p. 197

p. 194—"Not long after"—Davis, *This 'N That*, p. 186

p. 194–96—BOX: *Life* reported—*Life*, Dec. 21, 1959; during the tour—Leaming, p. 247; in San Francisco—Spada, p. 322; Ethel Barrymore—Margot Peters, *The House of Barrymore*, p. 520; "I sat and watched"—Merrill, p. 196; "she had totally"—Merrill, p. 197

CHAPTER 21

p. 198—The lights went down—unsourced clipping, Bette Davis scrapbook #50, BU

p. 199—Buzz in Hollywood—Spada, pp. 284–285

p. 199—Built on a scale—Black, p. 22

p. 200—Flood of telephone calls—*NY Times*, Oct. 14, 1950

p. 200—Ticket sales increased—*NY Herald Tribune*, Oct. 21, 1950

p. 200—*Variety* reported—*Variety*, Oct. 18, 1950

p. 200—"Eve, who would make"—*NY Times*, Oct. 14, 1950

p. 200—Leo Mishkin—quoted in Spada, p. 285

p. 200—Two servicemen—Riese, *Bette*, p. 199

p. 201—"The fans were treated"—*Hollywood Reporter*, Nov. 10, 1950

p. 201—As the stars arrived—*Hollywood Citizen News*, Nov. 9, 1950

p. 202—"I'm afraid some of"—*San Francisco Chronicle*, Apr. 16, 1950

p. 202—"It was a world"—Davis, *Glamour Factory*, p. 325

p. 202—"I love Hollywood"—McClelland, *Starspeak*, p. 50

p. 202—"My husband"—Considine, p. 255

p. 202—Sporadic applause—*LA Times*, Nov. 10, 1950

p. 202—When the movie ended—ibid.

p. 202—Dinner parties—*Hollywood Reporter*, Nov. 10, 1950

p. 202—The studio bash—Stine, *Mother*, p. 237

p. 202—"It was Bette's"—quoted in Considine, p. 256

p. 203—The new arrival—ibid.

p. 203—Joan took her phone—Considine, p. 426

CHAPTER 22

p. 206—Feeling ill—Considine, p. 257

p. 207—Joan Crawford's son—Considine, p. 258

p. 207—She campaigned hard—Levy, p. 61

p. 208—What a monster—Spada, p. 286

p. 208—The first two actresses—ibid.

p. 208—Later Mankiewicz said—ibid.

p. 209—"A symbol that captures—Levy, p. xi

p. 209—Sam Lesner—Swanson, p. 262

p. 211—Fellow starlets—Wiley, p. 208
p. 211—The only person—Wiley, p. 209
p. 211—Sanders accepted—VanDerBeets, p. 107
p. 211—"It is generally imagined"—Sanders, p. 69
p. 212—"I sat alone"—Gabor, *My Story*, pp. 183–184
p. 212—"The night I got"—Sanders, p. 70
p. 214—"Ran up to Sam Jaffe's table"—Wiley, p. 209
p. 214—Gloria hugged Judy—ibid.
p. 214—The radio network—Osborne, p. 170
p. 214—Gloria Swanson congratulated—ibid.
p. 214—In England—Wiley, p. 209
p. 214—But she left—Wiley, p. 210
p. 215—She felt she should—Levy, p. 218
p. 215—In support of—*Playboy*, July 1982, p. 76
p. 215—"Gary and I"—Riese, *Bette*, p. 412
p. 215—"Swanson was up"—*Playboy*, July 1982, p. 76
p. 215—Anne Baxter told—Riese, *Bette*, p. 38
p. 215–16—List of non-Oscar awards from Riese, *Bette*, p. 29
p. 216—*Samson and Delilah*—Riese, *Bette*, p. 60
p. 216—*Eve* brought in—Solomon, p. 73
p. 216—"In the golden years"—Solomon, p. xii

CHAPTER 23

p. 218—"Most of the guests"—Davis, *This 'N That*, p. 18
p. 219—"I begged the producer"—McBride, p. 108
p. 219—Someone asked Tallulah—Carrier, p. 35
p. 220—Tallulah called up—Quirk, *Fasten*, p. 334
p. 220—She had sued—Brown, p. 184
p. 220—Wrote letters, sent telegrams—Quirk, *Fasten*, p. 334
p. 220—"No intentional imitation"—Spada, p. 287
p. 220—Meyer Berger—quoted in Brian, p. 145
p. 221—"Someone in the audience"—*Dallas Times Herald*, Dec. 6, 1950
p. 221—The *Dallas Morning News*—*Dallas Morning News*, Dec. 6, 1950
p. 221—The following year—Israel, p. 287
p. 222—"Comedy of insult"—VanDerBeets, p. 109
p. 222—To guest George Sanders—Israel, p. 288
p. 222—"Whenever I'm in Hollywood"—VanDerBeets, p. 109
p. 222—"Forced to vote"—Bankhead, p. 2; p. 325
p. 224—Mary Orr still shudders—M O to S S, Apr. 16, 1996
p. 224—"Was there any truth"—*Playboy*, July 1982, p. 78
p. 224—Mankiewicz, too—Osborne, p. 171
p. 224—"I steeped myself"—Head and Calistro, p. 94
p. 224—"Multitude of reasons"—Israel, p. 236
p. 225—"Barrage of scurrility"—Israel, p. 237
p. 225—"I visited the set"—Carey, p. 74
p. 225—"Zanuck's choice for the role"—T M to S S, Aug. 21, 1997
p. 226—"What Dad tried"—T M to S S, Aug. 21, 1997
p. 226—"I've always told"—Carey, p. 72

p. 227—"When Tallulah decided"—Israel, p. 101

p. 227—"As scripts arrived"—Israel, p. 143

p. 227—"Dola was a wealthy Canadian"—Brian, pp. 128–129

p. 227—"Tallulah never traveled"—Brian, p. 256

p. 228—"Can I help her"—Israel, p. 220

p. 228—"She shopped"—ibid.

p. 228—"I know what people"—Israel, p. 221

p. 228—"By the time Tallulah"—Israel, p. 99

p. 229—She reportedly—Israel, p. 65

p. 230—"The Wise Old Man"—Campbell, p. 9

p. 230—"Occupy a prominent place"—Campbell, p. 10

p. 230—"Figure of the Tyrant-Monster"—Campbell, p. 15

p. 231—"I'm well-nigh besotted"—Carey, p. 41

p. 231—"Wonderful understanding"—Stempel, AFI

CHAPTER 24

p. 232—"The screenplay is"—*Dallas Morning News*, Oct. 11, 1997

p. 234—Film scholar, Bernard Dick—Dick, *Anatomy*, p. 83

p. 235—"Stream of juicy"—Winnington, p. 119

p. 235—"The fashionable viewers"—Truffaut, *The Films in My Life*, p. 129

p. 235—Mankiewicz only pretends"—quoted in Hochman, p. 314

p. 236—BOX: "That homely little girl?"—unsourced clipping, Davis scrapbook #50, BU

p. 236—"Triumphantly literary"—Andrew, p. 189

p. 236—"True and savage indictment"—Riese, *Bette*, p. 7

p. 236—"Elegant comedy"—Geist, p. 102

p. 236—"Théâtre filmé"—Dick, *Mankiewicz*, p. 151

p. 236—"Ersatz art"—Kael, *Kiss*, p. 283

p. 237—"We tried to make"—Behlmer, *America's Favorite*, p. 118

p. 237—This device goes all the way back—Slide, p. 322

p. 237—D. W. Griffith elaborated—Mast, p. 55

p. 237—Popularized the freeze-frame—Dick, *Mankiewicz*, p. 25; Geist, p. 101

p. 238—"The camera moves"—Dick, *Mankiewicz*, p. 155

p. 238—"The best direction"—Mérigeau, pp. 14–15

p. 239—"I was angry"—Taylor, p. 18

p. 239—"They entertained you"—Kael, *Kane*, p. 26; p. 52

p. 241—"We are transfixed"—Roen, p. 26

p. 242—"Male behavior"—*Films in Review*, Mar./Apr. 1991, p. 75

p. 242—"Based essentially on me"—*Films in Review*, Mar./Apr. 1991, p. 76

CHAPTER 25

p. 249—"One of Anne's greatest"—TM to SS, Aug. 21, 1997

p. 250—"I wanted Michael Caine"—Ciment, p. 155

p. 251—Still getting mail—Ciment, pp. 218–219

p. 253—"I'm not prepared"—*NY Post*, Feb. 24, 1973

CHAPTER 26

p. 257—Acting out favorite scenes—Gussow, p. 158

p. 257—Novelist, Joseph Hansen—JH, letter to SS, Oct. 11, 1997

p. 258—"Large volume" of letters—*NY Times*, Apr. 14, 1951

p. 258—J. R. Moser, et seq.—correspondence in Production Code files, AMPAS

p. 259—"I discovered that"—Davis, *This 'N That*, p. 90

p. 259—"All About Little Eva?"—*Variety*, Mar. 7, 1951

p. 259—Maria Zeppezauer—*Variety*, Mar. 5, 1952

p. 260—BOX: Local censor boards—Production Code files, AMPAS

p. 263—*Imitation of Life* screenplay—Fischer, p. 60

p. 263—Robert Alda—Fischer, p. 68

p. 265—"I was a kid"—GC to SS, Dec. 23, 1996

p. 265—James Baldwin—*Another Country*, p. 32

p. 269—Carey-Mankiewicz controversy—GC to SS, Dec. 23, 1996

p. 270—Mankiewicz told a reporter—*NY Post*, Feb. 24, 1973

p. 273—"Seven Deadly Sins Festival"—Robertson, p. 208

p. 275—Bradford Samuel—Jim Faraone, *2nd Fashion Doll Makeovers*, p. 68

p. 276—John Rechy—*Marilyn's Daughter*, pp. 83–84; 143; 180

p. 278—*MMII*—p. 161

p. 278—*Timequake*—p. 188

p. 278—Later that year—*TV Guide*, Aug. 8–14, 1998

p. 278—William Friedkin—Byrge, p. 57

p. 279—Isaac Mizrahi—*American Movie Classics* magazine, Aug. 1996

p. 279—E. Lynn Harris—*Publishers Weekly*, Apr. 9, 1999

p. 279—Gay filmmaker, Marc Huestis—Murray, p. 143

CHAPTER 27

p. 282—Cole Porter, in 1957—William McBrien, *Cole Porter*, p. 380

p. 282—A 1964 taped conversation—Spada, pp. 385–387

p. 283—"I had a tremendous"—CS to SS, June 26, 1998

p. 284—"I was working"—SM to SS, July 9, 1998

p. 285—"This time, at least,"—MO to SS, Apr. 16, 1996

p. 285—"The theatre has given"—*NY Times*, Nov. 19, 1982

p. 285—"We worked together"—SM to SS, July 9, 1998

p. 285—According to Lee Adams—LA to SS, Mar. 8, 1999

p. 285—To interest Anne Bancroft—Greenberger, p. 207

p. 286—"Lauren Bacall was"—SM to SS, July 9, 1998

p. 286—"I was approached"—Bacall, *Myself*, p. 339

p. 286—"We went to Ron Field"—SM to SS, July 9, 1998

p. 286—"I was bucking"—Field, SMU

p. 287—"Larry Kasha had"—SM to SS, July 9, 1998

p. 287—"My recollection"—LA to SS, Mar. 8, 1999

p. 287—"I hired Strouse and Adams"—Kasha, SMU

p. 287—"What happened"—CS to SS, June 26, 1998

p. 288—"A settlement"—Bacall, *Myself*, p. 353

p. 288—"I went to David Brown"—Kasha, SMU

p. 289—"A meeting was called"—SM to SS, July 9, 1998

p. 289—"A limited amount"—*NY Times*, Apr. 1, 1970

p. 290—Run-of-the-play contract—Greenberger, p. 207

p. 290—"We used very little"—*NY Times*, Apr. 1, 1970

p. 290—The decision to incorporate—Comden and Green, in Strouse, p. 73

p. 290—"Sometimes when you"—BC to SS, Sept. 16, 1998

p. 291—"I've heard that"—BC to SS, Sept. 16, 1998

p. 291—"A perfectly professional relationship"—BC to SS, Sept. 16, 1998

p. 292—"It is necessary"—Frankel, p. 75

p. 292—"The first meeting of actors"—Bacall, *Myself*, pp. 135–136

p. 293—"The Margo Channing of *Applause*"—Bacall, *Now*, p. 139

p. 294—"I've made an ass"—Greenberger, p. 207

p. 295—"I talked with Ron"—GL to SS, Oct. 3, 1998

p. 295—"It was tricky"—GL to SS, Oct. 3, 1998

p. 296—"I camped it up"—GL to SS, Oct. 3, 1998

p. 298—"During tryouts in Baltimore"—LRR to SS, July 14, 1998

p. 299—"You do the show"—Bacall, *Myself*, p. 359

p. 299—"Wonderful screaming acceptance"—DM to SS, July 8, 1998

p. 299—"I clasped her hands"—LRR to SS, July 14, 1998

p. 300—"The pressure was constant"—Bacall, *Myself*, p. 361

p. 301—Brandon Maggart, who played—DM to SS, July 8, 1998

p. 302—"The national is"—DM to SS, July 8, 1998

p. 302—"It's nice to dream"—DM to SS, July 8, 1998

p. 302—"The fourth row center"—Bacall, *Myself*, pp. 361–362

p. 304—"After the audition" et seq.—PF to SS, Sept. 23, 1998

p. 307—"The tenth musical"—Suskin, pp. 63–64

p. 307—"Whoever first-nighters are"—BC to SS, Sept. 16, 1998

p. 308—"Half of my royalties"—SM to SS, July 9, 1998

p. 308—"Whatever it is"—*NY Times*, Mar. 31, 1970

p. 308—"A splashy bitch"—*Hollywood Reporter*, Apr. 2, 1970

p. 309—"I always imagined"—*Playboy*, July 1982, p. 80

p. 309—Send Lauren Bacall a telegram—Greenberger, p. 210

p. 310—"I hope we meet"—Bacall, *Myself*, p. 20

p. 310—"Miss Bacall leaves out"—Moseley, p. 118

p. 310—"She sat on a chair"—Bacall, *Myself*, p. 369

p. 311—"Joe, you have to"—TM to SS, Aug. 21, 1997

p. 311—"He was happy"—Bacall, *Myself*, p. 272

p. 311—"I don't blame him"—CS to SS, June 26, 1998

p. 311—Mankiewicz said—CS to SS, June 26, 1998

p. 312—"Ladies and gentlemen"—PF to SS, Sept. 23, 1998

p. 312—"It has put"—*LA Times*, June 20, 1971

p. 313—"After a couple"—Field, SMU

p. 313—Penny Fuller describes—PF to SS, Sept. 23, 1998

p. 313—"Were very musical"—LRR to SS, July 14, 1998

p. 313—"A little silver apple"—PF to SS, Sept. 23, 1998

p. 313—"The theatre was very"—PF to SS, Sept. 23, 1998

p. 314—"Did one of the best"—LRR to SS, July 14, 1998

p. 314—"I hate what they did"—LRR to SS, July 14, 1998

p. 314—"A hard part to do"—PF to SS, Sept 23, 1998

p. 315—"Anne showed me"—AD to SS, Oct. 9, 1998

p. 315—"Oh my God"—Field, SMU
p. 316—"House taking summer off"—*Variety*, June 21, 1972
p. 317—"Every time I climbed"—Davis, *Lonely Life*, p. 67

POSTSCRIPT
p. 319—He played the tape—March 18, 1999
p. 320—He started out—HH to SS, Apr. 19, 1999
p. 320—"I have little interest"—ML to SS, Apr. 20, 1999
p. 321—"Let me ask you" et seq.—ML to SS, Apr. 24, 1999
p. 322—Rosemary Mankiewicz—RM to SS, May 19, 1999
p. 331—"I came to New York"—MD to SS, May 10, 1999
p. 333—Martina happened into town—ML to SS, Apr. 24, 1999

BRIEF LIVES. . . .
p. 340—Helena Mojeska—Mordden, *Fireside*, p. 191
p. 341—"The rudest person"—Denham, p. 217

Index